Policymaking in Latin America
How Politics Shapes Policies

Ernesto Stein and Mariano Tommasi
Editors
With Pablo T. Spiller and Carlos Scartascini

Inter-American Development Bank

David Rockefeller Center for Latin American Studies
Harvard University

©2008 Inter-American Development Bank
1300 New York Avenue, N.W.
Washington, D.C. 20577

Co-published by
David Rockefeller Center
for Latin American Studies
Harvard University
1730 Cambridge Street
Cambridge, MA 02138

To order this book, contact:
IDB Bookstore
Tel: (202) 623-1753
Fax: (202) 623-1709
E-mail: idb-books@iadb.org
www.iadb.org/pub

The views and opinions expressed in this publication are those of the authors and do not necessarily reflect the official position of the Inter-American Development Bank.

**Cataloging-in-Publication data provided by the
Inter-American Development Bank
Felipe Herrera Library**

Policymaking in Latin America : how politics shapes policies / Ernesto Stein and Mariano Tommasi, editors; with Pablo Spiller and Carlos Scartascini.

 p. cm.
 Includes bibliographical references.
 ISBN: 978-1-59782-061-5

1. Public administration—Latin America—Decision making. 2. Policy sciences. 3. Public policy. 4. Political planning—Latin America. 5. Pressure groups. 6. Political parties. I. Stein, Ernesto. II. Tommasi, Mariano, 1964-. III. Spiller, Pablo. IV. Scartascini, Carlos. V. Inter-American Development Bank. VI. David Rockefeller Center for Latin American Studies.

JL959.5 .D45 P84 2007   LCCN: 2007940418

Cover Image: Valérie Crausaz, France, Untitled, 1998, Color etching on Arches paper, 40-15/16 in. × 13-3/8 in., Inter-American Development Bank Art Collection

Cover Design: Ultradesigns.com

Contents

FIGURES

TABLES

Acknowledgments

The initial inspiration for this project came from the work on Argentina by two of the editors of this book, Pablo Spiller and Mariano Tommasi, reflected in their book *The Institutional Foundations of Public Policy in Argentina: A Transactions Cost Approach* (Cambridge University Press, 2007). In that work, Spiller and Tommasi developed a methodology that, with some refinements and adaptations, became the basis for the conceptual framework used in this project, in this case applied to a much larger set of countries in Latin America.

The book is part of a larger agenda on political institutions and policy outcomes in Latin America being carried out by the Research Department of the Inter-American Development Bank (IDB), which includes among other products the 2006 Economic and Social Progress Report, *The Politics of Policies*.

The country chapters in this book were produced by eight interdisciplinary country teams under the auspices of the IDB Latin American Research Network, and the coordination of the four editors. The process of writing the book was highly interactive, with ample opportunities for cross-fertilization among the authors of the country chapters, as well as frequent give and take (in both directions) between these authors and the project coordinators. In addition to the authors of the country chapters in the book, we are also indebted to Mario Bergara, and to Eduardo Moron and Cynthia Sanborn, who participated actively in this interactive process, but whose studies on Uruguay and Peru were ultimately not included in this volume for reasons of space.

Two seminars organized by the IDB, the initial one in Mexico City in October 2003 and the second one at Harvard University in May 2004, were very important focal points in this interactive process. For their help in organizing these seminars, as well as for their invaluable support during the whole process (from the initial call for proposals to the completion of the final drafts), we want to thank Norelis Betancourt and Raquel Gomez.

The second of these seminars was co-organized with Jeff Frieden, Stanfield Professor of International Peace at Harvard University, who helped us put together the seminar back to back with the prestigious biannual conference on Political Institutions and Economic Policy (co-organized with Ken Shepsle). Jeff assembled an all-star roster of political scientists (including, in addition to himself, Jim Alt, Robert Bates, Adam Przeworski, and Ken Shepsle) and asked them to provide feedback on different aspects of the overall project. Their invaluable contributions were a key input for the project. Beyond his role in the organization of this seminar, Jeff has provided constant encouragement and feedback, and we owe him a huge debt of gratitude. Similarly, we are very grateful to Fernando Carrillo from the IDB Office in Europe, and to Javier Santiso and BBVA, who hosted a workshop in Madrid so that we could disseminate our findings in Europe, and receive feedback from European scholars.

We would also like to recognize our colleagues at the Research Department of the IDB and at Universidad de San Andrés, for their support, their encouragement, and their feedback. Within the IDB, we want to especially recognize the support received from Guillermo Calvo, at the time the IDB's Chief Economist, and his Principal Advisor, Eduardo Lora. Without their support, this project would not have been possible. Tommasi acknowledges the support of the John Simon Guggenheim Memorial Foundation.

Apart from the authors of the chapters and those already recognized above, many others deserve recognition for their valuable comments at different stages of the process. This includes Carlos Acuña, Manuel Alcántara, Martín Ardanaz, Xosé Carlos Arias, Guillermo Cardoza, John Carey, Fernando Carrillo-Flores, Gerardo Della Paolera, Guillermo de la Dehesa, Carlos Elizondo, Jose Luis Escrivá, Ricardo Hausmann, Jacint Jordana, Marcelo Leiras, María Victoria Murillo, Alejandro Nuet, Mauricio Olivera, Charles Oman, Ludolfo Paramio, Santiago Pombo, Joan Prats, Jessica Seddon Wallak, Thierry Verdier, Andrés Velasco, Lawrence

Whitehead, and two anonymous referees. Participants in seminars at LACEA, LACEA Political Economy Group, IDB, and the Universidad de San Andrés, in which some of the papers were presented, should be recognized as well.

Ideas become successful books thanks to capable editorial and administrative support. For their invaluable support in this area, we would like to acknowledge Rita Funaro, María Helena Melasecca, Mariela Semidey, John Smith, and Luis Vélez. For pulling everything together we are most grateful to the main editor, Nancy Morrison, as well as the publications team at the IDB, led by Rafael Cruz and including Michael Harrup and Joanne Blake. Finally, this book would not have been possible without the exceptional contributions of Heather Berkman, who provided research assistance, managed the interaction with the country teams late in the process, and carefully followed the production process through the later stages of the project.

Foreword

Latin America is engaged in a constant search for policies to accelerate growth, reduce poverty, and otherwise further its economic and social progress. In its journey on the path to development, it has been offered, and often followed, celebrated road maps designed to speed it along in this tortuous trek. The state-run inward-looking policy package of the postwar era and the liberalization of the Washington Consensus were each hailed as tickets to sustainable, equitable development. Instead, they produced mixed results and ultimately fell short of the region's goals and expectations.

Were these policies flawed? Was something missing? To date, most of the discussion has been an exchange between those who argue that the transformation of the state has been incomplete and more reform is needed, and those who oppose reform and attribute the poor results to them. This book suggests an alternative view: the problem lies less in the policies than in the process behind these policies. Public policies are not simply items on a menu that policymakers pick and choose. Rather, they are cooked up by numerous political actors and must then be implemented and sustained over time. Each of these political actors at each stage of the process brings his personal interests to the table and is pressured by others in the process with their own respective interests. The quality of the outcomes in the policymaking process depends as much on how these different actors interact as on the merits of the policy being promoted. Thus, differently put, the issue is not only with the nature of the interventions pursued by the state ("Producing", "Regulating", or "Distributing"), but also with the institutions that constitute the state: their incentives, the rules that govern their day-to-day functioning, and their accountability.

This book focuses on the political dimension of the public policymaking process. It analyzes the results of a comparative study of political institutions, policymaking processes and policy outcomes in eight Latin American countries, which together account for nearly 80 percent of the population and 90 percent of the GDP of the region. Each country chapter provides a detailed description of the electoral, legislative, executive, judicial, and bureaucratic institutions of the country and analyzes how these political institutions interact as they go about the business of making economic policy. By comparing both the processes and the policy outcomes in these countries, the book goes a long way toward explaining why things work the way they do in different contexts.

Policymaking in Latin America: How Politics Shapes Policies comes at an opportune moment in Latin America. Political institutions and the political rules of the game are under scrutiny in many countries and in some of these countries are currently subject to change. Constitutional reforms are on the agenda in some countries, the role of the state is being reviewed and the balance of political power may be shifting. This book offers a wealth of information that can serve as valuable input for these discussions. The book is of great relevance to policymakers to the extent that it can help avoid costly mistakes of the past, on one hand. On the other, because it points out an issue at times underestimated by economists: that the interactions between actions and institutions in the policymaking process are as important as the nature of the policies being promoted in determining outcomes.

Santiago Levy
Chief Economist and General Manager
Department of Research
Inter-American Development Bank

1

Political Institutions, Policymaking, and Policy: An Introduction

Pablo T. Spiller, Ernesto Stein, and Mariano Tommasi

"The political process that underpins economic reform is no less important than the reform's content, and perhaps even more so."

—Dani Rodrik

This book is about the political economy of policymaking in Latin America. It is written for an audience of development practitioners, economists, and political scientists, as well as for students training in those disciplines with an interest in Latin America. The objects of study are institutions, political behavior, and public policies. In addressing the links between political institutions, policymaking processes, and policy outcomes in a variety of countries, the book builds bridges between the concerns of economists about the effects of public policies on economic and social outcomes, and the concerns of political scientists about the workings of democratic institutions and political outcomes.

Public policies have always been a central concern for development economists and other development practitioners. In fact, the work of the development community has been dominated by the search for policies that would help accelerate growth, reduce poverty, or achieve other noble economic and social goals. As a result of this search, Latin America has been repeatedly influenced by various waves of policy advice, from the state-run inward-looking development of the postwar era to the liberalization of the Washington Consensus in the 1990s. In both these cases, the results of these efforts have been diverse, and somewhat disappointing.

This book suggests a change of focus in this search. It starts from the premise that public policies are not simply objects of choice for a social planner trying to maximize the welfare of the population. Rather, public policies emerge from a decision-making process that involves a multiplicity of political actors who interact in a variety of arenas. Thus the studies in this book look beyond the specific content of policies and focus on the policymaking process (PMP): that is, on the critical *process* that shapes policies, carries them forward from idea to implementation, and sustains them over time. This focus is grounded in the belief that the potential of policy prescriptions to deliver better outcomes ultimately depends, to an important extent, on the *quality* of the policymaking process through which policies are discussed, approved, and implemented.

Policymaking processes affect the type and content of policies that are adopted. But these processes may also imprint some common characteristics on public policies. These characteristics may be as important as the policy content itself. Policymaking processes can contribute to policy stability or lead to large policy swings; they may facilitate policy adaptability or lead to excessive rigidity; they can produce policies that promote either the public welfare or private interests; they can affect the quality of policy implementation and enforcement. In short, policymaking processes can affect the nature and the quality of public policies in a variety of dimensions.

In the Latin American democracies studied in this book, the process of adopting and implementing public policies occurs in political systems in which a variety of actors participate, ranging from the president to voters in small rural communities, and including members of congress, judges, public opinion leaders, and business groups. The complex interaction among these actors—the subject of this book—is influenced by the institutions and political practices of each country. These institutions affect the roles and incentives of each of the actors, the characteristics of the arenas in which they interact, and the nature of the transactions they engage in.

The emphasis on the role of domestic political institutions as the explanatory variables of interest in this volume represents somewhat of a departure from the focus of much of the earlier work on Latin American political economy, which placed relatively more emphasis on the impact of foreign economic pressures and powerful special interest groups. That earlier emphasis was perhaps justified by the conditions prevailing in the 1960s and 1970s, when most of the region was characterized by undemocratic regimes dominated by powerful interest groups in a highly protectionist setting, where favored actors were often able to extract sizable rents and where foreign actors were practically the only meaningful counterweight to the ruling elites.[1] These conditions are long gone (at least in most of the region), and the countries of Latin America certainly deserve an open-minded analysis of the laws of motion of their political economies, and a more serious investigation of their formal political institutions.[2]

This book builds upon the efforts of important recent work on political institutions in Latin America. There are some excellent books on comparative politics of Latin America, focusing on specific institutional features in various countries. These include edited volumes such as Mainwaring and Scully (1995a) on party systems, Mainwaring and Shugart (1997a) on constitutional and partisan powers of the president, Carey and Shugart (1998b) on executive decree authority, and Morgenstern and Nacif (2002) on legislative politics. This book benefits from the insights of those volumes and of related work, but takes a more general look at the process of policymaking, including a wider set of actors and their interactions, and links these interactions with the resulting policy features.

The book presents the results of a comparative study of political institutions, policymaking processes, and policy outcomes in eight Latin

---

[1] In the words of Barbara Geddes in her survey on the study of politics in developing countries, "When authoritarian governments ruled most developing countries, few political scientists interested in these countries paid much attention to the development of theories of democratic politics" (Geddes 2002, p. 343).

[2] After several decades in which most Latin American countries frequently switched between democratic and military government, the countries of the region gradually returned to democratic rule in the 1980s.

American countries, which comprise nearly 80 percent of the population of Latin America and nearly 90 percent of its GDP. The countries are Argentina, Brazil, Chile, Colombia, Ecuador, Mexico, Paraguay, and Venezuela.[3] While similar in some dimensions (they all have presidential systems, for example, and most of them share important aspects of their cultural heritage), they offer substantial variation in terms of country size and level of development, as well as an array of political and institutional features. As the reader can verify by looking at the country cases, they also vary substantially in terms of the quality of their public policies, and thus offer a good basis for studying the impact of political institutions on policy outcomes.

The country chapters in this book are not just a collection of related papers. They are the result of a truly collective comparative enterprise in which various multidisciplinary country teams of local scholars, former policymakers, and foreign experts—interacting frequently and intensively—conducted a series of country studies structured around a common framework.

As coordinators of a complex comparative project such as the one presented in this book, we had to confront the question of how much guidance to provide the authors of the country chapters in terms of the methodological approach to study the links among political institutions, policymaking processes, and policy outcomes in their own countries. A minimalist approach would have entailed giving them freedom to tackle each study as they saw fit, stressing the factors that were particularly relevant to their own countries. At the other extreme, we could have imposed a rigid common methodology to maximize comparability across the country cases. We opted for an intermediate approach. We provided a guiding framework, inspired by the work of Spiller and Tommasi (2003) on Argentina. The framework, which emphasizes the role of cooperation among the political actors that participate in the PMP,

---

[3] The country chapters were written as part of an IDB Research Network project on "Political Institutions, Policymaking Processes and Policy Outcomes." In addition to these studies, the original project also included studies on Peru (Moron and Sanborn 2006) and Uruguay (Bergara et al. 2006).

provided a common lens with which to look at policymaking processes, their institutional determinants, and their impact on policies.[4] While we asked the authors to take this framework as a point of departure, we also encouraged them to combine it when necessary with other approaches, and to add as many dimensions as needed in order to capture the essence of the policymaking process in their own countries, and its impact on public policies.

The country chapters pay extremely detailed and systematic attention to political institutions. Each of them provides a comprehensive description of the electoral, legislative, executive, judicial, and bureaucratic institutions of the country, which in itself is of substantial value. Each chapter also goes on to present an integrative interpretation of how these institutions interact (together with voters and interest groups) in the making of economic policy. The result demonstrates the importance of going beyond simple partial equilibrium assertions about the impact of, say, presidential and parliamentary systems, or independent central banks, and of moving toward a more integrated analysis of how various components of the political-institutional environment interact.

Read together, the country studies provide a fascinating interpretation of the role of political competition, electoral institutions, legislative structure, judicial independence, and other crucial factors in the making of Latin American policies. We hope the reader will come away with an appreciation for the complexity of policymaking processes in these countries, and of the central importance of understanding these processes well as a prerequisite for venturing into the challenging territory of giving policy and institutional advice.

In this introductory chapter, we summarize the guiding framework and briefly discuss some key insights derived from the country studies.

---

[4] This framework, which draws from a rich literature on political economy both in economics and in political science, was provided to the country teams at the beginning of the IDB Research Network project on "Political Institutions, Policymaking Processes and Policy Outcomes." See Spiller, Stein, and Tommasi (2003) and references there, as well as in chapter 2 of this book.

A Guiding Framework

The objective of this book is to contribute to the understanding of the determinants of public policies. For example, we want to understand why some countries are able to implement policies that are stable over time, yet are flexible enough to adapt to changing economic conditions, while other countries tend to change policies whenever the political landscape changes, or must resort to highly inflexible and inefficient rules to give policies some stability and credibility. In order to understand these policy outcomes, we focus on the process of discussing, approving, and implementing public policies—**the policymaking process (PMP)**—and its grounding in political institutions and practices.

The methodological lens we suggested for these studies was based on the idea that several important features of public policies depend crucially on the ability of political actors to achieve cooperative outcomes: that is, their ability to strike political agreements and enforce them over time. In a sense, the whole game of democracy is based on agreement and cooperation at a deeper level: that of respecting the rules of the game and letting other people rule, if that is the voters' choice and the outcome of the electoral process.[5] In our analysis, within the democratic rules of the game, **intertemporal agreement** is the mechanism by which political power of the incumbent is not abused: that is, the mutual agreements over time prevent the prevalence of policies that favor the dominant actors of the moment and ignore others.[6] In environments that facilitate political agreements, policymaking will be more cooperative, leading to public policies that are more effective, more sustainable, and more flexible in responding to changing economic or social conditions. In contrast, in settings where cooperative behavior is harder to develop

---

[5] See, for instance, Weingast (1997), Wantchekon (2000), Przeworski (2005), and Fearon (2006).

[6] While our discussion focuses mostly on democracies, the framework used in this volume can be also applied to cases of dictatorship. The players may be different (the armed forces may play a big role while the legislature may be weak or nonexisting), but the logic of the framework remains the same. The discussion in chapter 9 of the *Stronismo* in Paraguay is a case in point.

and sustain, policies will be either too unstable (subject to political swings) or too inflexible; policies will be poorly coordinated; and there will be little investment in building up long-term capabilities.[7]

An important question within this framework is whether the workings of the PMP tend to facilitate or hinder cooperative outcomes in policymaking. As we will see in more detail below, the theory of cooperation in repeated games provides some useful insights regarding the type of features of the PMP that may foster cooperation. These include the number of key political actors, their time horizons and the frequency of their interaction, the nature of the arenas in which they interact, and the availability of enforcement mechanisms that bind them to their commitments. The authors of the country chapters were asked to keep these factors in mind when analyzing the PMP of their respective countries.

The workings of the PMP, in turn, are determined (to some extent) by the political institutions in place in each country, such as the presidential/parliamentary nature of the government, the electoral rules in place, the federal structure of the country, and the existence of an independent judiciary. In studying the connection of institutional variables with the workings of the PMP, we asked chapter authors to take a systemic "general equilibrium" approach. As we expected from our theoretical priors and from the pilot work we had done on Argentina, the chapters demonstrate that the characteristics of countries' PMPs do not depend on a single institutional factor, but rather on the interaction among a number of factors—a point we develop in more detail below.

The rest of this chapter traces the steps linking political institutions to policymaking processes to policy outcomes. These are the components and steps we requested from the country studies. These components and interconnections are illustrated in figure 1.1. The figure and

---

[7] Rigidity arises when political actors do not trust their opponents, and prefer to tie their opponents' (and perhaps their own) hands, rather than allow for political discretion. If there are multiple policymaking actors, lack of cooperation is analogous to lack of coordination. It is a standard result of repeated games that in noncooperative environments, agents are less willing to pay short-term cost for future benefits: that is, they are less willing to invest.

**Figure 1.1. Political Institutions, Policymaking Process, and
Policy Outcomes**

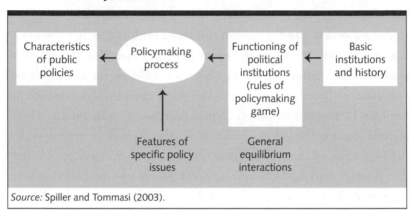

Source: Spiller and Tommasi (2003).

discussion that follow work backwards, starting from a definition of the dependent variable.[8]

The Dependent Variable: Public Policies

Policies are complex undertakings. Bringing any particular "policy reform" to fruition is a process that involves multiple actors through many stages of the policy process. It requires specific responses from economic and social agents, and therefore necessitates several forms of cooperation and positive beliefs about the durability and other properties of the policy. That is, policies require a good deal more than a magical moment of special politics to introduce "the right policy" in order to produce effective results.

A universal set of "right" policies does not exist. Policies are contingent responses to underlying states of the world. What might work at one point in time in a given country might not work in a differ-

---

[8] We use "steps" from political institutions to policymaking processes and from policymaking processes to features of policies. This schematic bears some resemblance to the notions of *structure, politics,* and *policy* of the comparison of the United States and Japan edited by Cowhey and McCubbins (1995).

ent place at another time. In some cases, particular characteristics of policies or details of their implementation might matter as much as the broad policy orientation in bringing up the desired outcomes. For instance, Dani Rodrik (1995) analyzed six countries that implemented a set of policies that shared the same generic title of "export subsidization," but had widely different degrees of success. Rodrik relates success to such features as the consistency with which the policy was implemented, which office was in charge, how this policy was bundled (or not) with other policy objectives, and how predictable the future of the policy was.

One important characteristic of policies that has been widely recognized in recent work in economics is policy credibility. The effects of policies on the final economic and social outcomes of interest depend on the actions and reactions of economic and social agents, who take into account their expectations about the future of the policies in question before deciding on their responses. As Rodrik (1989, p. 2) explains, in reference to trade reform, "it is not trade liberalization, but *credible* trade liberalization that is the source of efficiency benefits. The predictability of the incentives created by a trade regime, or lack thereof, is generally of greater importance than the *structure* of these incentives. In other words, a distorted, but stable set of incentives does much less damage to economic performance than an uncertain and unstable set of incentives generated by a process of trade reform lacking credibility."[9]

For those reasons, in the background work for this book, we suggested that country authors pay special attention not only to the content of public policies, but also to the characteristics of those policies, such as their predictability, their adaptability to changing economic circumstances, and other related qualities. Unlike the content of policies, such features have the advantage of allowing comparisons across multiple policy domains. In addition, they fit very naturally within the proposed theoretical framework. Consider the example of a hypothetical country with two similarly sized parties that are highly polarized, and with elec-

---

[9] For models studying the effects of policies of uncertain duration in several economic contexts, see Calvo (1996, section V) and Calvo and Drazen (1998).

toral rules that tend to endow the government with a legislative majority. In such a setting, if the PMP does not facilitate cooperation, as parties alternate in power, the content of some policies may be shifting all the time. Yet features such as policy stability (or, in this case, volatility) will be a constant as long as the institutional setting does not change.

We list below some of the policy characteristics ("**outer features**") upon which we suggested that authors place their focus. The list, of course, is not taxonomic, and country authors were encouraged to highlight additional features of policies that were considered to be particularly relevant in their own countries. (Several of them focused on the content of policies, as well.)

Policy Characteristics ("Outer Features")

Policy Stability. Some countries seem capable of sustaining policies over time. In other countries, policies are frequently reversed, often at each minor change of political winds (whether a change in administration or even a change in some key cabinet member or senior bureaucrat). By stable policies we do not mean that policies cannot change at all, but rather that changes tend to respond to changing economic conditions or to failure of previous policies, rather than to changes in political administrations, parties, or coalitions. In countries with stable policies, changes tend to be incremental, building upon achievements of previous administrations, and tend to be done through consensus and compromise. In contrast, volatile policy environments are characterized by large swings and by lack of consultation with different groups in society. We associate policy stability with the ability of political actors to strike and enforce intertemporal agreements that allow certain fundamental policies ("*Políticas de Estado*") to be preserved beyond the tenure of particular officeholders or coalitions. Thus the notion of policy stability is closely linked to the notion of policy credibility.[10]

---

[10] This notion of policy stability is also closely related to the notion of resoluteness in Cox and McCubbins (2001).

Policy Adaptability. It is desirable for countries to be able to adapt policies to changing economic conditions and to change policies when they are obviously failing. However, governments sometimes abuse the discretion to adapt policies by adopting opportunistic, one-sided policies that are closer to their own preferences or those of narrow constituencies. This can result in policy volatility, as policies may shift back and forth as different groups alternate in power. In political environments that are not cooperative, political actors sometimes attempt to limit such opportunism by resorting to fixed policy rules and mechanisms that are difficult to change.[11] This has the benefit of limiting policy volatility, but at the cost of reducing adaptability. In other cases, political systems tend to generate gridlock, making it difficult to achieve change, a point emphasized in the literature on veto players (Tsebelis 1995, 2002) and on divided government. Whatever the reason, countries with low policy adaptability will be unable to respond adequately to shocks, and may get stuck in bad policies for extended periods of time.

Coordination and Coherence. Public policies are the outcome of actions taken by multiple actors in the policymaking process. Ideally, different agents acting over the same policy domain should coordinate their actions to produce coherent policies. However, this is not always the case. In some countries on certain issues, policymaking involves a large number of agencies that do not communicate adequately with one another, leading to what Cox and McCubbins (2001) have called "balkanization" of public policies. Lack of coordination often reflects the noncooperative nature of political interactions. It may occur among different agencies within the central government; between agencies in the central government and others at the regional or municipal level; or even among agents that operate in different stages of the policymaking process (such as when the complications that the bureaucracy might face during the

---

[11] Some of the countries studied here, such as Brazil and Colombia, have embedded important policy dimensions such as pension policies or intergovernmental transfers into the constitution.

implementation phase of a given policy are not taken into account during the design and approval stage of policymaking).

Quality of Implementation and Enforcement. A policy could be very well designed, sail through the approval process unchanged, and yet be completely ineffective if it is not well implemented and enforced. In many countries in Latin America, the quality of implementation and enforcement is quite poor. This is associated in part with the lack of capable and independent bureaucracies, as well as the lack of strong judiciaries. To an important degree, the quality of implementation and enforcement will depend on the extent to which policymakers have incentives and resources to invest in policy capabilities.

Public Regardedness. This dimension, suggested by Cox and McCubbins (2001), refers to the extent to which policies produced by a given system promote the general welfare and resemble public goods (that is, are public regarding) or whether they tend to funnel private benefits to certain individuals, factions, or regions in the form of projects with concentrated benefits, subsidies, or tax loopholes.[12]

We have been referring to the features highlighted above as "common features" of public policies; although the same features tend to be present in most policy domains, not all policies are expected to have the exact same features. Differences in the nature of the policy issues themselves, in the actors that participate in the respective sector-specific PMPs, and in the arenas where the policymaking game is played may lead to different features across policy areas. As will be discussed below, several of the country chapters take advantage of these differences across sectors, which provide an interesting source of cross-sectional variation within a particular country.

---

[12] To the extent that those favored by private regarding policies tend to be the members of the elite, who are the ones who have the economic and political clout to skew policy decisions in their favor, private regardedness could relate to inequality.

The Policymaking Process

The process of discussing, approving, and implementing public policy is referred to as the policymaking process (PMP). In democratic systems such as those in Latin America, these processes play out on a political stage featuring a variety of political **actors** (or **players**, in the language of game theory). Players in this game include official state actors and professional politicians (presidents, party leaders, legislators, judges, governors, bureaucrats), as well as business groups, unions, the media, and other members of civil society. These actors interact in different **arenas**, which may be formal (such as the legislature or the cabinet) or informal (the street), and may be more or less transparent.

The PMP can be understood as a process of bargains and exchanges (or transactions) among political actors. Some of these exchanges are consummated on the spot or instantaneously (they are **spot transactions**). In many other cases, current actions or resources (such as votes) are exchanged for promises of future actions or resources (they are **intertemporal transactions**). The type of transaction that political actors are able to engage in will depend on the possibilities provided by the institutional environment. Issues of credibility and the capacity to enforce political and policy agreements are crucial for political actors to be able to engage in intertemporal transactions, and to cooperate more generally.

The behavior of political actors in these exchanges, and the nature of the exchanges themselves—such as support for the government in a crucial policy issue in exchange for a job in the public bureaucracy, or support for reform in a particular policy area in exchange for concessions in a different policy area—depend on the actors' preferences, on their incentives, and on the constraints they face. They also depend on the expectations various actors have regarding the behavior of other players. These interactive patterns of behavior constitute what in the parlance of game theory are called **equilibria**. Thus the characteristics of public policies depend on the equilibrium behavior of these actors in the policymaking game.

The behavior of political actors in the policymaking process—as shaped by their roles, incentives, and constraints—will depend, in turn, on the workings of **political institutions** (such as congress, the party system, or the judiciary) and on more basic **institutional rules** (such as electoral rules and constitutional rules) that determine the roles of each of the players, as well as the rules of engagement among them.

Policymaking processes are complex; multiple actors with diverse powers, time horizons, and incentives interact in various arenas with diverse rules of engagement. For these reasons, it is not possible to understand these processes fully by focusing on a few institutional characteristics. This level of complexity requires a more systemic approach. Such a systemic view can be accomplished only by means of detailed country studies, which take into account a variety of key institutions and their interaction, as well as historical and cultural legacies.[13] This is the reason why we assembled this comparative project, where teams of distinguished international and local scholars, guided by a common methodological lens, and interacting intensely with one another and with the project coordinators, immersed themselves into the details of political institutions, policymaking processes, and policy outcomes in each of the countries under study.

One very important building block in each of the studies was a careful characterization of the workings of the PMP, which the authors approached by answering questions such as the following:

- Who are the key actors that participate in the PMP?
- What powers and roles do they have?
- What are their preferences, incentives, and capabilities?
- What are their time horizons?[14]

---

[13] These legacies include fundamental cleavages, shared values, and whether a country has a history of stable democracy or has suffered frequent constitutional interruptions.

[14] Time horizons are very important determinants of political behavior. Actors with long horizons are much more likely to enter into the intertemporal agreements necessary to sustain effective policies. By contrast, actors with short horizons will tend to maximize short-term political and policy benefits, to the detriment of long-term institutional build-up, and of the credibility and quality of policies. This emphasis on time horizons draws inspiration from an important literature on institutional economics, and its application to politics. See, for instance, Dixit (1996) and references there.

■   What are the main arenas in which they interact, and what are
    the characteristics of those arenas?
■   What is the nature of the political exchanges/transactions they
    undertake?

Based on their answers to these questions, each of the country chapters provides a detailed discussion of the role played by each of the key
players in the policymaking game: the president, political parties, the
legislature, the judiciary, the bureaucracy, and in some cases, the governors. In each case, they discuss these players' roles, incentives, and
capabilities. More importantly, perhaps, they bring these actors to life by
showing how they engage in political transactions in order to advance
their objectives and, more generally, how they play the policymaking
game. All these ingredients add up to a thorough portrayal of the workings of the PMP in each case.

Having discussed the PMP and the features of public policies, the next
section discusses the link between the two. In particular, we highlight the
role of cooperation as a feature of the PMP that may help explain the
characteristics of public policies, as well as the factors that may foster—or
hinder—such cooperation.

Policymaking Processes and Policy Outcomes:
The Role of Cooperation

We have suggested that important features of public policies depend on
the ability of political actors to reach and enforce agreements; that is,
to cooperate. For this reason, in addition to other relevant features of
the PMP that may be key in shaping policy outcomes in their respective
countries, the authors of the country chapters were asked to pay particular attention to a number of factors that may foster—or hinder—cooperation among political actors.

Our emphasis on the role of cooperation does not mean that we
believe all forms of cooperation are always good. As in the case of collusion among firms in oligopolistic markets, cooperation in policymaking
may lead to undesirable outcomes, particularly when some sectors are

excluded from the cooperative agreements and the goals of those who are "in" (for example, retaining power) are different from those of society at large. For cooperation to deliver good outcomes, it needs to be combined with healthy doses of inclusion and political competition. In spite of this important caveat, the type of cooperation discussed in this framework seems to be a key ingredient—perhaps a necessary condition—for several desirable features of good policymaking.

Under what conditions is cooperation more likely? Drawing from intuitions from the theory of repeated games,[15] it can be argued that cooperative outcomes are more likely if: the immediate benefits from deviating from cooperative behavior are small; there are good "aggregation technologies" so that the number of actors with direct impact on policymaking is small;[16] these key actors have long horizons and they interact repeatedly; there are well-institutionalized arenas for political exchange; and there are credible enforcement technologies, such as an independent judiciary or a strong bureaucracy, to which certain public policies can be delegated. The discussion that follows examines each of these conditions in more detail. The elements listed below provide some rough guidance to observe the actual policymaking processes. Clearly, the list is suggestive, not taxonomic. Other important factors may be relevant in characterizing policymaking processes in general, as well as in specific countries. Several historical factors (beyond a specific configuration of political institutions at any moment), as well as cultural, social, and economic configurations, can foster or hinder cooperative political behavior, and affect the PMP in other important ways.

Conditions that Foster or Hinder Cooperation

Intraperiod Payoff Structure. If there are large immediate payoffs from deviating from cooperative agreements, cooperation will be hard to sustain.

---

[15] See Dixit (1996, p. 71), Spiller and Tommasi (2007, pp. 42–46, and references there).
[16] Gerring, Thacker, and Moreno (2005) emphasize a related concept: that of "centripetalism."

In oligopoly games, for instance, if a firm stands to gain very large short-term profits by lowering its price (for example, because there are a large number of rival firms from which they can attract customers), it is harder to sustain collusive oligopoly. The same is true in the case of cooperation among political actors. For instance, in the context of the Argentine federal fiscal system, a province's individual payoff for deviating from a cooperative agreement (for example, by attempting to get special benefits from the national government, which are paid from a common pool of resources) is quite high; hence the federal fiscal game has noncooperation as its equilibrium outcome (see chapter 3, on Argentina).

Number of Political Players. The larger the number of players, the harder it is to cooperate.[17] This relates to the previous point in that in many common pool situations, the intraperiod payoff structure is related to the number of players.[18] The case of Ecuador, with one of the most fragmented party systems in Latin America, clearly illustrates the difficulties that can be associated with a large number of players in the PMP (see chapter 7).

Time Horizons and Temporal Linkages among Key Political Actors. The intertemporal pattern of interactions among specific individuals in formal political positions (such as legislators, governors, and bureaucrats) mat

---

[17] Fudenberg and Maskin (1986) and Fudenberg and Tirole (1991, section 5.1.2) make this point, showing that, in repeated games, when the set of feasible payoffs is held constant, increasing the number of players reduces the set of equilibria toward less cooperative ones.

[18] Our notion of the number of players is different from the number of veto players in Tsebelis (2002). In Tsebelis, the number of veto players relates (roughly) to the number of actors holding institutional veto positions at a particular point in time. In contrast, we refer to the number of "permanent" players, even if they do not happen to be holding specific veto positions at a particular point in time. For instance, in a country with a stable party system dominated by two major parties that alternate in power, even if one party is out of power at a particular point in time, it is still a player in the intertemporal game. In such a case, we would concur with Tsebelis (2002) and with Cox and McCubbins (2001) in characterizing such a system as decisive. Whether we concur with them in calling that system nonresolute will depend on whether intertemporal cooperation prevents opportunistic short-term policy manipulation.

ters for achieving cooperative outcomes. It is not the same to have a leg-islature in which the same individuals interact repeatedly over extended periods of time as it is to have a legislature where individual legislators are frequently replaced.[19] Cooperation is less likely in the latter case, for a variety of reasons. First, longer time horizons tend to lead to lower discount rates, so the benefits of deviating from cooperation today will be smaller relative to the future gains of sustaining it. Second, repeated interaction makes it easier for other political actors to punish those who deviated from cooperation. Third, repeated interaction may also facilitate trust among the different political actors with key roles in the policymaking process. In addition to increasing the scope for coopera-tion, longer time horizons increase the incentives for political actors to invest in their policymaking capabilities. While there are other factors that affect the nature of the PMP and the features of public policies, it is perhaps not surprising that the countries in Latin America with longer lasting legislators—Uruguay, Chile, and to a lesser extent Brazil—are among the highest ranked in terms of the overall quality of public poli-cies, as measured by the Inter-American Development Bank in a com-parative study of the region (IDB 2005).[20]

Institutionalization of Policymaking Arenas. Arenas that make coopera-tion easier to enforce can facilitate the complex exchanges required to implement effective public policies. Seminal works on the U.S. Congress disagree on the role that different institutional arrangements (such as the committee system) have in facilitating legislative bargaining, but im-plicitly agree that somehow things are arranged in a way that facilitates intertemporal cooperation in political exchanges.[21] Whether the legis-lature—as the arena where these transactions take place—is adequately

---

[19] Beyond the actual tenure of political actors, some historical events, such as coups or frequent episodes of civil unrest, may also increase the discount rate of political actors and limit the scope for cooperation.

[20] See IDB (2005, tables 3.6 and 6.1).

[21] See Weingast and Marshall (1988); Shepsle and Weingast (1995); Shepsle and Bon-chek (1997).

institutionalized depends on several factors, including legislators' incentives and capabilities. There are some environments—several in the countries analyzed in this book—in which legislatures are much weaker than in the benchmark U.S. case. In these environments, when political exchanges are undertaken, they tend to take place in settings that are more informal, more uncertain, and more difficult to monitor, observe, and enforce.

Delegation. Repeated play encourages self-enforcement of agreements, but certain forms of cooperation can be achieved by alternative institutional means. One alternative is to delegate policy to independent technical agencies. While delegation has its problems, there are instances in which the cost of those problems is smaller than the cost of partisan policymaking. The feasibility of and benefits from such bureaucratic delegation may vary systematically depending on some features of the institutional environment of each country, such as the degree of professionalism of the civil service (Huber and McCarty 2001). The bureaucracy is a key actor for encouraging agreements, especially through its role in putting such agreements into practice over time. A neutral and professional bureaucracy limits the scope for the adoption of opportunistic policies and enhances the trust of actors that commitments made as part of policy agreements will be fulfilled.

Several of the country studies look in detail at issues of delegation, which typically introduce important changes into a sector's policymaking process. The Colombian case (chapter 6), for example, looks at the contrast between policymaking in the fiscal realm—which tends to involve the legislative arena—and in the realm of monetary and exchange rate matters, which were delegated to an autonomous central bank, following the 1991 Constitution.[22] Similarly, the Ecuador study (chapter 7) looks at successful delegation in the case of the tax administration, and compares policy features in this sector to those of other fiscal policies,

---

[22] Delegation to a strong autonomous central bank has also characterized monetary policy in Chile.

which are subject to the country's more general PMP. At the same time, the case of Ecuador, as well as that of Argentina (chapter 3), illustrates how fragile these agreements to delegate policy can be in the context of weak policymaking processes, when delegation becomes politically inconvenient for the incumbent government of the time.[23]

Availability of Enforcement Technologies. Cooperation is easier to achieve if there is good third-party enforcement. The presence and characteristics of an impartial referee and enforcer of political agreements, such as an independent judiciary, vary from country to country. As a result, the degree of enforcement of political cooperation—and the incentives to engage in cooperation—vary as well.

An Illustration

So far, we have discussed a number of factors that may lead to enhanced cooperation among the political actors that participate in the PMP. But we have not yet discussed how these factors (and cooperation more generally) can affect the features of public policies. While for the most part we leave this discussion to the country chapters themselves, it is worthwhile at this point to provide an example to see how some of these factors may come into play in explaining, for instance, policy stability.

Consider once more the hypothetical example of a country with two similarly sized parties that alternate in power. If these parties are highly polarized and their policy preferences differ very significantly, the gains from deviating during each period will be large. Unless there are other factors that lead to intertemporal cooperation, it is likely that each party will try to adopt its preferred policies when it is in office, leading to unstable policies. If in contrast their preferences are more closely aligned, the immediate gains from deviating from cooperation

---

[23] Costa Rica, a country not covered in this study, presents an interesting case, in which many areas of policy have been delegated to autonomous institutions. See Lehoucq (2007).

are smaller, and thus cooperation—and policy stability—will be more likely.

While the break-up of cooperation may yield immediate gains for incumbents, it also produces long-term costs for them, since deviating today means that policies will be further from their preferences when the opponent is in office, and that the costs associated with frequently switching policies will have to be borne, as well. Whether the immediate benefits compensate for the long-term costs will depend on the rate at which political actors discount the future. If discount rates are very high, cooperation is unlikely to arise. If discount rates are low, political actors will be more likely to agree on an intermediate policy—a "*Politica de Estado*"—that can be sustained over time. Discount rates, in turn, are determined in part by the length of the actor's horizons, including such factors as the tenure of presidents, legislators, and party leaders, and the degree to which political parties are long-lived.

If the immediate gains from implementing their preferred policies (rather than a compromise) are fairly low, and so are their discount rates, political actors will have incentives to behave cooperatively. Still, they will need some mechanism by which they can reach the necessary agreements and broker the necessary deals, which may involve compensation in other policy areas or across time. In the absence of adequately institutionalized arenas where these deals can be brokered and upheld over time, it will be difficult for the parties to reach these deals.

In some cases, the immediate benefits of deviating from cooperation—or the discount rates—may be large enough that cooperation will not be self-enforcing. While cooperation may lead to better results for everyone ex ante (for example, before the results of the elections are known), once an incumbent is in office, he or she may have incentives to deviate. In such cases, political actors may want to agree to an intermediate policy beforehand, and put in place mechanisms that will ensure that the deal is upheld. Delegating policymaking to a competent autonomous bureaucracy is one way to do this—provided the delegation is credible. An independent judiciary may help make such delegation or other forms of commitment more credible, by forcing political actors to stand by them.

Political Institutions and the Policymaking Process

The discussion so far has focused on public policies, the policymaking process, and on the connection between them. As figure 1.1 illustrates, the PMP is in turn determined by each country's political institutions, at least in part. But which specific institutions matter? And what are the channels through which they matter?

One of the main lessons from this comparative project is that there are a myriad of institutional dimensions that can have an impact on the workings of a country's policymaking process, and that the impact of each of those dimensions tends to be contingent on the configuration of other institutional dimensions.

Chapter 2 by Carlos Scartascini surveys the rich literature that addresses the way in which political institutions (such as constitutional norms and various aspects of electoral rules) shape the roles, incentives, and modes of engagement of the main players that participate in the policymaking process.

Chapter 2 is organized actor by actor, looking in turn at presidents, cabinets, the legislature, the judiciary, subnational actors, political parties, and bureaucracies. Thus the chapter tends to highlight the rules and practices that have an impact on the way each of these actors plays the policymaking game, rather than highlighting the interaction among different policy players and institutional dimensions. While this background is of course critical, one of the main points that we emphasized in the guiding framework and that comes across very clearly in the country studies is the importance of interactions, of configurations of institutions, and of the need for a systematic approach to the complex subject of policymaking. Looking at the eight country studies in this book, one gets the clear message that the impact of political institutions on the PMP is configural. Each country's policymaking process is the result of a configuration of political rules and practices, shaping the preferences, incentives, and constraints of policymaking actors. A focus on a few institutional characteristics—such as whether the country has a presidential or parliamentary system, whether the electoral rules are of the plurality or proportional representation variety, or whether the president has

more or less partisan or legislative powers—will provide only a very fragmented and unsatisfactory understanding of these processes. In order to
understand them fully, the institutional set-up needs to be looked upon
as a *system*.[24]

The point can be seen most clearly if the institutional factor one
focuses upon is the very "broad" category of presidentialism/parliamen-
tarism. All eight cases studied in this book are presidential, yet policymaking processes, as well as policy outcomes, are very different across
countries.[25] But even countries that look similar in several of the relevant
dimensions that have been emphasized in the literature (and that are
surveyed in chapter 2) may have very different PMPs and policy outcomes. Consider the cases of Brazil and Ecuador. In addition to being
presidential systems, both these countries share an extreme degree of
political party fragmentation. In fact, they have the most fragmented
party systems in Latin America, which translates into the lowest share
of seats controlled by the party of the president (see Jones 2005; IDB
2005). In both countries, legislators are elected under proportional representation, with open lists. Thus in both, legislators have incentives to
deliver benefits to their communities. In both, presidents have strong
legislative powers to compensate for the weak partisan powers. Yet in
spite of all these similarities, these countries are very different in terms
of their policymaking processes, as well as their political and policy outcomes. While Brazil has embarked on a path to good governance and
presents solid public policies in many areas, Ecuador is characterized by
political instability and policy ineffectiveness. A partial look at a few institutional dimensions, as important as these may be, is clearly insufficient

---

[24] Other authors have emphasized the importance of configurations and interactions
among different institutional dimensions: see Liphjart (1991); Tsebelis (1995, 2002);
Haggard and McCubbins (2001); and Fukuyama (2006). We believe that this is the
first book to study this point systematically in a number of integral and detailed country studies.

[23] Other studies taking advantage of variations within presidential regimes include
Mainwaring and Scully (1995a); Mainwaring and Shugart (1997a); Carey and Shugart
(1998b); Haggard and McCubbins (2001); Morgenstern and Nacif (2002); and Payne
and others (2002).

to explain the characteristics of the policymaking process and policy outcomes. Obviously, there are some other institutional dimensions that matter, and the interaction between these different dimensions matters as well. Sometimes seemingly smaller details of the institutional setting, such as the discretion of the president to allocate budget resources that generate local benefits (possible in Brazil, not in Ecuador), can play an important role (see chapters 4 and 7, as well as IDB 2005).

The chapters in this volume present various other instances in which institutional rules usually associated with some outcomes "in partial equilibrium" are not associated with those outcomes in specific country cases, since the configuration of political incentives make them operate differently. For instance, the president of Chile is constitutionally the most powerful president in the region. Yet the political dynamics of the country, as well as a wealth of complementary institutions, have led the presidents since the return to democracy to exercise that power in a careful and consensual manner, following a practice of negotiation, compromise, and consensus building. Such policies have fostered the development of credible and stable policies, while allowing presidents to (gradually) imprint their own priorities on the country's agenda (see chapter 5 on Chile; Weyland 1999). At the other extreme, the president of Mexico has traditionally been very weak in terms of his constitutional powers. Yet during the PRI era, he dominated the policymaking process, since the weak constitutional powers did not really matter much in the context of single-party rule.[26]

The Country Studies

The comparative research project reflected in this book steered a middle course between imposing a common methodological framework and giving the authors of the country studies the freedom to enrich the analysis of their cases both methodologically and empirically. The authors of the subsequent chapters have done a terrific job of judiciously applying the

---

[26] As chapter 8 on Mexico discusses, with the arrival of divided government, the constitutional weakness of Mexican presidents has come to the fore.

general methodological guidelines summarized in this introduction, while giving the idiosyncrasies of each case the weight they deserve in order to capture the essence of each country's policymaking process.

Some of the chapters have implicitly or explicitly broadened the basic guiding framework in some dimensions important to describe their cases better. Some country studies (such as Brazil and Ecuador) have framed the description of the policymaking game from the perspective of the ability of the president to pass his or her agenda through congress, and the ease or difficulty of implementing exchanges along alternative dimensions, such as making policy compromises, filling cabinet positions, and distributing resources to specific constituencies. Other studies have focused in more detail on the specific distribution of preferences represented in the PMP of their countries, enabling the simultaneous explanation of both general characteristics of and specific winners and losers from policy in different areas (Chile) or time periods (Mexico).

In order to characterize the policymaking process of each country, authors have combined firsthand knowledge of key policy actors and their interactions with secondary sources—and, in many cases, new empirical work. Each chapter contains a nuanced mix of quantitative and qualitative research techniques.

For example, in chapter 1 on Brazil, Lee J. Alston, Marcus André Melo, Bernardo Mueller, and Carlos Pereira discuss several episodes in which the supreme court ruled against the executive on issues of vital importance, in order to back up their claim that the Brazilian supreme court has been relatively independent. At the same time, they present novel empirical evidence about the connection between votes for the government in congress and the appropriation by the executive of legislators' budget amendments, providing support for their argument about the centrality of the exchange of pork for political support in the midst of a highly fragmented party system.

Similarly, the chapter on Ecuador provides a detailed account of the mechanics and the inducements with which the government attempts (not always successfully) to form and maintain coalitions, also in the context of a very fragmented party system that leads to considerable political and policy instability. In the chapters on Colombia and Paraguay, the authors illustrate their claims about the changing role of the legislature in the policymaking process by carrying out empirical analysis of legislative activity in the different periods they consider. This novel econometric analysis was enriched by the fact that in the Colombian case, two of the authors are former ministers with extensive experience in working with congress, and that the Paraguay team has drawn on background work based on extensive access to interviews with key actors.

A number of the studies exploit variations within a particular country, either across policy issues or across time. Variation of policy characteristics across issues is explained in the Brazilian case by arguing that those policies most important in the presidential agenda will be stable and adaptable; that many other policies will be volatile, since the resources devoted to them will depend on the budget situation; and that some policies with strong interests will be hard-wired into the constitution precisely to escape that volatility. The chapter on Chile argues that policies will have all the desirable properties (stability, adaptability, good implementation) in those cases where preferences are not too far apart (such as macroeconomic policies), but "veto-player" effects will dominate when preferences are very polarized (such as moral issues).

Several of the countries studied in this volume experienced major changes in their political institutions during the period under study. Colombia, for example, introduced a new constitution in 1991, which led to a more active role for congress, the judiciary, and subnational authorities, thus imposing increased constraints on the authority of the executive. Venezuela introduced elections for governors in 1989, which substantially changed the political and party dynamics, and led to important changes in policy outcomes. The 1999 Constitution introduced during the Chávez administration brought further changes that concentrated power in the hands of the president and considerably altered the nature of policymaking in this country once again. In Mexico and Paraguay, the process of policymaking changed significantly with the end of the PRI hegemonic period and the Stroessner dictatorship, respectively. The authors of these chapters take advantage of this variation across time, and attempt to pin down the impact of these changes on policy outcomes.

While the country studies that exploit variation of political institutions across time provide some insights into the reasons behind the changes in the relevant rules of the game, we should stress that the focus of this book is not on the dynamics of institutional change, but rather on the effects of political institutions on policymaking and on policies. That is, the country chapters by and large take political rules as given and focus on their implications.[27] We are aware, of course, that institutions are themselves endogenous and that a more complete understanding would also require an analysis of institutional change and of the endogenous determination of political rules. Yet from a rational choice perspective, any theory attempting to explain how institutions change should also understand, as a building block, the consequences associated with the different institutional settings (Diermeier and Khrebiel 2003). Since one project cannot cover all bases at the same time, we leave the study of the evolution of institutions for a later stage of our research agenda.

Parting Thoughts: The Challenges of Institutional Reform

To close this introduction, we come back to one of the original motivations behind this research agenda, and provide some brief reflections about institutional reform. There is a new wave of thinking about economic policy in developing countries that argues against universally applicable policy prescriptions being pushed in all countries, regardless of

---

[27] It is interesting to notice that some of the country studies suggest explanations of institutional change that draw from the framework of intertemporal cooperation of this project. For instance, in Venezuela, a cooperative power-sharing agreement between the two dominant parties that began in 1958 with the *Pacto de Punto Fijo*, started to break down during the Pérez administration (1974–78) in the context of the first oil crisis. As argued by Francisco Monaldi, Rosa Amelia González, Richard Obuchi, and Michael Penfold (chapter 10 in this volume), the huge windfall of oil resources increased the informal powers of the president, and gave way to presidential unilateralism, reflected in a dramatic expansion of the use of presidential decrees. This breakup of cooperation at a time of a windfall of oil money to the country is consistent with the prediction of the theory of repeated games that the benefits of deviating from cooperation are larger when short-term resources are greater than those expected in the future. Similarly, the case study of Paraguay relates the unraveling of the Stroessner-era equilibrium to the "last-period problem" during the late *Stronismo*.

the circumstance, time, and place where they are applied.[28] The previous discussion regarding the complexities involved in the link between political institutions and policymaking processes, as well as the important role of interactions between different institutional dimensions, suggests that one should adopt a similar logic when thinking about institutional reform.[29]

The merits of potential changes in political and institutional rules must be considered carefully, with an understanding of how these rules fit within the broader institutional configuration. Broad generalizations about the merits of different political regimes, electoral systems, or constitutional adjudication of powers among branches are not very useful. Partial equilibrium views that stress the importance of a single institutional dimension may lead to misguided institutional and policy reforms. Understanding the overall workings of the political process and of the policymaking process in each specific country, with its specific historical trajectory, is a crucial prerequisite for developing appropriate policy reform proposals, as well as institutional reform proposals.

In addition, we believe that one needs to be very cautious in attempting a technocratic solution to what are essentially political problems. The incentives of professional politicians such as presidents, legislators, and party leaders can impose important constraints on the type of reform that is feasible. Adopting the best civil service law in the world will not work if patronage involving positions in the bureaucracy remains an important currency used by politicians to reward their partisan base. Attempts to improve the policymaking capabilities of congress will not work if legislators themselves do not have incentives to develop such capabilities. This does not mean that such reforms cannot take place. It just means that success in this area may require creative ways of advancing reform that take the incentives of the key players into account.

---

[28] See, for instance, Evans (2001); Lindauer and Pritchett (2002); Hausmann, Rodrik, and Velasco (2005); and IDB (2005).

[29] For a similar view, see North (1994); Pistor (2000); Evans (2004); and Eggertsson (2005).

2

Who's Who in the PMP:
An Overview of Actors, Incentives,
and the Roles They Play

*Carlos Scartascini**

Introduction

Chapter 1 presents a framework linking political institutions, policymaking processes, and policy outcomes. Within that framework, public policies are seen as the outcome of the interaction among a variety of political actors. These actors, each with its own preferences and incentives—and within the constraints of the rules that frame their engagement—meet in different arenas to define public policies. This chapter looks at a number of those key actors, institutions, and arenas, with the aim of examining the roles, incentives, and capabilities of each of the actors in the policymaking process, and thus their impact on the features of public policies.

This chapter, which draws from an extensive literature in political science and political economy, does not pretend to be a complete survey; rather it highlights those institutions and actors that are important within the context of the framework developed in chapter 1, and that tend to have a key role in most of the countries studied in this volume.[1] While

*This chapter draws on Scartascini and Olivera (2003) and has benefited greatly from comments by Ernesto Stein, Mariano Tommasi, and two anonymous referees. Martin Ardanaz provided superb research assistance. The usual disclaimer applies.

[1] Other sources that should be considered for a complementary, more comprehensive, and substantial overview include Weaver and Rockman (1993); Mueller (1996a, 1996b, 2003); Carey (2000); Persson and Tabellini (2000, 2003); Haggard and McCubbins (2001); Payne and others (2002); Tsebelis (2002); and IDB (2005).

the framework emphasizes the interaction among actors, this chapter examines them individually, for the most part. The richness and complexity of interactions are more naturally addressed within the realm of the specific country cases, and therefore are mostly left to the country chapters that follow.

Each section of the chapter analyzes specific actors in the policymaking process, as well as the political institutions shaping their roles and incentives. For the most part, the order in which we present the institutional actors follows the traditional layout of institutions presented in the constitution of a country. Usually, democratic constitutions assign the role of policymaking to three separate but related branches—the executive (and cabinet), the legislature, and the judiciary—establishing the prerogatives, functions, and scope of these institutions. Additionally, there is sometimes a vertical dimension of institutions (federalism) that regulates the relationships between the central and subnational governments. Finally, the chapter analyzes the role of other actors with formally ascribed roles in the policymaking process, such as political parties and the bureaucracy.

The Executive Branch: Presidents and Cabinets

Countries can organize their executive branch along a "continuum" between two polar cases: presidential and parliamentary systems.[2] The choice of political regime between presidential and parliamentary systems can have important consequences for policymaking because it has an influence on the number and stability of the agents in charge of policymaking, the arenas where exchanges take place, the type of political exchanges that can take place between the executive and the

---

[2] Lijphart (1999) identifies three basic differences between presidential and parliamentary systems. First, the executive in a parliamentary system is responsible to the legislature and can be dismissed from office by a legislative vote of no confidence or censure. In a presidential system, the head of government is elected for a constitutionally prescribed period. Second, prime ministers are selected by the legislature, while presidents are popularly elected. Third, parliamentary systems have collective or collegial executives, whereas presidential systems have single person, noncollegial executives.

legislature, and some of the bargaining prerogatives of each of the actors.

Latin American countries have traditionally opted for presidential regimes, instead of the parliamentary systems that are more popular in Europe. Even though this study focuses on presidential systems, it is important to characterize both systems, insofar as this discussion helps introduce the literature and stylized facts on stability of governments and policies. In fact, some critics argue that some of the problems with policymaking in Latin America have their origin in the region's choice of political regime.

The stylized facts indicate that parliamentary systems tend to be less stable than presidential systems because political government leaders tend to change more frequently. However, when changes occur in parliamentary systems, they are usually smooth and do not involve a complete reshuffling of the government; some of the policymakers remain in place, along with their policies. On the other hand, changes in presidential systems are more dramatic when they occur because they entail either a democratic breakdown or a major reshuffle of the government. In that context, Linz (1990, 1994) has characterized presidential systems as "rigid" and parliamentary systems as "flexible." In his work, flexibility is to be preferred to rigidity, especially because flexibility is risk-minimizing (for example, crises in parliamentary systems would be government crises, and not regime crises). Thus the rigidity of presidentialism, crystallized in situations where presidents lack a majority of seats in legislatures, was thought to be one of the main determinants of the breakdown of democratic regimes in Latin America (Linz and Valenzuela 1994). This argument regarding the relationship between minority governments and regime survival has been tested empirically by recent scholarship.

On the one hand, based on data for all presidential democracies that existed between 1946 and 1996, Cheibub and collaborators show that minority presidents, minority governments, and deadlock situations do not affect the survival of democracies (Cheibub 2002; Cheibub and Limongi 2002; Cheibub, Przeworksi, and Saiegh 2004). On the other hand, based on a much smaller sample of Latin American governments between 1978 and 2005, Chasquetti (2004) and IDB (2005) note that in this period, a number of minority governments (defined as situations where governments control less than 45 percent of legislative seats) suffered constitutional interruptions (situations where either the president or congress does not finish the terms for which they were elected). For this selected group of countries, IDB (2005) finds that minority governments (whether single-party or coalitional) were five times more likely to suffer constitutional interruptions than governments with a majority or near majority of seats.

Considering the fact that the modal type of party system in Latin America is a multiparty one, the ability of governments to form and maintain majority coalitions should be considered an important factor that may affect political stability (or the lack thereof) in the region. In the case of Ecuador, a country where presidents usually have a minority of the seats in the legislature (lately around 25 percent) and where coalitions tend to be unstable, no president has finished his four-year constitutional mandate since 1996.

Presidents

The regime type adopted in Latin America makes **presidents** key players in the policymaking game. Therefore, it is important to understand their incentives and the factors affecting presidential behavior. Even though their personal qualities, ideology, and historical and cultural factors can shape the way presidents govern, the institutions that determine the way they are elected and their power to affect policy decisions tend to be at least as important in explaining their incentives and behavior. In some institutional contexts, presidents tend to be mostly interested in the public good and design their policies taking into account broad interests in society. In other institutional contexts, presidents have "mixed" incentives, and are driven by personal and political goals that may interfere with the goal of serving the general public interest. While differences in incentives are explained mostly by electoral rules, the capacity to transform policies depends on the powers bestowed on the presidents, which are discussed next.

Presidential Powers. The powers of the president determine the strategic actions the president may take, and the type of transactions he or she may engage in with the legislature and his or her political allies and opponents. Presidential powers can be classified as either *constitutional powers* or *partisan powers* (Shugart and Carey 1992; Mainwaring and Shugart 1997a).

Constitutional powers contribute to frame the relationship between the executive and the legislative. As the constitutional powers of the presidency increase, other things being equal, so does the president's discretion to introduce changes to the status quo. Higher constitutional powers make it easier for the president to take decisive action whenever it is necessary (such as adapting economic policy to shocks), but they also make it easier to change policies for political convenience, leading to a potential volatility of policies (such as changing policies before an election for political gain or discarding the policies of the previous administration and "starting all over" after taking office). *Constitutional* powers can be divided into *legislative* and *nonlegislative powers.*

Legislative powers include the package veto, the partial (line item) veto, the power to issue decrees or declare a bill "urgent,"[3] the exclusive initiative of legislation, budgetary powers, and the power to call a plebiscite or referendum. These powers can be further divided into *proactive* and *reactive,* according to whether the president can influence the adoption of policies that represent a change in the status quo or whether the president can stop or delay the implementation of policies that could modify the status quo (Carey and Shugart 1998b). If legislative presidential powers are important, policies will be closer to the preferences of the executive branch. For example, the president could obtain policies closer to his or her preferences by threatening to veto or actually vetoing the legislature, by issuing decrees and thus bypassing the legislature, and by using the prerogative to consult the citizenry through referendums to

---

[3] Decree is the authority of the executive to establish law without prior consent of the assembly (Carey and Shugart 1998b). This may include executive policy initiatives that eventually require legislative ratification. Urgency bills are proposals issued by the president and become law unless the legislature acts to reject them within a specified time period.

bypass the opposition of the legislature for those policies for which the president can ensure popular support (Mueller 1996a, 1996b).[4]

The president's *nonlegislative powers* include the power to nominate, appoint, and dismiss government officials. The rules for cabinet formation and cabinet dismissal affect not only the power of the president within the executive branch but also the relationship between the executive and legislative branches. If the rules provide the legislature with power over the appointment and dismissal of cabinet ministers, legislators could use those prerogatives as a bargaining mechanism with the executive over certain policies of their interest.[5] A related bargaining chip of the legislature is the mechanism for impeachment of the president, which could affect the degree of vulnerability of the president vis-à-vis congress (Pérez Liñán 2006). Constitutional rules are not the whole story for understanding the bargaining between the branches of government. In fact, these rules can be assessed only in interaction with the capacity of presidents to mobilize support among members of congress (Pérez Liñán 2006). This takes us into the realm of the partisan powers of presidents, a key variable whose importance goes far beyond the impeachment process, and to which we now turn.

Partisan powers relate to the degree of support for the president in congress. The standard measures are the size of the president's legislative contingent and the degree of party discipline (Mainwaring and Shugart 1997a). Dominant parties capable of ruling by themselves (in presidential systems, presidents and legislatures of the same party, especially if the party is a "centralized" one)[6] have the easiest time securing legislative

---

[4] The relevance of the elements of direct democracy (referendum, popular initiative) has been highlighted as one of the resources at the disposal of the executive branch to pass certain policies when the legislature is opposed to them. The literature on popular initiative, based on the tradition of Romer and Rosenthal (1978, 1979, 1982), shows that the agenda-setter has good possibilities of having its policies supported by maximizing support through popular votes, given the preferences of the voters and the status quo (reversionary position).

[5] See Shugart and Carey (1992); Amorim Neto (2002); Payne and others (2002); IDB (2005); Martínez Gallardo (2005).

[6] Centralized parties are those where national politicians have tight control over the valuable resources needed to further legislative and political careers.

support for their programs. Coalition governments fare less well, and presidential systems in which the president and legislature are of different parties have the greatest difficulty (Haggard and Webb 2000).

Sometimes, presidents can still govern in cases of minority government: they can circumvent potential opposition in the legislature by relying on the legitimacy provided by strong popular support. To a certain extent, the degree of support and legitimacy can be traced back to the electoral system that rules the election of presidents, the electoral system that rules the election of legislators, and the degree of concurrence of their elections.

Electoral Rules

Presidents can be directly elected using plurality voting or runoff elections, or they can be indirectly elected, either through an electoral college or by legislative decision (usually as a "second round" mechanism, as in Bolivia). The **method of election** of the president is particularly relevant, as it affects the degree of popular support of the president and determines whether forming a coalition is necessary for obtaining the presidency. Electoral systems that ensure a high share of the vote for the winning candidate (particularly in a first round) tend to increase the legitimacy and reduce the need for coalitions. As discussed in the next section, the electoral rules of the legislature also affect the extent to which coalitions are needed to govern by affecting the degree of fragmentation of congress—and thus the probability that the president could get a majority in congress. Having to rely on coalitions to govern usually creates restrictions for the president in the bargaining process, as the chapters on Brazil, Chile, and Ecuador show.

In addition to the formulas that transform votes into seats, other institutional aspects of electoral rules are important, including the **concurrence of elections** and the **use of midterm elections**. When elections are concurrent for the two branches, the president's party is likely to receive more votes, and fewer parties are likely to receive significant shares of the vote in legislative elections. This reduces fragmentation and increases the chance that the president can win strong legislative support (Jones 1997; Shugart

1995). Midterm elections, whether in systems with or without coterminous cycles, can contribute to difficulties in governing, mainly if opposition majorities result (Shugart 1995). These elections can weaken the policymaking effectiveness of the executive by altering the balance of partisan power mid-way through the term, and by shifting congressional attention from the policy agenda to electoral strategizing and campaigning.

In addition to explaining the president's relationship with the legislature, it is also relevant to explore the determinants of the president's relationship with the party. One of those determinants is the **nomination procedure** of presidential candidates. Some of the systems increase the allegiance of presidents to the party, while other systems tend to favor the appearance of "extra-party" candidates (Morgenstern and Siavelis 2004). For example, when the selection of presidential candidates is centralized (controlled by party elites) and high barriers for independent candidacies exist, it will be more likely for party insiders to become presidential candidates.[7] By contrast, decentralized recruitment and low barriers to independent candidacies may encourage the appearance of candidates known as "freewheeling independents." These candidates have no long-term identification with a party and typically use parties as mere electoral vehicles to reach the presidency. As a consequence, elected presidents will be less constrained by party ties, but they may be unable to build legislative coalitions (Morgenstern and Siavelis 2004). In this case, policies could become more unstable (because the policies pursued by the president are the president's own and do not follow a historic party stance) and less adaptable (because it will be harder—usually more costly—to respond to shocks).

The incentives behind some of the actions of the president may also be explained by the **tenure** of the presidency, given **term limits** and **reelection constraints**, because they explain their decisionmaking horizon. If presidents can serve consecutive terms and there is the possibility that presidents can be reelected, the policies pursued by the president will usually be influenced by the reelection campaign. If there is no possibility of reelection, the policies presidents will try to enact will be a mixture of

---

[7] Party insiders are candidates who emerge from long-standing, institutionalized, and programmatic parties, and who have held positions in the party before becoming candidates.

trying to help the candidate of the party (mainly if former presidents tend to keep some role in party politics) and trying to influence the set of policies that the next president will have at his or her disposal (Carey 2003).[8] Therefore, a candidate's potential post-tenure career path could be very important in defining the policies he or she pursues while in office.

Cabinets

The cabinet—even if it is not always an initiator of policies (which it is in many countries)—is usually a major player for the attainment of the government objectives because it is in charge of the actual implementation. Additionally, cabinets usually serve as a mechanism to cement coalitions. Given certain constitutional mandates that regulate the formation of the cabinet—which are usually determined by the type of political regime—the electoral system and the party system could have an impact on the number of ministers, the issues under their domain, the way in which they are appointed, their capacity for coordination, their responsibilities, and their political allegiance. More importantly, the electoral system and the party system could affect the duration of the ministers, their level of specialization and skills for the task at hand, and their mobility (Blondel 1985). Among the characteristics of cabinets relevant for policymaking, two are the most salient: *the process of cabinet formation and the stability of cabinets* (Martínez Gallardo 2005).

The process of cabinet formation affects the identity of the cabinet and the allegiance of its members to the president. The decisions on who to name to those (sometimes) key positions depend in part on the electoral system for the presidency. Electoral systems that ensure a majority for the president's party do not generate the need for the formation of coalitions and will usually result in compact cabinets (that is, cabinets made up entirely of members from the president's party).[9] On the other hand, when

---

[8] Offering past presidents a position in the party could be a mechanism for aligning their incentives when leaving office with those of the party.

[9] A compact cabinet would have fewer conflicts over policy. For example, Bawn and Rosenbluth (2006) find that the fewer the number of parties in the government coalition, the lower are public expenditures.

coalitions are needed, they can be cemented through positions in the cabinet, generating multiparty cabinets. The formation of the cabinet becomes more relevant the weaker the partisan powers of the president, or the more fragmented the party system. For example, in the case of Bolivia, there is a strong correlation among the number of ministries, the number of cabinet positions offered to coalition members, and the share of the votes obtained by the president in the general election (IDB 2005).

In cases of government coalitions, the degree of cabinet coalescence (that is, the extent to which cabinet posts reflect the distribution of seats held by the parties joining the executive in the legislature) may affect legislative voting behavior, and thus the ability of the president to pass his agenda. For example, Amorim Neto (2002) finds that cabinets in Brazil that display a high correspondence between cabinet portfolios and legislative seats held by the parties joining the executive foster coalition discipline, as they generate incentives for the parties to support executive initiatives in the legislature. While President Cardozo's cabinet maintained that correspondence, President Lula's cabinet was more partisan. According to Pereira and Power (2005), this is one of the reasons why his government had to cement the coalition through other means in congress.

Cabinet stability affects the stability and efficiency of policymaking, and thus of public policies.[10] One source of cabinet instability is frequent changes in government. In Latin America, it is common for each incoming president to change not only the people in charge of the ministries but also the overall structure of government by creating new ministries, eliminating others, changing their names, functions, and scope, and the like.[11] High cabinet instability ultimately leads to high policy instability, low accumulation of expertise, and thus low quality and less adaptable policies. When rotation is high, ministers have no time and incentives to accumulate expertise. These "negative" incentives usually trickle down to the lower levels of the bureaucracy.

---

[10] For example, Amorim Neto and Borsani (2004) find that cabinet stability (low ministerial turnover) is conducive to fiscal policy stability: that is, the ability to control spending and attain fiscal balance.

[11] In Latin America, it is common to see "failed innovations": ministries that are created and abolished a few years later (Blondel 1982).

The Legislative Branch

Two roles have traditionally been conferred on the legislature: to legislate and to restrain the executive branch. In terms of the framework of this study, the legislature, since its inception, has been considered an institution that would help reduce the volatility of polices and better represent the preferences of the populace. The legislature's effectiveness in doing so depends on the institutions of the executive just described and on the institutions of the legislature. Legislative institutions (broadly defined) can have important consequences for how policies are decided and implemented and the possibility of engaging in intertemporal cooperation. In terms of the approach followed in this book, those institutions could have an impact on the number of relevant political actors and their relative duration (and discount factor), tilt the results of the policymaking process in favor of some geographic or demographic minority, affect the "quality" of the representatives, and affect the arenas where decisions are made, among other possibilities. Among the legislative institutions that could affect the behavior of legislators, this discussion highlights two factors: *electoral rules*, the rules of access to the legislature, such as the electoral rules and party nomination procedures; and *legislative structure*, the rules that organize the workings of the legislature, such as whether the legislature is divided in two chambers, and the roles and prerogatives of committees.[12]

Electoral Rules

As is the case with the executive branch, the **method of election** of representatives is a very important determinant of the number of relevant policymakers and the incentives of policymakers.[13] One way the traditional

---

[12] These two groups are interdependent because the rules and workings of congress tend to be an endogenous response to the impact of the electoral rules on party discipline and organization. The study of the inner workings of congress and its interactions with the executive and other actors is one of the main focuses in the country cases covered in this volume.

[13] This discussion does not follow very strict criteria for classifying electoral systems. Using somewhat stricter criteria, Katz (1997) classifies electoral systems according to:

literature has analyzed the impact of electoral rules on policymaking has been primarily through their impact on representativeness, effectiveness, and participation.[14] An electoral system that fosters these features would basically ensure that a strong connection exists between citizens and representatives, that citizens' preferences are represented in the legislature according to their weight in society, and that legislators can work those preferences into policy effectively.

The first characteristic of the method of election is whether representatives to congress are directly elected, indirectly elected, or appointed. These options influence the number of relevant players. Because representatives have as one of their main objectives maximizing the returns on their political careers, they will usually try to satisfy those constituencies that provide them with the greatest benefit. This choice can differ according to the method of election. For example, if representatives are appointed by the executive branch, they are usually not potential veto players for executive branch initiatives; this reduces the number of relevant actors. If representatives are selected by the subnational legislatures, they could become highly relevant players when dealing with some issues, such as intergovernmental transfers; this increases the number of players, at least with regards to these issues.

In Latin America, indirect election and appointment have been gradually phased out in favor of direct election. While this reform alone could help to align the preferences of the representative with those of the citizenry, differences in the system used for the direct election of representatives play a role as well. The most common differences are those

---

translation of votes into seats (electoral formula and constituencies); nature of choice (object of choice, type and number of choices); access to the ballot box (suffrage, registration of voters, ease of voting); and control of candidacy (qualification and nomination, campaign activity, public subsidy).

[14] An electoral system that is optimally representative is one in which political groups obtain legislative seats in nearly exact proportion to their share of the vote. An electoral system fosters effectiveness if it produces sufficient concentration of power in the legislature to make it possible for diverse societal preferences to be aggregated and resolved into acts of government (Payne and others 2002). Finally, participation refers to how the form of voting affects the strength of the connection between the constituent and his or her representative. This is also called the agency dimension, and it could affect voter turnout (Grofman and Reynolds 2001).

with respect to the *electoral formula, the ballot structure, and/or the magnitude of the electoral districts.*[15] In some countries, each district is represented by a single legislator (single-member districts); in other countries, each district is represented by several legislators (multimember districts). In single-member districts, the seat is allocated to the candidate who had the largest number of votes (either in the first ballot or after a runoff election). In the case of multimember districts, candidates are usually part of a party list, and seats are allocated according to one of a variety of different formulas that relate the percentage of votes that the candidates or group of candidates received in the election to the percentage of seats. Ideally, candidates who receive a given share of votes would receive the same share of seats. However, the electoral formula plus the district size (how many legislators are elected from each district) and the thresholds of representation (the minimum percentage of votes that a party must reach to win representation) could introduce a wedge between the share of votes and the share of seats, increasing the degree of disproportionality, and thus affecting the degree of influence of different actors in society.[16]

The electoral rules, particularly the district magnitude, could also affect whether those who try to enter the legislature do so through an existing party or a new party (because of strategic voting).[17] Effectively,

---

[15] The *electoral formula* is the method by which vote totals are translated into claims upon seats. The main classes of electoral formula in democracies are plurality rule and proportional representation. The *ballot structure* consists of the number of votes each voter is entitled to cast; whether voters are allowed to abstain from using some of their votes, when they have more than one, or must cast them all; and whether voters can cumulate their votes or not. Finally, the *magnitude of the electoral district* refers to the number of seats to be filled by the voters of that district.

[16] The *disproportionality* for each party in a particular election is simply the difference between its vote share and its seat share. Disproportionality is usually larger in countries that use majority or plurality voting than in countries that use proportional representation systems. Among those that elect their legislators using proportionality, disproportionality would be larger the smaller the size of the district; the higher the threshold of representation; and if countries have presidential systems with concurrent elections.

[17] *Strategic voting* refers to a type of behavior induced by certain electoral rules in which voters choose not to vote their first order candidates, in order to prevent the least preferred candidates from winning (Shepsle and Bonchek 1997).

the number of effective parties (and potential players) is usually higher as the system becomes more proportional. In Latin America, the effective number of parties is close to two in Chile (with a district size of two) and almost eight in Brazil, where the average district is close to twenty (IDB 2005).[18] The relationship between the number of parties and the number of relevant players in the legislature depends on the degree of allegiance of candidates to parties.[19] If party discipline is high, the number of effective political parties would proxy the number of agents with power over decision making in the chamber. **Party discipline** is also affected by the electoral system because it shapes the incentives of those who must compete, particularly regarding their allegiance to the party bosses or to the constituency that elects them. Under a regime of multimember districts (large size districts) and proportional representation, party leaders have a higher number of "carrots and sticks" (particularly under closed lists); thus politicians respond to the party leadership's platform to increase their chances of nomination (Gallagher, Laver, and Mair 1992).[20] Under a regime of single-member districts and plurality rule (and to a lesser extent under proportional representation with small district size), politicians can usually act as political entrepreneurs who respond mostly to their local constituency to secure nomination and reelection.

---

[18] The degree of fragmentation of a legislature is usually measured one of two ways: through Rae's fragmentation index (Rae 1967), which indicates the probability that two randomly chosen legislators would belong to a different party; or through the effective number of parties (Laakso and Taagapera 1979). The major advantage of the effective number of parties is that it can be visualized more easily than the Rae index (it approximates the equivalent number of parties of equal size for a given fractionalization).

[19] One way to look at the incentives of candidates to conform to citizens or to their party is by looking at the degree of *particularism*: that is, the incentives to cultivate a personal or individual vote versus a party or collective vote (see Carey and Shugart 1995; Wallack and others 2003; Johnson and Wallack 2006).

[20] Rasch (1999) considers that holding equal other institutions, electoral systems have an impact on party discipline through three different channels: district magnitude, ballot, and decision rules or electoral formulas. Basically, parties represented in the legislature would be more disciplined if there is a large average number of seats per district, if the placement on party lists is centrally controlled or is controlled by the party branch of large regions, and if formulas are more proportional (there is a low threshold for election).

In addition to the size of the district, in the case of multimember districts, another important consideration is whether legislators are elected from closed or open lists (*ballot structure*). The ballot structure has important implications, as it could affect electoral strategies, the degree of party discipline, and the link between voters and representatives (Carey and Shugart 1995). Assuming that party labels are meaningful, closed list systems provide party leaders the greatest control over rank and file legislators, encouraging party discipline (Mainwaring and Shugart 1997a). As party leaders decide the order of the list, this may also weaken the nexus between legislators and voters.

By contrast, in open list systems, as candidates of the same party compete against one another, they face incentives to form *factions*: that is, organized groups within parties that compete for control of valued resources (Cox and McCubbins 2001). To sum up, while closed list systems encourage party votes, in open list systems legislators face incentives to cultivate personal votes (Ames 1995b).[21]

The overall degree of fractionalization of the legislature also depends on the incentives for coalition formation and stability generated by the electoral rules. Usually, coalitions will form in the pre-electoral stage in single-member districts, while coalitions will form in the post-electoral stage in multimember districts. However, there is much variation within the multimember district family, as some systems may encourage coalition formation at the pre-electoral stage as well. The binomial system used in Chile is a case in point.[22]

---

[21] A word of caution: the link between legislators and voters in open list systems should not be overestimated. In large multimember districts, as individual legislators are encouraged to focus on narrow constituencies, it is more costly for the voters to become informed about the contending candidates, and thus it may be more difficult to hold them accountable (Payne and others 2002).

[22] The *binomial system* is a proportional representation system with district magnitude of two in all districts. Each of the lists receiving the two highest vote shares wins one of the two available seats per district—unless the most voted list outplaces its second place rival by a ratio of more than two to one, in which case both seats go to the most voted list. In addition, coalitions are allowed only to the extent that they are national in scope (thus they are binding in every district in the country).

The binomial system provides parties a strong incentive to coalesce at the district level, as doubling the rival's vote share gives the winning list all seats, or securing a second place and avoiding being doubled gives the list half the seats. Additionally, given that the costs of defection for a party (such as leaving the coalition) are high, the binomial system also fosters coalition stability, as chapter 5 on Chile in this volume shows. The binomial system seems to be one of the main characteristics that explains some of the good features of public policy in Chile.

In contrast, multimember systems, where the thresholds of success are lower, make parties compete unilaterally, thus limiting their ability to form coalitions at the pre-electoral stage. As the related country chapters show, in these cases, the stability of coalitions varies across countries and across administrations; it depends at least in part on the extent to which there is a match between what the president is able to offer legislators to keep them within the coalition, and what legislators want. In the case of Ecuador, agreements are short-lived because legislators do not want to be associated with the president. In the case of Brazil, presidents use the distribution of projects with local benefits to gather political support.

Electoral rules also play a role in explaining the representation of ideologies and the polarization of the political system. Thus they also affect legislators' preferences. The electoral system can affect **representation** of ideologies, minority representation, and representation of local interests (*localism*), and whether politicians could compete successfully at the local or the national level (Grofman and Reynolds 2001) through their impact on barriers of entry and representation biases.[23] While some electoral systems favor the entry of small parties, others require a large presence in the electorate in order to win representation (high thresholds). Similarly, some electoral systems could overrepresent some parties and underrepresent others according to the distribution of their sup-

---

[23] The relationship between individual candidates and the party can also be changed through the practice of *gerrymandering*: dividing a territorial unit into election districts to give one political party an electoral majority in a large number of districts, while concentrating the voting strength of the opposition in as few districts as possible. Gerrymandering can affect the stability of legislators and their political allegiance, and thus it can affect the game of political transactions.

porters across districts (Saiz and Geser 1999; John and Saiz 1999; Calvo and Murillo 2004) and the degree of **malapportionment** (Samuels and Snyder 2001; Ansolabehere, Snyder, and Ting 2002).[24]

Electoral systems affect **polarization** through electoral formulas and district magnitudes (Sartori 1976; Mainwaring and Scully 1995a). In single-member district (SMD) electoral systems, policies are hardly ideological and a successful politician responds to the preferences of the median voter in his or her geographic district. By contrast, in regimes of multimember districts and proportional representation, parties are more ideologically oriented than in two-party systems and political parties' preferred policies usually deviate from that of the median voter. A higher degree of polarization could imply the existence of more extreme positions in government, the legislature, or the political spectrum. In some instances, this could lead to greater instability in the political system and more drastic changes in policies (Haggard 2000).

Some of the actions of legislators are explained by their expected duration, which affects the rate at which they discount the future (**discount rate**). Higher discount rates reduce the value of future benefits and reduce legislators' incentives to invest in their capabilities while in office. The duration is determined, among other factors, by term limits, reelection constraints, and the electoral system in place. The implications of the first two factors on duration are straightforward; the shorter the term and the harder it is to be reelected, the higher the discount rate. The electoral system affects duration through its impact on determining who has the power to reward or punish the legislators, that is, who is the legislator's principal.[25] In single-member districts such as in the

---

[24] *Malapportionment* is the inequitable or unsuitable apportioning of representatives to a legislative body. Some districts could be electing more than an equal share of legislators according to the population of the district. Even if malapportionment does not affect the number of relevant players, it can affect the legislator's identity, and thus the results of the policymaking process.

[25] The principal-agent problem is a particular description of a situation under game theory. There is a player called a principal, and one or more other players called agents with utility functions that are in some sense different from the principal's. The principal can act more effectively through the agents than directly, and must construct incentive schemes to get them to behave at least in part according to the principal's interests.

United States, it is the voters who are responsible for getting legislators reelected. Since seniority plays an important role in committee assignments, which in turn affect the ability of legislators to deliver benefits to their constituents, as a general rule voters have an incentive to reelect incumbent legislators. In contrast, in a country such as Argentina where the direct connection between voters and legislators is weaker, governors and other provincial party leaders tend to be responsible for putting together the party lists. They tend to be the "principals" of the legislators, and often have incentives to move legislators to other (often subnational) positions, which results in increased turnover in Congress. Some partial data support this hypothesis. The high rate of reelection of members of the U.S. Congress is not that common in Latin America legislatures. In Argentina, the number of incumbents running for reelection is close to 25 percent, and the reelection rate is below 20 percent (Jones and others 2002). In Chile, however, around three-quarters of incumbents have been renominated for the legislature within the same coalition, and three-fifths have won reelection (Carey 2002a). In the mid-1980s, the percentage of representatives seeking reelection in Argentina was as low as 26 percent, compared to 99 percent in the United States. For the same elections, the percentage of representatives returning to office was 17 percent in Argentina (proportional representation, closed lists) and 83 percent in the United States (plurality). These percentages were 70 and 43 in Brazil (proportional representation, open list), and 76 and 59 in Chile (binomial) (Morgenstern and Nacif 2002; IDB 2005).

As shown, the method of election, along with other complementary institutions, is relevant in this framework because it could have important implications for the number, characteristics, preferences, and stability of agents and groups that are in charge of policymaking.[26] Additionally, the electoral system could affect the pool of candidates willing to enter politics and the personal characteristics of individual legislators (such

---

[26] In addition to the electoral system, other determinants that could affect the personal characteristics (competence, honesty) of legislators are candidacy requirements, nomination procedures, term limits, and party organization. Additionally, gender and ethnic constraints could affect entry into politics.

as their competence and honesty) because different electoral systems affect the incentives faced by individual legislators to extract rents or engage in corrupt activities (Caselli and Morelli 2004).[27] According to standard criteria by which legislatures are compared, Chile's congress is reestablishing itself as an unusually professional and technically competent legislature (Carey 2002a; Saiegh 2005; IDB 2005). The same cannot be said of other legislative bodies in the region, where professional capacity is not common and politicians rotate without accumulating any institutional knowledge.

Legislative Structure: Unicameralism and Bicameralism

One of the most important characteristics regarding the structure of legislatures is whether they have a single chamber or are divided into two different chambers. In Latin America, more than half the countries have bicameral legislatures (Llanos 2003a; Sanchez, Nolte, and Llanos 2005). Nonetheless, there is little agreement in the literature on the benefits of having a bicameral legislature. While political philosophers like Montesquieu were in favor of the institution, others like Jeremy Bentham were not. Some of the advantages of having a bicameral legislature include the following: avoiding bad decisions made in haste,[28] avoiding actions that favor narrow interests (Buchanan and Tullock 1962); reducing the likelihood of voting cycles (Mueller 1996a); and representing different interests (Mueller 1996b).[29] Of course, the validity of these arguments

---

[27] First, while in proportional representation (PR) systems incumbent party leaders monopolize control over rents, in plurality systems the locus of rents is more evenly divided between the party leadership and individual legislators. Second, the ability of voters and opposition parties to control rent extraction under both systems is different. As plurality rule produces districts with smaller numbers of voters than proportional representation systems, collective action problems for voters and opposition groups in monitoring corrupt incumbents are less severe. Thus some authors argue that proportional representation systems are more susceptible to corruption relative to plurality systems (Rose, Ackerman, and Kunicova 2002).

[28] This was one of the reasons James Madison, John Jay, and Alexander Hamilton (1787) mentioned in *The Federalist Papers*.

[29] Of course, this begs the question of which interests these may be.

depends on the implementation of the system. In some cases, bicameralism could make the government incapable of responding decisively to a crisis, could increase wasteful redistribution (either to a geographic or to a corporate constituency), or could excessively increase the cost of reaching a decision (Mueller 1996b). In other cases, having a second chamber could provide the necessary balance of power. Because the strategies of the actors and the outcomes are affected by the presence or absence of a second chamber, the study of the policymaking process in countries with bicameral legislatures must focus not only on the bargaining of each one of the chambers separately, but on the interaction between chambers, as well.

Two institutions related to the legislature determine each chamber's strength or weakness, its relevance, and the basis of its representation. The first important aspect is the **constitutional powers** of each chamber (such as the order of voting, rules to overturn/modify decisions, and role in the confirmation/impeachment processes). Those powers determine the role of each chamber in the policymaking process, which one has the most power, and under which conditions both are relevant policy players. Constitutional powers could determine that in certain countries or policy areas both chambers are relevant, which would make it more difficult to pass new legislation. In other countries (or policy areas) one of the chambers could be "subservient" to the other and would not act as an additional veto player, which would make it easier to pass new legislation.

The second important feature is the **method of election**. While this chapter has already discussed the impact of this feature on the role of the legislature as a whole, here the emphasis is on the differential impact on a second chamber. On the one hand, the method of election could affect its political clout. For example, a second chamber that is not directly elected could lack the democratic legitimacy, and thus the real political influence, that popular election confers.[30] On the other hand,

---

[30] Currently in Latin America, there are no cases of indirect election. In Chile, until the constitutional reform of 2005, nine senators were appointed and one seat was reserved for former presidents.

the electoral rules may affect whether having two chambers adds players and interests to the bargaining, which interests those are, and thus the type of negotiation that ensues.

The method of selecting the representatives to each chamber and the basis of representation (type of constituency) determine the degree of congruence between the upper and lower houses in bicameral legislatures. If there is congruence, and the party composition of one chamber mimics the composition of the other, it is often assumed that preferences of the chambers will be similar or identical. However, congruence (and similarity) should not be equated with identity of positions. Legislators in each chamber could be representing different constituencies, as some geographic entities could be overrepresented in one of the chambers. Moreover, chambers could have different decision-making rules. In addition, opinions may vary even within the party.

One factor that can explain the divergence of positions across chambers is the degree of the legislature's malapportionment. Usually, the second chamber is elected by methods designed so as to overrepresent certain minorities. The greatest degree of overrepresentation occurs when there is equality of state representation regardless of states' population, as is usually the case in the upper chamber of federal governments.[31] A high degree of overrepresentation (malapportionment) usually produces two effects. First, state-level interests are favored in public policy, particularly on fiscal policy. Second, smaller states usually end up relatively better off. For example, the Brazilian and Argentinean congresses overrepresent the (mostly poor) less populated states (Samuels 2003; Gibson and Calvo 2000).

Therefore, even under congruence, the analysis indicates that compared with unicameralism, bicameralism could increase the number of relevant players, and thus make changes to the status quo more difficult (Tsebelis and Money 1997). If changes occur, they happen through a process of both cooperation and conflict between the two chambers. The outcome of the bargaining between the chambers depends on the

---

[31] Numerous explanations for this arrangement have been offered, both normative (in terms of equity) and positive (such as who held the power at the moment of drafting the constitutions).

relative power of each house, which is a function of the constitutional powers and institutional rules (such as in which chamber bills are introduced, which chamber has the last word on disputes, and the number of possible iterations for considering a bill) and the impatience of each chamber to reach a deal. We now turn to those factors.

Legislative Organization: Committees and Agenda-Setting Power

In a context where the legislature has an impact on policymaking, analysis of the practices and regulations that rule legislative activities matters because these practices and regulations may alter the number of players and their allegiance. By distributing power and resources, the voting rules, agenda-setting powers, rules for introducing bills, order of voting, presence or absence of roll call votes, and the relevance of committees and seniority all affect the actual number of agents that have influence over policy decisions, their incentives, the arenas in which they interact, and their discount rates. The legislature rules are usually endogenous because politicians—mainly party leaders—react to the deeper institutions commonly found in the constitutions, such as the electoral rules, by trying to shape the workings of the political institutions to their advantage (Shepsle and Weingast 1987; Carey 2006; Cox 2006).

One important aspect of legislative organization is the rules that guide the process and structure of legislation. **Agenda-setting power** refers to any special ability given to legislators to determine which bills are considered on the floor and under what procedures.[32] Because legislative rights and resources are not evenly distributed among legislators, agenda-setting power affects the structure of the policymaking process and the weight of legislators in policy decisions (Cheibub and Limongi 2002). Understanding agenda-setting power is fundamental to fully grasping the micro workings of legislatures.[33] First, it provides clues about the dis-

---

[32] Agenda power is positive/negative when a legislator or party has the ability to ensure/prevent the consideration of bills on the floor.

[33] Cox and McCubbins (2005) explain the workings of the U.S. Congress by analyzing agenda-setting rules. For applications of the agenda power framework in other institutional settings, see Figuereido and Limongi (2000); Amorim Neto, Cox, and Mc-

tribution of "power" in the legislatures. Second, it offers insights on the way majority parties or coalitions control the flow of legislation, and thus influence legislative outcomes (Cox and McCubbins 2005).[34] For example, in some countries, the president of the chamber controls which bills will be considered in a legislative year. That prerogative increases his or her power, which he or she can use to foster discipline of fellow party legislators and strike deals with the opposition.

The second aspect to analyze is the **role of committees**. Committee power depends on the rules governing the sequence of proposing, amending, and in some cases vetoing proposed bills in the legislative process. In most countries, committees are not only repositories of policy expertise but also gatekeepers and the point of origin of policies in their respective policy domains, which provides them with disproportionate control over the agenda. Therefore, committees are sometimes powerful and they are able to impose many of their policy preferences (Weingast and Marshall 1988; Shepsle and Bonchek 1997).

However, the extent of committee strength, the degree of specialization, and the technical capacities of committees vary widely and are shaped by a number of factors. First, committee rules determine the number and size of committees, thus affecting the supply of committee slots. If the number of committees per legislator is large, legislators are required to serve on several committees at the same time. As time and effort are limited resources, and legislators participate in more committees simultaneously, the level of specialization and the degree to which legislators accumulate policy expertise decreases (Jones and others 2002). Second, the process of committee and leadership assignment also affects specialization. While a seniority system in which legislators serve particular sectoral constituencies in order to be reelected fosters specialization, a partisan distribution of committee and leadership assignments, where party leaders practice rotating legislators from one

---

Cubbins (2003); and Jones and Hwang (2005). Tsebelis (2002) also analyzes agenda setting in parliamentary systems.

[34] Agenda-setting rules can usually be found in a legislature's formal procedures ("*reglamentos*"). Alemán (2006) provides a survey of the internal rules of procedure in Latin American legislatures.

committee to the other, undermines it. Finally, another factor shaping a committee system's technical capacities is the possession of resources, such as a competent committee staff (Saiegh 2005).

In those cases where committees are important for legislative policymaking, if party leaders retain control of committee nominations,[35] they could use those nominations to ensure a higher degree of party discipline (Cox and McCubbins 1994). Thus committees have gained importance in countries such as the United States, where party leaders and party seniority determine access to committee membership (Shepsle and Weingast 1987; Rasch 1999). In the case of Colombia (before a recent reform), the party label was not a relevant indicator of allegiance and factionalization was very high. Even campaign financing would flow directly to the factions, out of the control of party leaders. In that context, the only tool party leaders had for retaining some power over the legislators was through the selection of legislators for the committees (which are few and important).

Even though party leaders have usually tried to find ways to increase the importance of committees in order to increase their clout with the rank and file of their parties, in some countries they have chosen the opposite path to overcome problematic situations within their parties. For example, parties have chosen to create new positions and new offices within the parties and to increase the number of positions in the legislature, including increases in the number of committees. In Argentina, leaders use assignments to generate support, both within and among parties, and since reelection rates are low, the number of committee posts has grown to provide leaders more posts to offer to pliant legisla-

---

[35] There are other ways in which party leaders can increase party discipline, such as the allocation of party funds for the electoral campaigns of individual legislators or party nomination procedures. Opposition status also fosters party discipline, despite the fact that the opposition's party leadership controls fewer resources and is thus more vulnerable. Additionally, when there is an opposition party that is willing to block most of the government initiatives, the discipline in the governing party tends to increase. Members of governing parties in presidential systems tend to feel freer to vote against the executive on the assembly's floor than their counterparts in parliamentary systems. For details on party discipline in Europe, see Gallagher, Laver, and Mair (1992) and Sánchez de Dios (1999).

tors. The number of committees grew from 26 in the 1983–85 legislature to 39 in the 1993–95 legislature (Jones 2002; Jones and others 2002; Mustapic 2002). All of this has tended to conspire against the role of committees as repositories of technical expertise and policymaking capabilities (Jones and others 2006; chapter 3 on Argentina, this volume). In contrast, in Colombia, legislators can participate in only one committee for the entire four-year term. These features provide high incumbency rates and a high level of specialization.

Party leaders are not the only ones who use committees to their advantage. Legislators usually select to belong to those committees that would provide them with the greatest benefits, such as increasing their chance of reelection. Stratmann and Baur (2002) find empirical evidence of different behaviors across legislators for Germany, where half of the parliamentary seats are awarded from single-member constituencies and the other half through proportional voting. The legislators elected from single-member constituencies, regardless of individual expertise, tend to choose those legislative committees that deal with geographically based affairs, while the legislators elected by party lists tend to prefer those committees that deal with broad-based policies and transfers.

Finally, regarding the arenas in which transactions take place, an important characteristic of Latin American legislative institutions is that much negotiation and bargaining occurs behind closed doors (Morgenstern and Nacif 2002). In most instances, presidents prefer to shield disagreements with the legislature, as well as the concessions made to the legislature (or to individual legislators), from the public eye. In other cases, when the president's proposal enjoys strong popular support, he or she may prefer to override any legislative proposal by relying on public opinion and refusing to offer concessions.

The Role of the Legislature in the PMP and Congress's Capabilities

Recent studies have developed classifications or typologies of Latin American legislatures on the basis of variables and concepts like those emphasized above. By focusing on Argentina, Brazil, Chile, and Mexico,

Cox and Morgenstern (2001, 2002) classify Latin American legislatures as reactive instead of proactive. This implies that while the legislatures rarely initiate legislation, they are often involved in negotiating over policy issues behind the scenes and vetoing or amending executive initiatives. Accordingly, Latin American legislatures are not necessarily powerless or unimportant, and presidents must anticipate what the assemblies may accept and modify their strategies accordingly. The support for the presidents in the legislature varies greatly in Latin America, making it more difficult to establish a pattern of relationship between the two branches over time. While support for the president usually oscillates around half of the members of the legislature in the United States, in Latin America the amplitude is larger.

IDB (2005), drawing on Saiegh (2005) and Stein and Tommasi (2005b), develops an index of the policymaking capabilities of congresses. The index attempts to capture the factors that shape the role of legislatures in the policymaking process by focusing on the capabilities of congress as an organization, as well as on some personal characteristics of legislators. The quantitative and subjective variables that make up the index include: the level of confidence of citizens and business in the performance of congress, the average years of legislator experience, the percentage of legislators with university education, their technical expertise, the average number of committee memberships per legislator, the strength of committees, and the extent to which congress is a desirable place for politicians to build a career. The evidence indicates that those countries with high levels of congressional capabilities tend to score high on their features of public policies.

The impact of congress in policymaking is not independent of the role of the judiciary. The evidence seems to indicate that congressional capabilities particularly affect policies in the case of judicial independence; otherwise, there would be no regular enforcement of the acts of congress.

The Judiciary Branch

The role of the judiciary is framed by the choice of judicial system: that is, whether a country "chooses" to adopt civil law or common law. Common law is the body of customary law, based upon judicial decisions and embodied in reports of decided cases, that has been administered by the courts of England since the Middle Ages and has evolved into the type of legal system now found also in the United States and in most of the member states of the Commonwealth. Civil law, which has been adopted in much of Latin America, is a set of codes that sets forth general rules that are applied and interpreted taking into consideration the "spirit" of the code in an effort to apply to each case the solution that would have been desired by the legislator (Tullock 1997). This distinction is important, as it frames the relative importance of the judiciary branch vis-à-vis the other branches of government.

In terms of the framework of analysis of this study, the judiciary may play several policymaking roles.[36] It can be an **impartial referee**, as an enforcer of political transactions among different political actors; this can increase the durability and stability of policies. The judiciary can also be a **policy player**, shaping policies according to its preferences and/or society's, and sometimes providing a voice for marginalized or unorganized social sectors. The judiciary plays these roles through its reactive (veto) and proactive prerogatives. This distinction of the potential roles of the judiciary is important because it provides a more accurate depiction, moving beyond the analysis of its actions only as a veto player and highlighting its importance as enforcer of political transactions. These functions are not mutually exclusive, and some are closely connected.

The relevance of the judiciary as an actor in the PMP depends on the degree of judicial independence.[37] If the judiciary is independent, legislators and the executive must take into account the preferences of the judiciary when making policy. On the contrary, if the judiciary responds to one of the other branches of government, then its actions would

---

[36] The framework has been adapted from Sousa (2005).

[37] *Judicial independence* has four interrelated dimensions: *substantive independence*, or the power to make judicial decisions and exercise official duties subject to no other authority but the law; *personal independence*, or stability of tenure and freedom from intimidation or threats; *collective independence*, or judicial participation in the central administration of courts; and *internal independence*, or independence from judicial superiors and colleagues.

merely mimic (and probably strengthen) the actions of that branch of government.

Among the characteristics of the judiciary that affect judicial independence, several stand out: the extent of budgetary autonomy; the level of transparency and the extent of the use of meritocratic criteria in the process for nominating and appointing judges; the stability of the tenure of judges; and the reach of judicial review powers. Effective judicial independence also depends upon the behavior of other actors, such as whether the president or political parties regularly interfere with the courts. This, in turn, depends upon these actors' incentives (Sousa 2005).[38]

Given judiciary independence, the judiciary, as an **impartial referee**, can play the role of enforcer of political transactions. This offers an additional layer of durability to politicians' agreements by bounding them to their commitments. Thus, working mainly in reactive fashion, the judiciary can provide a "durability mechanism" that can increase the probability of reaching intertemporal agreements.[39] In this framework, related to the work first discussed by Landes and Posner (1975), the presence of an independent court generates intertemporal enforcement of the political agreements undertaken today, increasing the benefits of implementing policy exchanges.[40] In other words, an independent judiciary tends to resolve time inconsistency problems (that is, agreements made today have a higher discounted value because they are less likely to be changed in the future) because judges exhibit a pronounced ten-

---

[38] A topic related to the independence and duration of the judiciary is the existence and stability of, and respect for, the constitution. Whether or not a country has a written constitution, institutions such as the size of the majorities required for amendment and the type of judicial review for constitutional matters would all contribute to determining the durability of rules.

[39] By entering the bargaining with veto power similar to the rest of the agents, it could also facilitate cooperation by enforcing the transactions that facilitate long-term agreements (Crain 2001).

[40] Crain and Tollison (1979) show that as judicial independence and/or the tenure of judges increases, there are fewer incentives to use other, stricter rules to prevent time inconsistency problems. (In game theory and economics, time inconsistency is a situation in a dynamic game where a player's best plan for some future period will not be optimal when that future period arrives).

dency to resolve legal disputes and ambiguities in terms of the expressed intentions of the legislature that originally enacted the law. Therefore, an independent judiciary, even through vetoing new legislation, could be a facilitator of intertemporal agreements. In this context, a longer duration of judges could contribute to increasing the adaptability and stability of policies (Iaryczower, Spiller, and Tommasi 2002).

As a **policy player**, the judiciary branch can act in a reactive way (as a veto player) or in a proactive manner, molding policies according to its preferences by "ruling from the bench" in common law countries, or in civil law countries by interpreting laws according to the constitution.[41] For example, in a context where the judiciary is independent and able to veto new legislation, if the legislature and the executive wish to move policies out of the status quo they would have to approve policies that are closer than the status quo to the preferences of the median judge (Shepsle and Bonchek 1997). Additionally, judges (or constitutional courts, in the case of civil law countries) can introduce their preferences into policymaking by ruling on policies and new legislation if their preferences differ substantially from those of the other agents (Cox and McCubbins 2001; Tsebelis 2002).[42] In this role, the judiciary could contribute to making policies more public regarding and to ensuring that policies are more inclusive, if judges' preferences are aligned with those of the population at large.

The preferences and quality of the judges, which affect which interests they represent, are usually determined by the appointment procedure and the rules by which the judiciary is organized.[43] To predict their preferences and potential effects on the policymaking process, it is important to understand who judges are and what they want. Following the

---

[41] The judiciary can become a policy player by interpreting the statutes, not only in terms of what the legislature wrote at a particular time but also in light of the entire legal precedent.

[42] That is, if they are not "absorbed," in terms of the definition by Tsebelis (2002).

[43] Tsebelis (2002) discusses appointment procedures and impact on the preferences of the courts. Other factors that shape the judiciary's independence are the degree of judicial budget autonomy, the terms and tenure of judges, and the extent of judicial review powers (Sousa 2005).

work of Posner (1993), some of the motivations for judges are popularity, prestige, and reputation: popularity among fellow judges; prestige in the legal and larger political community; and reputation in the academic legal world (for example, the desire not to be reversed by a higher court or the legislature). Therefore, in this context, the method of nomination and appointment (by the president, by the legislature, by both of them, by a judicial council, or by some other means) makes the difference.

Summarizing, while the judiciary can constitute an additional veto player, making it harder for the government to change policies, or respond to crises, an independent judiciary can also favor the development of political transactions and move policies toward their (or society's) bliss point.[44] On one hand, it can provide enforcement for the agreements reached by other actors. This can increase the durability of agreements and policies, and thus the present value of cooperation: in this case, increasing the adaptability and stability of policies.[45] On the other, by acting as a policy player, the judiciary can move policies toward increasing public regardedness, if its incentives are right.

Federalism and Subnational Authorities

The basis of federalism is a national polity with dual (or multiple) levels of government; each level exercises exclusive authority over constitutionally determined policy areas, but only one level of government—the central government—is internationally sovereign (Gibson 2004). Federalism affects policymaking through the role that subnational authorities (governors) may play in the design and implementation of public policies and their interaction with national-level actors (presidents, legislators). For example, the introduction of subnational elections significantly changed political and party dynamics in Venezuela. The extent to which

---

[44] The bliss point is the point of maximum utility: the point that everyone wants to reach to maximize their utility according to their preferences.

[45] If there is no judicial independence and duration is low, actors would have to opt for other means to increase the durability of laws, such as introducing constitutional amendments and qualified majority rules. If this were the case, policies would tend to be more rigid.

subnational authorities influence national policymaking depends on a number of institutional variables, to which the discussion now turns.

The first important institutional variable is the **method of selecting subnational authorities**. If governors are popularly elected, they play a more important role than if they are appointed by the central government. If governors can be reelected, they have incentives to cater to their constituency and pursue regional goals at the expense of national objectives (Monaldi 2005).

Another important institutional variable is the existence of a **territorial chamber** in the national congress, as discussed in the section on bicameralism. Most federal countries allow for the representation of territories (states, provinces) in the national policymaking process through senates. These chambers tend to increase the power of subnational political actors, as they provide an additional veto point in the political system. This means that subnational interests need to be taken into account when national actors design and bargain over policies.

Another key factor is the overrepresentation of subnational units in the national legislature (malapportionment). **Malapportionment** strengthens the political power of the least populated states relative to the most populated units. Malapportionment is not a unique feature of territorial chambers. Several lower houses in federal systems show a certain degree of overrepresentation, even in population-based lower chambers.[46] As a consequence, overrepresented units may skew policies in their favor, and they typically receive higher resources per capita. This is the case in Argentina, which has the highest level of malapportionment in the upper chamber in Latin America and the third highest in the lower chamber (Samuels and Snyder 2001).

The **method used for selecting candidates to the national legislature** is important because it shapes the incentives of representatives once in office—and more generally, their political careers. If the candidates' names and order are decided at the subnational level, the potential for regional party leaders to use their influence and resources to influence

---

[46] This is a result of the existence of lower and upper limits to the number of deputies that a certain region may have, among other factors.

the election of legislators is high. In that case, the regional congressional delegation to the national legislature might vote more according to the governor's line than to the national party leader's or president's line, giving another tool to the regions for influencing national politics.

Moreover, when subnational authorities (such as governors) are important political players at the local level and parties are organized along territorial lines, national elections are heavily influenced by subnational-level politics, as governors may provide legislators and presidents with electoral coattails (Jones 1997; Samuels 2003). In cases where electoral districts coincide with territorial units (such as states and provinces), the degree of "partisan harmony" (the extent of support for the president throughout the territorial units) affects policymaking. For example, when national leaders lack support at the subnational level, a "vertically" divided government, combined with the absence of sufficient resources to buy support, could complicate the approval of a president's agenda (Rodden and Wibbels 2002). In Argentina, it contributes to sustaining a political system that operates on the basis of exchanges of provincial support of national policies for fiscal benefits to the provinces.

Finally, the link between federal and subnational politics is also fiscal. In particular, federal fiscal arrangements define tax and expenditure assignments between different levels of government, the design of intergovernmental transfers, and the borrowing autonomy of subnational units (Stein 1999). In situations of high fiscal decentralization, subnational authorities control resources that render them powerful actors, even affecting policy outcomes at the national level.[47] In Brazil, in the early 1990s, governors would challenge the central government fiscal sustainability to gain leverage in their negotiations (IDB 2005).

---

[47] For example, in many federal countries, while expenditure is decentralized, most revenues are collected at the center and then transferred to the subnational governments. This creates an incentive for subnational governments to overspend from the common pool of resources, enjoying the full benefits of overspending without internalizing its costs. If this tendency is not limited by the central government, the opportunistic behavior of subnational governments may result in dire economic consequences: excessive spending, fiscal deficits, debt crisis, and difficulties in macroeconomic management and fiscal adjustment at the national level (Wibbels 2000; Rodden and Wibbels 2002).

Political Parties and Party Systems

Political parties are organizations that seek influence in a state, often by attempting to occupy positions in government by "aggregating" interests in the society (Ware 1996). They have also been regarded as instruments used by politicians to gain political office by reducing transaction costs (Aldrich 1995). In terms of transactions with citizens, political parties reduce information costs by association with party labels and ideologies. In terms of transactions within the political system, political parties reduce the number of players in charge of transactions.

The role of political parties and party systems in the policymaking process is twofold. In some countries, political parties act directly in the policymaking process by contributing to the definition and articulation of policy programs and engaging effectively in public policy debates. In others, party system characteristics affect the policymaking process indirectly by influencing the workability of executive-legislative relations, the possibilities for coordination in congress, and the incentives of elected officials: that is, the extent to which they focus on adopting and implementing public policies consistent with a broader public good.

The characteristics identified in the literature, especially those that are most relevant for the focus of this volume, include the degree of party system institutionalization, the programmatic character of parties and party systems, the degree of fragmentation, the level of party discipline, and the degree of party system nationalization, as well as the nature of campaign finance.[48]

Party System Institutionalization

Party systems can be considered institutionalized when the patterns of interparty competition are relatively stable, parties have fairly stable and deep bases of societal support, parties and elections are viewed as legitimate and as the sole instruments for determining who governs,

---

[48] This chapter does not consider the impact of campaign finance because it is not relevant for the Latin American cases included in this book.

and party organizations are characterized by reasonably stable rules and structures (Mainwaring and Scully 1995a). In terms of the framework of this book, institutionalized party systems are likely to promote longer time horizons, greater policy consistency over time, and a greater potential for intertemporal agreements, since commitments made by current party leaders are more likely to be respected in the future. In contrast, electoral competition in noninstitutionalized party systems is volatile, and linkages between parties and voters are weaker, which may result in noncooperative outcomes in the policymaking process and a high degree of policy volatility.

Programmatic Character of Party Systems

Programmatic parties compete for and obtain support on the basis of their policy orientations and accomplishments, and parties distinguish themselves in terms of their policy proposals or ideological orientation. Programmatic parties are usually contrasted with *clientelistic parties*. The latter compete for and obtain support based on the distribution of selective material incentives to voters (such as public sector jobs, governmental contracts, cash, or meals) in networks of direct exchange and are judged by voters primarily on their ability to deliver these particularistic benefits (Kitschelt 2000).

These characteristics affect the outcomes of the policymaking process in contrasting ways. On the one hand, if an institutionalized party system is also programmatic, then political parties are likely to favor more public regarding policies, since parties represent different policy options and voters can hold them accountable on that basis. On the other hand, clientelistic parties are mostly interested in maintaining their narrow bases of support and keeping their electoral machines running. Thus the usual outcome of exchanges between clientelistic parties are private regarding policies.

Party System Fragmentation

The degree of fragmentation is usually captured through the number of parties that regularly obtain a significant share of the votes and/or seats in the legislature (Lijphart 1994). In terms of the framework developed in chapter 1, the level of fragmentation could influence the number of players in charge of policymaking. In presidential contexts, it limits the size of presidential legislative contingents and increases the number of partners with which the president must form coalitions. Higher fragmentation would be expected to complicate executive-legislative relations, increase the transaction costs of obtaining policy agreements, and limit policy adaptability.

As mentioned, party system fragmentation is a function of the electoral system: the proportional or majoritarian design of the system, the size of electoral districts, the nature of the formula for converting votes into seats, and the concurrence of presidential and legislative elections. However, electoral rules do not affect fragmentation in isolation. In fact, the number of parties is determined by the interaction of electoral systems, the number of salient social and economic cleavages, and the political history of each country (Cox and Amorim Neto 1997).

Party Discipline

Party discipline corresponds to the extent that representatives of the same party vote in similar ways in the assembly (Rasch 1999). As mentioned, party discipline is a key factor shaping the president's ability to pass his agenda, and it depends on several institutional configurations. For example, it is partly a result of the role party leaders play in nominating and influencing the reelection chances and future political careers of members of congress. However, factors other than candidate selection matter as well, including party leaders' roles in organizing the work of the legislature (such as appointing committee members and chairpersons, and agenda power).

Party System Nationalization

Another dimension of political party systems is their level of nationalization: that is, the extent to which parties are national in scope and receive similar levels of support throughout the country (Jones and Mainwaring

2003). Nationalization matters for policymaking because it affects the number of players interacting in the PMP, executive-legislative relations, and thus, the outer features of public policies.

When a party system is said to be nationalized, the executive (generally a nationally oriented political player) may be able to pass his or her agenda through the legislature more easily by negotiating with a few key national party leaders. The level of nationalization may also affect the quality of public policies. When the territorial distribution of a party's vote is relatively homogeneous, politicians will be more likely to treat its constituent units in a similar fashion in areas such as fiscal and social policy. Additionally, as national issues (such as macroeconomic stability) are central to the careers of both the executive and legislators, politicians have incentives to work for delivering national public goods, instead of focusing on delivering particularistic benefits. In contrast, in highly denationalized party systems, parties tend to favor their bases of support and may use different mechanisms (the budget process, discretionary handouts) to distribute resources asymmetrically.

Bureaucracies

Several characteristics of bureaucracies and public employment are important for policymaking because these characteristics can affect both the quality of implementation and the enforcement of political agreements (Zuvanic and Iacovello 2005). Two characteristics in particular help explain different bureaucratic types: the degree of *autonomy* (the extent to which effective guarantees of professionalism in the civil service are in place and the degree to which civil servants are protected from arbitrariness and politization); and the *technical capacities* of bureaucracies (the degree to which the bureaucracy has salary compensation and evaluation systems). *Meritocratic bureaucracies* are characterized by high levels of autonomy and capacity. In contrast, *clientelistic bureaucracies* lack both attributes, and thus function mainly as a private source of employment managed by governing political parties. Between these two extremes, *administrative bureaucracies* enjoy autonomy but lack a high degree of capacity, while *parallel bureaucracies* are characterized by high degrees of capacity and low autonomy.

The advantages of meritocratic bureaucracies for policymaking are numerous. First, an organized civil service can help politicians fortify their commitment by delegating decision-making authority to autonomous institutions,[49] reducing the capacity to reverse their decisions in response to short-term considerations. Because the effectiveness of policies depends on the widespread belief that they will be sustained over time, meritocratic bureaucracies, characterized by independence and long tenure of public employees, are an important part of the set of political institutions conducive to policy outcomes. The evidence seems to indicate that better bureaucratic types are strongly associated with better policy features (IDB 2005).

However, all bureaucracies are not created equal. In fact, the extent to which bureaucracies enjoy these characteristics depends on several factors. One important determinant of the organization of the civil service is the strategic interaction between other players in the policymaking process (such as legislatures and executives), their time horizons, the degree of interest alignment, and the distribution of the benefits of patronage (Geddes 1991; Spiller and Urbiztondo 1994).

Other Institutions

This chapter has focused on the workings of traditional political institutions. However, other relevant institutional dimensions play a role in defining the incentives and behavior of political actors in the design and implementation of policies—particularly in Latin America. This section considers a few examples.

A country's history of the voting franchise along dimensions such as age, gender, literacy, and geography has a potential impact on the economic and political landscape. This legacy may be important in understanding the interaction of voters with political parties, and the workings

---

[49] The analysis is somewhat similar to the rationale behind the literature on central bank independence and independent regulatory agencies.

of party systems, for example. In countries that lack a long-established democratic tradition, the link between voters and parties is weak, and party competition may be volatile. In such contexts, personalism (the personal draw of individual candidates because of their charisma, their background, or their status as a celebrity, for example) plays a much greater role in voting, increasing outsider candidates' chances of reaching high executive posts.

An additional element is the role played by institutional interruptions—particularly by the extent and frequency of military governments. Recurrent institutional interruptions tend to reduce the stability of rules and conspire against the development of policymaking capabilities of key democratic political institutions such as legislatures or supreme courts. Regardless of the de jure institution of the country, frequent institutional changes reduce the time horizons of political players, who may only prioritize short-term political benefits when bargaining over policy. Thus it would be more difficult to sustain intertemporal cooperation in this context.

Conclusion

This chapter has presented a survey of the political science and political economy literature to highlight the institutions and actors that are important within the context of the framework developed in the previous chapter. As chapter 1 points out, several characteristics of the policymaking game determine the features of policies. These include the number of actors, their incentives, their discount factors, and the arenas where transactions take place. Every one of the institutions presented in this chapter has some impact on these characteristics.

In the case of the executive branch, the type of political regime, the extent of presidential powers, and the method of election and selection can affect the number of agents with influence on policymaking, their stability (and discount rate), the availability of enforcement mechanisms, and the arenas where transactions take place. As the power of the president increases, the government's capacity to generate changes and new policies tends to increase as well. While a weak executive must work its policies through the legislature, in strong presidential systems the president can try to force policies unilaterally through executive decrees, and political transactions tend to occur in less formal environments.

The role of the legislature in the policymaking process is affected by the powers of the president but also by its own institutional framework; particularly, the rules of access to the legislature and the rules that organize the workings of the legislature. These institutions determine the number of relevant political actors and their relative duration by having some bearing on the number of political parties that can compete successfully for legislative seats, the term of the appointments, and the legislators' discipline to the party, their source of support and allegiance, and their incentives for specializing and building up their capabilities. These characteristics of the political system help to explain the type of negotiations that take place in Congress and whether Congress can become a relevant arena for policymaking.

The impact of congress in the policymaking process is not independent of the role of the judiciary. The judiciary can have a role as an impartial referee, enforcing the acts of the other branches, and can have its own role in the policymaking process as a policy player. While the judiciary has usually been regarded as an additional veto player, this book also stresses its role as facilitator of intertemporal cooperation. By providing enforcement to the agreements achieved by other actors, it increases the durability of agreements and policies, and consequently, the present value of cooperation. Thus it could facilitate the adoption of stable and adaptable policies. The comparative analysis of the country chapters shows that independent judiciaries tend to favor those features of public policies.

Even though this book focuses on policies at the national level, the organization of government at the local level matters as well, because subnational-level politicians can also influence national policies. The main channel of influence is the capacity of subnational-level politicians (local party bosses) to exercise control over national-level politicians (governors' influence on national legislators, for example). The method of selecting those national-level politicians is usually the main determinant: the degree of influence will be higher if national politicians are elected at the local level where local party bosses can influence the selection of candidates. The chapters on Argentina and Brazil show this vividly.

Across all the institutions surveyed, the role of political parties is essential to explain the particular dynamics in each branch of government—and across branches. The degree of institutionalization and nationalization of political parties, their programmatic character, the fragmentation of the party system, and their internal discipline are all characteristics that affect the number of players, their incentives, the arenas where decisions are taken, and so forth. As the country chapters show, the particular characteristics of each party system interact differently in each institutional context, creating a very distinct policymaking process.

The framework of chapter 1 stresses the need for a systemic approach, one that emphasizes configurations of institutions and interactive effects. The country cases in this volume will look in great detail into these configurations and interactions, offering a general equilibrium perspective on the workings of political institutions, policymaking processes, and policy outcomes in Latin America. Yet in order to understand these interactions among multiple institutional dimensions, it is important to first understand each of them individually, focusing on the variety of rules in place in Latin America, and the way they affect the incentives of political actors and the way they play the game. For this reason, this chapter has focused on a number of distinct institutional dimensions of democratic systems and studied them one at a time. We hope that the chapter will provide the reader with the tools necessary to embark on the fascinating reading of the country cases that follow.

3

Political Institutions, Policymaking Processes, and Policy Outcomes in Argentina

Pablo T. Spiller and Mariano Tommasi[*]

Introduction

In the 1990s, Argentina undertook a wide and profound process of market-oriented reforms. With its ambitious program of macroeconomic stabilization, financial liberalization, privatization, and deregulation, Argentina became the poster child of the Washington establishment. The cornerstone of that stabilization-cum-structural reform effort was a monetary regime known as "convertibility," which rigidly tied the peso to the dollar at a one-to-one rate. After decades of inward-looking policies, stagnation, and fiscal crises that led to hyperinflation in 1989, Argentina seemed to have found its way. The macroeconomic performance of Argentina for much of the 1990s was very strong. After GDP declined in the 1980s, growth performance was impressive from 1991 to early 1998. Inflation fell from hyperinflation levels in 1990 to around zero in 1997.

Despite the promising results in the 1990s, the Argentine economy entered a long recession in 1998, which exploded into one of the deepest crises in modern economic history in December 2001. In the end, the 1990s were just one more episode in the long history of hope and despair

[*] This chapter is based on Spiller and Tommasi (2003, 2005, and 2007). We thank two anonymous referees and Ernesto Stein for valuable comments and suggestions. Mariano Tommasi acknowledges the financial support of the John Simon Guggenheim Memorial Foundation.

that characterized Argentina for most of the twentieth century. Most economists who have evaluated the dismal performance of Argentina have pointed to poor economic policies as the culprit of these sad outcomes. We are inclined to agree with that characterization, but instead of blaming the *content* of economic policies, we blame the *characteristics* of policies and policymaking, including policy instability, inadequate enforcement, inadequate commitment capacities, and an inability to effect necessary adjustments.

Argentine policies are unstable in ways that weaken their credibility in the eyes of economic actors, rendering them far less effective in bringing about desired economic behavior, such as investment, savings, and job creation, and hence desired economic outcomes, such as sustainable growth and employment. Argentine policies are not only unstable but also poorly coordinated within the tiers of the country's federal structure and among ministries, secretaries, and programs of the national government. In many instances, it is also patently clear that the investments in capabilities required to produce effective policies are absent. The Argentine state is, in essence, ineffective in enforcing its policies.

We argue in this chapter that these undesirable properties of Argentine public policies are the result of a noncooperative policymaking process. Historical legacies and the constitutional context make the Argentine congress a weak policymaking arena that lacks professionalization. Legislators respond to provincial party elites who care little about the quality of national policies. Furthermore, presidential proactive powers are too extensive in practice. As a result, the relevant policymaking actors, such as the president, the provincial governors, and interest groups, lack an institutionalized arena in which they can make intertemporal policy agreements. Additionally, they cannot delegate the implementation of potential policy agreements to a professional bureaucracy because the Argentine bureaucracy has several intrinsic weaknesses. Nor can they rely on enforcement of contracts by the judiciary, because it is weak and easily politicized. Therefore, policymaking becomes the outcome of a noncooperative game in which each actor behaves opportunistically and tries to maximize short-term benefits. This causes policy volatility, poor coordination, and poor enforcement. Political and economic actors (both domestic and foreign) distrust the Argentine polity's ability to deliver credible policies. In order to overcome this credibility problem, policymakers occasionally resort to very rigid mechanisms, such as the convertibility regime. In the face of large adverse economic shocks, these solutions often turn out to be very costly.

Public Policies in Argentina

Perhaps the most noticeable characteristic of public policies in Argentina is their instability. One aggregate indicator of policy stability could be constructed from international indexes, such as the Fraser Index of Economic Freedom, which grades a country's economic policy according to market friendliness. Figure 3.1 plots the value of that index from 1970 to 2003 for a small number of countries. In the mid-1970s, Argentina went from being one of the most market friendly countries in this sample to being the least friendly after the Soviet Union, and then returned to market friendliness during the reform process of the 1990s. Argentina is one of the two countries in Latin America (with Venezuela) where there has been some recent "backsliding" from market-oriented reforms (Lora, Panizza, and Quispe-Agnoli 2004). Looking at the whole sample of 106 countries, Argentina appears as the seventh most volatile according to the coefficient of variation of the Fraser Index over time. Treating countries whose market friendliness goes up and down, like Argentina's, separately from countries like Chile or Russia whose policies moved in just one direction (toward market liberalization), Argentina ranks as the fourth most unstable.

Argentina exhibits policy instability not only at this aggregate level but also in more specific policies. In Spiller and Tommasi (2007, ch. 7), we document the volatility of antipoverty programs in the 1990s, describing how large policy changes were made without congressional mandates. Existing welfare programs are often reshuffled (refocusing or discontinuing existing programs, and creating new ones) when new ministers or secretaries take office, a frequent event in Argentina. Often, this reshuffling involves substantial tinkering with the geographic distribution of funds. The average tenure of department heads at the National

Figure 3.1. Volatility of Economic Policies, Selected Countries, 1970–2003

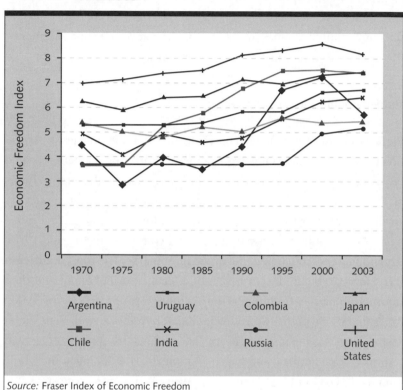

Source: Fraser Index of Economic Freedom

Secretariat for Social Development is less than a year. Furthermore, the agency has changed from secretariat to undersecretariat to ministry. The position of agency head has been occupied by highly qualified technocrats, by high-profile politicians, by the spouse of one president, and by the sister of another one. Argentina also shows high volatility in international comparisons of fiscal policy (Mody and Schindler 2004).

This policy volatility shortens the time horizons of the economic and social actors, thus reducing policy effectiveness and inducing poor economic and social outcomes. Businesspeople indicate in international surveys that they view Argentina's policy volatility as very costly for the operation of their businesses. According to the Global Competitiveness Report of the World Economic Forum, when businesspeople were asked how costly for the operation of their business were legal changes in the country, Argentina ranked 61 out of 75 countries in terms of the stability of its business environment.[1] Argentina's business community is reluctant to respond to export-promotion policies because their durability is so uncertain (Acuña 1991). Similarly, trade policy uncertainty has had a negative impact on the macroeconomic performance of Argentina. Uncertainty over trade policy was one of the key factors in the poor growth performance of Argentina in the second half of the twentieth century, according to Hopenhayn and Neumeyer (2003).

Argentina is also a weak enforcer of its policies, at the bottom of the international list in its ability to enforce tax collection, social security contributions, and payment of minimum wages (Argentina ranks 75th and 70th out of 75 countries in its enforcement of minimum wages and tax collection, respectively). This inadequate enforcement also weakens the credibility of Argentine policies. Unlike the case of other countries, such as Chile, as argued by Cristóbal Aninat and his colleagues in chapter 5, legislation is not a very hard currency for intertemporal policy exchanges in Argentina.

The lack of credibility leads, sometimes, to the adoption of highly rigid policies. A notable example was the 1991 adoption of the straightjacket monetary mechanism of convertibility, which prevented the authorities from undertaking monetary policies in response to adverse shocks throughout the 1990s. It is paradoxical that one of the few cross-country indicators in which Argentina looked good in the eyes of the international business community was exchange rate stability. An April 2001 survey (just eight months before the convertibility regime fell and the currency suffered a major devaluation) asked businesspeople whether they expected the exchange rate to be volatile, and Argentina ranked the sixth best country by this measure. After the fact, any measure of exchange rate volatility would have placed Argentina as the most volatile country in the sample. This suggests that credibility can be temporarily

---

[1] For details and references on all the statistics referred to in this section, see Spiller and Tommasi (2007, ch. 7).

achieved only through very rigid mechanisms. These mechanisms, however, may become very costly under some circumstances.

Another example of Argentina's inability to undertake efficient and flexible policies is provided by the history of fiscal federalism in the country (Tommasi 2006). In attempts to protect themselves from the opportunistic behavior of other political actors, national and provincial authorities have introduced all kinds of rigidities into the federal tax-sharing agreement. These rigidities, such as tying specific tax revenues to specific geographic distributions, created numerous microeconomic inefficiencies during the 1980s and 1990s. One of the most recent examples was the 2000 agreement by the national government to transfer fixed nominal amounts to the provinces. In the great economic downturn of 2001, with the convertibility straightjacket in effect and the reluctance of creditors to absorb fresh debt, it became impossible for the national government to honor those intergovernmental commitments. The political disputes over distribution of available fiscal funds and the state's inability to adjust the fiscal arrangement to the new adverse circumstances are seen as the proximate causes of the Argentine default and crisis of 2001–02.[2]

To give some texture to the description of policy characteristics, we summarize here one of the various examples analyzed in Spiller and Tommasi (2007, ch. 7): international trade negotiations. International trade negotiations are a crucial policy area for Argentina because access to international markets may hold the key to the country's development. Our summary of policymaking in this area draws on a recent assessment by one of the foremost Argentine experts in the field, Roberto Bouzas (Bouzas and Pagnotta 2003). As highlighted by Bouzas and Pagnotta, in international trade negotiations and international trade policy more generally, intertemporal capabilities—consensus building, policy consistency, capacity building, and institutionalization—are particularly important. These features, however, are lacking in Argentina.

Argentina participates in multiple trade negotiations with MERCO-SUR, the World Trade Organization, and the European Union, and

---

[2] See Eaton (2005) for references to international financial press accounts.

within the Americas in the framework of the Free Trade Area of the Americas. Bouzas and Pagnotta (2003, p. 81) describe Argentina's strategy this way:

> The strategy of external commercial negotiations by Argentina has had diffuse aims and has been ambiguous. The negotiating position has been guided by multiple, and often contradictory, priorities and interests. This is the result of the absence of a domestic consensus that ensures the continuity of those aims over time. Worse still, even for those topics on which there is consensus about the importance of the negotiation (as in the case of participation in the OMC), the ability to act in a consistent way has been very limited.

In terms of institutional organization, Bouzas and Pagnotta (2003) describe the design and execution of international commercial negotiations as highly fragmented, with diverse public offices having overlapping functions and with little coordination. The Ministry of the Economy is the executive office with the most extensive responsibilities, which include the design and in some cases application of several instruments of trade and related policies. Several secretaries under the Ministry of Production are in charge of the application of some of the instruments, and also participate in international commercial negotiations. The Ministry of Foreign Affairs is the main office in charge of international commercial negotiations and it also designs and implements commercial promotion policies. Other agencies linked to the executive also active in the area of trade policy are the National Commission of Foreign Trade, the Federal Administration of Public Revenues, the Investment and Foreign Trade Bank, and the Export-Ar Foundation. This complex organizational structure requires a high degree of coordination. Instead, according to Bouzas and Pagnotta, "there is no formal deliberative process in the elaboration of these policies." They go on (2003, pp. 91–92):

> The participation of Congress is sporadic and reactive. Although coordination inside the executive branch has changed over time

... the overlapping of functions, competition across offices, and interbureaucratic struggle have been the rule. This means that the efficiency of the routines and procedures depends strongly on particular circumstances, leadership, and personalities ... The bureaucratic structures are unstable, and there is high turnover among civil servants, as well as a low level of institutional learning. The high proportion of personnel under temporary contracts conspires against the accumulation of expertise, precisely in an area in which knowledge constitutes a strategic asset ... The institutional fragility of the policymaking process spreads to the absence of mechanisms for the systematic and organic participation of the private sector, which has promoted lobbying, in a context of a lack of transparent procedures and a general absence of routines.

Bouzas and Pagnotta's description of policy features and policymaking in international trade makes numerous points that are useful for the broader concerns of this chapter, and that are consistent with the insights glimpsed from several other policy areas in chapter 7 of Spiller and Tommasi (2007), including social policies, fiscal federalism, and regulation of utilities. We provide below a selected summary of the characteristics highlighted by those policy examples, which we take as "stylized facts" to be explained.

The characteristics of the policymaking process illustrated include: deficiencies of the budget process, which gives excessive discretion to some executive actors; insufficient involvement by congress; instability of the bureaucratic structures in charge of implementation; instability of top bureaucratic personnel; noncooperative interactions between national authorities and provincial authorities; noncooperative interactions among and within national ministries; provincial governors who appear as relevant actors in national policy; and promises that are not fulfilled.

Policies in Argentina, then, seem to present the following characteristics: They show a high level of volatility (they often change with low-level political rotation). Paradoxically, other policies are too rigid, not being adjusted when circumstances change. Sometimes they respond to changing circumstances in the wrong direction. They are poorly coordinated and poorly enforced, and they present poor qualities in dimensions beyond those captured by the previous points.[3]

All these policy characteristics are consistent with the predictions of the theory summarized in chapter 1 for cases in which the equilibrium of the game of policymaking is characterized as noncooperative. In the rest of this chapter we describe the workings of the political system in Argentina and we show that those interactions end up generating the conditions that the framework identifies as conducive to noncooperative policymaking.

The Policymaking Process in Argentina

In a nutshell, the national policymaking arena of Argentina is populated by actors who have little incentive and few instruments to engage in intertemporal policy agreements. In such an environment, noncooperative short-term strategies are the norm, leading to the policy characteristics described above.

The framework presented in chapter 1 suggests that efficient and effective intertemporal transactions require self-enforcement and/or institutional arrangements that facilitate enforcement. In the absence of either type of enforcement, political and policy actions will be characterized by short-termism, inflexible rules, inability to implement efficient policy changes, and underinvestment in capacities, all leading to low-quality policies. Argentina's historical political instability, basic constitutional features, electoral rules, and federal fiscal features are key determinants of its inability to develop efficient long-term public policies.

---

[3] In this section we have painted a fairly bleak picture of Argentine policies. Several indicators from international comparisons are consistent with our statements. There are other indicators in which Argentina does not fare so badly in global international comparisons. Yet the message of this paper is that Argentina has policies of very low quality, especially when compared with obvious determinants of policy quality, such as human capital or level of development. Berkman and others (2007) build an international index of policy quality. Argentina appears in the bottom 40 percent of countries in that index, but it moves down to the bottom 20 percent of countries when that index is adjusted by GDP per capita.

The theoretical discussion of chapter 1 identified various elements that affect the capacity to achieve efficient intertemporal exchanges. These elements include the number of political actors with power over a given decision, their intertemporal linkages (how long they are in office), the characteristics of the arenas in which they undertake their political exchanges, and the availability of enforcement technologies—such as an independent and capable bureaucracy or an independent supreme court. Most of these features of policymaking "take the wrong values" in Argentina.

Argentina's key political actors have tended to have short political horizons. The unusual political instability of the twentieth century contributed to that history. From the 1930 coup until 2007, there was only one transfer of power from one president to the next (from Menem to De la Rúa in 1999) that strictly followed constitutional norms. Political instability has left an imprint through path-dependent behavior in congress, the courts, the bureaucracy, and the federal fiscal system, as well as through the actions and expectations of nongovernmental actors. Political instability, however, is not the only factor contributing to short-sighted behavior. Electoral rules that transfer power away from congress and national parties toward provincial political patrons (who are not particularly interested in building a strong national congress) contribute to the shortening of legislators' political horizons, and, in an institutional general equilibrium way, affect the incentives of the rest of the polity.

The ability to enter into efficient intertemporal political agreements has also been eroded by weak constraints on unilateral moves by some actors. For instance, weak constitutional, judicial, and budgetary constraints on moves by the executive have led to unilateralism on the part of the president, which in turns weakens the incentives to achieve congressional agreements in the first place. A similar logic has been at work in intergovernmental relations: weak constraints on some moves by the national government on issues that affect the provinces have led to noncooperative behavior in the federal fiscal game (see the discussion on fiscal federalism below).

The history of political instability has contributed to the lack of judicial, and thus constitutional, constraints on executive action. A professional bureaucracy, well supervised by congress, could be an alternative channel for the intertemporal enforcement of political agreements. But Argentina does not have such a bureaucracy, either: in part because of its history of instability, but also because of current incentives of key political players.

The combination of lack of legislative incentives, the ability of the executive to act unilaterally, and the power of provincial leaders all have moved crucial political and policy bargaining away from the national legislature and into other arenas. Some key policy decisions take place in executive quarters (among the president, a key minister, advisers, and a few businesspeople), in meetings of the president with some governors, or in other closed groups. Not only are those arenas not transparent, but they also lack the required institutional stickiness to enforce bargains over time.

The Argentine policymaking process can, then, be summarized in a number of propositions about the behavior of some of the main institutional actors and about the characteristics of some of the main institutional arenas. We set forth these propositions below, and we devote the rest of the chapter to explaining and supporting them.

1. Congress is not an important policymaking arena.
2. The executive tends to have substantial leeway to take unilateral policy action.
3. Provincial political powers (especially provincial governors) are very important in national policymaking.
4. There is a symbiotic interaction between national and provincial policymaking that operates through political and federal fiscal channels.
5. Considerations of fiscal federalism are a factor in almost every policy issue, adding transaction difficulties and rigidities to policymaking.
6. Given the incentives of the executive of the day, of legislators, and of provincial governors, there is little investment in policymaking capacities in several spheres.

7. By and large, the bureaucracy is not an effective corps to which to delegate the technical implementation of policy bargains.

8. The judiciary does not provide much intertemporal "glue" to political or policy agreements.

9. Nongovernmental actors in the policy process (such as business groups and unions), lacking a well-institutionalized environment for political exchange, usually follow strategies that attempt to maximize short-term benefits.

The configuration of and interactions among the factors mentioned above is what, in our view, explain the characteristics of Argentine policies described in the previous section, and we explain those interactions in the rest of the chapter. We can, nonetheless, anticipate some direct policy implications arising from these propositions. The fact that the executive has wide leeway to take unilateral policy decisions means that policy is unstable and lacking in credibility. The importance of provincial political powers makes fiscal bargains particularly difficult to strike, with the consequent implications for the quality of fiscal and macroeconomic policy. One of the features of the Argentine bureaucracy is a high rate of turnover in top positions, including many outsiders who pass briefly through the public sector (having little more attachment than loyalty to the political patron who places them there). This turnover limits the extent of institutional knowledge and the development of cooperation across ministries and secretariats, deepens the heterogeneity in policy quality, and reinforces the lack of policy coherence.

In the rest of the chapter we argue that the deep determinants of the derived institutional characteristics and behavior summarized in the propositions above are some basic institutional characteristics of Argentina (including prominently some aspects of electoral rules), as well as some historical legacies at the return to democracy in 1983. We also argue that several of these characteristics tend to reinforce one another over time. For instance, the lack of judicial enforcement of previous political agreements reflected in laws or in the constitution diminishes the value of legislation and hence the political value of being in congress. This, in turn, affects legislators' incentives to invest in strengthening congress or in building long-term legislative careers. These congressional weaknesses reinforce the need and the temptation of the executive to undertake unilateral actions to deal with policy issues, and so forth.

In the next section, we provide a brief introduction to Argentina's political institutions and history, and in the rest of the chapter we bring some of the components of that picture into focus.

A Brief Introduction to Political Institutions in Argentina

Like the United States, Argentina is a federal republic, with a presidential form of government and a bicameral legislature. Given these similarities in some basic constitutional features, and the fact that the U.S. political system is the one most studied by positive political theorists, we will follow the expositional device of describing some features of Argentine institutions and Argentine political behavior by contrasting them with their U.S. counterparts.

A key difference between the political organization of the United States and Argentina is the way legislators are elected. The members of the Argentine chamber of deputies (currently 257) are elected from multimember districts (the 23 provinces and the capital city) for four-year terms. The deputies are elected from closed party lists. Half the chamber is renewed every two years, as each district replaces half its legislators (or the closest equivalent). Unlike in the United States, where each state is represented by a number of U.S. representatives proportional to its population, in Argentina the less populous provinces are highly overrepresented in the chamber. While chamber seats are technically allocated among the provinces on the basis of their population, each province has a minimum of five deputies. For ten provinces, this truncation leads to overrepresentation.

Overrepresentation is even higher in the upper chamber. Before the 1994 constitutional reform (and as in the United States), each district was represented by two senators. Unlike in the United States, however, senators were elected indirectly for nine-year terms by the provincial legislatures using the plurality formula. Since the constitutional reform of 1994, the senate is composed of 72 members, with every province represented by three senators (elected directly since 2001 using the incomplete list electoral rule), with the stipulation that no one party can occupy more than two of a province's seats in the senate.

The electoral connection in Argentina works quite differently than in the United States. In Argentina, electoral mechanisms make provincial governors (as provincial party leaders, with substantial control over party list formation) powerful actors in national politics, rather than individual legislators. At the same time, although provinces have large spending responsibilities, they raise little in taxes. Most of the provinces' funding comes from a common pool of resources collected by the national government for itself and for the provinces. These two features together—control by governors over their legislators, and the importance of the national government in provincial public finances—are the backbone of a symbiotic crisscrossing of national and provincial politics and policies, which is described in more detail later.

Argentina's first constitutional president took office in 1862. The formal machinery of democracy, elections, and checks and balances operated in Argentina until 1930, the first time that a military coup succeeded in removing a constitutionally elected president. Between 1930 and 1982, twelve presidents (both de jure and de facto) were removed from office by force.

Since the 1940s, the political scene has been dominated by two parties, the Peronist Party (*Partido Justicialista*, or PJ) and the *Unión Cívica Radical* (UCR). The UCR, the oldest active party, emerged during the 1890s to challenge oligarchic rule. It first captured the presidency in 1916, after the democratizing electoral reforms of 1912. The PJ emerged in the 1940s under the charismatic leadership of Juan Domingo Perón (president from 1946 to 1955, and from 1973 until his death in 1974) and has since become the main political party in Argentina. Historically, the socioeconomic base of UCR has been the middle class, and the socioeconomic base of PJ has been the working class. Even though those associations have remained accurate to some extent until the present, both are considered catchall parties whose positions nowadays revolve around the political "center." Peronism has traditionally combined a metropolitan coalition based on the urban working class with a peripheral coalition of provincial groups from the country's more "backward" interior (Gibson 1997; Gibson and Calvo 2000). Even though a majority of the voters in these peripheral provinces are poor, provincial PJ party machines tend to be dominated by political elites with ties to provincial economic power.

While third parties (of the left and right) have on occasion achieved some political prominence, to date all of these parties have had an ephemeral existence, rarely lasting more than five years as a relevant political force. This failure is due primarily to the parties' inability to build a territorial reach like that of the Peronist and (secondarily) Radical parties in a country where national politics have a strong "subnational" drag (Torre 2003; Calvo and Murillo 2004). Recent events, like the disastrous ending of the De la Rúa government, have weakened the UCR. The subnational drag on national politics described below and the overrepresentation of small backward provinces give inordinate weight in Argentine politics and policymaking to the clientelistic backwaters of the country, and underrepresents the more modern, urban, ideological, and programmatic segments of Argentine society.

Congress, Political Careers, and the Provincial Connection

Legislators in the United States enjoy long careers in congress and have high reelection rates, they specialize in powerful committees, and they tend to be high-quality politicians; the U.S. Congress is a central arena of policymaking. In Argentina, congress has exactly the opposite characteristics. Argentine legislators have very low reelection rates and tend to serve short terms in congress; congress is not a very important policymaking arena; it is not very institutionalized, and by and large, it is not the place where policy expertise resides.

The assessment of legislator quality in the United States is based on the extremely careful work of Diermeier, Keane, and Merlo (2005), who, using labor econometrics techniques, estimate the unobserved characteristics of U.S. legislators from 1947 to 1994. We have no way of replicating such detailed work at this point, but Stein and Tommasi (2005a) have constructed a preliminary indicator of the policymaking capabilities of

18 Latin American congresses. That index, built from input from Saiegh (2005) and references there, attempts to capture some characteristics of each legislature as an organization and of its legislators, which relate to the capacity to engage in substantive policymaking activity. Table 3.1 reproduces that index for the Latin American sample; Argentina is one of the five countries with the lowest value of the index.

The table highlights, in a comparative perspective, several points we want to make about the Argentine congress and about Argentine legislators, including the fact that congress is a weak institution in terms of legislative capabilities, the fact that legislators do not stay long in congress, and the fact that congress is not as important for political careers in Argentina as it is in some other countries. We address these issues in turn below.

Legislative Organization

As in most legislative bodies across the world, congressional committees in Argentina are the workhorses of the legislative process. Yet in the Argentine case, the policy jurisdictions of congressional committees do not parallel the structure of administrative or cabinet agencies. Some committees have far too vast (and others far too narrow) a focus. Not only are legislative committees poorly matched with the structure of the cabinet, but their number and size also bear no correspondence to the size of the legislature. Furthermore, even though from 1983 to 2004 the number of deputies increased only slightly (from 254 to 257), the number of standing committees increased from 27 to 45. Danesi (2004) argues that the creation of these new committees had more to do with the need to assign a committee chairmanship or other position to some important politician than to legislative needs. (This is reflected in the vague wording used to justify the creation of each new committee.) Not only has the number of committee slots increased monotonically, but so has the tendency of legislators to belong to them. In 1997 the typical Argentine deputy served on 3.5 committees, but by 2004 that deputy served on 4.5 committees: a much higher number than in neighboring countries like Chile or Brazil (Danesi 2004). This overstretching of legislators across

Table 3.1. Policymaking Capabilities of Latin American Congresses

Country	Confidence in congress, average 1996–2004	Effectiveness of law-making bodies	Average experience of legislators (years)	Percentage of legislators with university education	Average number of committee memberships per legislator	Strength of committees	Place to build career	Technical expertise	Congress Capability Index
Argentina	20.5	1.6	2.9	69.6	4.50	Medium	Low	Low	Low
Bolivia	19.9	1.8	3.3	78.4	1.66	Medium	Medium	Medium	Medium
Brazil	24.9	3.1	5.5	54.0	0.92	Medium	High	High	High
Chile	36.0	3.7	8.0	79.4	1.95	High	High	High	High
Colombia	20.3	2.7	4.0	91.6	0.86	High	High	Medium	High
Costa Rica	29.9	2.2	2.6	8.4	2.09	High	Medium	Low	Medium
Dominican Rep.	n.a.	2.0	3.1	49.6	3.54	Low	High	Low	Low
Ecuador	13.3	1.7	3.5	83.1	1.26	High	Medium	Low	Medium
El Salvador	27.7	2.1	3.9	64.0	2.44	Medium	High	Low	Medium
Guatemala	19.9	1.8	3.2	68.4	3.24	Low	Medium	Low	Low
Honduras	30.8	2.6	3.0	73.1	2.34	Low	Low	Low	Low
Mexico	27.4	2.0	1.9	89.5	2.43	High	Medium	Medium	Medium
Nicaragua	23.1	1.6	3.5	85.6	1.96	Low	Medium	Medium	Medium
Panama	22.5	1.8	5.8	81.3	1.86	Medium	High	Low	Medium
Paraguay	25.0	2.2	5.5	75.4	3.15	Low	High	Low	Medium
Peru	22.1	1.7	5.2	92.9	2.44	Low	Low	Low	Low
Uruguay	38.2	2.7	8.8	68.4	0.98	High	High	Low	High
Venezuela	27.8	1.4	4.9	74.6	0.98	Medium	Medium	Low	Medium

Source: Stein and Tommasi (2005a) and references there.

n.a.= not available

committees leads to little focus and specialization, especially given the brevity of legislative careers (as explained below).

Jones, Saiegh, Spiller, and Tommasi (2002) provide an empirical analysis of the composition of legislative committees in Argentina. Our objective was to test whether some of the theorics of legislative organization developed for the U.S. case applied to the Argentine case. We rejected the so-called "distributive hypothesis," according to which legislatures are organized so that legislators can obtain special decision power in those policy areas of more interest to their voters (Weingast and Marshall 1988). Constituency interests, although relevant to committee membership, are politically insignificant.

We also evaluated the "informational hypothesis," according to which legislators are sorted into committees in order to foster specialization and investment in knowledge necessary to deal with complex technical issues (Krehbiel 1991). A casual review of the empirical results in Jones, Saiegh, Spiller, and Tommasi (2002) may appear to provide support for that hypothesis, as the professional background of legislators is significant in the allocation of committee assignments. A closer examination of the results, however, leads to the conclusion that support for the informational hypothesis is also modest. Even though background may determine committee membership, short tenure and multiple memberships weaken any notion of specialization. As a consequence, informational advantages are not obtained. Additional knowledge of the Argentine legislature gained from extensive interviews with legislators, staffers, and other qualified observers supports this view (Danesi 2004). A more compelling explanation of these results is that legislators, required to serve on committees, simply choose those whose topic they find of greatest intrinsic interest and on which they can serve at the least personal cost.

The picture is slightly different when one analyzes committee chairmanships, as opposed to just committee membership. In contrast to serving on a committee as a general member, chairing a committee is highly valued. Most committee chairs receive extra resources, mostly for staff salaries, amounting to approximately 50 percent of the base allocation received by each legislator. The committee chair also controls the permanent staff assigned to the committee: a secretary, an administrative secretary, and two clerical assistants. These personnel perform only administrative functions, and should be seen as a way to compensate loyal legislators with patronage positions rather than as an indication of a chair's predisposition to conduct a committee's business in a professional manner. Committee chairmanships are more coveted positions given this access to greater resources. In our analysis we found that it is often the case that these positions are occupied by slightly more senior legislators with good relations with their provincial governors, and that these legislators tend to stay in such chairs a little longer than regular members do in committees (Jones, Saiegh, Spiller, and Tommasi 2002).

This evidence indicates that the Argentine legislature is not organized in a manner that maximizes its effectiveness in the policymaking process. Additional evidence of Argentine deputies' low level of interest in legislation is reflected in the allocation of resources within the chamber. Danesi (2004) presents evidence comparing the Argentine chamber of deputies with those of other Latin American countries (Chile, Paraguay, and Uruguay). Argentina ranks lowest in several indicators of the resources devoted to legislative functions.

Argentine legislators are simply not too worried about making the Argentine congress into a strong and capable policymaking body. This is an outcome of their career incentives, which in turn relates to the brevity of congressional careers, a point to which we turn next.

The Brevity of Legislative Careers

The first thing to note about the careers of Argentine legislators is that they are quite short. As of January 2001, only one legislator had served continuously in the chamber of deputies since the country's return to democracy in 1983. Since 1983, the overall stability of membership in the Argentine chamber of deputies has been relatively low. During the 1983–2003 period, the typical Argentine deputy served only one term in office, and only 20 percent of incumbents were reelected to their seats (see table 3.2). In contrast, during the twentieth century, the average U.S. House member served between five and six terms (Ornstein, Mann, and Malbin 1998).

Table 3.2. Reelection Rates to the Argentine Chamber of Deputies, 1985–2003

Year	Percentage of deputies reelected	Year	Percentage of deputies reelected
1985–87	29.2	1995–97	14.7
1987–89	22.0	1997–99	20.4
1989–91	18.9	1999–2001	23.6
1991–93	16.2	2001–2003	15.4
1993–95	14.2	1985–2003 average	19.4

Source: Authors' elaboration with data from Molinelli, Palanza, and Sin (1999) and from official records of the Argentine Chamber of Deputies.

The distribution of legislators' number of terms served in the Argentine congress is almost identical to that of Costa Rica, a country with term limits where legislators are forbidden from running for consecutive reelection. This can be seen in table 3.3, which shows the number of terms served by legislators in the Costa Rican Assembly from 1949 to 1990 alongside the same information for Argentine legislators from 1983 to 2001.

Reelection rates are quite low in comparative perspective. Table 3.4 shows reelection rates for a number of countries. Argentina presents the lowest reelection rate except for Mexico, where reelection is not allowed. Why are Argentine legislators not reelected? One possible reason is that the voters are throwing the rascals out. But a closer look at table 3.4 shows that the low reelection rate is not always the voters' choice: only

Table 3.3. Congressional Service by Argentine and Costa Rican Legislators

Number of terms served	Number of legislators Costa Rica (1949–90)	Argentina (1983–2001)
1	87	85
2	11	11
3+	3	4

Source: Carey (1996) for Costa Rica, and authors' elaboration from information in Molinelli, Palanza, and Sin (1999) and in official records of the Argentine Chamber of Deputies for Argentina.

Table 3.4. Reelection Rates in Selected Countries, Various Years

Country	Percent seeking reelection	Percentage of candidates reelected	Total percent reelected
Argentina (1997)	26	67	17
Brazil (1995)	70	62	43
Chile (1993)	76	78	59
Japan (1963–90)	91	82	74
Mexico (1997)	0	0	0
United States (1996)	88	94	83
Colombia (1990)			48
United Kingdom (1950–74)			81
Italy (1953–72)			82
Panama (1999)			49
Portugal (1991)			57.8
Turkey (1950–80)			56
West Germany (1957–76)			70–75

Source: Morgenstern (1998); Archer and Shugart (1997); Molinelli, Palanza, and Sin (1999).
Note: Empty cells reflect that figures are not available.

a small percentage of legislators seek reelection. Of those who sought reelection in Argentina, 67 percent succeeded: a number that is not particularly low in international comparison. But only 26 percent actually sought reelection.

Having established that the high rotation of Argentine legislators is not due to voter choice, in the next couple of sections we study in more detail the nature of Argentine political careers, as well as how the decision is made whether or not to renominate legislators to congress.

Political Careers

Members of the Argentine congress do not develop long "professionalized" legislative careers. Yet, they are not political outsiders either. That led us to describe them as "**amateur legislators but professional politicians**" in Jones, Saiegh, Spiller, and Tommasi (2002). Even though most deputies and senators serve only one term in congress, almost all of them occupy some government or party position before and after their congressional stint. These positions could be national, provincial, or municipal, but in most cases are tied to politics at the provincial level.

Jones (2004) provides information on the positions held by Argentine legislators before their congressional terms. He studies the prior positions held by deputies elected between 1991 and 1999 and senators elected between 1986 and 2001. One of the main conclusions stemming from his analysis is that virtually all deputies (97 percent) and all senators occupied either a governmental or party position immediately before their election. This fact underscores the presence of relatively stable career pathways in Argentine political parties. Another important fact that comes out of that analysis is that a majority of those governmental or party positions were in the home province of deputies (62 percent) and senators (54 percent). The province-centeredness of political careers is stronger among legislators from the dominant PJ and UCR parties (and obviously from provincial parties) than among the scarcely represented and often short-lived other national parties, such as FREPASO.

Jones, Saiegh, Spiller, and Tommasi (2003) performed an analysis of the position held by major party (PJ and UCR) deputies of the 1991–95 class as of mid-1988, two and a half years following the end of their term in office. That analysis also highlighted that a large percentage (85 percent) of deputies continued to occupy a partisan or governmental post, and that many of those posts were province-based. Nearly 60 percent of the deputies who had left congress held a political position at the provincial level.

The next section looks at the provincial connection in more detail.

The Subnational Connection:
The Role of Provincial Party Bosses

As the above discussion suggests, the keys to career advancement are held by the provincial leaders of the parties to which legislators belong. Therefore, it is worth taking a closer look at these leaders, who we call "provincial party bosses." That task is undertaken in Ardanaz, Leiras, and Tommasi (2007), studying who these bosses are, identifying their sources of power, and showing how they interact in national policymaking, especially through congress and in key policy events. The important role played by party bosses is suggestive of how subnational (provincial-level) politics influences national politics.

The 23 provinces plus the city of Buenos Aires serve as electoral constituencies for congressional elections. This makes the province the locus of party competition and the base of political support for politicians and parties.[4] As shown above, moreover, political careers are usually province-based, and even positions in the national government are often a consequence of provincial factors.

It is common for a single person or small group of politicians to dominate political parties at the provincial level. In provinces where the party controls the governorship, the governor is, with rare exceptions, the undisputed (or at least dominant) boss of the provincial-level party. In many other provinces where the party does not hold the governorship, the party is nonetheless dominated in a comparable manner by a single individual, but there is a greater amount of space for intraparty opponents. In the remaining provinces where the party does not control the governorship and there is not a single dominant leader, there is usually a small group of influential party leaders who predominate in party life.

Following the office of the president, the governorship is the most important institutional position in the Argentine political system. In fact, the governors—generally in a collective manner—have constituted a more relevant counterweight to the presidential authority than congress or the judiciary (De Luca 2004).

The two major parties have exerted a great dominance at the subnational level. The PJ controlled an average of 61.8 percent of the governorships between 1983 and 2003 (ranging from 54.6 percent to 77.3 percent), with the UCR placing second with an average of 23.3 percent (ranging from 9.1 percent to 33.3 percent). No other party ever possessed more than one governorship at any one time during this period.

---

[4] This fact has been highlighted by a spurt of recent literature, which is reviewed in Ardanaz, Leiras, and Tommasi (2007).

Another noticeable feature of provincial governorships is the high degree of name repetition (Ardanaz, Leiras, and Tommasi 2007). This is an indication of the fact that many provinces are controlled by single individuals or families over extensive periods of time.[5] Finally, a review of this name list shows that some of the most salient national political figures have been long-time provincial governors. In fact, all presidential candidates from the major parties (the PJ and UCR) were governors before running in presidential races.[6]

The power of provincial party bosses has been reinforced over time since the return of democracy by two channels. On the one hand, there have been political reforms, induced by these very leaders, which have increased their power within the provinces. For instance, no provincial constitution allowed governors to be reelected in 1983; by 2003 all but 6 of the 24 provinces had provided for the immediate reelection of the governor, 4 of them without imposing restrictions on the number of terms that a governor could serve.[7] Incumbent governors have also manipulated other institutional levers at their disposal in order to increase their control of the provincial political arena, including the timing of local elections vis-à-vis national ones. Electoral rules allow provincial

---

[5] Gibson (2004) provides a vivid account of one of the strongest examples of what he terms "subnational authoritarianism" in the province of Santiago del Estero, which has been "owned" by the Peronist caudillo Carlos Juárez since he first assumed the governorship in 1949. Bill Chavez (2003) provides a somewhat similar depiction for the province of San Luis, which has been dominated for many years by Adolfo Rodríguez Saá (briefly Argentine president during the December 2001 crisis) and his family. See also accounts by local political anthropologists about Misiones and San Luis, summarized in Cleary and Stokes (2006).

[6] More generally, some of the most salient national political figures since the return to democracy have been long-time provincial governors or members of family-run provincial governments. These include the cases of Angeloz (UCR, Córdoba, 1983–95), Duhalde (PJ, Buenos Aires, 1991–99), Kirchner (PJ, Santa Cruz, 1991–2003), Massaccesi (UCR, Río Negro, 1987–95), Menem (PJ, La Rioja, 1983–89), Rodríguez Saá (PJ, San Luis, 1983–2001), and Ramón Saadi and Vicente Saadi (PJ, Catamarca, 1983–91).

[7] Three of those four provinces with indefinite reelection are the provinces where the three Peronist presidential candidates in the 2003 election hail from—La Rioja, San Luis, and Santa Cruz. That is another indicator of the connection between subnational bailiwicks and national political power. See Calvo and Micozzi (2005) and Ardanaz, Leiras, and Tommasi (2007).

governments to set the date of local elections. Governors have exploited their control over local legislatures and manipulated the electoral calendar in order to avoid negative (coattail) externalities from the national arena and in order to take advantage of positive coattail externalities from the popularity of national presidents (Calvo and Micozzi 2005; Ardanaz, Leiras, and Tommasi 2007).

Additionally, the market-oriented reforms of the 1990s have increased the power of governors in at least two dimensions.[8] On the one hand, the decentralization of spending has transferred more fiscal (and hence political) resources to the provincial governments. On the other hand, welfare strategies have been transformed from national labor protection policies to compensatory social programs, programs that, even though national, are administered politically and clientelistically by provincial machineries (Weitz-Shapiro 2007; Levitsky 2007).

In sum, the dominance exercised by provincial party leaders over the political process in their respective provinces is based principally on patronage, pork barrel politics, and clientelism (Calvo and Murillo 2004). Campaigns, both primary and general election, are funded primarily through the use of resources gained from patronage, pork barrel, and clientelistic activities. Government financing of campaigns and party building also exists, although it represents only a very modest fraction of the resources used for campaign activity by the relevant parties (Jones 2004).

Patronage positions are particularly important for maintaining the support of second- and third-tier party leaders, who in turn possess the ability to mobilize voters, especially for party primaries. The ability to engage in pork barrel politics improves the party's reputation with key constituents and aids clientelistic practices through the provision of jobs to party supporters and the infusion of money into the party coffers, which in turn is employed to maintain clientelistic networks. Clientelism assists party leaders at all levels in maintaining a solid base of supporters.

Provincial party bosses are able to dominate local politics by mobilizing a variety of resources. Their powers are not restricted to the confines

---

[8] Ardanaz, Leiras, and Tommasi (2007) explore these two dynamics in more detail.

of their respective provinces. There are political and institutional variables that enable governors, through their control of legislative contingents in the national congress, to enjoy national leverage. One crucial such variable is the control of candidate selection methods.

Candidate Selection

Political parties, not the government, run party primaries for both party leadership positions and candidacies for national, provincial, and municipal public office.[9] Primaries involve a considerable amount of voter-mobilization efforts on the part of the competing intraparty lists. The electorate for these contests consists of either party members alone or party members and those unaffiliated with any party. When a primary is held, success thus depends almost entirely on candidates' financial or material resources. Whether or not a politician will faithfully represent (or has faithfully represented) the interests of his or her constituents normally has little impact on success in the primary contest.

It is in the best interest of the regional party boss to avoid internal conflict, since conflict increases the influence of the national party and the independence of its legislators. Because governors are likely to bear a disproportionate share of the costs of any divisive primary, they have both the incentive and the means to arrange a negotiated list of candidates. Most governors are able to impose their candidates, co-opt potential opponents, or successfully negotiate an agreement with other party factions. Given the high reelection rate of governors who seek continued office, the power of the governor depends in part on whether the provincial constitution restricts reelection. In contrast, where the provincial-level party is in opposition at the provincial level, the resources at the disposal of its leader are minimal in comparison to those held by a governor; its leader is therefore much less likely to be undisputed. In such circumstances, national-level organizations have more influence on the provincial list composition, and the chance that a primary will be held is higher.

---

[9] This subsection draws from De Luca, Jones, and Tula (2002) and Jones (2004).

The decision within the PJ and UCR to hold a primary depends first and foremost on whether the party controls the governorship at the provincial level and secondarily on whether the incumbent governor is eligible to seek reelection. Regardless of which method is used, the provincial-level party leaders are the key players in the nomination process, with the national party leadership and rank-and-file members playing a decidedly secondary role. Furthermore, even when a direct primary election is held, the weight of the party leadership in the outcome of the contest is quite powerful, since unlike in current U.S. primaries, Argentine primary elections are clashes of party machines, with the victory going to the machine that is able to mobilize the largest number of voters. As José Luis Lizurume, Chubut governor from 1999 to 2003, recently stated, "*La interna es aparato puro*" (The primary is just machine).[10]

The importance of province-level political variables in explaining the method used to select candidates for the national congress underscores the decentralized nature of the Argentine party system and highlights the prominent influence of provincial politics on national politics.

The Argentine Senate in Comparative Perspective

To give some comparative flavor to several of the points raised so far, we close this section with a brief comparison of the Argentine and Brazilian senates. We compare Argentina to another strongly federal country: a case which has been characterized as one in which provincial governors are very important in the national political arena, and in which political careers are supposed to center strongly in the subnational units (the Brazilian states) (Samuels 2000a, 2000b, 2003).

This discussion is based on a survey conducted and evaluated by Mariana Llanos (2003b). That survey of Argentine and Brazilian senators suggests that the Argentine senate is a weaker policymaking body with lower technical capabilities than its Brazilian counterpart. Committees in the Argentine senate are perceived to be less important than in Brazil. Argentine senators seem to look for instructions from provincial

---

[10] Jones (2004), citing the July 18, 2003 edition of *Diario El Chubut*.

governments to a much greater extent than do their Brazilian peers. They see their main job as obtaining resources for the province. When conflicts arise, they vote more according to the needs of their province and less according to the party line than do Brazilian senators. These are remarkable findings given the presumption in the specialized literature about the strong subnational drag to legislative careers and policymaking in Brazil (see, for instance, Samuels 2000b and 2003).[11] Some of the evidence in Llanos's study is summarized below.

Regarding the importance of the subnational connection, 85 percent of the surveyed Argentine senators expressed the view that the opinion of their provincial government is very important in their decisions, compared to just 64 percent of the senators surveyed in Brazil. Two-thirds of Argentine senators stated that obtaining resources for their respective provinces is a very important part of their legislative activity. Only 45 percent of the senators surveyed in Brazil shared this opinion. When asked whether they would side with their provincial interests or with their party in case there was a conflict of interest, 80 percent of Argentine senators said they would always favor their province's point of view, and only 6 percent said they would always vote with the party. In the case of Brazil, only 55 percent of the senators said they would always vote with their province, while 13 percent answered that they would always favor their party's point of view.

Regarding the importance of legislative committees, most of the Argentine senators expressed a negative opinion about the workings of the committee system in the Argentine senate. Nine out of ten respondents said that the functioning of the system was hindered by the existence of too many committees. In Brazil, only 21 percent of the senators offered a similar response. Also, more than half the respondents in Argentina said that committees are not an arena for the technical discussion of bills. Only 11 percent of the Brazilian senators expressed a similar response.

---

[11] That important interpretation of Brazilian politics is somewhat challenged in chapter 4 in this volume by Lee Alston, Marcus André Melo, Bernardo Mueller, and Carlos Pereira, who claim that the subnational dominance of Brazilian politics has been dwindling over time. Even in that more nuanced account, Brazil still appears as a country in which subnational politics is an important component of the overall system.

Finally, 87 percent of the senators in Argentina said that the work of committees is severely underappreciated by their peers, who seldom participate in the meetings. Half the senators in Brazil shared this opinion. In terms of legislative oversight, 70 percent of the Argentine senators expressed the opinion that investigative committees do not play an important role in making governmental activities more transparent. This opinion contrasts sharply with that of their Brazilian peers: 98 percent of them expressed the opposite opinion.

Regarding legislative work, floor debates seem to play a more important role in the voting decisions of Brazilian senators. Thirty-three percent of the Brazilian respondents, against only 9 percent of Argentine respondents, said that they took floor debates into consideration when deciding whether to support a bill. In every single category, the views of Brazilian senators with regard to the technical inputs at their disposal were significantly more favorable than those of Argentine senators. The inputs in question included technical assistance, the information office, computer services, the library, and infrastructure and equipment.

Summarizing, this section applies the insight that legislative behavior and the organization of legislative institutions are affected by electoral rules to reveal some basic features of Argentina's national legislature. By making legislators more beholden to the provincial party boss than to the voters, Argentina's electoral rules, along with a constitutional system that places limited constraints on unilateral executive actions, have created an amateur congress, one whose members have neither the expertise nor the incentives to initiate influential legislation, to control public administration, or even to invest in strengthening congressional institutions. These characteristics of the Argentine congress, in turn, have important implications for the qualities of public policy in Argentina.

The evidence presented here shows, though, that these legislators are not amateur politicians. Argentine legislators' progressive ambition causes them to leave congress, but not politics. The center of political careers is in the provinces. In turn, provincial politics is heavily influenced by the objectives and resources of provincial governors. The next section focuses on the interactions of provincial governors and national political actors in the crucial domain of fiscal federalism.

The Federal Fiscal Game

In Argentina, national and subnational politics and policies are intertwined to a much larger (and convoluted) extent than in other federal polities.[12] The main links are electoral and fiscal.

Provinces undertake a large fraction of total spending, yet collect only a small fraction of taxes. Provincial spending amounts to 50 percent of total consolidated public sector spending. This figure rises to close to 70 percent if one excludes the pension system and focuses on "more discretionary" spending. Furthermore, the type of spending in the hands of provincial governments tends to be politically attractive (such as public employment and social programs) because it is close to the interests of territorially based constituencies. Yet on average, provinces finance only 35 percent of that spending with their own revenues. The rest of their spending is financed from a common pool of resources, according to the "Federal Tax-Sharing Agreement." In a large number of small provinces, the proportion of funds from this common pool constitutes over 80 percent of their funding. Local politicians, then, enjoy a large share of the political benefit of spending and pay only a small fraction of the political cost of taxation.

This fiscal structure at the provincial level is one reason why many professional politicians are more interested in pursuing a career through appointments in the provincial government (or even the party at the provincial level) than in the national congress. But the powerful provincial brokers—that is, the governors—depend heavily on the allocation of "central" monies to their provinces to run both their political and their policy businesses. That is, they need central money to deliver particularistic political goods, as well as to provide general public goods in their province. There are several channels for funneling funds to the provinces; the main ones are the geographic allocation of the national budget and the Federal Tax-Sharing Agreement.

---

[12] This section is based on Saiegh, Spiller, and Tommasi (2007) and Tommasi (2006), and references there.

The game in which these allocations are determined is the source of many political and policy distortions, at both the national and the provincial levels. The game even affects the quality of democracy at the local level. The Argentine voter at the provincial level has an incentive to reward politicians who are effective at extracting resources from the center.[13] These are not necessarily the most competent or honest administrators.[14] Given the political mechanisms by which funds are allocated, this also adds uncertainty to provincial public finances, since it is not easy to project future allocations, and lowers the quality of provincial policies.

The history and evolution of the Tax-Sharing Agreement is fraught with examples of opportunistic manipulation, occasionally curtailed by fairly rigid and inefficient mechanisms (Tommasi 2006; Iaryczower, Saiegh, and Tommasi 1999). Unilateral, bilateral, and coalitional opportunism (by the national government, by a province, or by a set of provinces that turns out to be pivotal for an important vote in congress or for some other reason) has been common in the allocation of central government monies to the provinces. The national executive has enjoyed substantial discretion to allocate items in the federal budget geographically (Bercoff and Meloni 2007). In an attempt to prevent adverse changes in the future (for instance, a reduction in the amounts going to any specific province), political actors have tended to impose greater rigidity on the Tax-Sharing Agreement, reducing the government's capacity to adjust fiscal policy to changed economic circumstances. One example is the earmarking of taxes for specific programs with clear regional distributional effects. This earmarking led to a rigid and convoluted system of federal tax collection and distribution, which has been christened the "Argentine fiscal labyrinth."

Recent attempts to simplify that labyrinth, which also reflect the inability to strike efficient intertemporal agreements, led to the 1999 and 2000 "fiscal pacts" between the national and provincial governments.

---

[13] Jones, Meloni, and Tommasi (2007) show that voters in Argentina, unlike those in the United States, reward provincial spending in gubernatorial elections.

[14] On the heterogeneity of local democracy in Argentina, and its connection to fiscal federalism, see Sawers (1996), Cleary and Stokes (2006), and references there.

Those pacts generated a rigid commitment to a minimum of revenues from the center to the provinces, which turned out to be a very costly straightjacket for the De la Rúa government during the lead-up to the 2001 crisis. Similarly, the lack of cooperation from the provinces has been credited as the immediate cause of the country's move to default (Eaton 2005; Tommasi 2006).

That episode of the Argentine federal fiscal drama, which led to one of the largest defaults in modern world economic history, was a clear manifestation of one of the central points in our argument. Provincial governors, who are crucial players in national politics and policymaking, and who might have a slightly longer horizon than other players, have only secondary interest in national public goods (such as macroeconomic stability), and in the quality of national policies, and (hence) in investing in institutions (a professional congress, a stronger civil service) that might improve the quality of policies. Their primary interest—on the basis of which they grant or withdraw support to national governments and their policies—is the access to common-pool fiscal resources.

Weak Judicial Enforcement

The workings of judicial institutions have direct implications for the feasibility of private contracting, contracting among private and public actors, and arrangements among political agents. This section focuses on the latter, emphasizing the role of the supreme court as potential enforcer of constitutional and legislative contracts. Over the past several decades, the Argentine supreme court has not been a strong and impartial enforcer of political agreements. The reasons for weak judicial enforcement lie more in politics than in a lack of jurisprudence.[15] Iaryczower, Spiller, and Tommasi (2002, 2007) show that a strategic behavioral model similar to the one used to explain the U.S. supreme court explains quite well the behavior of Argentine supreme court justices. Furthermore, the fragmentation of the Argentine polity would suggest that the Argentine supreme court should be strong and independent.

---

[15] This section is based on Iaryczower, Spiller, and Tommasi (2002, 2006, 2007).

But Argentina's political history has resulted in a court with a much smaller role than the supreme court has in the United States.

In particular, since the mid-1940s, Argentine supreme court justices have had very short tenures—indeed, among the shortest in the world. From 1960 until the mid-1990s, the average Argentine justice lasted less than five years in his post. This short average tenure puts the country near the bottom of the ranking, alongside countries not usually associated with stability and the predominance of the rule of law (such as Malawi, Pakistan, and Peru), and a long distance from the United States, where supreme court justices serve an average of around 20 years, or Norway and New Zealand, where average tenure is longer than 15 years (see table 3.5).

Table 3.5. Supreme Court Justices' Average Tenure, Selected Countries, 1960–1990 *(number of years)*

Country	Judicial tenure	Country	Judicial tenure
USA	18.8	United Kingdom	6.4
Norway	16.2	Sri Lanka	5.8
New Zealand	15.3	Chile	5.7
Malaysia	14.7	Zambia	5.6
Ireland	14.7	Ghana	5.5
Australia	14.6	India	5.4
Singapore	14.5	Botswana	5.2
Canada	14.2	Philippines	4.9
Belgium	13.2	Zimbabwe	4.6
Guyana	12.7	Kenya	4.6
Germany, FR	12.2	Malawi	4.6
Netherlands	12.1	Pakistan	4.4
Italy	11.1	Argentina	4.4
Jamaica	10.9	Peru	4.0
Trinidad&Tobago	10.6	Dominican Rep.	3.6
Nigeria	10.1	Cameroon	3.3
South Africa	8.3	Mexico	3.3
Bangladesh	8.1	Honduras	2.8
Brazil	7.2	Colombia	1.9
Nicaragua	7.1	Ecuador	1.9
Sudan	6.8	Guatemala	1.8
France	6.6	Paraguay	1.1
Israel	6.5		

Source: Henisz (2000).

Short judicial tenure is a feature of the past 50 years. Indeed, after World War I the Argentine court was on a path of convergence with the U.S. supreme court. From the creation of the Argentine supreme court in 1863, the average tenure of justices increased systematically, reaching the same level as in the United States during the 1920s. Then during his first administration in 1946, President Perón impeached the sitting supreme court justices: an act that had a lasting impact. From that point on, the norm of not manipulating supreme court membership weakened substantially. The several military and civilian presidents who alternated in power appointed their own courts. In 1991, the first time since 1946 that a president might have faced an opposition court, President Carlos Menem expanded the size of the court from five to nine members, thereby granting him a "working" judicial majority. Indeed, control over the court was such that, since the mid-1940s until De la Rúa's inauguration in 1999, no president faced a court with a majority appointed by a political adversary. Similarly, since the mid-1940s until the present, no president, except for De la Rúa, has left the supreme court intact. All others have directly manipulated its composition, whether by removing justices (either directly or through threats of impeachment), or by expanding or shrinking its composition.

Courts with short judicial tenure naturally tend to be aligned with the sitting government, and hence are unlikely to strongly wield their power of judicial review. During a large part of the twentieth century—due mostly to de facto governments, but also to the political alignment during the interim democratic spells—executives often enjoyed a high level of political support in the legislature. This alignment is also a variable that leads the supreme court not to challenge the government.

The dynamics of a court without much clout are perverse. Lack of clout and loss of public respect are self-reinforcing. Indeed, during recent presidential elections, several presidential candidates promised to remove (some or all of) the sitting justices, and current president Néstor Kirchner has managed to alter the composition of the court in his favor.[16]

---

[16] Miller (1997) provides an interesting sociological interpretation of the historical weakening of the Argentine supreme court by comparing its trajectory to that of its U.S. counterpart.

A Bureaucracy without a Long-Term Principal

One possible way to enforce intertemporal political agreements is to delegate enforcement to a relatively independent, yet accountable bureaucracy. Argentina, however, does not have such a bureaucracy.[17] Even though Argentina has a more developed civil service system than some of the poorer Latin American countries, political shortsightedness and lack of consistency have contributed to weaken its bureaucratic apparatus way below what one could expect from a country with the level of human capital of Argentina. Figure 3.2 plots an index of "Weberianness" of the bureaucracy (from Rauch and Evans 2000) against an index of human development from the United Nations. Argentina appears as an outlier with a very weak bureaucracy compared to its level of development.

Even though from time to time there have been islands of bureaucratic excellence in the Argentine public administration, often those islands have not been respected when such independence collided with the short-term political interest of the government of the day. For instance, the current administration has not been keen on the independence of the central bank or of the National Statistics Office (INDEC), but has strengthened the Tax Collection Agency. Bambaci, Spiller, and Tommasi (2007) provide further evidence of the stop-and-go nature of capacity building in the Argentine public sector.

The absence of long-term principals hinders the building of a professional bureaucracy. Executives in almost all presidential systems are transient; but in Argentina, where the members of congress also are not long-term principals, they are not motivated to control the administration either. As Krehbiel (1991) argues, legislators everywhere tend to undersupply public goods such as controlling the administration. That effect is magnified in Argentina, where legislators' key incentive is to attend to the interests of provincial party leaders who, in turn, are not particularly interested in the quality (or in most cases even the content) of national policymaking.

---

[17] This section is based on Bambaci, Spiller, and Tommasi (2007).

Figure 3.2. "Weberianness" of the Bureaucracy in Relation to Human Development in 35 Developing Countries

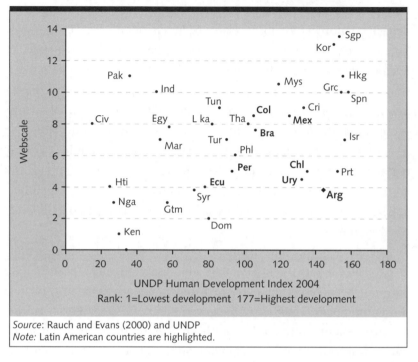

Source: Rauch and Evans (2000) and UNDP
Note: Latin American countries are highlighted.

When the bureaucracy, as a consequence, faces weak long-term incentives, its members tend to ignore their duties, and intrusive administrative controls to prevent corruption must be put in place, which further reduce the ability to generate timely and effective policies. Each new executive, unable to motivate (or fire) the permanent bureaucracy, nominates large numbers of additional political appointees, usually under much more flexible labor agreements; they can easily be fired, which they very often are after a change in their direct overseer. These practices have created a transient parallel bureaucracy. The parallel bureaucracy undertakes the same actions that the normal bureaucracy is designed to effect, but is unable (or unwilling) to undertake. The turnover at the ministerial and secretarial levels also implies turnover in the parallel bureaucracy. This turnover limits the extent of institutional knowledge and the development of cooperation across ministries and secretariats, deepens the heterogeneity in policy quality, and reinforces the lack of policy coherence.

It is well known that the parallel bureaucracy in Argentina is widespread, but its extent is difficult to measure. In Bambaci, Spiller, and Tommasi (2007), we present some evidence that the parallel bureaucracy constitutes a large fraction of the top echelons of the public sector. The members of the parallel bureaucracy tend to be better paid, but shorter-lived than permanent civil servants at similar levels. They are hired under a variety of temporary contracts. (For that reason within Argentina, they are known as *contratados*.)

Although in principle national parties could develop a cadre of potential bureaucrats, party fragmentation into provincial parties makes such cadre development ineffective in comparison with the practice of a parallel bureaucracy composed of individuals strongly aligned with the secretary or minister of the moment. Sometimes these loyalties correlate with the province of origin of the relevant political figure.[18]

The Leeway of the Executive

The previous sections have characterized a policymaking environment in which institutions (such as congress) designed to facilitate political debate, bargaining, and the intertemporal enforcement of agreements are weak; in which some key political players (the governors) care little about the quality of national policies; and in which complementary enforcement mechanisms such as a strong judiciary or a strong bureaucracy are also lacking. These factors are reinforced by, and reinforce—in a general equilibrium way—the capacity and tendency of the executive to act unilaterally.

The sources behind the executive's ability to effect unchecked moves and undo previous (say, legislative) agreements are various, in-

---

[18] A visible recent example is provided by the top echelons of President Kirchner's current administration, staffed by a proportionally large number of people from his sparsely populated province of origin, Santa Cruz. By the time of this writing, five out of eight state secretaries under the presidential office have been from the province of Santa Cruz, which contributes less than 1 percent of the country's population.

cluding the supreme court's tendency to be politically aligned with the president, the lack of a strong and independent bureaucracy, and the "general equilibrium" result that congress has not built strong technical capacities.

The budget process manifests this last feature. The inability of congress to monitor and control the budget has given the administration substantial budgetary discretion. Since the beginning of the twentieth century, congress has often failed to approve the budget sent by the executive on time, which in practice has meant that the administration functioned independently of congress. In years of high inflation, the executive often did not even bother to submit a budget. Even in the low-inflation period of the 1990s, although budgets began to be approved on time, congress did not exercise its ex post control. Indeed, the budget verification process ("*Cuenta de Inversión*") has not traditionally been initiated promptly enough to be an operational instrument for congress to verify the fulfillment of the budget "contract" by the executive. Jones (2001, p. 161) indicates that almost all of the substantial budget activity happens in executive quarters and not in congress: "…relatively little modification of the budget proposed by the executive branch occurs at any time during the treatment of the budget bill in Congress." Furthermore, Jones indicates that while ministries and other entities submit detailed disaggregated budget plans to the (executive) National Budget Office, the draft finally sent to congress contains expenditure only at a very macro level.[19]

Budget practices during the 1990s tended to overestimate revenues, and the (nonlegislative) follow-up adjustment mechanism gave substantial leeway to the secretary of the treasury to allocate scarce funds. Secretaries of the treasury have exercised the prerogative to allocate funds ex post according to a mix of their own whims and pressure from the various ministries, occasionally arbitrated by the president.[20] A similar

---

[19] See also Abuelafia and others (2005).

[20] Based on personal interviews by the authors with the then-secretary of the treasury (1999), Pablo Guidotti. See also Baldrich (2003), who in 2001 was secretary of the treasury, and Abuelafia and others (2005).

pattern has emerged during the Kirchner administration, with underestimation of revenues leading to discretionary executive allocation of the additional funds.

The unilateral power of the executive has also been based on practices that have tended to grant the president more power in fact than he has on paper. A common practice has been that of congress explicitly delegating power over some legislation; that is in part a "general equilibrium" consequence of the lack of interest by legislators in policymaking. Another factor that has contributed in this direction is the history of democratic instability. The absence of a legislative power during the frequent military dictatorships of the twentieth century has tended to centralize the actions and expectations of multiple societal actors on the executive (Acuña 1995; De Riz 1986; Llanos 2002a).

There are also explicit constitutional stipulations that have endowed the president with the capacity to "regulate" the laws from congress ("rulemaking" decrees in the course of implementing legislation); as well as constitutional vagaries, favorably interpreted by a weak supreme court, that granted the president the power to issue Decrees of Urgency and Necessity (DNUs) (Carey and Shugart 1998b; Molinelli, Palanza, and Sin 1999). DNUs are regulations dictated by the executive through which decisions are made that normally can only be taken through an act passed by congress. Before 1994, decree authority was not explicitly granted by the constitution, and legal experts disagreed over its constitutionality. These decrees are valid as long as they are dictated in response to situations of extreme gravity that endanger the continuity of the state or imply social breakdown. This ambiguous wording opens the way to all sorts of interpretations and therefore to presidential discretion, especially under subservient supreme courts. In the 130 years from the 1853 Constitution to the 1983 return to democracy, 25 DNUs have been counted; President Alfonsín signed 10 DNUs during his 1983–89 administration. It was President Menem who used and abused this legislative resource 166 times (or more, depending how one counts), a resource that was validated by a supreme court that he had packed (Mustapic 2002). That practice has continued in subsequent administrations.

President Kirchner produced 193 DNUs in his first three years in office (2003–06).[21]

The ability of the executive to "purchase" policies (through fiscal federalism and other political channels) also depends on electoral results. Institutional actors such as congress and crucial political actors such as governors tend to follow one of two strategies: one is confrontational, making the life of the president as hard as possible; the other is to cooperate "blindly" with the executive in exchange for short-term favors. The choice between those two strategies tends to be guided by a combination of partisan and resource availability considerations. When the party in executive power does not coincide with the colors of governors (and congressional majorities), and when the (fiscal) resources in the hands of the executive are low and declining, a confrontational strategy (like the one used by Peronist governors and leaders during the demise of the De la Rúa government in 2001) is more likely. In other (more "normal") times, exchanging votes for cash is the most common strategy. In either case, intertemporal cooperation necessary to build effective public policies is lacking.

Calvo and Murillo (2005) provide a detailed analysis of the partisan channels for the exchanges of votes for fiscal resources. They show that Peronist presidents have an advantage at this game, given the better grip of their party on subnational politics and clientelistic exchange networks, as well as the connection of national congress to subnational power. Interestingly, this has led to a pattern that Calvo and Murillo have christened "a new iron law of Argentine politics." A couple of decades ago, it was said that it was an iron law of Argentine politics that only Peronists could win the presidency in free and open elections. After the victories of Alfonsín in 1983 and De la Rúa in 1999, that law no longer holds, but might have been replaced by: "Others can win, but they cannot govern."

---

[21] Counting DNUs is not a trivial exercise, since all types of presidential decrees receive a consecutive number, whether they are DNUs or whether they are other, more run-of-the-mill presidential activities. For details on the different sources and figures see Braguinsky and Araujo (2006), Serrafero (2005), Ferreira Rubio and Goretti (1998) and references there.

Conclusion

This chapter began with the observation that Argentina's policies have shifted dramatically over time, and with the claim that its inability to produce consistent public policies is the reason behind its economic misfortunes. We argued that the deficiencies of Argentine public policies are the outcome of a policymaking process in which key actors have little incentive to cooperate with one another over time, leading to myopic political and policy choices. Argentina has thus been unable to steer a consistent path in crucial areas such as economic, social, or international strategies.

Argentina has a national policymaking environment dominated by executives who tend to have much leeway to pursue whatever policies they fancy, provided they can buy the support of quasi-feudal provincial governors with fiscal largesse. Such a depiction is somewhat surprising for a country that has a basic constitutional structure with separation of powers similar to that of the United States. In spite of a common basic constitutional structure, the workings of political institutions in Argentina could not be more different than in the United States. The Argentine congress is neither the arena where key policies are negotiated nor a very attractive place to develop a political career. The Argentine supreme court is not a respected institution with the power to act as a real check on executive power. In Argentina, there is no policy delegation to well-staffed independent professional agencies supervised by congress through the power of the purse. The Argentine president often seeks the support of provincial governors for his national policies, and provincial governors' main objective is to increase the amount of federal funds they obtain to finance provincial public sector activities as well as their political machineries (both things often coincide).

In such a scenario, interest groups such as business and unions also follow noncooperative short-term strategies, trying to maximize short-term payoffs whenever they have access to state resources. This was clear during the "reform" experience of the 1990s, in which many reform measures amounted to a front-loading of payoffs to many key actors, such as local business groups favored by privatizations, key unions favored by reforms in the health and pension system, and pension funds that charged high up-front commissions. So, socioeconomic actors also undertake shortsighted political strategies. Short-term maximization of political opportunities also shortens their horizons as economic actors. The short-term nature of most policy and institutional arrangements seems well understood by economic agents, who, for instance, did not contribute much to the "privatized" pension system. Some short-term credibility in monetary and exchange rate policy was bought through the rigid (and in the end, costly) convertibility system.[22]

In the 1990s Argentina undertook a rather surprising sharp turn toward market-oriented policies. According to the logic of policymaking described here, that turn was not the outcome of reasoned public debate in which most relevant political actors considered whether this policy shift was the most desirable course of action. It was a decision of the executive of the day, approved by congress through votes that were largely purchased through the federal fiscal system and related mechanisms.[23]

The implementation of these reforms carried the imprint of the non-cooperative policymaking process described here. This was reflected in several peculiar characteristics of the policies of the 1990s, such as the rigidity of the convertibility regime, the inefficiencies of federal fiscal arrangements, the lack of enforcement of some policies, and the incoherence of privatization and regulatory policies across sectors. The overall experiment, including the convertibility regime, did not end well, at least as evaluated by the Argentine public at the time of this writing. The current Kirchner administration is fairly outspoken against several aspects of the reform process of the 1990s. It seems clear that unless some fundamental changes in the rules of the political game take place, Argentina will continue to experience low quality policies, independent of their political orientation.

---

[22] Etchemendy (2002), Murillo (1997, 2001), and Kay (2003) provide evidence on the short-term beneficiaries of the political exchanges behind market-oriented reforms (see also Acuña and others 2007). Galiani, Heymann, and Tommasi (2003) describe the political and economic dynamics behind the origin and maintenance of convertibility and its demise.

[23] See Acuña and others (2007).

4

On the Road to Good Governance: Recovering from Economic and Political Shocks in Brazil

Lee J. Alston, Marcus André Melo,
Bernardo Mueller, and Carlos Pereira

Introduction

The Brazilian Constitution of 1988 defined the political institutions in Brazil and the powers of the political actors in the policymaking process following the end of the military government in 1985. As a result, 1988 is used as the point of departure for this analysis. In Brazil, strong presidential powers drive the policymaking process; though they are checked by the constitutionally defined powers of congress, the judiciary, state governors, and the *Ministério Público* (public prosecutors). Policymaking starts with an interaction between the president and members of congress, though it is always in the shadow of the other political actors. Significantly, the president's electoral connection relies on a strong economy that is perceived as satisfying the goals of economic growth, economic opportunity, and the reduction of poverty. Members of congress generally care more about redistributing gains to their constituents, especially along geographic lines.

Given the different preferences and relative powers of the legislative and executive branches, they can both benefit by exploiting the gains from trade. To achieve the goal of a strong economy, presidents focus first on fiscal and monetary stability (such as the *Real* plan), as well as on pension reform and tax reform.[1] To achieve these ends, presidents

---

[1] Fernando Henrique Cardoso as finance minister put in place the *Real* plan, which led to price stability. The success of the *Real* plan was also instrumental in Cardoso winning his first presidential election.

have used pork as well as other benefits as the mediums of exchange with members of congress in return for their votes on critical pieces of legislation. A key element in this exchange is the allocation of selected ministerial positions and appointments in the bureaucracy. Given that a large proportion of the budget is "hard-wired" with policies such as pensions, health, and education, once the trades of pork-for-policy reform on monetary and fiscal policies have been consummated, the surplus will be spent on more ideological policies such as land reform and the environment. The residual policies have different electoral effects on the president and members of congress depending on the degree to which they achieve national goals (whereby the president can claim more credit) or geographic goals, such as poverty reduction in the Northeast (in which case the deputies and senators receive relatively more electoral benefits).

This "game" can be viewed as sequential, with veto players as well as external shocks constraining the president and congress. Constraints from the other political actors and external shocks have budgetary implications, either positive or negative. This analysis views the policymaking "game" as one in which the president has an overriding incentive to keep the budget as a percentage of GDP within some target range, because greatly exceeding the budget to GDP ratio can have serious monetary and fiscal penalties imposed through international capital markets. This tendency to strive toward a target range of debt to GDP is called the budgetary equilibrium. The dynamics of the policymaking game yield policy outcomes that are classified as falling into four broad categories: "stable but adaptable," pork, hard-wired, and residual.

The second section of this chapter describes the outer features of public policies in more detail. The third section examines the political institutions and how they constrain the political actors. The passage of the 1988 Constitution is viewed as a "foundational" moment from which the president, congress, judiciary, governors, *Ministério Público*, and the *Tribunais de Contas* derive their powers.[2] The third section also illustrates

---

[2] The *Tribunais de Contas* is analogous to the General Accounting Office in the United States.

how the institutional players enter the game, constraining the executive and congress, and provides examples along with systematic evidence on the impact of the other players on policy outcomes. The fourth section uses the framework to analyze specific policy outcomes: stable monetary policy and the fiscal responsibility law, with stable but adaptable outcomes; land reform and other social policies, with volatile outcomes; and health and education policies, with rigid outcomes. The final section offers some concluding remarks about the overall policymaking process in Brazil since 1988.

The Dependent Variable: Outer Features of Public Policies

The purpose of this study is not to analyze the details of any specific policy adopted in Brazil, but rather to explain the outer features of public policies: that is, the common characteristics that systematically permeate those policies. The analysis of these outer features follows the framework developed in the opening chapter. The political institutions determine the key players, the payoffs to the players, the arena in which they interact, and the frequency of their interaction.

The characteristics of policies in Brazil vary markedly across specific policy issues. The policies have been separated into four categories according to those characteristics. The first category consists of policies that are stable and adaptable to shocks. These are basically macroeconomic policies, such as fiscal and monetary policies: that is, those with a direct impact on stabilization and economic growth. The second category involves policies used by the president to provide patronage to other political actors in exchange for support in approving his agenda of reforms: that is, geographically concentrated transfers, or "pork." The third category includes policies that, having been hard-wired, cannot be easily changed and are consequently rigid and less susceptible to economic and political shocks. In Brazil, policies such as education and health that have national purpose and important second-round effects have been hard-wired. "Second-round effects" refers to the fact that these policies generate important positive externalities for society that are realized not in the short term but in future periods. Thus there is always a temptation for shortsighted policymakers to postpone them in favor of policies in the first category, which is why at some point a consensus was reached to insulate those expenditures. The final category consists of residual policies, which include issues that are given priority only once the objectives of the policies in the first category have been secured. These are policies related to issues such as security, environment, poverty, and land reform. These policies tend to be volatile, oscillating according to political shocks, such as when a new president comes to office. In general it is expected that policies with a larger ideological component, such as land reform and poverty alleviation, will be in this group. However, infrastructure has also increasingly been treated as a residual policy. It is significant to note that Brazil is pushing strongly for expenditures on infrastructure to count as meeting fiscal targets.

The analytical task is to show how the same set of political institutions leads to political transactions that result in public policies with the characteristics described in each of the four categories when mapping across specific policy issues with different features.[3] The key features of Brazilian political institutions can be understood in terms of separation of power and separation of purpose (Haggard and McCubbins 2001). Although the details changed, the Constitution of 1988 maintained the notion of strong powers for the president inherited from the military dictatorship of 1964–85.[4] The next section will present details of the political institu-

---

[3] The point of departure of this analysis is the 1988 Constitution, which defined the current set of political institutions that determines players and their powers. Although this analysis technically covers the entire period since 1988, the fit is clearly stronger in the post-1994 period, which includes the two terms of President Fernando Henrique Cardoso, as well as the current term of President Luiz Inácio Lula da Silva. It is more difficult to see a pattern in the period from 1988 to 1994, since it covered the final year of the Sarney presidency (1989), the impeachment of the Collor presidency (1990–92), and the interim years of Itamar Franco (1992–93). During this time, the new political institutions were still in the process of being implemented and developed. Nevertheless, the model presented here applies to this period as well, since many of the subsequent changes were built on institutional changes that occurred during this time, which was also an important period for political players to define and learn the rules of the game. Therefore this study's claim that presidents have incentives to pursue sensible macroeconomic policy is not invalidated by unorthodox behavior during this early period.

tions that underlie those powers (including decree power, veto power, legislative rules, and the budgetary process) and evidence of their effects. This section simply states that strong presidential powers have generally allowed the president to initiate, pursue, and approve much of his policy agenda. Whereas such a scenario may seem perilous given Latin America's history with strong presidents, Brazilian political institutions provide two sets of safeguards against abuse of those powers. The first is that the electoral connection for the president is such that he has incentives to pursue sensible macroeconomic policies, as he is seen by the electorate as being responsible for outcomes related to basic issues such as a strong economy, economic growth, and stabilization. Given the strong presidential powers, failure in these areas cannot be credibly blamed on other political actors such as congress or the judiciary. The second safeguard is that although the separation of powers is clearly biased toward the president, several other political actors with different motivations (separation of purpose) are able to check the president's actions in different ways. Thus if an incompetent or ill-intentioned president were to come to power, strong presidentialism would not mean a blank check to pursue misguided policy. The next section will describe in detail the roles played in this balance of power by the other main players, particularly congress and the judiciary, and to a lesser degree, state governors, the *Ministério Público*, the bureaucracy, and regulatory agencies, showing that they can and often do constrain the president's actions.

The president uses his powers to pursue an agenda of stable and adaptable policies and reforms. Because the separation of purpose inherent in the political institutions has the president pursuing broad national public goods—as opposed to other actors with a say in producing legislation who have more narrow constituencies (particularly congress and to a lesser degree governors)—there is the potential for conflict.

---

[4] This resulted from the peaceful and voluntary transition from a military dictatorship to a civilian government. As a result, the Constitution of 1988 was written by congress, but with considerable input from President Sarney, who inherited strong presidential powers. It is logical that a strong military president would want to assure that the new constitution would not reduce those powers. In fact, one of his greatest concerns at the time was to be granted an additional year in office by the constitution.

However, this conflict is diffused by legislative rules that result in trades of support for patronage between congress and the president (Alston and Mueller 2006). The president is able to use his powers to control the legislative agenda and to create a stable supporting coalition that enables policy reform. Any other coalition not coordinated by the president would be inherently unstable, as it would not have any enforcement mechanism to ensure compliance and prevent defections. In addition, the president possesses considerable discretion over patronage (such as jobs and individual budget amendments), which, together with the career incentives of members of congress (discussed in the third section), lead to the well-institutionalized trade of policy support for patronage. Although these exchanges are often seen as being less than legitimate by the press and much of society, they form the basis of executive-legislative relations in Brazil, and this study argues that they lead to high levels of governability that allow important reforms to get accomplished. Furthermore it can also be argued that this comes at relatively low cost to the executive because political institutions facilitate the trades (see discussion of individual budget amendments in the next section), and the patronage that is dispensed is a very small part of the budget (Pereira and Mueller 2002, 2003).

The result is that congress tends to approve many of the policy reforms proposed by the executive, yet congress still holds checks on the powers of the president.[5] It is this interaction that determines the qualities of policies in the first and second categories discussed above: stable macro policies on the one hand and pork on the other. Only when the divergence of preferences over specific policy issues between the president and members of congress is sufficiently high will there be no gains to trade. That is, the cost of the patronage necessary to approve those reforms is higher than the benefits to the president. This may lead to gridlock over that issue; presidential action to drop the issue or significantly water it down; or attempts by the executive to get around congress, for example

---

[5] This interaction between the president and congress in Brazil is formally modeled in Alston and Mueller (2006). See Melo (2002) for the executive's recent success in amending the constitution.

through decree power (discussed in the next section), which may then prompt other political actors such as the judiciary to intervene. The next sections argue and present evidence, however, that, except in a few high-profile cases such as pension reform during the Cardoso presidency and tax reform during President Lula's term, the president has generally gotten what he wanted, with these other outcomes being exceptional.

Depending on his success in achieving the top priority policy objectives, the president will decide which residual policies will be pursued, and how. Thus the residual policies are contingent on there being space in the legislative agenda, as well as on budgetary availability. These in turn are affected by both economic and political shocks. The fifth section provides one example of each shock: the effect of the 1999 devaluation of the *real* and the uncertainty resulting from the election of Luiz Inácio Lula da Silva ("Lula") as president. In each of these cases it will be shown how the budgetary process was used to bring about a recovery by reducing the execution of the residual policies in the budget. This implies that many of these residual policies will be characterized by high volatility. Given this inherent tendency toward volatility of the residual policies, political actors may often choose to hard-wire some policies where it is considered that the volatility can be particularly damaging. This is especially the case with education and health policies that are crucial for social and economic well-being, since some politicians may nevertheless be tempted to withhold resources because the effects of these policies are not generally felt in the short term. Thus at some "constitutional moment," politicians establish impediments to changing these policies by tying the hands of future political actors. This results in rigid policies, which are advantageous when this rigidity constrains opportunistic behavior but which comes at the cost of reducing the ability to adapt to unforeseen future contingencies.

Political Institutions

This section provides an overview of Brazilian political institutions and how they affect the policymaking process. The section describes the key political actors, the payoffs for political cooperation, where and how frequently the political actors undertake their exchanges, and the properties of the arenas in which exchanges take place. The discussion begins with an analysis of the way in which the 1988 Constitution established the current political institutions and how it has endogenously changed as an important mechanism for providing commitment for policy reform. Next the section describes the powers of the president and of congress and analyzes how their interaction generates policies and how the electoral and legislative rules influence the behavior of the president and members of congress. Finally the section concludes with an examination of other political actors that shape the policymaking process in many different ways, constraining what the president can do.

The Constitution

The Constitution of 1988 established the rules of the current political game in Brazil. A Constituent Assembly convened in 1987 drafted the constitution. The Constituent Assembly was set up by conferring special powers on the ordinary legislature rather than by holding new elections for the purpose of writing a new constitution. The new constitution reflects a number of principles long advocated by the opposition: decentralization, transparency, participation, social control, and redistribution. These principles produced a significant transformation in the patterns of policymaking and implementation. In terms of fiscal and intergovernmental relations, the constitution devolved administrative autonomy to subnational governments and mandated a new redistribution of functional responsibilities. In addition, it mandated a new regime of tax assignments whereby the states and municipalities were given not only new tax powers but also managed to secure a larger share of federal tax revenues. The constitution created new funds for states and *municípios* by mandating automatic transfers of federal money. It also mandated the decentralization of public policy in a great number of sectors ranging from health to education to environmental policy. Furthermore, the constitution mandated multilevel participatory arrangements aimed at social control. They include an enhanced role for the *Tribunais de Contas* (Court of Accounts) and the *Ministério Público* (public prosecutors), as well as the decentralization of the judiciary branch.

While the new Constituent Assembly was characterized by the strong desire to break away from a long period of authoritarian rule, a number of institutional innovations represented an element of continuity. Although the new constitution (by virtue of Article 2 of the provisional clauses) mandated a plebiscite on the regime and system of government that was set to take place in 1993, most of its features presupposed a strong presidency.

The adoption of the constitution can be seen as a pivotal moment in time, with important path-dependent developments. Because it was formulated during a unique historical juncture, it incorporated a vast array of political, social, and corporatist demands that had been kept silent under centralized military rule. As a result, with 250 articles in the main text and an additional 75 provisional articles, the constitution is unusually long and covers many very specific nonconstitutional issues of policy. The decision to create such a wide-ranging and detailed constitution could be attributed to the lack of any sort of political trust and credibility at that time. Thus writing a constitutional article was a "safe" institutional method by which political players could undertake political transactions with some degree of certainty that their arrangements and agreements would be enforced. As a result, the constitution emerged with many policy issues hard-wired, meaning that changes would require constitutional amendments. Indeed much of the political capital of Presidents Cardoso and Lula was spent in deconstitutionalizing certain issues: that is, deleting articles from the constitution and subsequently (but not always) legislating issues through ordinary laws. The initial high level of constitutionalization of public policy produced great rigidity in public policy in general. This did not preclude the Cardoso or Lula da Silva administrations from passing their reform programs, however.

The previous discussion helps explain why the Constitution of 1988 is the most amended constitution in the country's history. Brazil's first constitution, passed in 1824, lasted 65 years and was amended once. Brazil's second constitution, which established the republican form of government, lasted from 1891 to 1930, and also was amended only once.

The Constitution of 1946 lasted 21 years and was amended 27 times. The military constitutions of 1967 and 1969 were amended 26 times in a period of 21 years. By contrast, the Constitution of 1988 was amended 37 times in 12 years. Between 1988 and February 2001, 2,424 constitutional amendments were presented to congress. Under President Lula da Silva's first term, three new constitutional amendments were passed. The yearly average amendment rate for the Constitution of 1988 through 2003 reached 3.5. For the period from 1992 (when the first amendment was approved) to 2003, the average yearly rate of amendment was 4.4—an extremely high rate by any standard.

These rates are all the more significant because constitutional change requires approval in two rounds of voting in each house by an absolute majority of three-fifths. Other procedural requirements include the following: the executive is not allowed to change the constitution by provisional decrees (*medida provisória*). Similarly, the executive cannot resort to special urgency procedures through which it could unilaterally require a vote on a bill ahead of any other legislative proposals. Moreover, the vote must proceed by roll call (thus increasing the political costs of approving unpopular proposals). The political transaction costs of securing legislative approval are therefore much higher for constitutional amendments than for ordinary legislation. Comparatively speaking, however, the requirements for approving constitutional amendments are not very strict; Brazil is in a cluster of countries whose constitutions are the most easily amended (Melo 1998).

In addition to the procedural difficulties, it should be noted that constitutionalization and deconstitutionalization (inserting and deleting provisions from the constitution) are very distinct and asymmetrical political processes. For consitutionalization, collective action problems undermine the ability of the public to insert particularistic interests. For deconstitutionalization, the opposite holds; withdrawing benefits and rent-seeking privileges from the constitution requires overcoming the resistance of organized and sectoral interests. Reforms that deconstitutionalize issues initially lead to legislation regarding the issuing of a *medida provisória*. In this climate, a lack of trust and opportunistic behavior have precluded some welfare-enhancing deals from taking place. Two examples include tax reform initiatives involving the assignment of the power to collect value added taxes across local, state, and federal governments; and the elimination of taxes by states on exports. These potential policies were not implemented because no credible compensation mechanisms could be put in place by the federal government during a transition stage. The lack of trust arose because the executive holds great agenda powers and decree authority. Many members of congress saw the deletion of articles from the constitution as a mechanism by which the executive can unilaterally impose its preferences. In other words, some regard deconstitutionalization as the equivalent of giving a blank check to the executive.

Many constitutional issues have a direct bearing on fiscal and financial stability, and therefore put the constitution in the center stage of the political game described earlier. These include the rules defining social security benefits, the provisions stipulating levels of pay and of hiring/ dismissing personnel, the stipulation of areas not open to foreign ownership, rules defining tax and fiscal matters of subnational governments, and central bank independence. Thus, we argue that the political game described herein is largely a "constitutional change game." Granting constitutional status to certain policy areas is an integral part of hardwiring. As discussed below, this was the strategy pursued in the areas of education and health. In these cases, hard-wiring represented a strategy of precommitment on the part of the executive and the legislators.

In this game, the supreme court plays the role of a veto power because of the institution of judicial review in the country. Two instruments can be used by players in the judicial review game: the *ação direta de inconstitucionalidade* (ADIN, a petition for nullifying a decision or legal norm because it is assumed to be unconstitutional) and the *ação declaratória de constitucionalidade* (a petition for the confirmation of constitutionality of a decision or legal norm). Both are to be decided by the supreme court (*Supremo Tribunal Federal*). The first type of petition can be initiated by the president, congressional parties, the attorney general, the speakers (*mesas*) of the senate, the chamber of deputies and of the state legislative assemblies, the governors, the bar association, trade unions, and professional bodies. The second type of petition can be initiated by the president, the secretariats (*mesas*) of the senate or chamber of deputies, and the attorney general.

The Executive, Congress, Parties, Committees, and Electoral Rules[6]

Since redemocratization, and especially after the new Constitution of 1988, all elected presidents have been able to build reasonably stable post-electoral majority coalitions within congress with a high level of governability by means of strong party discipline of the governing coalition (Figueiredo and Limongi 1999; Pereira and Mueller 2003). The only period without a stable majority coalition was from March 1990 to October 1992, under President Collor. Collor preferred to work through ad hoc coalitions and this undoubtedly added to the support for his impeachment. Although none of the elected presidents belonged to a party with a pre-electoral absolute majority of the seats, they have, nevertheless, been able to achieve congressional support by use of their extensive legislative and nonlegislative powers.

Despite the presence of a decentralized electoral system and a fragmented party system, the optimal electoral strategy in the Brazilian legislature has not been concentrated in personal votes, but rather, the party vote in congress (Figueiredo and Limongi 1999; Pereira 2000; Nicolau 2000). At first glance, this assertion seems paradoxical, given the premise that legislators are subject to electoral incentives to behave individually. Indeed, Brazilian legislators vote according to their party leader's indication in order to accumulate greater benefits in the congressional arena and thus to strengthen their electoral probability of political survival in the local sphere (Pereira and Renno 2003). This claim is also corroborated by Amorim Neto and Santos (2001b, p. 213), who argue, "Party

---

[6] New regulatory agencies and the activities of the *Ministério Público* are two increasingly important checks on the ability of the executive and congress to change policies quickly. Since 1997 Brazil has created 10 new regulatory agencies varying in their independence. The budgets of the *Ministérios Públicos* are hard-wired at both the state and federal levels, giving them considerable independence. Unfortunately, space constraints preclude a discussion of their roles. For more information, see the discussion in Alston and others (2007).

discipline was above all a function of the President's legislative coalition-building strategies based on dispersion of patronage to parties."[7]

Scholars who analyze the Brazilian political system, especially its electoral rules and political parties, usually affirm that they provide significant obstacles for the executive to approve its agenda, thus creating tremendous governance problems (Mainwaring and Scully 1995a; Mainwaring and Shugart 1997a; Haggard 1995; Haggard and Kaufman 1992; Ames 1995a, 1995b, 2001). For these authors, the electoral rules offer strong incentives for candidates to develop direct links with their constituency groups rather than mediating such relations through political parties. Additionally, this institutional context generates incentives that lead to a personalized vote, as opposed to voting for political parties, and to a high saliency of constituency pressures in incumbents' electoral calculus (Ames 1995a, 1995b; Samuels 2002).

By contrast, a second group of authors has strongly questioned this predominant view. Rather than stressing the decentralizing effect of electoral rules, they emphasize the institutional rules and structures that centralize the legislative process itself and the powers held by the executive (Figueiredo and Limongi 1995, 1997, 1999; Meneguello 1998; Pereira and Mueller 2000). These authors attempt to explain how institutional variables internal to the decision-making process (the distribution of power inside congress) and the institutional legislative and nonlegislative powers held by the president (including decree and veto powers, the right to introduce new legislation, permission to request an urgency time limit to certain bills, discretionary power on the budget appropriation) work as key determinants for legislators to behave according to the preferences of party leaders.

The Brazilian political system can be characterized neither as a purely decentralized nor as a purely concentrated system (Pereira and Mueller 2002, 2004). While some features such as electoral rules, a multiparty sys-

---

[7] In 12 consecutive elections (from 1950 to 1998) for the Brazilian chamber of deputies, the great majority of incumbents (70 percent, on average) have decided to run for reelection and almost 70 percent of them have been successful, more than most other countries in Latin America (Morgenstern 2002). This suggests that it is incorrect to ignore static ambition as the main goal among Brazilian legislators.

tem, and federalism act toward decentralizing the political system, other features such as the internal rules of the decision-making process in congress, the constitutional powers of the president, and his or her capacity to selectively distribute political and financial resources (most of them locally allocated), act toward centralizing it. In fact, the electoral rules provide incentives for politicians to behave individually, while the internal rules of congress, the president's power to legislate, and the centralization of benefits by the president render legislator behavior extremely dependent on loyalty to the party and on presidential preferences. It is claimed that even a political system with incentives for opposing behaviors, like the Brazilian one, provides equilibrium and stability. However, in this case it is a very dynamic equilibrium that can change from one issue to another and it depends on the capacity of the president and his party leaders to offer appropriate incentives (political and economic benefits) that can ensure the best electoral returns to individual legislators. This combination of institutional rules is key to understanding how it is possible for weak political parties in the electoral arena to coexist with strong political parties inside congress (Pereira and Mueller 2003). As a result, an underlying premise of our analysis is that there is no contradiction between party and individual behavior in the Brazilian political system at the same time. Legislators behave according to the preferences of party leaders within congress so as to have access to benefits that will increase their individual chance of surviving politically.

Party leaders hold important institutional prerogatives: the ability to appoint and substitute members of committees at any time, to add or withdraw proposals in the legislative agenda, to decide if a bill will have urgency procedure, to indicate the position of the party regarding a bill on the floor, and, fundamentally, to negotiate with the executive the demands of the members of his party. In other words, party leaders are the bridges that link individual legislators with the preferences of the executive. This is why political parties are so strong within the legislative arena. It is not rational for legislators to act individually inside congress, just as it is not rational for the executive to negotiate or bargain for support with each member of his or her coalition on every bill. The role of intermediary between the executive and the individual legislators cements the fragile links between voters and representatives in the electoral sphere. Because the Brazilian political system works in the peculiar manner described above, one might observe a false contradiction between the "personal vote" and "party vote" approaches in the literature. But the two explanations are faces of the same coin.

The most striking proactive power (which enables presidents to legislate and to establish a new status quo) in the Brazilian constitution is the ability of the president to legislate through provisional decrees (*medidas provisórias*). This institutional device allows the president to enact new legislation promptly and without congressional approval. Provisional decrees not only give the president the power to legislate, they also give him influence over the congressional agenda. If congress fails to act on a provisional decree within 30 days, it automatically goes to the top of the legislative agenda, displacing issues that congress may have been discussing. According to the constitution, a provisional decree should be used only in specific situations, although in practice the executive has made indiscriminate use of this device. Not only have a large number of provisional decrees been issued in past legislatures, but individual decrees have typically been reissued and amended at numerous times, since congress rarely challenges them. The supreme court tolerated this practice as long as presidents did not try to reintroduce any decree that congress had specifically rejected. In congress, serious disagreements over the extent of decree authority were not resolved until September 2001, when, in an accord with President Cardoso, congress amended Article 62 so as to limit presidents to a single reissue of a lapsed decree. The amendment also reduced constitutional ambiguity by specifying a list of issue-areas in which the executive may not resort to decrees. The partial rollback of presidential decree authority in late 2001 has altered the game of executive-legislative relations, and new patterns have yet to emerge (Pereira, Power, and Rennó 2005).

The most common reactive power is the veto; it allows the president to defend the status quo by reacting to the legislature's attempt to change it. The most common veto is the *package veto*, with which the president can reject the entire legislative bill sent by congress. Besides allowing the president to veto entire bills, the Brazilian constitution also allows *partial vetoes.* The president may promulgate the articles of the bill with which he agrees, while vetoing the rest of the legislation and returning only the vetoed portions to congress for reconsideration. The 1988 Constitution makes it relatively easy for congress to override a presidential veto, given that an override requires only an absolute majority of the joint chambers. Nevertheless, the Brazilian congress has seldom used its veto power. This suggests that a majority of members of congress benefit from the status quo as compared to a counterfactual world of multiple parties facing a severe collective action problem in the legislative arena.

In addition to provisional decree and veto power, the Brazilian constitution defines some policy areas where the executive has exclusive power to initiate legislation. Only the president can introduce bills concerning budgetary and public administration matters, as well as bills in an array of other important policy areas. In terms of budgetary law, although the congressional majority has the right to amend bills that were introduced by the president, it can do so only if those amendments are compatible with the multiyear budget plan elaborated by the executive, as well as with the law on budgetary guidelines. In addition, congress may not authorize expenditures that exceed the budgetary revenue. In practice, these rules enable the president to preserve the status quo on budgetary matters simply by not initiating a bill.

The internal rules of the chamber of deputies give party leaders in the Steering Body (*Mesa Diretora*) and Board of Leaders (*Colégio de Líderes*) central roles in the legislative process and in the definition of the committee system. Roughly speaking, it is the prerogative of party leaders to appoint a committee's members, as well as substitute them at any time (Article 10). There are no restrictions regarding how long a legislator can be a member of a committee. There may be some extent of self-selection to committee appointments, but there is evidence of significant interference by party leaders in the process of appointing and substituting committee members. Turnover of legislators from one committee to the next is typically extensive. Legislators change committees frequently, not only between years but also within years. Additionally the executive, through party leaders in congress, stacks certain committees with loyal members.

Besides centralizing decision-making processes inside congress and allocating huge powers of legislating to the executive, the Brazilian political system also allows the president to control the distribution of political and financial resources. This provides colossal electoral consequences for those who have the chance to exploit them appropriately. In Brazil, the executive has exclusive power to initiate the annual budget. Although legislators have the right to propose individual amendments to the annual budget, the executive determines which amendments will be appropriated, making the budget contingent on the amount of available resources in the national treasury. The Brazilian president rewards those legislators who most vote for his interests by executing their individual amendments to the annual budget; at the same time, he punishes those who vote less frequently for his preferences.[8] This is done by selectively executing their individual amendments (pork barrel policies).

Legislators who are most successful in delivering pork barrel politics demonstrate a pattern of party behavior inside congress of consistently favoring the president's preferences. To what extent has this legislative strategy been producing electoral returns? Pereira and Renno (2003) tested this question. They found that all other things held equal, the greater the amount of individual legislator amendments appropriated by the president, the higher will be the probability of a legislator's re-election. Pereira and Renno also found that the greater the number of individual amendments approved (but not appropriated) by the president, the lower is the probability that this legislator will be reelected. In other words, claiming credit is not enough to increase the chances of being reelected. The money has to be delivered. An additional result of the analysis indicates that there is no direct effect if a legislator votes in line with the wishes of the president; rather, the voting behavior matters for the indirect effect it has through pork. This leads to the inference that, in the electoral arena, the great majority of voters do not care about their representative's legislative behavior overall. Therefore, when legislators are deciding how they should vote on the floor, they are

---

[8] See Pereira (2000), Pereira and Mueller (2002, 2004), and Alston and Mueller (2006).

less inclined to take into consideration their constituency's preference because it provides few benefits for their future political careers. Instead, their strategy is to access the benefits controlled by party leaders and by the executive.

The Judiciary

Eleven judges serve on the supreme court. The president nominates judges for life terms, though with compulsory retirement at 70, and the senate confirms or denies nominations. The composition of the court has changed very slowly over time. Each president typically has the chance to appoint only a small number of judges, which makes it difficult to appoint the median voter in most issues, thus limiting the influence of the executive.

The Constitution of 1988 further enhanced the independence of the judiciary by establishing that the judiciary determines its own annual budget, and the judicial courts appoint lower court judges. Both these rights removed potential instruments of control over the judiciary from other branches of government. The supreme court influences legislation both directly and indirectly: directly by ruling that legislation is unconstitutional, and indirectly by shaping what congress will consider passing. In other words, legislative and executive activities transpire "in the shadow of the courts."

If the supreme court were truly independent, then it should be possible to observe occasions whereby it directly contradicted the interests of the executive and congress. There have been a few high-profile cases in which the court ruled against the executive on issues that were of extreme importance to the executive. These are issues over which there can be no doubt of the executive's preferences and will to prevail, so that if the judiciary were not truly independent, the executive would have used its power to change the court's decision. The best example of this was the attempt by the Cardoso government to tax retired workers. The Cardoso administration envisioned this as an important component of the solution to the fiscal crisis of the government. The social security system in Brazil was seen as one of the main sources of the country's large internal deficit. Taxing the transfers to retired workers proved highly controversial because it involved acquired rights and entitlements, and the executive was able to pass this measure through congress only with much effort (Alston and Mueller 2006). The supreme court, however, declared the measure unconstitutional. This decision enraged the administration and its supporters in congress. Initially, congress and the president threatened to deal with the supreme court's decision by changing the constitution. The reversal of the pension reforms also prompted a return to the episodic debate on the need for external control of the judiciary. This debate is revived every time a ruling by the supreme court or other parts of the judiciary gets in the way of governmental policy. Despite its threats to change the constitution, the Cardoso government abandoned the idea. The Lula government passed the same pension reform measure through congress in 2003. President Lula dealt with the potential challenge of the supreme court by making exceptions in the pension rules for the judicial branch and by counting on the support of the three members he had recently appointed.[9]

Given the independence of the supreme court, what can be said about its preferences and how can it be expected to act? Mueller (2001) analyzed the existence of commitment mechanisms for the government in the privatization and regulatory process in Brazil. His working assumption was that the court could be expected to act in a nonpolitical and unbiased manner in concession contracts, ruling closely to the letter of the contracts.[10] The evidence is not yet in, but the current political debate over regulatory pricing is clearly taking place "in the shadow of the courts."

---

[9] Other important rulings by the supreme court include the mandate in 1997 by the court to increase the wages of federal civil servants to compensate them for losses due to previous stabilization programs, and the frequency with which the court prevented expropriations of land for land reform (see Alston, Libecap, and Mueller 2000). For a list and discussion of cases entailing conflicts between administrations and the court between 1988 and 1994, see Castro (1997).

[10] This assumption does not mean that the Brazilian judiciary functions well in other aspects. Indeed there is evidence that the overall judicial system has a negative impact on the economy. See Pinheiro (1997) and Pinheiro and Cabral (1998).

More generally, the main problem cited by companies, individuals, and judges themselves is the slowness of the judiciary (Pinheiro 2000).[11] Courts at all levels, including the supreme court, are typically overloaded with cases, and decisions can take years. Companies often use this slowness strategically, taking actions that they know will be struck down in the distant future. For the government, this type of strategic behavior is even more appealing since the consequences of actions taken today may be left for future administrations. Governments have used the expected court delays successfully in tax legislation. If the courts rule against the government, it is future governments who will have to rebate taxes. In short, court delays act as a quick and cheap emergency means of government financing.

Governors

Unlike the other actors discussed in this section, governors do not have an independent and constitutionally defined power that can *directly* counter executive preferences. Governors are not veto players, in the sense that their agreement is not necessary for approval of legislative proposals, nor do they hold powers to reverse legislative decisions. They can, however, have some indirect power over policy by their influence.

The constitution vested a number of policy domains (such as public safety) to the states, which also enjoy certain autonomy in the area of taxes and administration. The policy preferences of governors and the executive may diverge in the political game described in the preceding section. Governors are not primarily concerned with fiscal stability at the national level and have a preference for higher federal public spending and geographically concentrated investments. Governors are also interested in more social transfers because these can be presented as state government's spending and local programs. The preferences of governors and the executive clash over fiscal policy.

It is necessary to distinguish two phases in the discussion of the ways in which governors, and federalism at large, have constrained the execu-

---

[11] Another well-cited problem is the lack of access to the judiciary by the poor.

tive. The first phase was transitional, when the rules of the political game were not yet fully institutionalized. In this period, governors derived their power by virtue of the role they played in the democratic transition. The second phase dates from the Cardoso administration, when the new constitutional rules of the game were in place.

Governors have derived their powers from two sources. First, as previously mentioned, they enjoyed great political power in the 1980s because of the role they played in the democratic transition. In addition, while there is much dispute in the political science literature, governors tend to have some, albeit declining, influence over the behavior of federal deputies and senators in congress. The degree of influence they hold varies across areas, with governors playing a crucial role in issues with important state-wide effects, such as tax and regional infrastructure. Governors can also play an important role in the electoral career of legislators at the state level. Samuels (2003), for example, claims that congressional candidates tend to coordinate their campaigns around gubernatorial candidates and not presidential candidates. That is what he calls the "gubernatorial coat-tails effect," in which the race for governor shapes the race for federal deputy because Brazilian politicians do not obtain much of the electoral resources they need from national parties or presidential candidates, but from state-level connections.

However, the broker's role attributed to governors and their control over their state's legislative delegations have been greatly exaggerated by the media and by the literature, especially during the Cardoso administration. It is true that governors can constrain the executive in indirect ways, but they do not wield veto power in any federal arena. There is no evidence that state loyalties on the part of legislators undermine party lines or create trouble for the executive (Cheibub, Figueiredo, and Limongi 2002). The indirect ways in which governors influence policy formation range from lobbying activities on specific issues affecting states, such as tax policy, to control over specific appointments in the federal bureaucracy. Governors can also resist the implementation of federal policy, such as when a number of state governors refused to privatize state-owned energy firms. These episodes are unusual and have become even more so because states have become less and less autonomous and more dependent on the federal government.

Another declining institutional source of a state's power has to do with the state's prerogative to own banks and public enterprises. The state banks were created in the 1960s as part of the developmental strategies pursued by the military government. With the democratization of the country in the 1980s, the governors became more autonomous from the federal government and therefore were able to use the state banks for pork. This included granting subsidized loans to the private sector and more importantly, financing state government projects that are fiscally unsound. The state treasuries also issued bonds that were purchased by the banks. Thus during the Sarney, Collor, and Itamar administrations, the states operated under a soft budget constraint because of their ability to undermine the supervision of the central bank. In 1994, before the establishment of the privatization program (PROES), there were 35 state banks. Currently, there are four small state banks.

In addition to the state banks, governors control a vast network of sources of pork, ranging from public sector jobs to infrastructure programs and state-owned enterprises. In state-owned enterprises, a pattern similar to what occurred in the banking sector can be observed. Most public utilities companies in energy were privatized, leaving governors without an important instrument of power. The resources controlled by the states are important assets that are instrumental to winning elections, and they are coveted by the federal government. In the large states, the administrative *apparati* are large machines that can be even larger than the federal government machine itself, as in São Paulo.

Because of the fiscal problems facing the states following monetary stabilization, the federal government was able to impose the privatization of the banks and public enterprises, thereby dramatically undercutting the power of governors. With inflation under control, the state banks lost their principal source of revenue (the floating of financial assets), and a surge in interest rates caused a rapid deterioration of the states' fiscal situation. State debt reached a peak in 1997 (three years after the *Plano Real* was phased in) and represented a significant part of the GDP. The *Plano Real* was therefore an exogenous shock that undermined the ability of the states to resist the preferences of the executive. The federal government implemented a program aimed at renegotiating the states' debts. It included debt swapping under favorable conditions, though it was linked to a number of conditionalities.[12] Before 1994, a number of incentives such as federal bailouts encouraged states to behave fiscally irresponsibly and indulge in opportunistic behavior.

In sum, while it is clear that federalism matters and that governors play an important role, throughout most of the last decade the executive has been able to have its agenda implemented by recentralizing the political game. This includes passing legislation that adversely affected the state governors and initiating measures that have led to a political recentralization of the country (Melo 2002).[13]

The Bureaucracy

This chapter views the Brazilian bureaucracy as an important institutional player and institutional constraint in the political game. The bureaucracy is an institutional actor that constrains the executive but at the same time plays an integral part in the management of the government coalition. The bureaucracy has been undergoing significant change in response to the changing economic and political environment. In particular, the role of the bureaucracy within regulatory agencies is increasingly important. Overall, the changes in bureaucratic structures following the enactment of the Constitution of 1988 have led to policy outcomes that are stable and adaptable.

Brazil has been discussed in the literature on comparative bureaucracy as a fairly successful case. During the so-called *Estado Novo* (1937–45), President Vargas implemented a significant administrative reform. It set up the *Departamento Administrativo do Serviço Público* (DASP, or Adminis-

---

[12] This was accomplished by the *Programa de Recuperação Fiscal e Financeira* (RFF) and through Law 9496 in 1997. A stock of debts corresponding to 11 percent of the Brazilian GDP was renegotiated (Mora 2002).

[13] For a contrasting view that argues that resistance from the states and governors undermines much of Cardoso's reform efforts, see Samuels (2003).

trative Department for the Civil Service) in 1938 as the key administrative agency responsible for the competitive selection of federal personnel and for the rationalization of administrative practices and procedures. The DASP reforms led to the formation of a hybrid, two-level administrative structure in Brazil. The first level consisted of the core developmental bureaucracies in agencies in state-owned enterprises, state-owned banks, and in planning, taxation, and budgeting. The second level consisted of the administrative structures of the line ministries, particularly in the social sectors. The first level was insulated from competitive politics. The second level was part and parcel of patronage games and highly clientelistic arrangements (Geddes 1995; Nunes 1997). Examples of the first type of insulated bureaucracies in the 1950s include the National Bank for Economic Development (BNDES), the Bank for the Brazilian Northeast (BNB), the Bank of Brazil, the Brazilian Institute for Geography and Statistics (IBGE), the Northeast Development Agency (SUDENE), and the Ministry of Foreign Relations (Itamaraty).

Despite the insulation of some bureaucracies, the president still retains a large degree of power to make appointments, especially at the cabinet level. As noted earlier, the president uses both pork and patronage as ways of solidifying the support of his coalition. In order to obtain his preferences for fiscal stability, the president faces the dilemma of delegating bureaucratic discretion to coalition party members while reducing the associated agency losses. The institutional rules governing the bureaucracy have enabled presidents to successfully play this game. The president can resort to 18,000 political appointments (known as DAS posts); a considerable number of these are low-rank posts. The key high-rank posts (approximately 3,000) are filled by the DAS 4, 5, and 6 appointments, representing less than 2 percent of federal public employees. Presidents have recruited personnel for these positions from within the civil service, from nontenured but highly qualified professionals currently holding positions in the bureaucracy, from public universities, and from the private sector.

The president delegates less in the areas of taxation, budgeting, and planning in the ministries of finance and planning. Top-rank bureaucrats in these ministries are typically appointed from a pool of career civil servants in the central bank, the Internal Revenue Service, and the Itamaraty, among other institutions, and less frequently from outside government. Unlike countries such as the United States or France, appointments are made across career lines (Loureiro and Abrucio 1999). The president can then combine distinct criteria while making these appointments. These include personal loyalty and technical expertise. The latter is assured in these careers by extremely competitive entrance examinations and subsequent training in a number of civil service schools, including the *Escola de Administração Fazendária* and *Escola Nacional de Administração Pública.*

The rest of the ministries have a less endogenous source of recruitment, and ministerial posts are assigned on a partisan basis. Presidents have usually kept the prerogative of appointing the ministries' secretary-general—second in line to the minister, and in charge of managing the ministries' positions—as a mechanism for reducing agency losses. The ministry of finance, however, is a key institution in this regard. By controlling budget execution and the cash flow of government expenditures, presidential control over the ministry is crucial (Loureiro and Abrucio 1999).

Critical factors that explain the ability of bureaucratic executives to ensure a reasonable level of technical expertise in the Brazilian federal bureaucracy include the following: the widespread use of competitive entrance examinations in the areas of tax administration, budgeting, control, economic planning, accounting, central banking, social security, and legal positions within the executive; and favorable employment conditions in the public sector. These include tenure and reasonably competitive salaries. In the 1990s public employees' real salaries eroded, but they were raised significantly during the Cardoso administration.

The government also managed to change the civil service rules enshrined in the Constitution of 1988. The constitution introduced important changes in the Brazilian administrative state. The extension of tenure to all state employees (formerly called CLT workers) through *Regime Jurídico Único* (the Unified Legal System, or RJU) created a rigid system of personnel that exacerbated state inefficiency. The RJU prohibited different pay levels for distinct performance levels by state employees. It established the principle of equal pay for categories of functions at the municipal, state, and federal government levels. It also granted tenure and a secured 100 percent replacement rate for civil servant pensions (in several cases, up to 130 percent). The 1988 Constitution also created or strengthened bureaucratic and time-consuming mechanisms for competitive bidding and personnel recruitment, thereby creating an incentive structure that encouraged inefficiency.

The administrative reform package was approved in 1998 and included revamping the RJU, setting up the legal foundations for social organizations and executive agencies—institutions with managerial autonomy and with social control mechanisms, establishing performance contracts within the public sector, and making tenure more flexible. A number of measures also boosted the attractiveness of public employment: the ratio between initial pay and top grade pay within specific civil service career tracks was expanded significantly. The reform aimed at the low and middle ranks of the bureaucracy, where the pay is high, performance is poor, and the fiscal costs are very significant because of the sheer numbers of employees.

Another important positive development under the Cardoso administration was the extension of professionalization outside the core of the economic, planning, finance, and infrastructure ministries. The ministries for the social sectors, particularly the ministry of health and education, also underwent important changes. For the first time, the ministers, secretary-general, and key managers were economists and were much more qualified than their predecessors.

Policy Outcomes

Rather than generating consistent policy outcomes, the political institutions in Brazil generate policies in four broad but distinct categories: stable but adaptable policies; pork, or geographically distinct projects; volatile and unstable policies; and rigid and hard-wired policies. Consistent with this study's claims that the government has incentives and instruments to pursue sound fiscal and monetary policy, the first subsection below describes those policies and the recent Fiscal Responsibility Law. Pork is also examined in this context, because it is often given by the president in exchange for other actors' support on certain stable but adaptable policies. Then the discussion turns to the volatile and unstable policies, including social and poverty policies, as well as land reform. Finally, education policy and health policy are analyzed. These are examples of policies that are hard-wired, given the long lag that exists between spending and outcomes in these sectors, which may tempt policymakers to divert spending to other, less fundamental areas that have more immediate dividends.

Stable and Adaptable Policies, Along with Pork

Stable but adaptable means that should outside conditions be stable, policy in these areas would be automatic. But exogenous events occur sporadically and unpredictably, so the government adapts to the events so as to minimize the damage to fiscal and monetary stability. The policies that best fit into this category relate to economic growth, inflation, and unemployment. To achieve policies such as pension reform, the president exchanges pork for policy support with members of his coalition. The following subsections first discuss why we consider macroeconomic policy to be generally stable and adaptable, even though economic performance has not been stellar (although recently growth has increased). The discussion then turns to the Fiscal Responsibility Law, which reined in state government debt.

Macroeconomic Policy and Economic Performance. The framework presented in this chapter states that political institutions give the executive incentives to be concerned primarily with macroeconomic policy. In addition, strong presidential powers give the executive the means to pursue those policies which, when combined with the incentives and checks by other political actors, result in stable and adaptable policy. Meanwhile other policies, described in the next section, remain contingent on the success of macroeconomic policies to be executed.

The framework presents a rather positive picture of the Brazilian policymaking process, especially when compared to most other Latin

American countries. Although there are clearly several problems with this policymaking process, we maintain that overall the process provides a reasonably good means for intertemporal political transaction to be realized. The result is a system of checks and balances where a strong president achieves high levels of governability, positively constrained by several other political actors. These claims, however, may seem to many observers to clash with actual facts. An examination of real GDP growth rates shows economic growth has been less than spectacular: 0.7 percent on average for Brazil from 1990 to 1999, less than the average of 1.4 percent for Latin America as a whole.[14] In addition, public sector debt, which is a key variable for gauging the sustainability of public policy, presents a trend that is a serious cause for concern: since 1999 the ratio of government debt to GDP has been above 50 percent. However, we argue that legitimate political change does not translate instantaneously into economic growth: policy changes create disruptions, and it takes time for the positive growth results to materialize. The growth record for the twenty-first century, especially in the past few years, has been a good indication that past policies are having a positive impact.

This chapter does not claim that economic outcomes have been as positive as can be desired, but rather that the underlying policymaking process has had some very positive characteristics. Clearly a functional policymaking process should lead on average to good economic outcomes—although the fundamental link between these two is not immediate, since history (path-dependence) and other intervening factors may delay the effect of new political institutions on economic outcomes. The policymaking process portrayed here has evolved gradually over time and is still evolving. Many of the positive incentives tied to that policymaking process, which enable political transactions to be realized, have been functioning for only a relatively short period of time. The ma-

---

[14] In March 2007 the Brazilian census bureau released revised figures for past GDP growth, incorporating improved methodologies in the calculation. The new numbers showed markedly better outcomes. GDP growth from 2000 to 2005 was revised from 4.4 to 4.3 percent (2000), 1.3 to 1.3 percent (2001), 1.9 to 2.7 percent (2002), 0.5 to 1.1 percent (2003), 4.9 to 5.7 percent (2004), and 2.3 to 2.9 percent (2005).

jor process of institutional change that has led to this system started only in 1985 with redemocratization, and especially with the new Constitution of 1988. However, these changes did not come into effect immediately. Even after the promulgation of the constitution, there was still a long period in which complementary laws were being created and voted on in congress. More importantly a process of gradual changes has occurred, as discussed above. Furthermore, in the first years after the adoption of the constitution, the political process underwent a convoluted period because of shocks not directly influenced by the new institutions.

Most of the important institutional changes began only in 1995, which is why most of our analysis focuses on the Cardoso and Lula administrations. Since 1995, many of the formal and informal rules that currently permeate executive-legislative relations were consolidated and became routine. In addition, several important reforms began to be implemented, representing not only important policy outcomes, but also altering the nature of the policymaking process by changing the political actors' incentives and constraints: that is, shaping the political institutions themselves. The following changes have been among the most important: administrative reform, which changed the rules governing civil servants; privatization and the creation of regulatory agencies in several sectors; passage of the Fiscal Responsibility Law, which constrains political actors, especially governors (see discussion below); the evolution of the role of the *Ministério Público*, which has become an important veto player; and deconstitutionalizing many policies originally embedded in the constitution, such as pension reform. Yet to come is reform of the judiciary, already initiated by the Lula government.

Fiscal Responsibility Law (FRL). Congress and the president enacted the FRL in 2000. The FRL represented the apex of a relatively successful set of measures to control the state governments' indebtedness. The FRL illustrates the kinds of policy outcomes that reflect the executive's ability to implement its policy preferences in the political game, discussed in the previous sections. Furthermore, it reflects a learning process arising from a repeated game between the federal government and the states.

As Braun and Tommasi (2004) point out, fiscal rules to be enforced require self-enforcement by the players (states) or an external enforcer with the power to ensure compliance. We argue that the Brazilian case approximates the second case. As discussed in this chapter, the current depiction of the Brazilian political system as a federal structure in which governors wield vast powers is inaccurate. In fact, the circumstances that originally produced strong powers at the state level were extraordinary: a Constituent Assembly in which the executive played a minor role; the political conjuncture of the transition to democratic rule, in which fiscal decentralization and increased social spending were important banners; and the specific sequence through which the political transition (demo-cratic elections) occurred first at the state level (1982) and subsequently at the national level, converting the governors into key political figures in the transition. However, unlike pre-1994 Argentina, the political sur-vival of the president or of the senators does not depend on subnational institutions such as the electoral college, in provincial assemblies in which governors play a key role.[15] Because there was no constitutional basis for the power of governors, the *Real* plan represented a shock that restored the dominant power of the president. Among other things, it laid bare the states' fiscal imbalances, made it impossible for the states to resort to floating and other financial mechanisms to finance their fiscal deficits, and caused a further deterioration of the deficits because of the sharp increase in interest rates. The executive was able to impose its fiscal preferences because it could offer advances from the federal development bank, BNDES, in exchange for fiscal reforms, including privatization of state banks and utilitiesz it had agenda powers and other legislative prerogatives to implement its agenda; and it was helped by the approval of the reelection amendment, which strengthened not only the president vis-à-vis the governors, but also helped extend the governors' time horizons (19 governors ran for reelection), thus introducing some

---

[15] Current views on fiscal rules fail to recognize these crucial differences and instead categorize Brazil and Argentina as examples of the same perverse fiscal federal game (Melo 2004). These contributions fail to recognize the great preponderance of the executive in the fiscal game. For analyses of the Brazilian case along these lines, see Rodden (2003), Braun and Tommasi (2004), and Webb (2004).

element of self-enforcement in the fiscal game.[16] In addition, because of the devastating impact of hyperinflation in the mid-1990s, the president's policies were viewed favorably by a great majority of the public, which became strongly inflation-averse.

The sustainability of the current fiscal situation is therefore not dependent on the states' cooperation. Although the FRL could be reversed, there is some rigidity in it, since a three-fifths majority in two rounds of voting in the two chambers is required for a change in the law. The FRL specifies in great detail the fiscal rules governing public sector indebtedness, credit operations, and public account's reporting. The law prohibits the federal government from financing subnational governments, therefore eliminating the possibility of bailouts as well as any changes in the financial clauses of the existing debt-restructuring agreement. The FRL imposes debt ceilings for each level of government. The executive branch proposes the ceilings and the senate must approve. The law stipulates that in the context of economic instability or drastic changes in monetary or exchange rate policy, the federal government can submit to the senate a proposal for changing these limits. Any excesses to the limits are to be eliminated within one year, otherwise new financing and voluntary transfers from the central government are prohibited. Other sanctions include withholding federal transfers by the federal government, denial of credit guarantees, and banning of new debt (Nascimento and Debus n.d.). In addition, the financing arrangements are transparent to all parties, including the public, and the FRL contains a golden rule provision for capital spending, that is, annual credit disbursement cannot exceed capital spending.

It would be misleading to conclude that the impressive fiscal costs to the central government meant that the initiatives were in the interest of subnational governments. Furthermore, the fact that most of the fiscal adjustment was generated by raising tax revenue rather than by significant cuts in expenditures does not mean that there has not been a radical change in the intergovernmental balance of power. The states had to

---

[16] Without the reelection amendment, incumbent governors would have an incentive to exacerbate the common pool problem by leaving the fiscal problem to future governors.

privatize or close their banks, embark on a program of fiscal modernization, reduce the relative importance of payroll (for which governors were
required at least to refrain from hiring more personnel), sell enterprises,
as well as to adapt their pension regimes to the federal rules (in addition
to being prohibited from creating new pension institutions or legislating
in this area). In sum, the states lost significant degrees of autonomy. As
Mora (2002) argues, the states have become more and more dependent
on the federal government because voluntary (that is, discretionary)
transfers from the federal government have become essential for their
fiscal survival. Many observers have praised the FRL because it laid the
foundation for a new formidable system of rules for fiscal management.
The IMF (2001, p. 1) described the new fiscal institutions as follows:

> In the last few years Brazil has achieved a high degree of fiscal trans-
> parency, together with major improvements in the management
> of its public finances. This was done against the background of an
> international and domestic macroeconomic environment that has
> posed substantial challenges to the country's economic policymak-
> ers. The cornerstone of these achievements has been the enactment
> in May 2000 of the Fiscal Responsibility Law, which sets out for all
> levels of government fiscal rules designed to ensure medium-term fis-
> cal sustainability, and strict transparency requirements to underpin
> the effectiveness and credibility of such rules. Another pillar of the
> improved fiscal management has been the medium-term expendi-
> ture framework aimed at better aligning the allocation of budgetary
> resources over time to the government's priorities and regional de-
> velopment strategy. Also instrumental in promoting sustained fiscal
> adjustment of sub-national governments has been the firm enforce-
> ment by the federal government of the debt restructuring agree-
> ments with most states and many municipalities.

Volatile and Unstable Policy

We categorize certain policies as being volatile and unstable. Policies
are unstable because some have a strong ideological component and as

such will oscillate with changes—in the executive branch, in particular; and some are residual, in that the appropriations are determined so as to meet a budgetary target that does not upset the overarching goal of stable monetary and fiscal policy.

The mechanism by which receipts and expenditures are balanced by the government throughout the budgetary year so as to achieve the target primary surplus is known as *contingenciamento*. At the beginning of each fiscal year, the government passes a decree impounding part of the discretionary expenditures in the budget: that is, those pending expenditures that are not hard-wired. As the year proceeds, these resources can be "unimpounded" if tax receipts are greater than expected and if hard-wired expenditures have not been greater than expected.

The size of the cuts are set for each ministry and it is then up to each minister—together with the executive, but without consulting congress—to determine which programs and projects will be hit. Because these are necessarily in the "investment" part of the budget, which is the only part that is not hard-wired, these projects typically affect the policies that we label volatile residual policies. They become volatile because they undergo a process where they will be executed more fully in good fiscal years than in bad fiscal years. The next two subsections will discuss two sets of policies that fall into this category: land reform and poverty alleviation.

Land Reform Policies. Land reform is the prototypical social policy. It is perhaps the most ideologically charged policy issue in all of Latin America. In addition, it is the kind of issue where the economic benefits of well-conducted policy materialize only in the long run. That is, land reform has those characteristics that the framework presented here predicts will lead to volatile policy, with changes in emphasis, design, and implementation coming about with each change in government. In Brazil, this is clearly a predominant characteristic of land reform policies. Since the 1960s every government has had a specific land reform program, although more than 40 years of effort have not managed to budge the indices of land ownership concentration.

Each new administration has created a new land reform program with a different name and has set ambitious targets of how many families it planned to settle. The executive includes resources in his budget proposal to congress and congress typically adds amendments to increase expenditures. But at the beginning of each fiscal year, the executive issues a decree that impounds (*contingenciamento*) part of the resources from several areas, so as to assure that the government's expenditures and receipts are compatible with the primary fiscal surplus target, as described above. For example, the percentages of the budgets for land reform that Presidents Cardoso and Lula impounded from 2001 to 2004 were 11, 25, 36, and 6 percent. In short, the budgets for land reform demonstrate considerable volatility over time and within a term of a given president.[17] As predicted by this chapter's model, the Lula government cut expenditures on land reform, a residual ideological issue, despite its ideological preferences for greater spending on land reform. The rationale for the cut was to meet the fiscal imperatives of a particularly troublesome year.

Poverty Alleviation. Brazilian antipoverty programs exemplify the kinds of policy areas that have exhibited highly unstable patterns in the last decade. According to the political game discussed earlier, they are residual policies. There is ample evidence of instability in the period from 1988 until the end of the Cardoso government. The evidence during Lula's administration is more mixed and hinges on the interpretation of the high visibility received by the flagship program *Fome Zero* (zero hunger).

The Brazilian constitution stipulates a clear role for the state in terms of poverty alleviation. According to Article 23 of the constitution, poverty alleviation is the joint mandate of the federal government, the states, and the municipal governments. In the 1980s there were two federal institutions aimed at reducing poverty: the Legião Brasileira de Assistência (LBA) and the Centro Brasileiro para a Infância e Adolescência (CEBIA). The Collor administration (1990–92) transferred many of the programs to a newly created *Ministério do Bem Estar Social* and also closed a large number of programs. In the area of food and nutrition, the administra-

---

[17] Budgetary data, including that on impoundments, comes from several technical notes of the *Consultoria de Orçamento e Fiscalização Financeira* of the house of representatives, http://www.camara.gov.br/internet/orcament/Principal/exibe.asp?idePai=16&cadeia=0@.

tion terminated the eight subprograms that had existed in the 1980s from which children and expectant mothers had benefited (Resende 2000). At the same time, President Collor phased out the *Programa de Alimentação do Trabalhador* (PAT), a food program for low-income workers.

Upon taking office, President Itamar Franco announced poverty alleviation as one of his top priorities, dramatically changing course from the Collor administration. IPEA, the planning ministry's economic think tank, prepared a "map of hunger." The announcement of the map and the publication of figures pointing to the existence of 32 million people living in extreme poverty led Franco to declare the country to be in a "state of social calamity." The next step was the announcement of a number of emergency measures and the setting up, in 1993, of the *Conselho Nacional de Segurança Alimentar* (CONSEA, the National Council for Food Security), consisting of 8 ministers and 21 representatives from civil society.

Under President Cardoso, *Comunidade Solidária* became the main antipoverty initiative. The programs consisted of public and private partnerships and included volunteer groups. Overall, *Comunidade Solidária* functioned as a coordination mechanism designed to take place on two levels: it would encourage and facilitate the participation of civil society institutions in the formulation and implementation of social assistance programs, and it would identify current social spending programs that had a higher impact on poverty and channel resources to those programs. The programs identified received the "priority seal," which protected them from expenditure cuts.

The Lula administration initiated a reversal of Cardoso's antipoverty programs, at least on paper. The Lula administration phased out *Comunidade Solidária* and launched a new antipoverty program, under the auspices of the *Ministério Extraordinário para a Segurança Alimentar e Combate a Fome* (MESA, an ad hoc ministry for food security). The *Fome Zero* program became the centerpiece of the new ministry. However, President Lula reduced the resources earmarked for the program because of his fiscal targets.[18] At the same time, the government decided

---

[18] The budget law for 2003 contained R$1.8 billion for the *Fome Zero*, whereas the budget estimate for its full implementation was R$5.0 billion.

to introduce a single card, the *cartão família*, which was to be used by families to receive the food benefit plus three other current conditional income transfer benefits. To receive the benefits, families must engage in a number of activities, including vaccination and school attendance. In practice, the government discontinued its initiatives and promoted the merger of cash transfer programs created under President Cardoso: the school attendance program (*Bolsa Escola*), food aid (*Bolsa Alimentação*), and the gas benefit. By creating the card, the Lula government could present the achievements of *Fome Zero*—that is, the number of families that received the card—in the same package with the figures for the much larger existing programs. The same applies to the funds allocated to the family card. The net result was that the political visibility of the modest resources allocated to the food benefit was reduced.

Before Lula's administration, during President Cardoso's second term, an attempt was made to hard-wire funds for poverty alleviation. While acknowledging the gravity of the poverty situation, the Cardoso administration opposed the idea of a fund because it would imply "budget rigidity." The prima facie attempt to introduce rigidity in the budget for the purposes of poverty alleviation can be understood as part of the logrolling between the executive and legislative branches. The executive maintained fiscal stability by increasing taxes at the subnational level. In return, congress received some poverty alleviation programs sheltered from discretionary executive budget cuts. This is consistent with the political game described in this chapter. The executive prefers hard-wiring subnational spending so as to allow for fiscal discretion at the national level.

Rigid or Hard-Wired Policy

This section provides examples of hard-wired policies. These are policies specified in the constitution over which the executive has no discretion. In 2003, approximately 94 percent of the expenditures in the budget were "rigid," that is, they could not be changed. The largest portion of these expenditures included types of expenditures whose shares grew over time and whose amounts were most probably not foreseen at the time of hard-wiring. The best example is pensions, which now account for 33 percent of the budget. Other types of hard-wired expenditures occurred intentionally; they are the outcomes of the deals between the legislature and the executive. They include transfers to states and municipalities (18 percent), the Unified Health System or SUS (7 percent), miscellaneous subsidies, including subsidies for small farmers and small enterprises, rural development, computer technology law, and many more diverse subsidies (2 percent), social assistance (1 percent), export tax breaks (Kandir Law) (1 percent), and other expenditures (11 percent). Only 6 percent of the expenditures were subject to being withheld by the executive to reach fiscal targets. However, the total value, which is approximately R$20 billion, is still significant.

There has been much debate over what powers the constitution and the Fiscal Responsibility Law actually confer on the president in terms of discretion to execute the budget (Lima 2004). There has also been much debate on whether and how hard-wired items should be made flexible. As the rigidities imposed in the past on current public expenditures become more constraining and impede efficient adjustment to current circumstances, the pressure for decoupling some expenditures has increased. Also, as more expenditures become hard-wired, there are fewer resources left over for use as pork by the president for trades with congress. The only mechanism that remains largely unaffected by these fiscal trends is the political allocation of patronage to members of the governing coalition. But as indicated before, the increasing professionalization of the line ministries of the social sectors (the largest bureaucracies of the state machinery) has also restricted patronage to a certain extent. This has created an incentive for the president to try to find creative ways to increase his leeway for determining expenditures. The most frequent mechanism used by Presidents Cardoso and Lula has been "deconstitutionalization."

Hard-wired policies generally include those with little ideological content, and are perceived in society as entitlements. The two that best fit this description and that will be discussed in the next two subsections are education and health policies.

Health Policy. The Constitution of 1988 created a unified budget for pensions, social assistance benefits, and health care, the so-called social security budget. This was part of the demand for a universal social protection system advanced by the opposition during the military regime and an important sectoral banner during the Constituent Assembly. A diversified source of funding was set up. This institutional arrangement was viewed by the groups supporting the idea as a mechanism that would delink contributions and access to the system, making it more democratic and redistributive. To this end, the constitution gave universal access to health care through the newly created Unified Health System (SUS). It also introduced generous social assistance benefits. The social security budget was made up of the CSLL, the contribution on net profits paid by corporations (*Cofins*), and the employers' and employees' payroll contributions.

The fusion of expenditures for health care and pensions in the same budget produced a dynamic over time that has been highly detrimental to health care, because pensions are contractual disbursements and are not compressible. They are a flux of future commitments that ends only with the death of the pensioners. By contrast, health expenditures are mostly current expenditures that are by definition vulnerable in the context of fiscal management. Over time, social security commitments crowded out health expenditures. It did not take long before this process became critical. This occurred because fiscal imbalances in the pension schemes were not very significant before the Constitution of 1988, and, more importantly, pensions were not indexed. This gradually resulted in a sharp reduction in the real values of pensions. By mandating that pensions were to keep their real value, the Constitution of 1988 resulted in future fiscal imbalances. It dramatically expanded the mass of workers under the civil service regime, upgraded rural noncontributory pensions and social benefits to the level of urban pensions, and set the lowest value of pensions at the minimum salary level. This produced a shock to the system and caused a crowding out of health expenditures shortly after its implementation.

At the same time that the fiscal burden of pensions was growing, Brazil decentralized health care. The decentralization was very significant.

The *municípios* were responsible for 9.6 percent of total spending in health care in 1985 (Arretche 2003). This share reached 35 percent in 1996 and 43 percent in 2000. The flip side of the coin is that the federal government's share declined from 73 percent to 53 percent over the same period (Arretche 2003).

The recurrent crisis in the funding of the health sector enhanced the visibility of health issues in the country. Brazil's infant mortality rates are far above countries with comparable levels of per capita income. Policy elites have been increasingly sensitive to the need to address health issues as a precondition for development. Many proposals have been advanced for earmarking resources for the health sector. These have been criticized by the finance and planning circles as a move backward that would cause more fiscal rigidities in a context of rapidly declining degrees of freedom in the budget.

The measures to secure financing for the health sector culminated in a proposal to create the CPMF, the provisional contribution on financial transactions. The CPMF was created by Constitutional Amendment 3 in 1993 and was a "sunset" provision that would be valid for only two years. In 1996, Constitutional Amendment 12 reinstated the CPMF and earmarked it for the health sector. In 2000, Constitutional Amendment 29 stipulated minimum values for investments in the health sector for the three tiers of government: municipal, state, and federal. For the federal government, the budget for 2000 was set at the 1999 level plus 5 percent. For the period 2001 to 2004, the value of health expenditures was readjusted by the annual variation of the nominal GDP. Of these, 15 percent was to be spent in the municipalities on basic health care, and distributed according to their population. In the case of the states, 12 percent of the revenue (after legal transfers to the municipalities) was to be spent in the health sector. In turn the municipalities were required to spend 15 percent of their budget on health care. The states and municipalities, which in 2000 had expenditures levels below those stipulated, were to reduce the difference at the rate of one-fifth per year. Noncompliance would allow federal intervention in subnational governments. The law stipulated that all transfers would be channeled to a fund and subject to auditing.

The initiatives aiming to hard-wire health care resources may be interpreted as attempts at controlling and securing subnational spending in a context of rapid decentralization and consequently high uncertainty over outcomes in an increasingly salient issue for the executive. It is significant that in the context of fiscal adjustment, discretionary health transfers—which are by far the largest of their kind in the country—have become crucial for the fiscal survival of subnational governments. This made the control of subnational spending all the more critical for the central executive.

Education Policy. Education policy is another area that illustrates the use of institutional innovations as a precommitment device to ensure that they are preserved. As in the case of health care, primary (*ensino fundamental*) and secondary education are viewed by the governing coalition as crucial, thereby requiring insulation from political logrolls. Similarly, the key issue here for the executive is guaranteeing that the resources earmarked for primary and secondary education are in fact applied by the subnational governments in the sector and in specific ways. Article 30 of the Constitution states that primary education is to be provided by the municipalities, with the financial and technical assistance of the federal government and of the state. Constitutional Amendment 14 contains articles calling for priorities to be given by each level of government, but does not mandate specialization of competence. This definition provides an incentive structure that discourages efficiency because it diffuses responsibility and accountability.

In the late 1980s and 1990s, the centrality of education to development became a recurrent issue in the public agenda. From business interests to social movements, a consensus emerged that was reflected in the executive's preference for insulation of the educational sector. This was combined with the increasing need to enhance control mechanisms in the context of an accelerated program of decentralization. The furor over the quality of education finally resulted in the passage of Constitutional Amendment 14 in 1996 and the approval of the LDB (the complementary law of basic guidelines for education) in the same year. Constitutional Amendment 14 required that for 10 years, at least

60 percent of the 25 percent of the subnational resources mandated for education were to be spent on the payment of teachers actively involved in classroom activities. The federal government was to play an equalization role. This has become the Achilles' heel of the new arrangements. Consistent with their preferences for fiscal expansion at the local level, subnational governments have pressured the federal government to raise its transfers. However, fiscal needs have led the national government to not readjust it. The Lula administration did not increase its funding, notwithstanding the intense criticism by the Workers' Party (PT) of inadequate funding by the Cardoso government. The federal government's desire is to control subnational priorities and spending, while keeping its own preferred federal fiscal targets as the ultimate adjustment variable.

The incentive structure led mayors to actively engage in attracting pupils because this would lead to more transfers from the fund. In addition, it encouraged decentralization from states to municipalities because there would be negative transfers in some municipalities if the educational services were provided by the states. The rationale for the education initiatives by the federal government is similar to those that underlie the health care system: attempts to control and secure subnational spending in a context of rapid decentralization and consequently high uncertainty over outcomes. Control by the federal government over subnational spending is therefore critical to ensure that the federal government meets its preferences.

Conclusion

This study has found that the driving force behind policies in Brazil is the strong set of powers given to the president by the Constitution of 1988. To have strong powers does not mean unbridled powers. Several institutions constrain and check the power of the president, in particular, the legislature, the judiciary, the public prosecutors, the auditing office, the state governors, and the constitution itself. The electorate of Brazil holds the president accountable for economic growth, inflation, and unemployment. Because of the electoral connection, and perhaps because of reputational effects, presidents in Brazil have a strong incentive to pursue stable fiscal and monetary policies as their first priority. At least for the past 10 years and especially during the Lula administration, executive power has been aimed at pushing policy towards macro orthodoxy. Although orthodoxy may not lead to short-term growth, international financial markets provide additional incentives for discipline, as deviations are instantly punished with unfavorable consequences that are readily recognized by the electorate. Achieving stable macro policies required constitutional amendments as well as considerable legislation. To attain their goals, past administrations (Cardoso and Lula in particular) used their property rights to pork to trade for policy changes. The rationale for members of congress to exchange votes on policy for pork is that the electorates reward or punish members of congress based on the degree to which pork lands in their district. With the exception of the devaluation of 1999, macro policy has become more stable over time. Macro policies in Brazil can be characterized as "stable but adaptable."

The pursuit of macro orthodoxy comes at a cost; some policies in Brazil are "volatile and unstable." This analysis has found volatility and instability in policies that have an ideological component, such as land reform and poverty alleviation, or whose gains accrue at the congressional district level, such as infrastructure projects. The volatility on ideological policies is no surprise and happens most when administrations change. For policies having a local rather than national impact, the volatility results from the fact that spending is based on the residual left in the budget after the president takes care of hard-wired and pork expenditures. The negative side of this arrangement is that many infrastructure projects have fallen into this residual category, notably sanitation and local roads.

The Constitution of 1988 is a detailed political document rather than a set of principles. It has constrained and still constrains policymaking. Its biggest constraint comes from hard-wiring expenditures in certain policy areas, most importantly those in health and education. The constraints from the constitution bind because the judiciary has been relatively independent in ruling on issues of constitutionality. This has led to a perception that the constitutional amendments will be permanent. Reinforcing the role of the judiciary is the independent and increasingly powerful role played by the *Ministério Público*. Public prosecutors have been most active in enforcing social policies, such as legislation concerning education, health, and the environment.

Despite the perception in the press, the power of governors to influence national policies is relatively weak and is becoming weaker. In large part this resulted from the enforcement of a law on fiscal responsibility. State and local political actors still play a role that affects economic performance. Considerable federal and state funds are diverted from public spending intended for public goods and infrastructure toward campaign finance. Future research by the authors will investigate the role of the courts and auditors' offices in allowing corruption (the misuse of public funds for private gain) to persist.

Overall, this study has painted a relatively rosy picture of the policy-making process in Brazil. Importantly, pork was found to be a relatively cheap and effective means to ensure stable but adaptable macro policy. The actions to date of the Lula administration bolster this view. Of course there are deficiencies: most prominently in the inflexibility of health and education policies, the volatility of social programs and infrastructure investments, and the persistence of corruption. But social programs can be advanced in a permanent fashion only when the government has ensured stable macro policy and the confidence of world capital markets. Brazil is currently in a relatively stable political equilibrium, but this equilibrium can be upset by a sufficiently large exogenous shock.[19] A shock of sufficient magnitude could tip Brazil back to its former populist ways.

---

[19] For a discussion of Brazil's use of fiscal and monetary policy as an equilibrating mechanism in response to a monetary shock (the 1999 devaluation) and a political shock (the election of Lula), see Alston and others (2007). The actions taken in response to those shocks were consistent with the framework presented in this chapter.

5

Political Institutions, Policymaking Processes, and Policy Outcomes in Chile

*Cristóbal Aninat, John Londregan,
Patricio Navia, and Joaquín Vial*

Introduction

This chapter focuses on the policymaking process (PMP) in Chile since 1990, when the military dictator Augusto Pinochet turned over the presidency to his democratically elected successor, Patricio Aylwin. That moment represents a sharp change in Chile's institutional framework, so it makes sense to treat the ensuing period as a distinct policymaking regime. Since the restoration of democracy, Chile's institutional system of checks and balances has worked well in terms of promoting intertemporal political transactions. Chile has a presidential system with a bicameral congress, a proportional electoral system, an independent judiciary, and other enforcement technologies. The system produces a PMP favorable to intertemporal political transactions in most policy areas, as it favors a small number of political actors who interact repeatedly with long time horizons, and there are good enforcement technologies overseeing the process.

Four salient institutional features together have shaped policymaking in Chile during this period. First, there is the party system, which consists of two closely knit and stable coalitions, one on the left and the other on the right. This party system is strongly shaped by the electoral system, which creates pressures for moderate polarization in legislative elections through the use of the d'Hondt rule with open-party lists and a district magnitude of two. A "dual ballot" system for electing the executive discourages extremist presidential candidates.[1]

The second salient feature of the PMP is a powerful agenda-setting executive. The president of the republic has near-monopoly control over the legislative agenda, with proposal and veto powers that make him a de facto agenda setter.

Third, the PMP is studded with veto players, some of them written into the constitution by the outgoing military government in order to make policy changes by subsequent elected governments more difficult. These include a bicameral congress, a comptroller general, and independent loci of judicial power, including the regular courts, a constitutional tribunal, and an electoral tribunal. Several significant veto points were removed by a constitutional reform in 2005, including a provision for unelected senators in the upper chamber of congress and the relative autonomy of the armed forces (the heads of the armed forces could not be removed by the president of the republic, and they were a dominating presence on the National Security Council, or COSENA).[2]

A fourth key feature of the Chilean PMP is the existence of a well-functioning mechanism for policy implementation, including an independent judiciary and an honest and reasonably efficient bureaucracy (although there is variation across policy areas on this last score).

As discussed further in the chapter, because the party system shrinks the de facto set of decision makers and because the parties are long lived, the Chilean system is characterized by a relatively small set of decision makers who repeatedly interact. The relatively honest and well-working bureaucracy and judiciary facilitate cooperation by enhancing transparency (through adherence to standardized procedures), and providing reliable enforcement of the policies that are put in place. The existence

---

[1] In a dual ballot system, if no candidate obtains an absolute majority of the popular vote, there is a second round between the candidates who obtained the two highest vote shares.

[2] These undemocratic institutions were introduced by Pinochet in the 1980 Constitution. After 15 years of negotiations between the center-left government coalition and the right-wing opposition coalition, they were eliminated by a constitutional reform in 2005.

of a transparent enforcement technology also limits the benefits obtainable by defecting from agreed-upon policies. The degree to which policymakers' interests align differs across issues. However, two features of the Chilean polity are worthy of particular note. First, Chile has a small open economy, so that the consequences of poor economic policy are particularly keenly felt. Second, there is the "hangover" from the civil strife of the early 1970s and from more than a decade and a half of military rule; certain sensitive issues create a shared interest in avoiding conflict. Beyond these two features, the alignment of interests among policymakers varies from issue to issue.

The framework for this chapter is based on work by Spiller and Tommasi (2003) intended to identify features of the PMP that tend to produce cooperative outcomes. Cooperation means working together for a common purpose or benefit, and this can happen only when there is at least some alignment of interest among the participants, and when the degree of alignment between the parties places a ceiling on the amount of cooperation that one can expect to observe. The Spiller and Tommasi (2003) framework emphasizes five factors identified in the game theoretic industrial economics literature as facilitating cooperative outcomes:[3] first, there is only a small number of decision makers; second, there is repeated interaction among decision makers; third, deviations from agreed-upon behavior are easily observed; fourth, the immediate benefits from reneging on agreements are small; fifth, credible enforcement mechanisms exist. Left off their list is the degree to which agents' interests align, though the alignment of interests is central in the industrial organization literature from which the list is derived. Accordingly, we take the advice of Spiller, Stein, and Tommasi (2003, p. 6, footnote 8) to combine the "lens with which authors ... can focus the analysis of the PMP" with "others that they believe relevant for understanding key features of their respective countries," and add a sixth factor to the list of those facilitating cooperative outcomes: sixth, the degree to which the parties' interests are shared. While all six of these factors play an

---

[3] For more on this literature, see Friedman (1971); Green and Porter (1984); Abreu (1986).

important role in the Chilean policymaking process, the first, second, and sixth factors are particularly salient.

An additional consideration bearing on the repeated games literature from which the unifying theoretical framework of this chapter springs is that the factors it identifies as facilitating cooperation are factors that expand the set of possible equilibria to include cooperative outcomes, along with "uncooperative" myopic equilibria. That is, in the parlance of game theory, the oligopoly models that allow for possible cooperation also have other equilibria consisting of endless price wars. The game-theoretic models provide little guidance as to which of the possible equilibria will actually occur. Thus one may think of the factors identified by the framework applied here as identifying an upper bound on the level of cooperation that can emerge in a given political system. It may be that some significant differences between, say, Uruguay and Chile—both of which have relatively small and stable party systems and independent courts—result from policymakers having coordinated on different equilibria among the set that are supported by their institutional framework.

Thus one may think of the six elements identified by the preceding discussion as "risk factors" for the emergence of cooperation. While the presence of these factors does not guarantee that political actors will successfully coordinate on one of the cooperative equilibria, it does at least hold out the possibility that they will do so.

The second section describes Chile's policy outcomes and the policymaking capabilities of the Chilean state from a comparative perspective. It focuses on the outer features of policies following the criteria set by Scartascini and Olivera (2003). The third section describes and analyzes Chile's institutional setting and the incentives it sets for political actors. First, it analyzes the combined effects of the two different electoral systems, for presidential and legislative elections, and the congressional rules over the party system and the number of political actors. The subsections that follow describe the powers of the executive and its role in the legislative process, review the role of enforcement technologies and the civil service on policy implementation, and analyze the interactions of the different actors in the policymaking process. The fourth section concludes.

Policy Outputs and Policymaking Capabilities

Stability and Flexibility

Public policy in Chile has shown a remarkable level of stability since the last years of the dictatorship, in the face of major political changes entailed by the transition to democracy and three later changes of government. The four different *Concertación* administrations that have governed the country since 1990 have maintained fiscal discipline and avoided manipulation of fiscal policy for political purposes. A fiscal surplus was consistently maintained between 1990 and 1998. During the Asian Crisis, recession pushed the budget into a deficit of 1.4 percent of GDP in 1999, but the budget was again balanced the following year. The government quickly addressed the problem and proposed the adoption of a new fiscal rule in March 2000. The new rule seeks a "structural" surplus of 1 percent of GDP. It was designed to prevent inefficiencies produced by erratic and discretionary government spending, maintain stability in fiscal policy, and increase transparency in government spending.[4] However, unlike other public policy features, the "1 percent fiscal surplus rule" is a discretionary policy self-imposed by the last two administrations and might not survive beyond the end of Bachelet's term in March 2010.

High rates of GDP growth during the 1990s allowed governments to increase public expenditure while repaying most foreign debt, thus assuring a solid macroeconomic position to foreign investors. The ratio of government debt to GDP decreased from 42.7 percent of GDP in 1990 to 13.3 percent in 2003 (DIPRES 2004). The relatively conservative fiscal response of the Chilean government to the "boom" years of the 1990s can be examined in the context of Latin American countries' tendency to pursue procyclical fiscal policy, and runs counter to the stereotype of developing country governments trapped in "boom and bust" cycles.

Monetary policy has also been conservative since the restoration of democracy. The central bank applied restrictive monetary policies dur-

---

[4] For more details regarding the structural balance rule, see Marcel and others (2001).

ing most of the 1990s, achieving a gradual reduction in average inflation rates from 26 percent in 1990 to 1.1 percent in 2004.[5] Between 1989 and 2000, the central bank worked with one-year inflation forecasts to lower expectations of future inflation. In 1999, the central bank announced a policy shift, effective in 2001, to an inflation-targeting framework (IT). The IT reduces the central bank's discretion and puts automatic stabilization mechanisms in place to maintain inflation within the target band of 2 to 4 percent. This simple targeting rule tends to protect the central bank from political pressure. The IT framework for monetary policy has been successful, as inflation has remained within the band since the inception of the system in 2001. Chile today enjoys a stable and very low level of price inflation, and its fiscal and monetary institutions have earned praise from multilateral institutions, credit rating agencies, and international investors.

Trade policy is another example of stable policymaking with successful results. The military dictatorship initiated an aggressive unilateral liberalization strategy in the mid-1970s to eliminate the high trade barriers that had protected domestic economic production for most of the twentieth century. The *Concertación* governments continued with the unilateral liberalization policy. Tariff rates averaged 11 percent during the 1990s. Then a four-year-long series of tariff reductions beginning in 1999 lowered across-the-board tariffs to 6 percent in 2003. The *Concertación* administrations complemented the unilateral liberalization policy with bilateral economic agreements during the first half of the 1990s with several Latin American countries, including the Mercosur trading bloc. Since 1996, Chile has signed free trade agreements with Canada, the European Union, the United States, the Republic of Korea, and other countries. Today Chile has one of the freest economies in the world, trade volumes closely follow the evolution of terms of trade, and the share of trade in GDP has risen steadily from 28 percent of GDP in the 1960s and early 1970s to more than 70 percent today.

In September 1999, the central bank decided to abandon an exchange rate policy based on a price band and instead adopted a free-

---

[5] Central Bank of Chile, www.bcentral.cl.

Figure 5.1. Trade Liberalization, Chile, 1974–2004

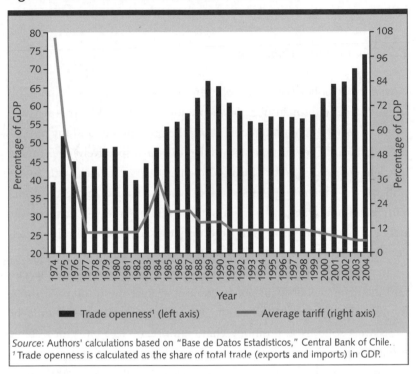

Source: Authors' calculations based on "Base de Datos Estadisticos," Central Bank of Chile.
[1] Trade openness is calculated as the share of total trade (exports and imports) in GDP.

floating exchange rate policy. The floating exchange rate policy gives the economy enough flexibility to face external shocks and reduces the discretionary power of the central bank. The central bank has twice intervened in the exchange market in recent years: in July 2001 because of the crisis in Argentina, and in October 2002 because of a crisis in Brazil. However, on both occasions, the interventions have been transparent and well founded, with the central bank providing a public rationale for its actions and providing full disclosure as to the amounts involved in the operations and the timeframe for the unusual action.

Cross-national indexes of economic policy also reflect the stability of Chile's policy outcomes. Since its transition to democracy, Chile has improved consistently in indexes such as the Heritage Foundation's Index of Economic Freedom, the World Economic Forum's Growth Competitiveness Index, Transparency International's Corruption Perceptions Index, and the World Bank's Governance Indicators.[6]

Coordination and Coherence

Government policy has been coherent across policy areas. In part this suggests a long-term strategy for economic policy, and in part it is the result of a shared commitment by both the government and the opposition coalitions (the *Concertación* and the *Alianza*, respectively) to promote efficient economic policy. During these past years, changes made in key policy areas—including the structural balance rule, a monetary policy with inflation targets, and a free-floating exchange rate—have made the entire public policy process more transparent, coherent, and internally consistent.

In a country with a flexible exchange rate like Chile, the inefficacies and inefficiencies of fiscal policy counsel against using them as instruments to bring about stabilization. Instead, their main role should be to secure a solid fiscal position. That better serves as a basis for a stable monetary policy and serves to consolidate long-term economic growth. In this way, the fiscal rule of government surplus adopted in 2001 under the tenure of Finance Minister Nicolás Eyzaguirre is a significant innovation, as it acts as an automatic stabilization tool.

Similarly, since the free-floating exchange rate was adopted in 1999, a potential source of incoherence in the formation of public policy has been eliminated. Before that decision, the central bank had to worry about keeping the exchange rate within the target band at the same time that it sought to control inflation, which occasionally produced competing and contradicting objectives. The costs of these tensions between competing objectives became evident in 1999, when the central bank was forced to raise interest rates well beyond prudent limits when the exchange rate band came under pressure after the Russian debt default. The only central bank objective now is to meet inflation target goals.

---

[6] See Kaufmann, Kraay, and Mastruzzi (2003); Miles, Feulner, and O'Grady (2003); Transparency International (2003); World Economic Forum (2003).

While the military government left what Navia and Velasco (2003) refer to as a "first generation of reforms" in place, subsequent democratically elected governments continued the reform process with what have been called second-generation reforms, including privatization of the port sector and utilities, introduction of private concessions in public works, and educational, health, and labor reforms.

These reforms, however, have been achieved with varying degrees of success. The most advanced areas correspond to macroeconomic policy, where there is considerable consensus. Also, substantial success has been achieved in improving the regulatory framework, the transparency of government policies, and state capabilities. Areas where success has been more elusive are those related to human rights, social issues (such as divorce), and efforts at reforming the labor code and the import-competing agricultural sector (wheat, vegetable oils, and sugar).

The introduction of public works concession programs has been a successful innovation. Historically, the state was in charge of building and operating public infrastructure works. In the 1990s, however, the state initiated an aggressive concessions plan through a system of Build, Operate, and Transfer contracts (BOT). The use of such a system brings about huge improvements in efficiency and welfare. From a distributive approach, it is convenient that the users of the new infrastructure pay for it, rather than placing the burden on all taxpayers. Finally, the design of the contract seeks to generate competition and helps discard ideas where the expected demand does not justify the construction of the new infrastructure (MOPTT 2003).

There are also a large number of public policies that work in a manner directly opposed to the above-mentioned concessions program: they carry very heavy political costs in the short term, but yield enormous long-term benefits. If those political property rights are not protected, it will be difficult for governments to undertake those kinds of reforms. Two sectors that clearly present these kinds of challenges are health and education. Not surprisingly, progress in these areas has been far slower than in concessions of public works.

In the education sector, spending has increased by more than 220 percent between 1990 and 2003 (DIPRES 2004). That trend has allowed the government to reverse the decline in educational spending observed in the 1980s. As a result of a correct diagnosis of the bad state of Chilean education, an educational reform (elementary and secondary) was adopted in the 1990s. A number of initiatives to improve the system were undertaken: improvements in working conditions and salaries for teachers, improvements in structure and equipment for existing schools, improvements in access to education (reflected in an increase in enrollment figures), and the most comprehensive curriculum reform in 25 years. Together with improving the quality of education, enormous efforts have been made to reduce school dropout rates. Yet much remains to be done. Access to higher education remains highly discriminatory against low-income youth. Because the public funding scheme for university education covers only public institutions, many capable young students who attend private universities are left without access to public funding for their university education. In summary, although some important reforms have been undertaken in recent years with the objective of giving more autonomy to educational institutions, linking teachers' pay with their performance, providing more information to parents on school performance, and improving access to higher education to all students, the successes in this field have been positive but largely insufficient.

In the health sector, there are some signs of progress, but some worrying signs of neglect as well. In the early 1990s, there were significant deficiencies in infrastructure and equipment in the public health system, a lack of qualified human resources, and administrative inefficiencies. To correct those problems, the government invested more in the public health system than it had at any previous time in the country's history. Health spending went from 1.9 percent of GDP in 1990 to 3.0 percent in 2003. The increase is also evident when comparing health spending as a share of total expenditures; it went from 9 percent of total expenditures to 14 percent during the same period (DIPRES 2004).

Even though Chile has achieved health indicators (lifetime expectancy at the time of birth, infant mortality, and mother's mortality) higher than what its economic development level would predict, public satisfaction with health coverage remains low. One of the main criticisms against the system is that it does not constitute a system per se. Instead, there are two systems (one public, one private) that function in parallel, with little coordination and insufficient cooperation between them. A partial health reform guaranteeing speedy access to the public system in case of a limited number of illnesses was approved in 2004, but it falls far short of what is needed to improve the efficiency and coordination of the whole system. Opposition by the *Alianza* and by other interested parties—including doctors' and health workers' unions, with the tacit or explicit support of members of congress belonging to the government coalition—was able to derail important structural changes initially proposed by the *Concertación* administration.[7]

Despite repeated efforts to improve labor markets, success has been moderate. The first labor reforms adopted after the restoration of democracy (1990 and 1991) sought to correct the imbalance between workers and employers. That imbalance was inherited from the labor reforms adopted by the Pinochet dictatorship during the 1970s and 1980s. The lack of legitimacy of the labor system inherited from the dictatorship weakened its long-term stability. Thus while the new democratic government sought to maintain some of the improvements made in the 1970s and 1980s regarding flexibility and modernization, other rules on individual contracts, collective bargaining, and the operations of labor unions were introduced to bring legitimacy to the system and to bring labor unions on board as allies of labor market reform efforts, rather than enemies (Mizala and Romaguera 2001).

Yet during the last year of the Frei administration, a labor reform was launched in an effort to reverse the low levels of labor union participation and collective bargaining by seeking to bring some additional protection to workers and labor unions. The labor reform initiative was rejected by the legislature in the midst of the 1999 presidential campaign, to no one's surprise. Yet President Lagos, after taking office, sent

---

[7] The former chairman of the doctors' union is now a member of congress representing the PPD (the president's party), and was very active in the health commission of the chamber of deputies, which is almost completely monopolized by medical doctors.

a new labor legislative initiative to congress that eventually passed. The new legislation had two objectives. First, it sought to increase the legal protection of workers (by formally recognizing a number of rights that were not clearly spelled out in the existing legislation). Second, it sought to reduce the costs of hiring new labor. These dual—and somewhat contradictory—goals have made it difficult to appropriately evaluate the success of the reform.

A significant improvement in labor market regulation was achieved in 2002. A mandatory unemployment insurance scheme for those who enter the labor market during or after 2002 was passed into law after some tough negotiation and bargaining with the opposition and left-wing *Concertación* legislators. Eventually, the newly created unemployment insurance scheme should replace the existing dismissal compensation scheme. A novel feature of this system is the introduction of individual savings accounts with contributions by both the workers themselves and companies to fund compensation during the unemployment period. However, the law did not include a revision of the high dismissal compensation scheme, which puts a very heavy burden on companies that seek to lay off workers and introduces severe distortions into the Chilean labor market.[8]

According to Lora's structural reform index for the 1985–2001 period (Lora 2001), reforms in Chile have increased the efficiency of the public policies and have strengthened free markets for the five economic sectors considered. The level of progress and liberalization of each of those five sectors is different, but there is no incoherence in the reforms implemented in each one of those sectors. The most important advances took place in the commercial and financial arenas. The labor index is the only indicator that arguably showed a decline toward the end of the 1990s. Yet as discussed in the previous section, the labor reforms implemented during the 1990s sought to restore certain workers' rights that were lost in the previous decade.

---

[8] For more information on this topic, see Cowan and others (2003).

Public Regardedness of Public Policy

Government spending in Chile by and large reaches those in most need. The last poll on poverty and inequality, CASEN 2000,[9] shows that fiscal spending on health, education, and direct subsidies for the poor was well spent; 68.8 percent of all spending on these items went to the poorest 40 percent, and an impressive 80.2 percent of public spending in health benefited the poorest 40 percent of the population. In terms of education, 62.8 percent of spending went to the poorest 40 percent of the population. In terms of direct subsidies, 73.1 percent of all that was spent went to the poorest 40 percent of the population. Altogether, the subsidies and benefits that the state offers to the poorest Chileans allowed the first decile (the poorest 10 percent) to increase its share of income from 3.7 percent before taxes and subsidies to 6.4 percent of total pre-tax income, while the wealthiest 20 percent saw its share of income reduced from 57.5 percent before subsidies to 53.4 percent after subsidies.

The distribution of social transfers per quintile in Chile as well as nine other Latin American countries is presented in figure 5.2. The figure shows a stark contrast between the focus of social spending in Chile and in other countries of the region. While in Chile transfers steadily decline from the poorest quintile (quintile I) to the richest one (quintile V), in the other countries, without exception, transfers tend to favor the rich.

However, there are some areas where highly intense private interests have captured the policymaking process. A notable example of this is the price bands for some agricultural goods. Chile introduced price bands for some agricultural products with the aim of reducing tensions in politically sensitive southern regions of the country. The price bands are applied to wheat, sugar, and vegetable oil. The argument behind the decision was that highly fluctuating international prices for these goods placed an overwhelming burden on producers. A protectionist neutral band was adopted so that the government could impose tariffs when international prices were too low and reduce tariffs when international

---

[9] See MIDEPLAN (2000).

Figure 5.2. Distribution of Social Transfers by Income Quintile,
1997–2001[a]

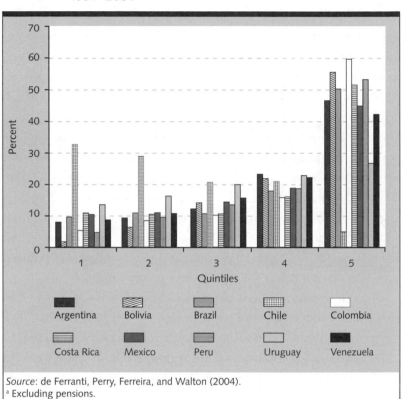

Source: de Ferranti, Perry, Ferreira, and Walton (2004).
[a] Excluding pensions.

prices were too high. The scheme was not deemed protectionist, but rather was defended on the grounds that it would reduce price volatility, thus improving the welfare of agriculture workers. Yet this mechanism has not functioned correctly. Lobbying by agricultural producers has prevented the government from reducing tariffs when international prices have increased and has even effectively altered the scheme by which the government calculates the appropriate price bands for these products.

The benefits from price intervention go primarily to well-off agricultural producers, not to minimum-wage agricultural workers. Galetovic (2001) showed that 63 percent of small sugar beet producers produce only 4 percent of the national production and receive less than 1 percent of the total amount overpaid by consumers for imported sugar (US$258 million in the 1998–2000 period). Taking into account its effect on consumers and producers, this price intervention policy is probably one of the most regressive policies that exist today in Chile.

State Capabilities and Overall Quality of Public Policy

Chile's policy schemes and regulation are relatively transparent. There is a simple tax code, tax evasion is low, and rates of effective and total trade protection are very similar. The procedures and time required to open new businesses and to comply with government regulations are much lower than regional averages (but are still higher than in OECD countries). The regulatory burden is moderate. While survey data reveal that the time and government fees needed to comply with regulations when a new business is opened are low by international standards, the total number of regulations that must be complied with exceeds the international average. The staff of the regulatory agencies, tax collection agencies, central bank, and finance ministry tend to be more prepared, better trained, and more professional than that of other government agencies.

It is well known that the liberalization of the economy and of the financial system, the privatization of companies that offer public services, and the consolidation of markets must be accompanied by the strengthening of the institutions in charge of regulating those activities. Otherwise, there will be high risks of capture where the regulator works to advance the interests of the regulated industries rather than to defend the interest of consumers and to secure more competitive markets. The option of choice for Chile's regulatory scheme has been based on reducing entry barriers and on selective, rather than structural, intervention executed by antimonopoly commissions that bring more flexibility to the system. It would be far-fetched, however, to suggest that regulatory policies have changed since 1990. The so-called "rules of the game" have not undergone significant changes. Instead, there has been an effort to improve the regulatory framework in light of specific problems that have arisen over time.

With regard to the quality of the personnel who work for the central government, there is a high degree of centralization of relevant decisions. There is a limited margin for decision making at the regional and local institutional levels, and there is a high level of inflexibility, with little room for discretion for those responsible for the management of the respective institutions and offices. Moreover, there is a single and uniform regime of human resources for the entire public sector. That makes it more difficult to adjust to the specific needs and demands of particular institutions and public services. There is a very rigid employment stability framework, which in practice amounts to an inability to fire public workers. Salary and public compensation also respond to a rigid and nationally controlled scheme that often favors those who have been employed by the public sector the longest.

Since 1994, there have been several attempts to modernize the state bureaucracy. The most remarkable was the creation in 2003 of a public civil service division (*Nuevo Trato y Dirección Pública*). This new office will fill between 1,900 and 3,500 positions that were previously considered presidential-appointed positions. Two autonomous institutions were created to appoint the new public sector employees for those positions: the *Consejo de Alta Dirección Pública* and the *Dirección Nacional del Servicio Civil.*

Other institutional changes of note adopted in Chile since 2003 are a new law on government remuneration and spending that regulates salaries for high-level officials and caps their discretionary budgets; new legislation that requires the government to maintain a registry of all individuals, institutions, and companies that receive public funds; and a new law on political party and campaign financing that has brought the issue of money and politics to the forefront of debate in Chile. Most recently, the legislature also began to debate a proposal to regulate lobbying. Among the noteworthy features of that legislative package are the proposal to register and identify all official lobbying organizations and individuals as well as meetings between lobbyists and public authorities, the provision of equal access to authorities for all lobbyists, restrictions on public sector employment and electoral eligibility for those who work as lobbyists, and restrictions on political contributions by lobbyists.

Lastly, indexes that measure corruption, governance, business environment, and quality of institutions are useful proxies to assess the overall quality of public policies from a comparative perspective. The "Doing Business" Index prepared by the World Bank ranks Chile above Latin American countries, but well below OECD averages.[10] This index assesses regulations and policies insofar as they foster (or hinder) investment, productivity, and growth. Some of the regulations in Chile include the following. In order to start a business in Chile, a person must complete 10 steps (procedures). That is below the Latin American average, but is significantly higher than in OECD countries. In order to enforce a contract, 21 procedures are needed in Chile, requiring an average time of 200 days and costing an expected 14.7 percent of GDP per capita. Although those values are also lower than the Latin America average, the cost of enforcing contracts is much higher than in OECD countries, where it stands at 7.1 percent of GDP per capita. Chilean courts normally take 5.8 years to rule on insolvencies, much longer than in OECD countries, where courts take on average 1.8 years.

The Corruption Perception Index, produced by Transparency International, ranks Chile among the 25 least corrupt countries in the world, and as the least corrupt country in Latin America.[11] According to the Global Competitiveness Report, Chile ranks 26th among 123 countries in the world.[12] This report, prepared by the World Economic Forum, analyzes three fundamental pillars for growth: business environment, good institutions, and technological development. Chile's highest ranking comes from the quality of its institutions.

Political Institutions and the PMP in Chile

This section argues that Chile has an institutional system of checks and balances—with some similarities to the United States, but with some important differences—that has worked well in terms of promoting intertemporal political transactions since democracy was restored in 1990. Chile has a presidential system with a bicameral congress, a proportional

---

[10] See World Bank (2004a).

[11] See Transparency International (2003).

[12] See World Economic Forum (2003).

electoral system with a district magnitude of two, an independent judiciary, and other enforcement technologies. The ensuing PMP is conducive to political cooperation in most policy areas, as it favors a small number of political actors who interact repeatedly with long time horizons, and there are good enforcement technologies overseeing the process. Some "undemocratic enclaves," established in the 1980 Constitution left behind by the Pinochet regime (eliminated through a constitutional reform in October 2005), reduced the "issue space" for policymaking during the period under analysis, restricting cooperation in areas regarding human rights and some military-related issues. After describing the main components of Chile's political system and analyzing the incentives they establish for political actors, the section explores their interactions and the combined effect on the policymaking process.

Chile has a presidential system similar to that of the United States, with a bicameral congress as part of a system of checks and balances. Such systems are designed to allow for slow but incremental change, preventing policy instability as a result of changes in the balance of political power. If these systems are well designed, however, they also allow for decisiveness when there are external shocks that change the relative value of political issues for the relevant actors.

The crucial issue here is not the existence of institutions designed to be checks and balances, but the precise design that determines the workings of those institutions. Several comparative studies note that policies are of very different quality in countries with similar institutional settings. The effectiveness of the institutional design is in its details; these will determine the possibility of finding loopholes or bypassing the checks and balances—which ultimately will determine the real incentives for political actors.

Systems of checks and balances are designed to produce good policies in areas of relative consensus or in cases where compensation could possibly be worked out; to produce a bias toward the status quo in policy issues that are more conflictive; and to produce relative gridlock on issues where political actors have strong opposing views. In that regard, the Chilean system seems to be well designed. It has allowed for a constant and incremental improvement of policies, institutions, and rules and regulations since the restoration of democracy. It has allowed for stability with respect to political shocks and for decisiveness with respect to socioeconomic shocks. As expected in a system of checks and balances, the quality of policies varies across policy areas. It tends to be higher with regard to macroeconomic issues, international integration, financial markets, and regulations, as opposed to social issues like labor markets, social security, health, and education. On moral issues, human rights, and military-related issues, policies show higher rigidity and overall lower quality.

Effects of the Electoral System, Electoral Cycle, and Congressional Rules on the Party System

Chile has two different electoral systems for legislative and presidential elections, which give different incentives to political actors and cross-pressure them in their electoral strategies. For legislative elections, Chile has the so-called binomial electoral system, which is a proportional representation system with a district magnitude of two in all districts. It uses open lists (with an upper limit of two candidates per list) and the d'Hondt seat allocation formula. It allows for coalition formation, but coalitions are nationally binding.[13] In practice, each of the lists (coalition/parties) receiving the two highest vote shares wins one of the two available seats per district—unless the list receiving the most votes outpolls its second place rival by a ratio of more than two to one, in which case it receives both seats.

Chile's electoral system has a twofold effect on the party system: it reduces the number of relevant actors by encouraging parties to coalesce, and it strengthens the national leadership of parties. At a district level, a magnitude of two determines an upper bound of three parties (Cox

---

[13] When a coalition has more than two parties, the provision that limits the number of candidates to be presented in each district by each list forces them to negotiate the districts in which each party presents a candidate. By the end of the period under study, this provision has led to high tensions in the *Concertación*, stressing their capacity for cooperation.

1997).[14] At the national level there can be many parties presenting candidates in just a few districts; hence the system allows for the existence of several parties. But at the same time, there is a strong incentive to coalesce at the district level, since if the list receiving the most votes doubles the second place rival, it obtains 100 percent of the seats available in the district. If a list secures second place and avoids being doubled, it gets 50 percent of the seats being contested. The provision that coalitions are binding at a national level leads parties to form broad-based national coalitions. Since it is difficult to form coalitions that can secure more than two-thirds of the votes in each district, and it is relatively easy to secure one-third of the vote share, the most likely outcome is the formation of two national coalitions, which in most districts obtain one of the two seats available. Under this scenario, if coalitions are already formed, any given party would pay a high toll if it unilaterally left its coalition. On the other hand, this sets a high entry barrier for a third national coalition or independent party.

Since 1990 there have been six parties with congressional representation, organized into two national coalitions. The 1988 plebiscite to decide whether General Pinochet should remain in power for eight more years organized the existing political actors into two blocs supporting the "yes" and "no" votes. These blocs have remained during the subsequent democratic elections, with the center and left-wing parties that opposed Pinochet in one coalition, and the right-wing parties that supported the general in the other: the *Concertación de Partidos por la Democracia* and the *Alianza por Chile*, respectively.[15] The *Concertación* and the *Alianza* are

---

[14] The district magnitude (DM) determines the minimum vote share required to secure a seat in each district. (For example, when DM equals two, a candidate can secure a seat with about one-third of the votes. The exact percentage depends on the electoral formula being used.) Regardless of the initial number of parties, in the absence of other influences, parties tend to consolidate in fewer and larger parties in order to maximize their chances to gain congressional seats. In a repeated game—as periodic elections are—this process continues until the number of parties equals DM + 1.

[15] The *Concertación* originally consisted of 17 parties that opposed the Pinochet regime. During the 1990s, these parties merged or disappeared. The *Concertación* currently consists of the centrist Christian Democratic Party (PDC), the leftist Party for Democracy (PPD), the Socialist Party (PS), and the Radical Social Democratic Party

still the only two coalitions with congressional representation, and have become the longest-standing coalitions in Chile's long history as a republic.

The existence of these coalitions provides political parties with several incentives and restrictions. Since only one-third of the vote is needed to secure 50 percent of the seats in each district, it drives parties' platforms away from the median voter, potentially polarizing the party system. (As indicated below, this effect is mediated by the effects of the presidential electoral system, which reduces its centrifugal incentives.) Also, the potentially high price a party would pay in terms of its share of the national vote if it unilaterally leaves its coalition enforces high intracoalition discipline. This has been important for maintaining unity in both coalitions throughout the democratic period, since they each include parties with different platforms on several issues, as well as political leaders with deep personal rivalries. Despite publicized intracoalition bickering between parties, both coalitions have remained united by the pressure of their congress members on their respective party's leaderships. Congress members know that their chances for reelection would be jeopardized should their coalitions break up.

The binomial system also encourages continuous intracoalition party negotiations to decide which candidates will be nominated to the coalition's lists in every district. This strengthens the national leadership of parties, but only to a certain extent. In high-magnitude proportional representation systems, candidates must respond to their party leadership to be included in the ballot. In single-member districts, politicians are political entrepreneurs since they must respond to their local constituencies. Under the binomial system, politicians and parties have mixed incentives. The national party leadership must negotiate with its partners as to the districts in which it should present candidates while responding to both national and local considerations: on the one hand, parties must negotiate their share of the coalition's candidate list, and on

---

(PRSD). Since 1989, the *Alianza* has had several names, but it has always consisted of two parties: the moderate right-wing National Renovation (RN), and the more rightist Independent Democratic Union (UDI).

the other, they must try to get the districts where the party has candidates with strong local support.[16]

The legislative electoral system does not have term limit provisions, which, together with the need for candidates with strong local support, encourage politicians to seek long legislative careers. In Chile 75 percent of congress members are renominated and about 60 percent are reelected (Carey 2002a). This reelection rate is much higher than in other Latin American countries, but it is lower than in the United States, where 99 percent of representatives seek reelection and about 80 percent succeed. (This issue is examined further in the section on the role of seniority in congress.)

Summing up, the main effects of the binomial system for the workings of the policymaking process are that it reduces the number of relevant actors to a few parties organized into two broad-based stable coalitions, and strengthens the party leadership while encouraging politicians to respond to their constituencies to a certain extent, and to have long legislative careers. Finally, given the difficulty of one coalition doubling the vote share of the other in any given district, under the binominal system congressional representation for each coalition oscillates at around 50 percent of the members of each chamber of congress.[17]

For presidential elections, there is a majoritarian electoral system with runoff provisions if no candidate obtains a majority of the votes

---

[16] Even though the electoral system is the main determinant of the party system, the structure and behavior of political parties is determined by the incentives and restrictions established by the relevant institutional setting as a whole. The Political Parties Law, campaign finance laws, and internal rules of congress, among other factors, also influence political parties' behavior.

[17] In addition to the positive effects the binomial system produces for the workings of the PMP, it produces a negative effect on the degree of competitiveness of the party system, and its responsiveness to changes in the electorate's preferences. Given the difficulty of one coalition doubling the vote share of the other in any given district, the binomial system leads to a situation in which each one of the two main coalitions has a secure seat in most districts. This implies low levels of intercoalition competition, which in turn allows coalitions to present candidates responding to strategic national interests instead of voters' preferences. Also, the congressional overrepresentation of the right-wing coalition, together with the existence of institutional senators, protected the status quo left behind by the Pinochet dictatorship for 16 years, until the constitutional reform of 2005 did away with the so-called undemocratic enclaves.

in the first ballot. This system induces the nomination of moderate candidates who seek the median voter position. In the context of only two large coalitions having congressional representation, this system induces intracoalition negotiations to nominate one candidate for each coalition, which in turn reinforces coalition cohesion and discipline.[18] Municipal elections in Chile are held nationwide on the same day. This makes them another arena for the electoral contest between the coalitions, and provides another opportunity for intracoalition negotiation to agree upon a common list of candidates (which distributes seats for each party.)

The combined effect of the three electoral systems on politicians, parties, and coalitions is a set of incentives that cross-pressure them and multiply the opportunities for electoral competition and intracoalition negotiation. There is a twelve-year electoral cycle for concurrence of presidential and legislative elections; municipal elections are never concurrent. Hence between 1989 and 2005, there have been ten different electoral contests, no more than three years apart, and often held every other year or even in consecutive years, as in 1992–93, 1996–97, 1999–2000–2001, and 2004–2005.[19]

Different electoral systems functioning under a continuous electoral cycle have a moderating effect over the coalitions. The binomial system is the core of the electoral system, and is the main force leading parties to coalesce. However, the existence of municipal and presidential elections mediates the moderate polarizing effect of the binomial system, which induces parties to design their electoral platforms aiming at one-third of the electorate, and encourages coalitions to aim closer to the median voter. On the other hand, the high sequence of elections forces parties

---

[18] In the 2006 elections, however, the *Alianza* presented two candidates, using the first ballot as a de facto primary. In the second ballot, both parties of the *Alianza* supported the same candidate.

[19] The constitutional reform of 2005 reduced the length of the presidency to four years and introduced simultaneity in congressional and presidential elections. This will facilitate the operation of coalitions, allowing for "compensations" in congressional elections to the parties that must resign their presidential options within each coalition.

to successfully reach intracoalitions agreements, reinforcing coalition discipline and increasing the power of party leadership, and hence party discipline as well.

Finally, the informal rules that determine the actual workings of congress reflect the power of both parties and coalitions. The two main institutions that shape the workings of congress are the executive boards (*mesas*) of each chamber and the chambers' committees. Formal rules determine that committee assignments are nominated by the *mesas* and ratified by the respective chambers, and shall proportionally reflect the partisan composition of each chamber. In actuality, however, the *mesas* consider the parties' requests for committee assignments. Proportionality is not strictly maintained, but coalitions work out agreements. Also, the chairmanship of committees is not proportionally assigned, but is agreed upon by the coalitions and normally rotates from one congress to the next. In this respect, it can be argued that the workings of congress reinforce the importance of both parties and coalitions, and that both coalitions and parties as well are central to Chilean politics—contrary to Carey (2002a), who states that the only relevant unit of analysis is coalitions.[20]

An Agenda-Setting Executive with an Array of Negotiating Tools Confronted by Several Checks and Balances

The Chilean presidential system has one of the strongest agenda-setting presidents in Latin America. The executive has exclusive legislative initiative on several policy areas, has a highly hierarchical control of the budget process, and has an array of urgency and veto options, which makes it a de facto agenda setter. Yet there are a number of institutional actors that are able to block executive policy initiatives (Londregan 2000). These include an independent judiciary, a constitutional tribunal, a comptroller general, and until the constitutional reform of 2005, the "National Security Council" (COSENA), which gave the armed forces

---

[20] For evidence of the interplay between coalitions and political parties in Chile, see Aninat and Londregan (2004).

a direct institutional role in the government. The bicameral congress, which until 2005 had almost a dozen nonelected senators in the upper chamber, requires supermajority thresholds to change many laws, enabling various minorities to block policy changes.

Until 2005, presidents were elected for six-year terms and were prevented from running for immediate reelection. During the past 16 years, the process of nominating candidates has varied across elections and parties, but the two main coalitions have presented candidates for every presidential election. Despite the fact that in all elections several candidates have competed, in all three elections the candidates of the main two coalitions—which include all the parties with congressional representation—have dominated the elections. The four presidential elections have been won by *Concertación* candidates.

The constitutionally mandated agenda-setting powers enjoyed by the Chilean president are quite substantial. Issues are divided into "matters of law" and "matters of administration." All legislation related to the daily running of the government is considered a "matter of administration." Members of congress can only propose legislation that is considered a "matter of law." This restricts the legislative initiative of congress. Within matters of law, the executive has the sole legislative initiative over legislation concerning the political and administrative divisions of the state, its financial administration, the budget process, and the selling of state assets. The executive also has sole initiative in areas such as taxation, labor regulation, social security, and legislation related to the armed forces. Therefore, the executive has sole authority to initiate legislation that requires budget increases or allocation of new funds, which gives it exclusive legislative initiative over most economic policy areas.

Furthermore, until 2005, the executive could convene an extraordinary legislative period, during which the executive determined the legislation congress was allowed to consider—in addition to the constitutionally mandated legislative period from May 21 to September 18 of each year.[21]

---

[21] In the absence of a presidential request for an extraordinary legislative period, congress could convene for an extraordinary legislative period, in which case the legislation to be considered was determined by the legislature.

Perhaps the constitutional provisions that best reflect the strong powers vested in the presidency are those governing the budget process.[22] The formal rules governing the budget process give strong powers to the executive, making Chile one of the countries with the most hierarchical budget institutions in Latin America (Alesina and others 1999; Vial 2001). The constitutional responsibility for the financial administration of the state belongs to the president via the finance minister, assisted by the budget director. They are in charge of setting the spending limits and leading the negotiations with the spending agencies during the preparation stage of the annual budget process, and of overseeing the execution and control stages. Legislators are not allowed to introduce amendments that raise spending or create any financial commitments. Every legislative proposal by congress that has financial implications must be accompanied by a financial report prepared by the budget office (ministry of finance) with an estimate of the financial impact of the project and the sources of financing under the current budget law. The Public Finances Committee of each chamber must review the specific articles carrying financial implications.

The executive has the sole responsibility for the overall revenue estimates and the presentation of a medium-term macroeconomic program, which is presented to the Special Budget Committee of congress by the finance minister at the opening of the budget debate. Congress cannot increase expenses in any item; it can only reduce or reject expenses proposed by the executive, as long as it does not interfere with the ability of the government to run state policies or meet previous legal commitments. Additionally, congress has 60 days to approve the budget law sent by the executive, or the original proposal becomes law. The tight control of the executive over the budget process, and all matters of legislation with fiscal impact, gives it control over side payments to compensate members of congress negatively affected by new legislation. For example, the executive was able to successfully implement a major

---

[22] For a detailed discussion of the political economy of the budget process in Chile, see Aninat and Vial (2005).

port reform and to sign a partial accession to Mercosur, given its ability to financially compensate the losers of those reforms.[23]

In addition to its agenda-setting powers, the executive controls the flow of legislation through the use of "urgencies"—a constitutional mechanism designed to give the executive the power to force the legislature to vote on an initiative within a fixed time limit. There are three different types of urgencies that can be introduced and withdrawn solely by the executive at any moment during the legislative process: *simple urgency, summa urgency,* and *immediate discussion.* They require the chamber in which the bill is being considered to vote the bill in thirty days, ten days, and three days, respectively. If the bill is already in a mixed senate-chamber of deputies committee, the indicated timeframes must be divided between the vote in the mixed committee, and the subsequent votes in each chamber of congress. Therefore under simple urgency, the mixed committee and each chamber have ten days to vote the bill; under summa urgency, the mixed committee has four days to vote the bill, and each chamber has three days to do it; and under immediate discussion, the mixed committee, the senate, and the chamber of deputies have one day each to vote the legislative initiative.

The executive can also exercise a wide range of veto options.[24] If a president vetoes a bill, or part of it, congress needs a two-thirds majority of members present in both chambers to insist on its preferred version of the bill. In addition, the use of the amendatory veto (*veto sustitutivo*) gives the president the power to amend legislation that has already been passed, thus allowing the executive to exercise a last-minute bargaining tool with the legislature after the preferences of both chambers have already been made public in the floor vote of the legislation. For the approval of the partially amended vetoed bill, however, the president needs the favorable vote of a simple majority of both chambers of congress. If a majority is not reached, the amendatory veto is equivalent

---

[23] For more on this, see the working paper version of this chapter (Aninat and others 2006) and Aninat and Londregan (2004).

[24] See Ley Orgánica Constitucional del Congreso Nacional, http://www.senado.cl/site/institucion/normativa/ley/.

to a simple partial veto, and the bill is approved without the contested articles. As a consequence, this power has seldom been exercised in the last 15 years, except to amend technical errors in the legal text (Aleman 2003).

The president's nonlegislative powers include broad authority to nominate, appoint, and dismiss government officials. The president nominates the supreme court justices, the central bank's governing board members, one of the seven members of the constitutional tribunal, and the comptroller general, who must be ratified by a supermajority of votes in the senate. This procedure ensures nonpartisan—or at least politically balanced—nominations to these key institutional posts. The executive also had the authority to nominate two of nine so-called "institutional senators" every eight years, and all former presidents who serve for at least six years were entitled to a lifetime voting seat in the senate[25] (more on this below, in the section on the undemocratic enclaves of the 1980 Constitution).

The president directly appoints all cabinet ministers, regional and provincial governors, ambassadors, and heads of government agencies and state companies. Given that the party system fosters coalition governments, cabinet formation might be negatively affected by reducing the cabinet's cohesion. However, the highly hierarchical structure of the cabinet, combined with the president's authority to appoint and dismiss the cabinet ministers and the prominent role of the finance minister in determining the budget of each ministry, has produced highly efficient cabinets in the four administrations since the restoration of democracy. There has been a stable number of ministries and a low rotation of ministers and undersecretaries (there were eighteen ministries until 2004; since then, three new ministries have been created).

The president, however, could not exercise discretionary power over the high command of the armed forces until the constitutional reform of 2005. The president could not remove the heads of the armed forces without the approval of the COSENA. The heads of the army, air force, navy, and *Carabineros* (national police) are appointed by the president

---

[25] Former President Aylwin did not have that capacity, since he held office during a special transitional term of only four years.

for four-year terms from a list consisting of the five highest-ranking officers of each branch.

The degree of support for the Chilean president in congress is relatively high and constant under the current electoral system. As mentioned above, the binomial electoral system encourages coalition formation, and leads to rather similar congressional representation for each coalition in both chambers of congress. Therefore, support for the executive in congress oscillates around 50 percent in all legislatures.

Because presidents are the de facto leaders of the multiparty coalitions that have characterized Chilean politics since 1989, presidents exercise significant influence over the decisions made by the government coalition (Carey 2002a; Montes, Mainwaring, and Ortega 2000). In all legislative and municipal elections, sitting presidents have been called upon as the ultimate arbiter in disputes among party leaders over the composition of the *Concertación* electoral lists (Carey and Siavelis 2003). Because they assume the role of coalition leaders, presidents have actively sought to distance themselves from the political parties they belong to in order to avoid the impression that they are benefiting their own parties and hurting the other parties that comprise the government coalition.

Offsetting the powerful Chilean president is the national congress. Although it is weak in comparison to the U.S. Congress, the Chilean legislature is unusually professional and technically competent by Latin American standards. Embedded in a well-designed system of checks and balances, the legislature has an active and decisive role in the Chilean policymaking process. The bicameral legislature consists of a 120-seat chamber of deputies and a senate with 38 members (in addition to the 9 institutional senators). Deputies are elected to four-year terms, while senators serve for eight-year terms, both elected in two-member districts, with no term limit provisions.

The Chilean legislature makes extensive use of committees. Only the Finance Committee is required by law to exist; other committees are established by each chamber at its own discretion, though traditionally there are 19 permanent committees in each chamber. The legislative committee system in use in Chile gives committees less power to influence the final composition of a bill than the U.S. House of Representatives sometimes grants its committees under closed rules provisions. Moreover, senate rules permit the floor to easily overturn committee decisions (the signatures of ten senators suffice to force a floor vote on a provision rejected in committee).

The legislative process consists of three "constitutional" steps (*trámite constitucional*). The first constitutional step begins when a legislative initiative is submitted by the president to a chamber of his or her choice. Individual legislators and groups of legislators can also submit legislative initiatives to their respective chamber. The chamber assigns the initiative to one of its established committees or to a specially assigned joint committee depending on the nature of the initiative. The committee then discusses the bill "in general" and can modify the initiative at will. Regardless of the committee's vote on the initiative, the chamber votes on the amended initiative presented to the floor by the committee. If amendments are offered during the general discussion, this triggers a second reading of the bill, called discussion in particular. At this stage, the bill is returned to the committee, and all amendments are discussed. Typically the chamber will agree to extend the deadline for presenting amendments. Once this has passed, the committee meets, discusses, and votes on the new amendments. The bill, along with any adopted amendments, then returns to the floor. In the senate there are easy procedures to "renew" amendments rejected by the committee (with the signatures of ten senators, less than a quarter of the chamber). Any member of the legislature can introduce amendments in advance of the second reading, and in the senate, committee members must put each proposed amendment to a publicly reported vote.

Once the first legislative step is completed, the initiative moves on to the other chamber for the second legislative step. A similar process ensues. After this stage, if both chambers have approved exactly the same version of the bill, it is sent to the president for signature or veto. However, if the chambers have approved distinct versions of the bill (if the revising chamber has sustained any amendments, for example), the bill is returned to the chamber of origin, which votes on the bill article by article. If differences persist, the bill is referred to a conference committee made up of equal numbers from both chambers and chaired by a member of the senate. The senate conferees are typically the members of the relevant committee. Deputies' committees tend to be larger (thirteen members, compared to five for the senate), so not all the deputies from the relevant committee will be involved in the conference committee. The bill put forth by the conference committee is put to an up or down vote in each chamber, without the possibility of amendment.

If and when both chambers have approved the same version of the bill, it goes to the president, who can sign the bill, in which case it often goes to the constitutional tribunal for approval of its consistency with existing constitutional provisions, if a minimum number of members of congress or the president ask for it, and if provisions about the constitutionality of the objected part of the bill have been raised during the legislative process. (Objections at this stage tend to be genuinely related to constitutional issues, so that the constitutional tribunal does not act as a third legislative chamber—as it could if it were to abuse its authority.) As mentioned, if the president does not wish to sign the bill, he can veto it in whole, in part, or offer amendments and send it back to congress. If the veto is overridden, or if the amendments are accepted, the bill is promulgated. If a successful presidential veto applies only to part of a bill, then the remainder of the bill is promulgated.

Constitutionally mandated supermajority thresholds for some special legislation contribute to offsetting the executive's substantial agenda-setting power. They range from an absolute majority of the total membership (as opposed to a majority of those present) up to two-thirds of the members.[26] Constitutional reforms and laws that interpret the constitution require the highest supermajorities. A high threshold of four-sevenths of both chambers is required to reform organic constitutional laws, which

---

[26] There are four types of laws in Chile. A simple majority of the members of each chamber of congress present at the time of the vote is required for ordinary laws. Laws of qualified quorum require a majority of the total number of members of each chamber. Organic constitutional laws require a supermajority of four-sevenths of the total number of members of congress. Laws that interpret the constitution and constitutional reforms require a three-fifths supermajority; to reform some chapters of the constitution, a two-thirds supermajority is required.

cover a wide range of issues, such as education, the electoral system, regulation of political parties, and the laws that regulate the central bank and the comptroller general. Social security issues also require a special quorum of an absolute majority of the total membership of both chambers.

At the core of the policymaking process in Chile since 1990 has been the combination of the binominal system—which induces the formation of party coalitions that regularly win between 40 and 60 percent of the seats in congress—with the supermajority provisions. Those provisions permit the minority coalition to block legislation, forcing the government to build consensus across coalition lines in order to approve its legislative agenda. With the exception of ordinary legislation that requires the weakest thresholds, the *Concertación* has always faced the need to negotiate changes to legislation that require supermajority approval with the conservative opposition in at least one legislative chamber.

In sum, the Chilean executive has strong agenda-setting powers and good negotiating tools that allow it to implement most of its preferred legislation. But the Chilean president cannot bypass congress through its veto, decree, or plebiscite powers, as it is the case in other Latin American countries (Aninat 2007). Besides the budget bills, which have special legislative procedures, all legislation needs at least a majority of both chambers to be approved.

Independent and Politically Insulated Enforcement Technologies and Other Veto Players

In addition to the legislature, the Chilean political system has several constitutionally mandated checks and balances offsetting the executive's substantial powers. Of the number of veto players the executive faces, some are "traditional" checks and balances present in most of today's successful democracies, and others were "undemocratic enclaves" entrenched by the Pinochet regime in the 1980 Constitution. They were in place from 1990 until the constitutional reform of 2005. Among the former are the bicameral congress with supermajority provisions for some legislative matters that were analyzed in the previous section, and several enforcement technologies such as the judiciary, the constitutional tribunal, and the comptroller general. These institutions are independent and politically insulated. They do not play any active role in legislation, but are strong independent checks on the executive. Among the latter were the semi-autonomous armed forces; the National Security Council (COSENA), in which the armed forces were heavily represented; and the institutional senators (nine nonelected senators appointed by different state institutions, which gave undue political power to the armed forces).

As mentioned, the three main enforcement institutions of the system are the judiciary, the constitutional tribunal, and the comptroller general. The 1980 Constitution establishes their absolute independence from other powers of the state, and their institutional design successfully accomplishes that goal. Even though all three institutions are nominated by other branches of the state, the correct combination of checks and balances assures their political independence and avoids partisan biases in their composition. In all cases, the people who aspire to hold these offices cannot cater to the interests of one branch of the state alone and, once nominated, the stipulation that they cannot be removed from their posts insulates them politically so they may carry out their duties.

The judiciary, headed by the supreme court, is the final and most important enforcement institution. It has to review all legal disputes in the country, enforce property rights, and hear all cases brought by the comptroller general regarding the legality of government actions. Even though the judiciary in Chile does not have judicial review powers—and hence has no legislative role—as the main enforcement technology, it is an important check on the executive for policy implementation. The judicial branch is composed of the supreme court, the courts of appeals, and ordinary courts. The supreme court is the highest tribunal in the country and is composed of 21 judges. They are nominated by the president from a five-person list proposed by the supreme court, and must be approved by two-thirds of the senate. Judges cannot be removed until they are 75 years old, unless sanctioned for misdemeanors. There are 17 courts of appeals throughout the country, and their judges are designated by the president from a three-person list proposed by the supreme court.

The constitutional reform of 2005 increased the composition and strengthened the powers of the constitutional tribunal (TC). Before the reform, the TC consisted of seven members—three supreme court judges and four lawyers—who were appointed in staggered terms, served eight-year terms, and could not be removed unless impeached. A quorum of at least five members was needed to convene. The supreme court nominated the three judges through simple majority voting in successive and secret ballots, the president and the senate nominated one lawyer each, and the COSENA nominated two lawyers. Following the reform, the president and the supreme court now nominate three members each and the senate nominates four members. These nominating procedures ensure the tribunal's technical capability and avoid partisanship in its rulings. The rulings of the tribunal are not subject to appeals of any kind, though it can rectify previous rulings if it independently decides to do so.

The Constitution of 1980 mandated that constitutional review for *preventive control* be performed by the constitutional tribunal, and for *repressive control* (ex post review), by the constitutional tribunal together with the supreme court. In practice, however, given that the Chilean legal system is based on civil law, supreme court rulings do not set a valid precedent for other similar cases, giving the constitutional tribunal de facto sole power to review for ex ante constitutionality of laws.

The constitutional reform established that both ex ante and ex post constitutional reviews be performed by the constitutional tribunal.[27] The TC must review the constitutionality of all organic constitutional laws and laws interpreting the constitution before they are promulgated. As mentioned, it can also review specific articles of any bill if requested by a certain number of members of congress during the discussion of a bill. In that way, the constitutional tribunal exerts ex ante jurisdiction over legislation, so it can prevent legislation from being enacted if it violates the constitution. For example, in 2001 the TC declared unconstitutional a bill to reform the pension system that was a high priority of the Lagos administration and that had been under legislative discussion for six years. The government had to redraft the bill almost entirely to overcome that ruling and carry out the pension reform (Aninat 2006).

---

[27] Constitución Política de la Republica (CPR), article 93, numbers 1, 3, 4, 6, 7, and 16.

Given its nonpartisan composition, the tribunal does not take an active role in shaping legislation by itself. However, it can be used by legislators to delay the discussion of a bill. A small number of legislators can temporarily stop the discussion of the bill by sending it to the tribunal to review its constitutionality, as was the case in the pension reform.

The *Contraloría General de la República* consists of the comptroller general and the *Contralorías regionales*. The comptroller general is appointed by the president with the approval of three-fifths of the senate, and cannot be removed until she or he is 75 years old, unless impeached by the senate based on a constitutional accusation by the chamber of deputies. The comptroller general controls the lawfulness of the state administration. It oversees the centralized and decentralized organs and services of the state, as well as any private entities that deal with the state and receive public funds of any kind. The comptroller general verifies the constitutionality and legality of the actions of administration, but it does not have punishing powers; it proposes measures to the appropriate authorities or presents a case to the courts. It regularly publishes bulletins setting the correct interpretation of norms and administrative procedures. The comptroller general is in charge of the general accounting of the nation and calculates the annual balance of the financial administration of the state. It also provides information and advice to the executive and congress.

Several nondemocratic veto players exerted a significant role in the Chilean policymaking process until their removal by the constitutional reform of 2005. The armed forces were given a political role as "guarantors of the constitution"—whatever that may mean—by the 1980 Constitution. Among the undemocratic means through which the armed forces could interfere with the executive's policy agenda were their semiautonomous status (the president could not dismiss the head of the four branches of the armed forces at will, and they could dispose of their budgets without government oversight),[28] their role in the COSENA, and their power to nominate four of the nine institutional senators.

---

[28] Even though the constitutional reform eliminated the political role of the armed forces, they are still entitled to receive 10 percent of the revenues of the state-owned copper company, CODELCO.

The National Security Council (COSENA) was also drastically modified by the constitutional reform, leaving it as a consulting body for the president. During the previous 16 years, however, it wielded significant influence in Chilean politics. It was comprised of eight members: the president of the republic, the president of the senate, the president of the supreme court, the comptroller general, and the heads of the armed forces. The COSENA appointed four of the nine institutional senators (who have to be themselves former heads of each branch of the armed forces) for eight-year terms to the highly contested and narrowly divided senate, and also appointed two members of the constitutional tribunal. While the COSENA did not take an active role in the formulation of economic policy, it was actively engaged in shaping the policies related to the human rights record of the former military regime, including the government's response to the arrest of General Pinochet in the United Kingdom in 1998.

The nine "institutional senators" were selected as follows: two were chosen by the outgoing president, three by the supreme court (two had to be former supreme court justices, and one a former comptroller general), and four were appointed by the COSENA. The outgoing dictatorship nominated all nine institutional senators in 1990, giving the right-wing coalition a majority in the upper chamber throughout the 1990s and early 2000s without commanding a majority of the popular vote. As time passed, the *Concertación* administrations were able to nominate some institutional senators. In 1997, President Frei nominated two senators, significantly altering the composition of the senate for the remaining two years of his term, and in 2000 he became senator for life. The constitutional reform of 2005 eliminated the institutional senators and allowed the *Concertación* to have a legislative majority in both chambers of congress for the first time since the return to democracy.

In sum, the combined effect of a de facto agenda-setting president, who has effective negotiating tools but is confronted with several checks and balances, produces a policymaking process in which legislation is not easily approved. But the very difficulty of approving legislation means that once a measure is approved, it is hard to overturn. Passing a law in Chile represents a genuine policy commitment.

Capabilities of the State Bureaucracy

Chile is a unitary state; its main political divisions are 13 regions subdivided into provinces. The administration of the state is centralized in the central government in Santiago, with local branches of the central government located throughout the country. There is some degree of local decision making at the municipal level, but there is no fiscal decentralization. Communities have some opportunity to participate in local decision making through consulting councils at the regional and provincial levels.

The head of the administration of the state is the president of the republic. The bureaucracy is divided into ministries for sectoral administration, and intendances (*Intendentes*) and governorships for regional and provincial matters, respectively. The president can appoint and dismiss at will all ministers, all *Intendentes*, and all governors. Coordinating sectoral decision at the regional and local levels are the *Secretarías Regionales Ministeriales* (SEREMIs), which administratively depend on the ministries but work with the *Intendentes* to implement the sectoral policies at the regional level. Finally, there are councils for local consulting at different levels, which incorporate local concerns, but have no decision-making power.

Chile's bureaucracy has undergone a profound process of reform in the last 30 years. During the twentieth century it developed a reputation for low levels of corruption by Latin American standards, but also was marked by strong centralization, an emphasis more on procedures than on outputs, and no participation of civil society or market mechanisms in the provision of public services, making it rigid and not very efficient. The major economic transformations carried out by the military dictatorship in the mid-1970s started a slow but incremental process of reform that led to major reforms in the late 1990s and early and mid-2000s during the Frei, Lagos, and Bachelet administrations. The military implemented structural economic reforms and reduced the size of the state by privatizing public companies and the social security system, deregulating several markets, and improving the tax system. These reforms, however, were carried out in an ideological environment contrary to empowering the state, which led to underinvesting in state capabilities and no effort to modernize the provision of public services.

Since the end of the dictatorship, as both the nascent democracy and the new economic institutions have gained popular support and consolidated, a gradual reform of the civil service has been taking place. The Frei administration initiated a significant modernization of the state, which has been further developed by the Lagos and Bachelet administrations after corruption scandals broke out in 2003 and 2006. The most important pieces of state reform legislation approved during the Lagos administration addressed the following issues: simplifying administrative procedures (Law 19.880), updating the level of remuneration of high public officials to make it more in line with the private sector, reducing the amount of undisclosed funds (Law 19.863), professionalizing the public service in order to improve and develop long-term careers in the civil service regardless of political changes (Law 19.882), and increasing the transparency of government procurement and the concessions system (Law 19.886).

In November 2006 the Bachelet administration introduced to congress a wide-ranging legislative package focusing on anticorruption and transparency. Its main focus was on regulating lobbying activities, political campaign finance, and conflicts of interest among members of congress; legislating to protect the right to access to public information; deepening the civil service reform; and modernizing the comptroller general. As of July 2007, these bills were under legislative discussion. Other bills still under discussion in congress are intended to decentralize the execution of social spending, modernize municipal financing, reorganize the state holding of public companies, and improve the capabilities of regional governments.

Changes to the administration of the state that do not require legislation and that are already in place include a wide range of e-government initiatives,[29] and improvements in the performance indexes for civil servants. The latter were introduced in the mid-1990s as experimental pro-

---

[29] www.gobiernodechile.cl, www.presidencia.cl, www.elecciones.gov.cl, www.chilecompra.cl, www.dipres.cl, www.senado.cl, www.camara.cl.

grams, but have evolved to cover all central government institutions and are currently used to partially link salaries to measures of performance. They are regularly scrutinized by congress during the annual discussion of appropriations as part of the budget allocation process.

Despite the ongoing effort to improve the capabilities of the state, Chile's bureaucracy is still rigid and procedure-oriented, and wages at the professional and high-responsibility levels in the public sector are lower than their counterparts in the private sector. These shortcomings lead to lower performance and at the end of the day contribute to a lower quality of public policy. It is important to emphasize that these criticisms of Chile's civil service are based on a comparison with OECD best practices and that the Chilean bureaucracy is highly competent by Latin American standards.

Interactions: The Policymaking Process in Chile

While numerous features of the Chilean system have thus far been mentioned, two are most salient from the standpoint of implementing cooperative policies. The first is the existence of a small number of long lived political parties that interact repeatedly with one another and with the voters. The second is the existence of implementing institutions—the bureaucracy and the judiciary—that function honestly and with some degree of efficiency and transparency.

Repeated interaction between the parties not only makes it possible for them to make (and keep) policy deals, but more importantly it creates an incentive for the parties to maintain their ideological "brand names" with the voters—thus constraining the sorts of policy changes with which they align themselves. Because the laws passed and executive decrees handed down are actually implemented, deals are credible, opening the door for policy agreements that involve intertemporal trades.

While other noteworthy institutional features such as the agenda-setting powers of the executive, the number and disposition of the veto players, and the degree to which policymakers' interests align on a given issue are important to the details of the policymaking process, Chile would achieve a much less cooperative policymaking process without its party structure and implementation technology. Neither changes in the executive's agenda-setting power, nor in the blocking capacity of the various veto players (insofar as it did not interfere with the equilibrium party structure or the integrity of the judiciary or the bureaucracy), nor a variation in the degree of interest-group alignment would rule out at least some degree of cooperation in policymaking.

To illustrate the relative impacts of the salient features of the Chilean PMP, it is useful to consider some examples of policy compromises. Two important reforms—the partial privatization of Chile's major port facilities (Law 19.542) and the approval of Chile's special relationship with Mercosur—each led to improvements for the general public, and each came at the cost of a disadvantaged group. In neither case did the disadvantaged group enjoy a policy veto, yet in both cases the government committed itself to compensating the losers from the reform.

In the case of port modernization, the government faced the need for an expensive upgrading of Chile's outdated port facilities. The massive capital outlay required would have placed enormous strain on the public budget, and so the government chose instead to grant long-term concessions to private investors in return for the investors undertaking specific construction projects. This route actually relieved the strain on the budget, since the private concession holders paid for the privilege of running the port facilities. The government calculated that the higher rates charged by the private service providers would be compensated by a more rapid processing of ships through the port, leaving overall shipping costs lower. This has happened; transfers from port operators to the government have far exceeded initial estimations. However, this reform entailed replacing the existing state-owned enterprise EMPORCHI, which controlled most of Chile's ports, and it meant that existing EMPORCHI employees would lose their jobs. Given that the great majority of Chileans would be better off as a result of the proposed reform, the government could have simply scrapped EMPORCHI, lived with the ensuing strike, and gone on with the reform.

However, the dominant *Concertación* coalition of left-of-center parties could only choose to abandon the EMPORCHI workers at the cost of violating some of their basic ideological premises regarding the treatment of workers, thus sending a signal to the rest of the labor movement that the government was not to be trusted. Because the *Concertación* parties were in a long-term relationship with organized labor, which they needed for electoral purposes, it was politically costly to simply abandon the port workers. Accordingly, the port reform included expensive "parachutes" for the dismissed dockworkers, such as educational benefits for their children, occupational retraining, and funds for dismissed longshoremen to start small businesses.

The right-of-center opposition was much less ideologically constrained to compensate the dock workers, and the president could have formed a coalition of opposition legislators and some members of his own party coalition to push through the reform without expensive concessions to the dock workers. However, the constraining effects of ideology and of party reputation prevented the president from doing so.

A similar process played out in 1996 on an even larger scale with the passage of the government's trade agreement with Mercosur. This treaty would open attractive markets for Chilean pharmaceutical manufacturers and reduce the price of food in Chile. The Mercosur countries were among the world's most efficient producers of vegetable oils, wheat, and sugar. This threatened Chile's "traditional" agricultural sector, which was involved in the production of sugar beets and wheat. Both the *Concertación* and the opposition *Alianza* were electorally competitive in the adversely affected regions, so the government risked long-term alienation among adversely affected farm voters and eventual seat losses if it pushed the policy through with a majority coalition of legislators from outside the affected areas. Instead, the government persuaded almost all of its adversely affected legislators to vote in favor of the treaty, promising economic compensation to the affected farm areas.[30] This compensation actually arrived in the form of a budget reallocation equal to 3 percent of the 1999 budget, and in the form of redesigned price supports in 2003 that had the effect of extending temporary tariff protection to sugar beet

---

[30] The fact that electoral districts in the affected regions were heavily biased in favor of rural areas was also a key factor.

growers. These latter shifts of resources were not trivial (the sugar tariff fell disproportionately on the poor) but the *Concertación* sustained them in order to preserve its reputation; long-term interaction with the voters made reneging too costly.

In the case of the legislative approval of the government budget, the executive enjoys stronger powers relative to congress than in other policy areas. Nevertheless, congressional approval is required to pass a new budget (but if congress does not address the government's budget on time the government's initial proposal automatically becomes law). One possible outcome of Chile's institutional structure would be for the opposition to follow a "scorched-earth" policy of voting against the government's budget and forcing a constitutional impasse, given the practical ambiguities of the constitutional norm. However, this is not what happens; instead, budgets typically pass with majority support from both the government coalition and from the opposition. This is partly facilitated by rules limiting the government's discretion in allocating funds, and by the independent supervision of expenditures by the *Contraloría General.* Any efforts by the government to act in bad faith regarding budgetary allocations would be quickly detected.

But why would there be good faith to begin with? First of all, it exists because even the opposition wants to avoid a constitutional crisis caused by gridlock.[31] Moreover, the actual budgets reflect compromise solutions with the opposition, in which spending growth for favored government programs is slower than the executive would prefer, giving the opposition something to point to as an achievement and restraining the growth of spending, even as the government can deliver a balanced budget and pass its programs. Without the ongoing reputations of the ruling coalitions, the temptation for individual legislators to play "blame games" by sabotaging new budgets and arguing over who was responsible might become overwhelming. Voters would then be stuck trying to sort out which maverick legislators were really to blame and which were in fact

---

[31] Something that is often on the minds of members of congress when the final deadline approaches is the memory of the 1891 Civil War (the bloodiest conflict in Chilean history), which started after congress rejected President Balmaceda's budget.

defending voters' interests. The organization of the legislature and the executive within the rubric of two electoral coalitions makes allocating blame much easier, and so increases the incentives for politicians to implement cooperative solutions.

Looking across policy areas, one can see that when the executive has greater control over policy, as in the budgetmaking process, policies are closer to the executive's preferred outcome. Likewise, an alignment of interests facilitates the passage of legislation and reduces the probability of gridlock, which delayed resolution of the military government's human rights legacy, and which has hampered reform in areas such as education. As education reform requires a four-sevenths supermajority of both houses of congress for its approval, the Bachelet administration has been unable to pass one of its top priority reforms. However, even when the president is in a position to impose his or her will, he or she often makes concessions to adversely affected minorities. These concessions arise from the governing coalition's need to maintain its ideological "brand name" and its reputation for keeping its policy promises (as in the case of its favorable treatment of sugar beet farmers). The need to maintain a reputation, for the sake of ideological consistency and for the sake of being able to keep one's word, stems from the stability of Chile's political parties and their small number. This cooperative behavior is facilitated by the existence of good institutions for enforcement and implementation, and it responds, on margin, to variations in the institutional structure of the legislative process and to differences in the alignment of interest. However, it is the organization of policymaking around a small number of long-lived parties that is a decisive factor in the cooperative nature of policymaking in Chile.

Conclusion

The policymaking process in Chile is characterized by an institutional structure in which a gauntlet of institutional veto players opposes an agenda-setting executive. The institutions responsible for enacting policies into law are relatively transparent, honest, and efficient, though there is significant variation on this last score. The electoral system (which is open-list d'Hondt with two member districts, and has selection within lists by plurality rule) has fostered the development of two ideologically distinct coalitions of political parties.

The small number of parties (there are five major parties) and their longevity make them vehicles for accountability, staking out credible ideological positions with the voters and cultivating reputations for fulfilling promises. Within this framework, the relative divergence or alignment of interests by the major actors influences the ease with which cooperative outcomes are reached.

The legislative institutions create pressures for selective gridlock, punctuated by policy changes that strain the tolerance of the veto players. However, the capacity of the system to actually implement the laws that are passed makes negotiations over policy outcomes meaningful: policy debts are paid in the hard currency of policies that will actually be carried out, with verifiable contents. The party system, which is shaped by the electoral laws, creates an environment in which policymakers can break out of the structure of an agenda-setting president and a gauntlet of veto players to implement cooperative policy choices. Because there are relatively few parties and because they are longer lived than the individual politicians, they are willing to invest in their long-term reputations, which facilitates intertemporal bargaining.

While any change in the institutional details would influence the behavior of the system, we believe that it is the political party system that is the essential foundation for cooperation. Change other features of the process (by weakening the executive's agenda-setting power, or by removing some of the veto players, for example) and the parties (and voters) would adapt, but they would continue to cultivate their reputations, and this would lead them to continue to act as guarantors of intertemporal bargains. Fracture the party system (by adopting a higher-magnitude electoral rule, or implementing a federal structure with powerful governors, for example) and the status quo legislative institutions and bureaucratic capacity would fail to support cooperative policy outcomes.

6

Political Institutions and Policy Outcomes in Colombia: The Effects of the 1991 Constitution

Mauricio Cárdenas, Roberto Junguito, and Mónica Pachón

Introduction

In an influential volume edited by Rudiger Dornbusch and Sebastian Edwards (1991) on the macroeconomics of populism in Latin America, Miguel Urrutia (1991) argued that populist macroeconomics were absent in Colombia, contrary to the norm in the rest of South America. According to the definition used in that volume, one feature of populist economics is the presence of large fiscal deficits, reflecting the use of budget expenditures for redistributive purposes without a concurrent effort to raise tax revenues. Fiscal deficits in Colombia were relatively small (rarely exceeding 4 percent of GDP) for most of the past century and, when present, were rapidly corrected (see figure 6.1). Moreover, the public sector was relatively small by regional standards (aggregate expenditures and revenues of the consolidated public sector were around 20 percent of GDP between 1960 and 1990).

However, since the early 1990s, fiscal policy outcomes have changed significantly. There has been a strong deterioration of the fiscal balance, as figure 6.1 also shows. The deficit of the central government has been close to 5 percent of GDP since the late 1990s, without a clear indication of a major correction. Aggregate public expenditures grew to 33.7 percent of GDP in 2003 from 21.2 percent in 1990, reflecting a deliber-

Figure 6.1. Fiscal Balance of Central Government, Colombia, 1905–2005

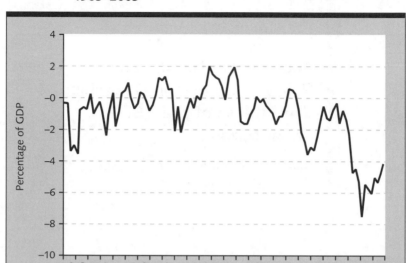

Source: Junguito and Rincón (2004) and Ministerio de Hacienda y Crédito Público.

ate effort to increase the size of the state and use fiscal expenditures for redistribution. Although total fiscal revenues grew to 29.7 percent of GDP in 2003 from 20.6 percent in 1990, the data are unequivocal on the greater tolerance toward fiscal deficits in recent times.[1] In the words of Alberto Carrasquilla (2003, p. 23), "It has not been feasible to consolidate a political agreement that excludes fiscal disequilibrium as an option for public and private agents."

The presence of large and structural fiscal deficits contrasts with Colombia's previous experience in terms of macroeconomic management.

---

[1] Ocampo (2004) argues that "the Gaviria (1990–94) and Samper Administrations (1994–98) did not have the explicit purpose of raising the fiscal deficit, but rather to increase the size of the state in an orderly manner," concluding that recent fiscal policy in Colombia cannot be characterized as populist macroeconomics in the sense of Dornbusch and Edwards (1991).

Economic fluctuations have been much larger since 1990, while GPD growth has decelerated (to 2.9 percent per year during the 1990s from a 4.7 percent annual average between 1950 and 1990). However, inflation rates have fallen since 1990, reflecting the effectiveness of new political institutions that ruled out high inflation as an outcome (see figure 6.2). The purpose of this chapter is to understand the causes of the change in the quality of policies as well as their outcomes: improvement in some areas and deterioration in others. We focus on fiscal and monetary policies, but the analysis can easily be extended to other areas, such as trade policy and the regulation of public utilities. Rather than analyzing the details, we identify some common characteristics of policies and the policymaking process (PMP) that can be related to changes in the political institutions. More precisely, our goal is to understand how relevant political institutions such as the constitution map into political behavior, political behavior maps into policymaking processes, and policymaking processes map into policies and policy outcomes.

Figure 6.2. Inflation in Colombia, 1950–2006

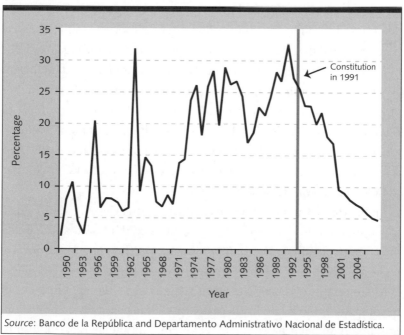

Source: Banco de la República and Departamento Administrativo Nacional de Estadística.

It is analytically tempting to focus on the effects of the 1991 Constitution, which changed the rules of the political game along multiple dimensions. The new constitution strengthened the checks and balances of the political system in an effort to endow political institutions with greater legitimacy after decades of limited participation and low representation. Although remaining extremely powerful even by Latin American standards—surpassed only by the Brazilian executive—the president lost some capacity as an agenda-setter relative to the previous period, while congress and the constitutional court (CC) gained relative power. As a consequence of the larger number of relevant players and the diminished presidential powers, political transaction costs increased in several policy areas, so the gains in representation came at a cost in terms of cooperation.

In addition to the changes in the number of key players, as well as in the rules of the political game, the new constitution covered many specific, previously nonconstitutional, aspects of policy. This is particularly the case of fiscal policy, where key components of public expenditures—such as pensions, fiscal transfers for education and health, and public sector wages—were either "hard-wired" into the constitution or have been determined through the constitutional review process. Many observers have suggested that these embedded rigidities have been a major source of growing fiscal deficits and public debt, tax uncertainty, and inefficient government expenditures, which are frequently mentioned as the causes of macroeconomic instability and low growth. In an extreme form of rigidity, changes in fiscal policy often require constitutional reform, which by definition involves transactions that are slow and costly. As a result, fiscal policies are not adaptable to economic shocks, in contrast to Colombia's own previous experience.

In the case of monetary and exchange rate policies, the 1991 Constitution granted independence to the central bank's board and banned direct monetary financing to the private sector. (Lending to the government is allowed but requires unanimity of all board members.) These constitutional provisions have been reinforced by the appointment of technocrats to the board by successive presidents. As a result, policies in this area have been more stable, coherent, and public regarding since

1991. Policies have also been adaptable to external shocks, especially after the central bank's success in bringing down inflation (there is some indication that flexibility was initially sacrificed to gain credibility).

To develop the argument, the chapter proceeds in the following way. The second section familiarizes the reader with some historical background about Colombia. The third section describes the key political actors in Colombia: the president, congress, political parties, and the constitutional court. The idea is to show how the relative powers of the different players have evolved throughout time. The fourth section discusses the policymaking process in Colombia, with special emphasis on those aspects that changed after the 1991 Constitution. The fifth section presents the empirical exercises, using a database containing 3,428 bills discussed in congress during the last 20 years. The main point of the exercise is to document the relative reduction in presidential powers, measured by the increased difficulty of the executive in enacting laws in congress. More importantly, the evidence suggests that the fragmentation of congress (through more lists and more parties) explains the greater difficulty in passing laws. The sixth and seventh sections discuss in more detail the salient features or outer characteristics of fiscal and monetary policies, respectively, and illustrate the policymaking processes in both cases. The eighth section contains a summary of the main findings and some thoughts on the policy implications of two recent institutional changes: the possibility of presidential reelection and the reform of electoral rules.

Historical Background: Toward the 1991 Constitution

In 1958, after ten years of political violence between the two traditional parties (*Liberal* and *Conservador*), and four years of a military government (1953–57), the parties agreed to share power during four presidential terms between 1958 and 1974, in what was called the *Frente Nacional.* In addition to alternation in the party affiliation of presidents, the agreement (initially a referendum and later a constitutional amendment) included strict "parity" between the two parties in the key policymaking arenas, such as congress, cabinet positions, courts, governors, and mayors. Many features of this agreement survived after its formal end in 1974.

In spite of their apparent success in terms of economic policy outcomes, the political institutions and the consequent rules of the political game derived from the agreement were unsustainable. The left did not have access to a democratic channel for participating in the political process, weakening the legitimacy of the *Frente Nacional* and resulting in high rates of abstention. Popular support for the existing political institutions was also eroded by problems of patronage and corruption, as well as by the escalating violence and the growing political influence of drug money—in particular, the Medellin and Cali cartels—at both the regional and national levels.[2] Capturing this discontent, and benefiting from the weak presence of the state in parts of the country, guerrilla groups—such as the M19, EPL, ELN, and FARC—gained momentum in urban and rural areas, along with labor and social movements.

Early on, President Belisario Betancur (1982–86) proposed a political rather than military solution to the guerrilla problem. In 1984, his government signed a truce agreement with the FARC and started the negotiations with the M19, the two largest guerrilla groups at the time. These efforts failed, and the confrontation escalated to a higher level. In 1989, during the Barco administration, the M19 (and other smaller insurgent groups) finally laid down their arms and successfully entered the political process.

However, the assassination of three presidential candidates in 1989, including the likely winner, Luis Carlos Galán, elicited popular demand for political reform.[3] The long-debated idea of a constitutional reform gained popular support as a response to the political unrest, at

---

[2] Drug trafficking activities and crime rates escalated during the 1980s: the production of cocaine increased by 672 percent between 1981 and 1990 (Rocha 1999), while the homicide rate rose from 42 to 89 per 100,000 inhabitants from 1981 to 1991. The negative economic implications of these trends have been well documented. See, for example, Levitt and Rubio (2005) and Cárdenas (2007).

[3] The other two candidates represented the left: Bernardo Jaramillo (UP) and Carlos Pizarro (AD-M19).

a time when great importance was given to the successful incorporation of guerrilla groups, especially the M19, into the political system.[4] Ultimately, it was the students' initiative through the *movimiento séptima papeleta* that succeeded in this effort.[5]

President Virgilio Barco, in recognition of the people's will, issued Decree 927 of 1990 to authorize the introduction of a referendum onto the ballot of the May presidential elections calling for a constitutional assembly to reform the national constitution. The supreme court declared the constitutionality of the decree by admitting, at the same time, the state's incapacity to confront the different types of violence facing the nation (Lleras and Tangarife 1996). The ballot, which became an official plebiscite, resulted in more than 5 million votes in favor of the national constituent assembly. President-elect Gaviria called for elections in December to organize the constituent assembly. The new constitution was adopted on July 4, 1991.

Key Political Actors in the Policymaking Processes

The entire set of characteristics of the PMPs underwent important modifications during the late 1980s and early 1990s, including the role of key and veto players, the policy initiation process, and the effective number of parties. These changes mostly related to the end of the rules imposed by the *Frente Nacional* and the emergence of new political institutions. Since the drafting of the new constitution in 1991 is the most salient of these transformations, it is convenient to characterize key political actors and the corresponding PMPs before and after that year.[6]

---

[4] Previous reform proposals for institutionalizing political parties, providing guarantees to opposition parties, and improving the electoral system had not prospered. See Hartlyn (1993).

[5] This refers to a seventh extra-legal ballot in the March 1990 elections in favor of summoning a national constituent assembly. See Dugas (2001).

[6] Some of the changes in the underlying political institutions preceded the 1991 Constitution, such as the direct election of majors (1986). Other factors have also had an impact on the PMP, such as market-oriented reforms introduced in the early 1990s and the greater interest of the United States in Colombia in recent years.

The President

As has been the case in most Latin American presidential regimes, an important number of constitutional prerogatives make the Colombian president the main agenda setter in most policy areas. This has remained true even after the 1991 Constitution, which reduced presidential powers in a number of dimensions. Table 6.1 compares constitutional presidential powers before and after the 1991 Constitution.

Proactive Powers. The 1886 Constitution established a highly centralized power structure, which was elevated to a new level with the 1968 constitutional reform promoted by President Lleras-Restrepo. In addi-

Table 6.1. Constitutional Presidential Powers, Colombia, 1958–2004

	National Front and transition (1958–1980s)	After the 1991 Constitution (1991–2004)
Proactive powers	High decree powers, urgency petition, ex post judicial review, areas of exclusive introduction of legislation (from 1968), declaration of unrestricted state of siege and state of economic emergency	Restricted decree powers with ex ante judicial review, call for joint permanent committees along with urgency petition. Declaration of state of siege for periods of 90 days, for a maximum of 180 days, subject to approval by the constitutional court
Integrative powers	Appointment powers in the governorships, various autonomous agencies, cabinet (highly centralized)	Appointment of the cabinet, autonomous agencies (highly decentralized)
Reactive powers	Required supermajority to override in economic bills (2/3 of the members of each house)	Required majority to override: 1/2 of the members of the house
Partisan powers	Relatively low due to electoral rules (no vote pooling across lists, no limit in the number of lists per party). Majority of 2/3 required in congress (until 1974).	Extremely low. No nomination power, electoral rules. Nonconcurrent elections: congressional elections first, majority runoff system.

Source: Authors' compilations.

tion to strengthening the capacity of the president to initiate legislation by augmenting the constitutionally delegated decree power, the 1968 reform significantly increased executives' control over the budget. The president could exclusively introduce legislation in key areas, issue decree-laws when in crisis, and issue administrative decrees with limited judicial review.

The 1991 Constitution deliberately curbed the legislative powers of the president by limiting to 90 days the declaration of either a state of internal commotion or a state of economic emergency (extendable for another 90 days if considered necessary). The constitutional court may revoke decrees issued, including the declaration of the emergency or commotion, if they are considered unconstitutional in any way. Previously, decrees issued under a state of siege became law, even after their special status had expired. Since 1991, decrees remain in force only if congress enacts them in regular sessions, while the pro tempore powers cannot be used to decree codes, statutes, organic laws, or taxes (see Archer and Shugart 1997).

The presence of the constitutional court has restrained the use of the president's special powers. Before 1991, the president needed only the signatures of all his cabinet members to use extraordinary powers to issue decree-laws in a 90-day time frame. Although the subject matter was supposedly narrow, in practice the president could freely use the emergency powers to make policy. The supreme court was the only veto gate, as it had the duty of reviewing each decree enacted, but it was not as active and independent as the current constitutional court. The judicial budget was determined by the executive, and justices to the supreme court were elected from lists submitted by the president to congress. A critical aspect was that magistrates had short terms of five years, with the possibility of reelection. In contrast, the constitutional court is elected by the senate only for longer terms (eight years without reelection), with only one-third of the lists submitted to the senate originating in the executive.

One important aspect in which there has been no change is the president's permanent control over the legislative agenda by using the discharge or urgency petition. This petition enables the president to prioritize a bill in the legislators' agenda. Congress then has 30 days to debate and pass or reject the bill. To speed up the process, the president can also ask for joint sessions of house and senate committees in charge of the law, thereby limiting debates to two instead of the regular four. The executive has retained the exclusive right to introduce bills concerning the structure of the ministries, salaries of public employees, foreign exchange, budget, external trade and tariffs, and national debt, among other areas.

Integrative Powers. Before 1991, the president had greater appointment powers (governors, justices, and heads of control entities, among others). The president also appointed the governor of the central bank.

Reactive Powers. The president can either veto legislation, on procedural and substantive grounds, or suggest changes to the text approved by congress. However, congress can override the executive's veto or annotations with a simple majority. Before 1991, a two-thirds majority was required to overrule a presidential veto.

Electoral Rules. Finally, a majority runoff electoral rule replaced the plurality rule. The majority runoff, along with the timing of congressional elections (which take place before the first round presidential election), have changed the patterns of coalition building. After 1991, one can observe a clear pattern of post-electoral coalitions, and a greater role of legislators in the election of the president.

Congress

The symmetric two-chamber Colombian congress can be classified as reactive more than proactive, given its lack of organization and resources and the substantial legislative powers of the executive (see Payne 1968). A powerful executive, combined with an extremely personalistic electoral system, implicitly delegates the national agenda to the president and the cabinet members. Nonetheless, the legislature has always been an important veto player for the president, especially in areas where the executive does not have complete jurisdiction.

Figure 6.3. Number of Lists Running Per Election, Colombia, 1958–2006

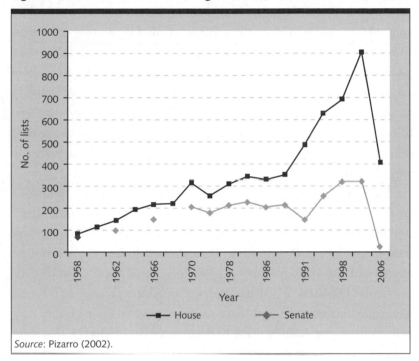

Source: Pizarro (2002).

The 1991 reform reduced the number of representatives from 199 to 165, and the number of senators from 113 to 102. The reform also transformed the national territories (large portions of the territory with low population density) into *departamentos* and established a minimum representation of two house members per *departamento*. Thus seven districts achieved representation in the house for the first time. Since 1991, senators have been elected in national, rather than departmental, constituencies.[7]

Electoral Rules. Congressional elections have become increasingly contested since 1991 (see figure 6.3). The rapid growth in the number of

_____

[7] The house has five members elected from special districts (two from indigenous communities, two from Afro-Colombian communities, and one from Colombians living abroad). Two senators are elected from special indigenous districts.

lists competing in congressional elections has also implied that a large number of successful lists elect only one legislator. For example, in 2002 only three lists, out of more than 300, succeeded in electing more than one senator. To a large extent, this was the result of the electoral rules used for 40 years, until the 2003 political reform. With the formula of largest remainders (LR) or Hare system, seat quotas were calculated by dividing the number of votes by the number of seats. Seats were first allocated to lists that surpassed the quota. The remaining seats are then allocated to the largest remainders, generating incentives for parties to fragment into factions.[8]

The key point is that the largest remainder formula was applied in each district to factional lists rather than party lists (Payne, Adsera, and Boix 2003). The electoral law allowed multiple factions to present lists under the same party label. Thus, though the factional lists were closed and blocked, in effect the system was equivalent to unblocked party lists. The result was that parties increased the number of lists over time, maximizing their seat share while enhancing their decentralization and fractionalization. The 1991 reform did not change this situation, mainly because no representation thresholds were put in place to discourage small lists. The largest remainders-Hare system remained in place, encouraging fragmentation and election by largest remainders. Furthermore, state campaign funding is given directly to candidates, creating additional incentives to form factions or movements, instead of depending on national party resources. The combination of the incentives created by the electoral system and by campaign funding resulted in a large number of movements that were essentially electoral machines.

---

[8] To illustrate the point, take the case of a district with 1,000 voters and ten seats, so the quota is 100. Party A has 650 votes, party B has 240, party C has 70, and party D has 40. Accordingly, party A would get seven seats (six by quota, one by remainder); B would get two (by quota); C would get one (by remainder); and D would get none. Now, if party B subdivides into three factions, it would get three seats (all by remainder), taking one away from party A, which would get six. Party C would not benefit from fragmenting, however. This shows that this strategy is beneficial only for parties that are large enough to get at least one seat allocated by quota (in fact, if party C splits into two equal parts, it gets nothing). Now, if party A splits into eight factions and party B into three, they will capture all ten seats (eight and two, respectively).

For example, 72 movements obtained at least one seat in the house of representatives in the 2002 election. Although these movements are typically affiliated with a major party, the excessive fragmentation of legislators was a key characteristic of congress, with an important impact on the policymaking process. The 2003 electoral reform limited the number of parties by requiring a minimum share of the total votes in order to have legislative representation (2 percent in the case of the senate). As a result, only 14 parties won representation in the congress elected in 2006.

Organization. Each chamber is organized into seven *Comisiones* (eight before the 1991 Constitution), which have a significant role in the workings of congress. The small number of standing committees contrasts with the Mexican or Argentinean legislatures, which have more than 35 committees with overlapping jurisdictions.

Legislators can belong to only one permanent committee and must remain on that committee for their entire four-year term; committee membership is determined by elections. Party membership is indispensable in order to access the committee of first preference (Pachón Buitrago 2003). This is important because it shows that behind a veil of fragmentation and atomization, party structures play a role in organizing legislative activity. Plenary sessions rely heavily on what is approved by the committees, especially in economic and budget matters. Membership in the economic and budget committees is highly valued because of proximity to government funds. The committee in charge of constitutional and political affairs is also highly visible, with highly valued membership.

When compared to other Latin American countries, Colombia has one of the highest incumbency rates. Certain committees (such as the constitutional, economic, and budgetary committees) offer legislators an incumbency advantage, as well as a higher level of professionalization in comparison to other committees. As a result, members of those committees are the natural leaders of congress. Incumbency rates for members of these committees can be as high as 69 percent, while the rates are on average between 30 and 41 for other legislators. Professionalization thus seems to provide an advantage to incumbents.

Political Parties

The Colombian party system is considered one of the oldest and most institutionalized in Latin America (Mainwaring and Scully 1995b). The system is characterized by high intraparty competition, functional party coalitions in congress, and significant party discipline in presidential elections. Although intraparty competition was always part of Colombia's political history, lack of vote pooling since 1974, political decentralization since the early 1980s, and the 1991 constitutional reform brought it to new levels.[9] To make politics even more candidate-based, the 1991 Constitution confirmed the independent electoral authority (*Consejo Nacional Electoral*), in charge of elaborating and distributing the ballot (*tarjetón*) with the name and picture of all aspiring candidates. Before 1986, candidates were responsible for handing out their lists on pieces of paper (called *papeletas*) that were used to cast a vote, and party infrastructure was useful for their distribution among voters. By 1998, 67 parties and movements were recognized by the electoral authorities and were receiving public funding for campaign expenditures (Posada-Carbó 2001).

However, the internal rules of congress enhance the role of the parties and recentralize power in a few hands. Parties are determinant for accession to membership on specific committees, hierarchical positions (presidents and vice presidents of the senate, house, and their respective committees), and strategic roles such as sponsorship of key bills. Sponsors play a key role as political brokers between the executive and other legislators.

Finally, congress has become more fragmented as measured by the Laakso-Taagepera index of Effective Number of Parties (ENP) shown in figure 6.4.[10] The ENP increased from two political parties in the 1970s (Liberal and Conservative), to three in the post-1991 period (Liberals,

---

[9] See Pizarro (1995); Archer and Shugart (1997); Nielson and Shugart (1999); Gutiérrez (1999, 2001); Rodríguez-Raga (1999, 2001); Shugart and others (2006).

[10] We consolidate movements and factions into parties based on the party affiliation of their leaders.

Figure 6.4. Effective Number of Political Parties in the House of Representatives, 1974–2006 (Laakso-Taagepera Index)

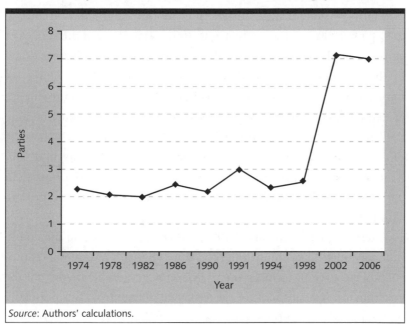

Source: Authors' calculations.

Conservatives, and the AD-M19), to four in 2002: Liberals (official), Liberals (*uribistas*), Conservatives, and the *Polo Democrático* center-left coalition, which includes the AD-M19. By restricting parties to present a single list, the 2003 political reform reduced the number of parties with congressional representation (to 10 from 70). Furthermore, the *Ley de Bancadas*, has devolved to parties in congress the power to sanction their members and facilitate more programmatic stances because of vote pooling and the regained value of the party label.

Courts

In the Colombian system of separation of powers, the judiciary has always been a key player in the policymaking process. In the 1886 Constitution, the supreme court was in charge of constitutional review and dispute settlement between the executive and congress (for instance after a presidential veto on the grounds of unconstitutionality). The supreme court also reviewed ex officio all decrees issued by the executive during a state of siege or state of economic emergency. According to Cepeda (2004), between 1886 and 1991, 60 percent of the rulings of constitutional review (1,489 out of 2,496) were related to decrees issued by the executive during periods of exceptional legislative power (of these 25 percent were found unconstitutional). Due to the constant use of extraordinary powers by the executive, the supreme court became the last resort for very controversial and difficult decisions (such as the one that declared unconstitutional the Extradition Treaty in 1986). Nonetheless, the appointment mechanism, as well as strict bipartisan parity, restricted the independence of the judicial defense of the constitution.

After the major reforms of 1991, the key player became the constitutional court. The nomination procedure changed radically, as part of an explicit attempt to make the judiciary more independent from the government. Nine justices are elected by the senate from lists presented by the president, supreme court, and *Consejo de Estado*, for periods of eight years without the possibility of reelection. Instead of an abstract a posteriori review of the law, the new system is based on abstract ex officio and ex ante review of the statutes, treaties, and organic bills. In addition, the CC revises ex officio the declaration of any state of emergency by the executive, as well as the decrees issued under such status. Although ex post judicial review had been in the judicial system since 1904, the number of bills that are reviewed each year has increased greatly since 1991. Between 1991 and 2003, the CC issued 2,923 rulings on abstract constitutional review—more than the supreme court in 104 years. This shows that the CC has a larger jurisdiction (in 27 percent of the cases, the reviewed laws or decrees have been declared unconstitutional). The majority of these rulings result from citizens' use of the *Acción Pública de Inconstitucionalidad*. Moreover, 39 percent of the decrees issued by the executive under special legislative powers were found unconstitutional. In sum, the CC exercises great influence over policymaking. The main reason is that many policy issues have been elevated to the constitutional rank, especially after the constitutional revision of laws. In practice, this implies that constitutional reforms are necessary to change policies in certain areas.

Technocracy

Technocrats made their first appearance in Colombia as a result of the creation of the monetary board and the National Planning Department (DNP) in the early 1960s. With some exceptions, the head of DNP (a cabinet-level position) has been a Ph.D. economist with recognition in academic circles. The role of the technocracy is strengthened by the wide use of the CONPES (*Consejo de Política Económica y Social*) as a vehicle to formulate policies, based on documents prepared by DNP. Finance ministers have for the most part also been technocrats, at least since the mid-1970s.

Although technocrats have on occasions been appointed to other ministries, their influence has been much less important than in the economic policy arena. The career path of technocrats often involves academic work at independent institutions such as FEDESARROLLO and the Universidad de los Andes, or the central bank and international organizations. Very few have embarked on successful political careers.

A Characterization of the Policymaking Processes (PMP)

Before the 1991 Constitution

Although congress was not formally excluded from economic policymaking during the *Frente Nacional*, the frequent use of states of economic emergency to bypass legislative discussion left the executive with few checks.[11] In practice, this provided governments with more discretion in macroeconomic policies. There is no evidence of major macro policy reversals, while policies were rapidly adjusted in light of external conditions. In other words, policies tended to be stable and adaptable.

---

[11] See Hoskin, Leal, and Kline (1976).

Presidents had a free hand to implement policy. While the executive faced some limited opposition in congress, ample majorities were always secured, and presidents had leverage to pass their bills. Cabinet and gubernatorial appointments were critical in the coalition-building process. The appointment of a prominent political leader in congress (typically a regional party boss) to the cabinet or a governorship was the most effective way of securing the coalition. Presidents had the difficult task of implementing the "*milimetría*," which ensured that cabinets and governorships had adequate representation, by regions, political parties, and factions.

The rules of the political game imbued the minister of finance with immense power. Other prominent actors in economic policymaking were the governor of the central bank and the manager of the Coffee Federation (representing a key source of fiscal revenue and foreign exchange). The very nature of the power-sharing agreement, as well as the usually long tenures of these key players, prevented opportunistic behavior and favored a long-term perspective in policymaking. The insulation of fiscal and monetary policies from political cycles, for example, was effective.[12]

After the 1991 Constitution

The central implication of the 1991 Constitution for the PMP is that, although the president continues to initiate policies in the most relevant areas, congress is increasingly involved in their discussion, oftentimes introducing significant changes. The Coffee Federation has lost importance as key actor, in part because of a more market-oriented economy and the declining economic importance of coffee exports.

Congress, on the other hand, has strengthened its position as a key player, enhancing its role in the policymaking process. The 1991 Constitution severely curtailed the use of special powers to bypass congressional discussion. Nevertheless, presidents elected after 1991 have been able to secure a post-electoral majority coalition in congress, regardless of their political affiliation. Budget allocations and appointments to government positions are regularly used to form and hold coalitions. As congress has

---

[12] On the absence of political business cycles in Colombia, see Escobar (1996).

Figure 6.5. Average Number of Legislative Sponsors, Colombia, 1982–2003

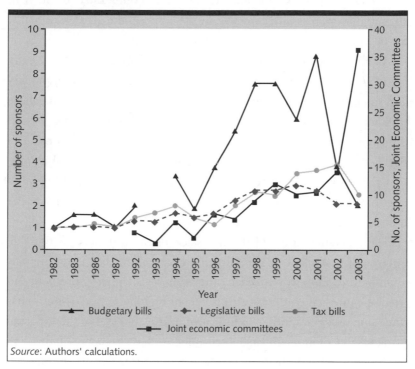

Source: Authors' calculations.

become more fragmented, these costs have tended to increase. Figure 6.5 shows the number of sponsors assigned to each bill discussed in congress, which is a good proxy for the amount of pork that the executive has to deliver to pass a law.[13]

The PMP does not end with the enactment of legislation in congress. The constitutional court acquired the status of a key player and, on occasion, a veto player in the PMP. The constitutional revision of laws allows the CC to intervene in critical areas, such as fiscal policy. The introduction of the CC's review has furthered the transaction costs for the executive, which can no longer rely on "short-term alignments" with congress to enact its policy. Although the president still retains the exclusive right

---

[13] Cardenas, Mejía, and Olivera (2006) follow the budgetary process through different stages and conclude that since 1991 congressional approval has implied greater increases in the size of the budget.

to introduce economic bills, the polity has become more resolute with the presence of the CC as a powerful veto gate. Even if the executive can align its preferences with congress, the CC imposes the greatest difficulty for the president's attempt to change the status quo.

Another prominent actor in the economic PMP is the central bank board, given its constitutional responsibilities as authority on monetary and foreign exchange matters. These two areas of policymaking have traditionally been considered highly specialized, and both congress and the courts have had little involvement in their policy formulation. The significant change undertaken as a result of the constitutional change that granted independence to the central bank is the diminishing influence of the executive in monetary decisions, despite the presence of the minister of finance as president of the board.

The PMP since the mid-1990s has also been influenced by the U.S. government. While U.S.-Colombian relations have been traditionally amicable and supportive of each other's interests, the drug problem and domestic internal conflict—with potential regional repercussions—has put them on a new footing, as indicated by the approval of the U.S.-supported Plan Colombia in 1999. U.S. influence has also been felt through the backing of Colombian government economic programs, monitored by the International Monetary Fund (IMF) (between 1999 and 2006). It is worth adding that, despite the well-known insecurity situation of the country, neither the armed forces nor the illegal groups have become veto players.

Finally, interest groups and business associations have had a very active role in the PMP. The president often invites the main private sector leaders for consultative sessions, in which important policy decisions are made. With some ups and downs, this has been customary both before and after 1991.

Key Implications of the 1991 Constitution for the PMP

A number of important policy issues were directly included in the constitution so that they essentially became off limits in terms of the regular legislation. The PMP in these areas now takes the form of constitutional amendments, which by definition are more difficult to pass than regular legislation.[14] In addition, constitutional amendments, as well as regular lawmaking, have to face a more contested, fragmented, and polarized congress. As we will document below, this has implied a lower probability of approving bills in congress, particularly for bills initiated by the executive. Before 1991, it was easier for the executive to put together a winning coalition because the president had greater partisan powers and the legislature was less fragmented. Also, the loss of the president's power to appoint governors, the shift in the financing of campaigns (from party-based to candidate-based), and the use of a ballot system that lowered the value of the party had a negative impact on party discipline and may have also made it more difficult for the president to enact his agenda. In addition, once the president is able to get laws passed through congress, constitutional review by the constitutional court can derail or modify what comes out of the legislative.

As before, presidents have been able to bypass legislative debate by invoking exceptional circumstances (*estados de excepción*). Since 1991, there have been stricter checks on whether emergencies were declared appropriately (by the CC), and limits (in terms of the duration of the emergency and the type of legislative decrees that can be adopted). More relevantly, before 1991 decrees issued during the emergency became laws automatically, whereas now they must go through the normal legislative approval process to remain in effect after the emergency expires.

Finally, the president's reactive powers to block legislation also changed. The president's veto power was weakened by the 1991 Constitution. Before 1991, the president's veto was hard to override, as a two-thirds majority was required. Since 1991, only a simple majority is required to override a presidential veto.

---

[14] Article 375 of the constitution restricts the initiation of constitutional amendments to the executive, 10 members of congress, 20 percent of city councils and departmental legislators, or 5 percent of the electorate. The amendments must be discussed in two ordinary and consecutive legislative periods, approved in the first round by the majority of the legislators present. In the second round, amendments must be approved by the majority of the members of congress. In the second round, debate is limited to initiatives discussed in the first round. In contrast, regular laws require only one round and a simple majority of the legislators present during the debate.

Empirical Evidence

This section provides some empirical content to the previous discussion by using a legislative output database covering 14 legislative years between 1982 and 2003.[15] Legislative output is the information about the bills that have been presented and enacted in a given legislature. The database consists of 3,428 bills presented in the house of representatives, and comes—since 1992—from its annual *Informe Legislativo*. Before 1992 the information comes from the archives at the Library of Congress.[16]

We focus on the variables that explain why bills become laws and compare the executive and legislative capacity of enacting policy before and after 1991. Specifically, we want to test whether the changes in the agenda-setting power of the executive have lowered success rates for bills initiated by the government after 1991. On average 179 laws were initiated annually, before the enactment of the 1991 Constitution. Since then, congressional activity has intensified: 271 laws have been initiated per year. Bills initiated by the executive represent around 19 percent of the total, regardless of the time period.[17]

To gain insight into the database, we borrowed the detailed typology from Taylor-Robinson and Díaz (1999) to classify bills according to their scope: individual, local, regional, sectoral, national, and international treaties. Bills that have a local or regional target are classified as "local scope" in our database, while sectoral or national bills are classified as "national scope."[18] Table 6.2 shows some basic information from the

---

[15] Legislative years begin on July 20 and end on June 20 of the following calendar year, with a scheduled recess from December 16 to March 16. For 1986 and 1987, we have complete information only for the bills introduced in the first six months of the legislative year.

[16] See Mejía Acosta (1998), Amorim Neto (1998b), Morgenstern and Nacif (2002), and Amorim Neto and Borsani (2004) for similar data and analyses for other Latin American countries.

[17] We have information only on bills initiated in the house, but we can track the outcome of these bills in the senate as well. Our unit of analysis is the bill instead of the legislator (as in the case of the databases constructed with roll call data), which does not allow any measure of party unity or party cohesion within congress.

[18] This allows us to differentiate bills such as the "celebración de los 462 años de la fundación del municipio de Charalá" (PL. 091/2002C) from bills that have a national

database. Success ratios (enacted bills over presented bills) have fallen for all bill types after 1991. Bills initiated by the executive systematically have higher success ratios, as well as bills that have a national scope.

Econometric Tests and Results

This section presents the results of a logit regression on the success of bills. As mentioned above, at the end of the legislative year a bill can be enacted (our definition of "success" regardless of the impact of the law), filed (which means that the initiative was defeated), or allowed to remain in process for consideration in the next legislative year. We exclude bills that are still in process, as it would be imprecise to treat them as cases of failure or success, as well as bills dealing with the ratification of international treaties, where congress essentially rubber-stamps negotiations conducted by the executive.

The purpose of the econometric exercise is twofold. First, we want to identify the factors that determine success rates in legislative activity in general. Second, we want to disentangle the effects of the 1991 Constitution. In particular, we explore the role of greater polarization and fragmentation—as well as diminished presidential powers—discussed in the previous section. In all cases, the dependent variable takes a value equal to one in the case of initiatives that become laws, and zero otherwise. The explanatory variables include a dummy that takes a value of one when bills are initiated after 1991 and zero otherwise (*Post 1991*), a dummy that takes a value of one when bills are initiated by the executive (*Executive*), a dummy with a value of one when the bill is initiated during the last year of the administration (*Last Year*), a dummy for bills that have a national scope (*National*), a dummy for bills that are discussed in the constitutional committee (*Constitutional*), a dummy for bills that are discussed in the economic committee (*Economic*), and a variable that measures each bill's number of sponsors (*Sponsors*). In addition, we also

or a sector-specific impact, such as those regulating professional activities. These classifications are based on the limited information contained in the title of the bill. We also used the information contained in the title to classify bills by policy area (see the working paper version for the results [Cárdenas, Junguito, and Pachón 2004]).

Table 6.2. Legislative Database, Colombia, 1982–2003

	Initiative[1]						Scope[2]					
	Congress			Executive			Local			National		
	Before 1991	After 1991	All Periods	Before 1991	After 1991	All Periods	Before 1991	After 1991	All Periods	Before 1991	After 1991	All Periods
Number of bills[3]												
Presented	567	2,150	2,717	137	494	631	714	822	1,536	432	1,682	2,114
Enacted	137	212	349	88	253	341	109	103	212	93	268	361
Success ratio (enacted/presented) (percent)	24	10	13	64	51	54	15	13	14	22	16	17

Source: Authors' calculations. Information for the period 1991–2003 is based on *Informes Legislativos del Congreso* produced by the House of Representatives, Oficina de Leyes. Information previous to 1991 was obtained in the congressional archives.

Note: Selected legislative years are presented.

[1] Excludes 79 bills presented by other instances and bills in process at the end of each year.

[2] National bills also include those with a sector-specific scope, and exclude international treaties.

[3] The unit of analysis is each bill introduced in the House of Representatives. The legislative periods selected previous to 1991 are 1982–1983, and 1986–1987. The legislative years included after 1991 include 1992 until 2003.

used two variables that capture the polarization and fragmentation of the political system. This is the case of the effective number of political parties (*Parties*) and the number of lists competing in the previous election (*Lists*).

Table 6.3 presents the results. Equation 1, which tests our basic hypotheses, shows that success rates have fallen significantly since 1991, while initiatives originated by the executive have a higher probability of success, relative to those initiated by congress. The interaction of these two variables has a positive and significant coefficient, suggesting that after 1991 the executive has been more effective in enacting laws than before. The other variables in the equation show that bills introduced during the last year of the administration and bills that have a national scope are less likely to pass, suggesting the presence of a "lame duck" effect, and a bias in favor of laws that have a local or regional scope. Interestingly, bills that begin legislative discussion in the constitutional committee have a lower probability of success. This is important because, as mentioned above, much of the PMP after 1991 requires constitutional amendments (due to the level of detail and specificity of the constitution). By definition legislative discussion on these amendments is initiated in the constitutional committees. Therefore, constitutional amendments are harder to pass than regular legislation. Bills that enter congress through the economic committees do not seem to be any different than the rest.

The hypothesis is that a larger number of sponsors (a proxy of the amount of pork that the administration is willing to provide) increases the chances of approval by the floor. This is precisely what we obtain in equation 2 when we add the number of sponsors as an explanatory variable. Importantly, the interacted term between the dummy *Post 1991* and the executive variable loses all significance. This suggests that the more apparent success of the executive is the result of greater use of sponsors (that is, pork) since 1991 to assist the legislative process. Equations 3 and 4 add the effective number of parties and the number of lists, respectively. As expected, both variables have a negative impact on the bill's chances of success, implying that greater fragmentation and polarization make the legislative process more difficult. All other variables remain signifi-

Table 6.3. "Determinants of Legislative Success Rates," Colombia, 1982–2003 (Logit Model)

Equation Sample	1 All bills	2 All bills	3 All bills	4 All bills	5 All bills	6 Bills after 1991
Dependent variable	=1 if enacted, 0 if filed	=1 if enacted, 0 if filed	=1 if enacted, 0 if filed	=1 if enacted, 0 if filed	Marginal effects (4)[a]	=1 if in process, 0 otherwise
Constant	-0.427***	-0.419***	1.459***	0.328		-0.458***
	(0.123)	(0.131)	(0.390)	(0.246)		[3.42]
Post-1991	-0.550***	-0.636***	-0.295**	0.063	0.012	
	(0.125)	(0.137)	(0.150)	(0.233)	(0.046)	
Executive's initiative	2.059***	2.020***	2.011***	2.032***	0.462***	-0.208
	(0.258)	(0.274)	(0.275)	(0.275)	(0.058)	[0.82]
Post-1991* Executive's initiative	0.642**	0.388	0.532	0.344	0.072	
	(0.305)	(0.334)	(0.337)	(0.335)	(0.074)	
Last year in office	-0.792***	-1.026***	-1.087***	-1.020***	-0.160***	1.358***
	(0.253)	(0.279)	(0.282)	(0.280)	(0.033)	[8.15]
National scope	-0.593***	-0.704***	-0.752***	-0.734***	-0.153***	-0.641***
	(0.119)	(0.129)	(0.130)	(0.129)	(0.028)	[4.93]
Constitutional committee	-0.891***	-0.772***	-0.743***	-0.794***	-0.146***	-0.735***
	(0.136)	(0.148)	(0.149)	(0.148)	(0.025)	[5.41]
Economic committee	-0.150	-0.237	-0.253	-0.218	-0.042	-0.007
	(0.154)	(0.166)	(0.167)	(0.167)	(0.031)	[0.05]
Number of sponsors		0.205***	0.176***	0.231***	0.046***	0.165***
		(0.044)	(0.043)	(0.045)	(0.009)	[4.43]
Effective number of parties			-0.820***			
			(0.161)			
Number of lists (x100)				-0.225***	-0.045***	-0.178***
				(0.063)	(0.012)	[3.30]
Number of Sponsors* Executive						
Number of obs	2278	1789	1789	1789		1831
LR chi2	415.74	365.88	395.14	379.27		179.15
Pseudo R2	0.162	0.167	0.180	0.173		0.077
Log likelihood	-1,076.96	-913.51	-898.89	-906.818		-1071.443
Marginal effect after logit[b]					0.272	

Source: Authors' calculations.

[a] Marginal effects on the probabilities based on the logit regression (in the case of dummy dy/dx corresponds to discrete change from 0 to 1).

[b] Estimated probability of the model for a bill to became law [y = Pr(bill_law) (predict)].

***significant at 1%, **significant at 5%, *significant at 10%

224 Mauricio Cárdenas, Roberto Junguito, and Mónica Pachón

cant, except in equation 4 for the *Post 1991* dummy, suggesting that the decrease in the probability of success after 1991 is effectively explained by the increase in the number of lists (a measure of fragmentation) that has taken place since the enactment of the new constitution.

Transforming the estimated coefficients into marginal effects on the probability is a straightforward exercise. According to equation 4, the estimated probability is 27.2 percent, which is marginally affected by changes in the explanatory variables. For instance, when the bill is initiated by the executive, the probability increases by 46.2 percent; in contrast, when the bill is introduced during the administration's last year, the probability falls by 16 percent. If it has a national scope the probability falls by 15.3 percent, and if it is introduced through the constitutional committee, the probability diminishes by 14.6 percent. At the same time, an extra sponsor raises the probability by 4.6 percent. The increment of party lists (both interparty and intraparty competition) and a higher "effective number of parties" lowers the probability of success by 4.5 and 16.1 percent, respectively.

Given the large number of bills that are still in process at the end of each legislative year, it is worth exploring the factors that can lead to delay. Equation 5 shows the results of the logit estimation when the dependent variable is the probability that a bill is postponed into the following legislative year. The exercise, which is done with post 1991 data (there is no information on bills in process before 1991), shows that bills that are presented during the last year of an administration have a greater probability of remaining in process for the next legislative cycle. Bills that are introduced in the constitutional committee, as well as those that deal with national issues, are less likely to remain in process. In the case of bills that are introduced by the executive, the larger the number of sponsors, the lower the probability that a bill is delayed or postponed.

The remaining sections of this chapter describe key policy features of some important policy areas. With the purpose of exploiting variation across time and across sectors, we focus on specific aspects of fiscal, monetary, and exchange rate policies. The idea is not to provide a detailed account of these policies or a complete taxonomy, but to identify those features and characteristics that can be related to the workings of the political institutions and the policymaking process. Given that lens, the implicit notion of optimal policy involves policies that are resilient to *political* shocks (or, more generally, to changes in the political landscape), but that are flexible enough to adjust to *economic* shocks. Finally, the description also highlights some specific aspects of those policy areas, other than political institutions, that are useful in understanding their outer features.

Fiscal Policy

To identify the outer features of fiscal policy, we will divide the analysis into three parts. We start by discussing fiscal policies in relation to oil and coffee exports. Analytically, this is a rich area because of variation across sectors (the number of relevant actors is larger in the oil sector than in the coffee sector, for example) and time (coffee was a critical source of fiscal and foreign exchange revenues until the 1980s, and oil has been since then). Second, we discuss issues related to the national government, which handles most tax revenues and transfers a significant share of those revenues to the regions. Third, we look into pensions, which are the fastest growing public expenditure.

Oil and Coffee Exports

Public finances in Colombia have been highly dependent on taxation on coffee and oil exports. In particular, coffee policy was a key component of fiscal policies before 1991, while oil has been a key element of public finances since 1991. Incidentally, the constitution was written during a time of major oil discoveries, potentially explaining the generosity in terms of protection of social rights and lack of emphasis on aspects related to fiscal sustainability.

Oil and coffee export revenues are intrinsically volatile. Thus the ability of the policymaking processes specific to these policy domains to facilitate intertemporal agreements is critical for the adoption of consistent fiscal policies (that is, policies that prevent overconsumption during booms). However, the outer features of the policies that address these issues are very different in the case of oil (after 1991), compared to coffee (before 1991), reflecting differences in the underlying political institutions, but also diversity in the specific characteristics of these two policy areas.

The rules of the political game during the *Frente Nacional* facilitated the adoption of intertemporally consistent fiscal policy (that is, coffee policy). In 1958, the same year that the *Frente Nacional* was agreed upon, world coffee prices collapsed, sending producers into a deep crisis. That year, the National Coffee Fund (NCF) became the instrument for the stabilization of producers' incomes. By its very nature, stabilization implied savings during booms and dis-saving during busts. The minister of finance and the leadership of coffee producers were the only relevant players in negotiating prices paid to domestic producers. Technocrats and coffee leaders shared similar objectives and mutually reinforced their respective powers. Bates (1997) argues that coffee producers were pivotal in electoral turnouts, so liberal and conservative governments adopted similar policies in relation to coffee.[19] In sum, coffee policies were stable (intertemporal agreements were sustained) and flexible (they adjusted rapidly to changes in international and domestic conditions).

In light of the potentially destabilizing effects of an oil boom, congress approved the creation of the Oil Stabilization Fund (OSF) in 1995. In contrast to coffee, redistribution is based on a rigid system of royalties allocated among the producing departments and municipalities (including those where ports are located) and the National Royalties Fund (NRF), which in turn redistributes royalties to other departments and municipalities. Depending on the value of exports, the OSF forces saving by all recipients of oil rents and invests the proceeds abroad. The large number of players with power over a given decision (national and local governments, as well as the state-owned Ecopetrol), the short-term nature of the interaction between the key actors (governors, mayors, and the executive), the high discount rate of these actors, and the difficulty in delegating policies to a third party create an environment with high

---

[19] Cárdenas and Partow (1998) show that electoral and partisan cycles did not play a role in the redistribution of coffee revenues to other groups in society.

transactions costs. The natural consequence is that the cooperative solution that provides some stability (savings during high export years) is embodied in a rigid system of rules and is costly to change, even if those changes are desirable.

Issues Related to the National Government

Total expenditures by the central government have doubled from an average of 10 percent of GDP during the 1980s to over 20 percent since 1999. As a result of eight tax reforms since the 1991 Constitution, current revenues rose to 15.3 percent of GDP in 2003, up from 8.8 percent in 1990. The net result has been an increase in the central government's fiscal deficit, especially after 1995. The growing gap between the overall and the primary deficit reflects the large increase in public debt and interest payments during the second half of the 1990s.

We argue that the capacity to conduct stable and predictable fiscal policies (avoiding and rapidly correcting deficits) has been severely hindered since the 1991 Constitution. This is not only the result of additional expenditures mandated by the constitution, but also a consequence of the reduction in the degree of flexibility and adaptability of fiscal policies. In turn, rigidity is a natural consequence of the difficulty in reaching cooperative solutions in the environment created by the 1991 Constitution, characterized by less presidential power and a larger number of relevant political actors.

On the revenue side, tax reforms have been frequent (on average every 20 months since 1990), distortionary (introducing anachronistic taxes as well as tax expenditures), and incomplete (never closing the gap with expenditures). Policies in this area have shown high volatility (there have been some policy reversals in relation to tax rates and exemptions), low coherence (little consistency between reforms), and low capacity to adopt structural reforms with short-term upfront political costs but high long-term economic payoffs.

Fiscal Transfers to Local Governments. The process of decentralization has evolved rapidly since 1980. In Colombia, over 40 percent of total government spending is allocated by subnational governments, compared to an average of 15 percent in Latin America (see Daughters and Harper 2006). Articles 356 and 357 of the 1991 Constitution ordered a gradual increase in fiscal transfers, which were 29 percent of the central government's current revenues in 1990 and were expected to rise to 46.5 percent by the end of that decade.[20] In practice, fiscal transfers rose faster, to nearly 60 percent of current revenues, suggesting the presence of other factors beyond the constitutional mandate.[21]

In July 1999, worsening economic conditions at home and abroad led the Pastrana administration to initiate formal talks with the IMF. The core of the program agreed upon was to lower the consolidated public sector (CPS) deficit to 3.5 percent of GDP in 2000, 2.5 percent in 2001, and 1.5 percent in 2002.[22] The IMF program emphasized the need for a constitutional amendment to reduce the growth in fiscal transfers.

The amendment was finally approved by congress in July 2001. The workings of that policy change illustrate well the incentives and constraints of the political actors. The government's initial proposal was to replace the old system (a fixed fraction of the central government's current revenues) with a guaranteed 1.5 percent real annual increase in fiscal transfers (equivalent to population growth), regardless of economic conditions. In an effort to gather the sympathy of the political class, the government modified the initial proposal and introduced another article, extending the term in office of elected mayors and governors from three to four years. Negotiations in congress raised real growth in fiscal transfers to 2 percent per year between 2002 and 2005, and 2.5 percent

---

[20] The goal was to enhance political participation by redistributing power from the national government to the municipalities and departments (see Wiesner 1995 and Acosta and Bird 2003). Critics emphasize low accountability and waste of resources (see Echavarría, Renteria, and Steiner 2003) and the excessive earmarking of expenditures on health and education, which has interfered with an efficient use of resources to reduce poverty (Perotti 2005).

[21] For example, Law 188 (1995) incorporated new teachers into the system and reclassified them into higher salary categories (effectively increasing salaries by 26 percent in real terms). The national government paid the extra cost through greater fiscal transfers.

[22] At the end of 2002, the program was extended for another three-year term.

between 2006 and 2008.[23] The end result was that the executive had to pay a high price (ensuring regions with a high growth rate in fiscal transfers) in order to gain a few years of independence between revenues and transfers. This shows that changing the rigid clauses of the constitution regarding fiscal transfers is politically costly. This, of course, limits the executive's maneuver room in economic matters, which cannot adjust expenditures to overall economic conditions.[24]

Other Examples of Embedded Rigidity. In a recent paper, Echeverry, Fergusson, and Querubín (2004) discuss other sources of inflexibility in the central government's budget. They distinguish between mandatory expenditures and earmarked revenues. As they rightly point out, these rigidities have a long tradition in Colombian economic history.[25] Apart from pensions and transfers to local governments, earmarked expenditures currently represent nearly 1.7 percent of GDP. These expenditures cover almost every single sector from sports to security; they are earmarked in the sense that the budget law cannot change them. Another source of rigidity is earmarked taxation (taxes that are introduced with the purpose of financing specific expenditures). In this case, the estimated amount for 2003 is 3.7 percent of GDP, suggesting that it is a larger problem (79 percent of the current earmarked rents were created after 1991). Thus the evidence strongly suggests that the rules of the political game favor rigidities, given the high political transaction costs.

High transaction costs also result in the constitutionalization of fiscal policies. A good example is wage policy in the public sector. Based

---

[23] After 2009 transfers will grow at a rate equal to the real growth in current revenues of the central government during the previous four years.

[24] A number of reforms introduced in the past few years redirecting the use of the fiscal transfers (creating a fund to cover pension liabilities and improving the criteria for allocation across jurisdictions) improved efficiency in the use of these resources, but provided no additional flexibility regarding their overall level. See Zapata, Acosta, and González (2001).

[25] Almost every minister of finance in the twentieth century complained about the fiscal problems caused by congressional initiatives in relation to expenditures and earmarked taxation. See the survey of Memorias de Hacienda, collected in Serna (1988).

on its interpretation of Article 53 of the constitution (which says that minimum vital remuneration is a right), the constitutional court has overruled the budget and has mandated minimum public-sector salary increases.[26] Rigidities are so pervasive that the executive had to call a referendum in 2003 to freeze government expenditures for two years. The referendum failed.

Taxation. As discussed above, there has been a deliberate, although insufficient, effort to raise revenues to finance larger expenditures. The analysis of the contents of recent tax reforms, as well as the formal objectives established in the draft projects, confirm that the major objective of the executive in the tax reform process has been to increase tax revenues as a means of reestablishing fiscal balances. Even though the priority has been the increase in fiscal revenues, the draft tax reform projects submitted to congress have given importance to the structure of the tax system, an area in which governments have been only partially successful. There has been an increasing reliance on the rate of the value-added tax (VAT), which has increased from 10 percent to 16 percent through various reforms since 1990. However, the most recent attempts to increase the VAT have systematically failed. More importantly, most of the draft projects submitted to congress have sought to widen the VAT base, with limited success.

As a consequence of congress' reluctance to widen the income and VAT tax base, the executive has introduced new—and highly distortionary—tax sources. In 1998, a temporary 0.2 percent financial transactions tax was adopted through an emergency decree, which was raised to 0.3 percent and made permanent in the 2000 tax reform, and raised again to 0.4 percent in the 2003 reform. In the same vein, in 2002 the Uribe government, using an extraordinary internal commotion decree, adopted a transitory net wealth tax earmarked to the strengthening of democratic security in Colombia. This tax was extended for three additional years in 2003. The conclusion is that revenue pressures have

---

[26] There have been four different rulings on this matter, suggesting that constitutionalization does not imply stability of policies.

led to decisions that disregard the basic principles of an equitable and efficient tax structure.

The role of congress as a political actor in tax reform has been significant. While in earlier decades, congress largely rubber-stamped the tax reforms submitted by the executive, often through emergency legislation, its involvement in the design of tax packages has been increasing since the early 1990s. On the positive side, congress has a solid group of distinguished members with knowledge and expertise on fiscal affairs who lead the debate and who are influential in the outcome of the legislation. On the negative side, congress could be partly blamed for the insufficiency of revenues that come forth from the reforms, for the increase in expenditures, and for the deficiencies in the structure of the taxing system. An analysis of tax legislation submitted by the executive reveals that congress tends to water down proposals during debate, both in terms of revenues and, more importantly, in terms of the quality of the reforms.

The growing involvement of congress in fiscal issues is also illustrated in the significant number of sponsors who are assigned to the analysis of the draft proposals from the executive. As discussed above, the interest in becoming sponsor also has to do with the distribution of pork, or with benefits obtained from the private sector as a result of political favors. The constitutional court has also been a significant actor in tax policy outcomes. Tax issues have represented around 10 percent of the total legal claims on economic matters handled by the CC since 1991. For example, in 1999, a ruling on the financial transactions tax limited the scope in the use of revenues, while in 2003 the CC denied the approval of the generalization of the VAT and the taxation of specific activities. At the same time, the CC has given its full legal support to other important reforms in this policy area.

Pension Policy

The policymaking process in the area of pensions provides another example of an entrenched status quo—unsustainable and unequal, yet extremely hard to reform. A good illustration of the workings of the political process is Law 100 of 1993, a major reform that had as its main goal replacing the pay-as-you-go defined benefit (DB) system with a defined contribution (DC) and individual capitalization scheme. What emerged from the legislative discussion is quite different from the initial government proposal. The initial proposal eliminated the defined benefit system, leveled the benefits of all systems by 2004, and excluded only the military from the standard regime. Under Law 100, the defined contribution regime is not mandatory for new entrants and was offered only as an alternative to the defined benefit system. The political compromise was to phase in the new conditions very slowly; they will be fully effective only in 2014. Such a long transitional period has implied growing fiscal deficits. In addition, legislators, workers in the oil sector, teachers, and members of the armed forces, among others, were able to keep their privileged pension regimes.

Even though the reform lowered the implicit pension debt by 38 percent of GDP, mainly as a result of the increase in contribution rates from 6.6 percent to 13.5 percent of wages, the fiscal costs of the new pension system were still unsustainable. The *Comisión* (*Comisión de Racionalización del Gasto y de las Finanzas Públicas* 1997), among others, proposed shortening the transitional period, raising the retirement age, increasing contributions, reducing the replacement rate, and adopting stricter eligibility criteria.[27] Although in the 1999 IMF program the Colombian authorities had made strict commitments to submit to congress a second-generation pension reform, it was not until December 2002, under the Uribe administration, that the pension reform was finally approved in congress. Notwithstanding the high political capital of the new administration, congress rejected the proposed increase in retirement ages starting on 2009. Contributions went from 13.5 percent of wages to 15.5 percent by 2006, while the minimum required number of weeks of contribution was increased. The replacement ratio was also reduced gradually from levels in the range of 65 to 85 percent to the range of 50 to 70 percent, and new public workers were forced to remain in the public pension system for at least the three initial years. Here also, the

---

[27] Other early advocates included Ayala (1998) and Clavijo (1998).

constitutional court rejected some of the changes, such as the increase in the minimum number of weeks of contributions, which was declared unconstitutional.[28]

Many aspects of the pension regime have been set by rulings of the constitutional court. To deal with some of these features, the 2003 referendum included a specific question, proposing the elimination of all exempt and special public sector pension regimes and the enrollment of all new entrants in the general pension regime as of 2008; it was not approved. When the initial version of this chapter was being written in 2005, the government was promoting a constitutional amendment in congress. A balance of results in pension reform indicates this is a politically delicate and costly issue. As in the case of tax reform, draft proposals submitted by the administration are watered down in the congressional debate, especially in relation to changes in benefits, and in some cases rejected by the constitutional court. The conclusion is that the executive has the power to initiate measures but not necessarily to control the final output.

Monetary and Exchange Rate Policies

Players and Policy Framework

Before 1963, monetary and exchange rate policies were made by a board chaired by the minister of finance and composed mostly of prominent private sector bankers. In 1963, these policies were transferred to the government-controlled monetary board, presided over by the minister of finance and with the presence of other economic cabinet members, the central bank governor, and support from two technical advisors. From 1963 to 1991, in practice, monetary and exchange rate policies were in the hands of the executive.

The 1991 Constitution (Article 372) established the seven-member central bank board as the monetary and exchange rate authority. The

---

[28] It was subsequently approved again in the following legislature (Law 860/2003), and again rejected by the constitutional court in 2004.

members include the minister of finance, who serves as chair, the governor of the central bank, who is elected by the board, and five independent members named by the president for a period of four years (renewable for two additional periods). Only two of the independent members can be changed every four years.

Even though the central bank board makes its decisions by majority rule, where each member has one vote, the two most prominent actors within the board are the governor of the central bank and the minister of finance, both of whom act as de facto agenda setters. The governor instructs the central bank's staff on the preparation and submission to the board of the technical papers, which gives him great influence. Even though the minister has only one vote in the board decision process, in practice the board has almost always acted with the support of the minister in regard to exchange rate issues, and very often at his request.[29]

In terms of executive-legislative relations, congress has fared well with the independence of the central bank to the extent that it gained relative power, since the executive is no longer able to resort to monetary financing from the central bank, and thus is forced to confer with the legislative branch, both in the case of taxes and in authorizations to undertake public lending.

Initiatives to modify the mandate of the central bank have not been uncommon.[30] However, only one initiative out of 70 was approved by congress, and it was later rejected by the constitutional court. The one approved was presented by the Samper administration in 1996 and was clearly directed to modify the role of the board of Banco de la República as the exchange rate authority of the country. Other initiatives have been geared toward the explicit acceptance of the "employment" objective as one of the main goals of the board's actions and to subject board members to a censure vote—a political action that congress can apply to cabinet ministers. Ultimately, however, congress has not been successful

---

[29] For a critical analysis of the presence of the minister of finance in the Board, see Alesina (2004).

[30] For a complete list of initiatives, see the working paper version of this chapter (Cárdenas, Junguito, and Pachón 2004).

in reforming the framework established by the 1991 Constitution and by the central bank law.

The constitutional court has generally ruled in favor of the central bank's independence by limiting the role of the government in exchange rate and monetary matters, although the CC has also become more active in issues such as caps on mortgage interest rates. In one of the most relevant rulings, the constitutional court in 1999 stated that the objectives of the central bank include both inflation control and economic growth. The *Consejo de Estado* in general has confirmed and reiterated the role of the bank's board as the foreign exchange and exchange rate authority in the country.

The role of multilateral organizations, particularly the IMF, has also been important. In 1999, during the final stages of negotiation of the IMF program, both the IMF and the U.S. Treasury held that Colombia should switch from the exchange rate band system to a flexible regime, and this view ultimately prevailed. Colombian private sector interest groups, the academic community, the press, and public opinion in general have limited influence on the formulation of monetary and exchange rate policies.

Features and Outcomes

Monetary and exchange rate policies have tended to be stable in Colombia. Before 1991, political interference was limited to the president (and ministers in charge of agriculture and industry), while congress was excluded from this policy area. After 1991, policies have been formally delegated and have thus become more independent. Volatility or policy reversals associated with changes in the political landscape have been prevented by an institutional design that has favored the role of technocrats, both before and after 1991.

However, the pre-1991 monetary framework presented smaller fluctuations in interest rates, at the cost of inflation rates in the range of 20 to 30 percent from the 1960s to the mid-1990s. With the adoption of the inflation-targeting framework in 1999, deliberate interest rate adjustments adopted by the central bank board have been more frequent, with resulting gains in terms of reducing inflationary expectations and achieving single-digit inflation. A final distinguishing aspect between the pre- and post-1991 regimes relates to differences in the policies' public or private regardedness. Before 1991, subsidized credit was directed toward certain politically favored sectors of the economy that not always were chosen on technical grounds.

Finally, it does not appear that changes in administrations or in political ideology have made a substantial difference in the way monetary and exchange rate policies have been conducted and implemented. Under the crawling-peg exchange rate regime, the variation of the nominal exchange rate responded to discretionary management, but the real rate followed economic fundamentals. The behavior of the exchange rate between 1991 and 1999 and afterward, when the exchange rate band was eliminated, was more strongly determined by fundamentals and market perceptions. There is no evidence that political pressures or party orientation have influenced the evolution of these policies.

A General Characterization of Policies' Outer Features

The main findings in relation to the outer features of fiscal, monetary, and exchange rate policies in Colombia before and after 1991 are summarized in table 6.4. In the case of fiscal policies, the main changes are related to the adaptability of policies. In most areas, fiscal policies became more rigid after the 1991 Constitution (except in the area of pensions, where policies have been always rigid). There has been a slight deterioration regarding stability vis-à-vis political shocks, but also an improvement in terms of public regardedness.

Monetary and exchange rate management policies have been more isolated from political shocks since 1991. Compared to the period before 1991, monetary policy (at least since 1999) has been more adaptable to external shocks, while the exchange rate has also been more flexible. There is more coordination/coherence in these two policy areas, and both have clearly gained in terms of public regardedness. An indication of this last point is the fact that special privileges such as differentiated exchange rates and subsidized credit facilities were eliminated after 1991.

A more general view of the effects of the 1991 Constitution can be provided by a brief exploration of other policy areas. Trade policy is an area that has remained relatively isolated from political changes. It is less used now than in the past to deal with economic shocks, for reasons that have to do with the trade agreements signed since 1991. Trade policies still display private regardedness, in the sense of including some forms of protection that are not openly discussed outside the executive.

Regulation of public utilities is an area where much progress has been achieved since the 1991 Constitution. The regulatory commissions operate with relative autonomy from the executive, although not to the point observed in monetary policies. With the important exception of the water commission, these commissions have largely been able to produce regulation that is stable and adaptable. However, the most important advancement in these areas is related to the public regardedness of the decisions made.

Finally, in the case of financial policies, certain decisions are made by the constitutional court, which limits the response to economic shocks. This has been especially the case with mortgage interest rates, which has limited the degree of financial stability, adaptability, and coherence since 1991. Labor policies are still very rigid, although isolated from political shocks. Social policies have lost adaptability, as in the case of fiscal policies in general.

In short, the evidence is mixed; some policies areas have improved while others have deteriorated. Clearly, the 1991 Constitution has brought positive changes in many policy areas. The main conclusion is that policy features have tended to improve when authority has been delegated to an autonomous agency, as has been the case in public utilities and monetary policy. Absent delegation, adaptability seems to have suffered.

Conclusion

At the end of the 1980s, Colombian political institutions were under severe strain. After decades of bipartisan control, large segments of

Table 6.4. Characterization of Policies Before and After the 1991 Constitution: Outer Features, Colombia

	Stability[1] Before	Stability[1] After	Adaptability[2] Before	Adaptability[2] After	Coherence Before	Coherence After	Public regardedness Before	Public regardedness After
Fiscal policy								
Fiscal transfers	Medium	Medium	Medium	Low	Medium	Medium	Medium	High
Pensions	Medium	Medium	Low	Low	Medium	Medium	Low	Medium
Other expenditures	Medium	Low	Medium	Low	Medium	Medium	Medium	Medium
Taxes	Medium	Medium	Medium	Low	Medium	Low	Medium	Medium
Coffee	High	High	High		High		High	High
Oil		High		Medium	Medium	High	Low	High
Monetary policy	Medium	High	High	Medium	Medium	High	Low	High
Exchange rate policy	Medium	High	High	Medium	Medium	High	Medium	High
Other areas not covered in the paper								
Trade policy	Low	Low	High	Medium	Low	Medium	Low	Low
Regulation of public utilities	Low	Medium	Low	Medium	Low	Medium	Low	High
Financial policies	Medium	Medium	Medium	Medium	Medium	Medium	Low	High
Labor policies	High	High	Low	Low	Medium	Medium	High	High
Social policies (health and education)	Medium	Medium	Medium	Low	Medium	Medium	Medium	Medium

Source: Authors.

[1] Vis-à-vis political shocks.

[2] Vis-à-vis economic shocks.

the population demanded more political participation and inclusion. Regional political leaders, with the support of the electorate, advocated fiscal and political decentralization. The call for increased security and political stability was particularly loud after a decade of growing unrest and conflict that ended with the assassination of three presidential candidates in 1989. Moreover, the expectation of greater resources available from the discovery of oil, as well as the exacerbation of social tensions, created momentum for a new constitution, which had long been debated. The elections of 1990 included an unofficial vote in favor of rewriting the constitution. With the enactment of the new Constitution in 1991, more sectors were brought into democratic life, barriers to political participation were lowered, and regions gained autonomy and greater administrative independence.

The new political institutions have had a significant effect on the policymaking process and policy outcomes in a variety of areas. The constitution reduced presidential powers, enhanced the role of congress, lowered the costs of political participation, and brought two new key players into the policymaking processes: the constitutional court and the board of the central bank. In addition, some policy areas were embedded in the constitution, such as fiscal transfers, social expenditures, wages, and pensions, thus restricting the executive's room to maneuver. Moreover, in those cases in which there is some constitutional flexibility, the executive has faced a more divided and fragmented congress; this has increased political transaction costs and has lowered the probability of approving the preferences of the executive. Those bills that are approved are typically watered down relative to executive proposals.

In addition, the use of special legislative powers by the executive was severely restricted, while the regular constitutional review of laws is now more active, independent, and detailed. As a result, fiscal policies have become less adaptable and less flexible. We argue that removing some aspects of fiscal policy from the constitution could improve policy outcomes in this area.

The reduction in presidential powers has also affected monetary policy. Although the president is still influential, through the presence of the minister of finance on the board of the central bank, policies do not always reflect the preferences of the executive. Although disinflation has been the overriding goal of monetary policy since 1991, the evidence suggests that monetary policy has become more flexible and adaptable since 1999, the year when inflation returned to single-digit figures. Hence we do not propose major reforms of the political institutions that are relevant for monetary policy.

Recently, congress approved two constitutional amendments. The first, in 2003, entailed a significant reform of the electoral rules for all legislative bodies, for the first time in Colombia's modern history. In 2004 congress considerably strengthened the powers of the president, approving a constitutional amendment allowing the president to run for a consecutive second term. Although there were attempts in congress to extend the possibility of reelection to all executive offices, including mayors and governors, this was finally rejected.

These reforms will change Colombia's political institutions in important ways. Instead of choosing across hundreds of lists, voters now choose candidates from single-party lists. This will encourage formal pre-electoral coalitions and more policy-based campaigns. Although post-electoral coalitions will remain a relatively salient feature of the system, due to the existence of the preferential vote (voters can chose their preferred name on the party list), changes across party lines will imply more costs to members who decide to move from their pre-electoral coalition. Thus, we anticipate a reduction in the number of lists and the consolidation of a multiparty system.[31]

In addition, because the president can now run for a second consecutive term, we expect an increased role of the president in congressional elections. Depending on the president's level of popularity, elections will allow voters to punish or reward the government, as well as legislators aligned with the executive. It will also increase the likelihood of intertemporal agreements, because members of both congress and the executive will have longer time horizons. The existence of a second term will reinforce the party organizations at the national level. However, the fact that reelection for other offices is not allowed might leave the lo-

---

[31] See also Shugart and others (2006).

cal and regional party apparatus somehow disjointed from this process. In addition, the reelection of the president will somewhat limit the independence of the central bank, although this risk can be mitigated if presidents continue to appoint technocrats as board members.

To conclude, the 1991 Constitution was a clear gain in terms of representativeness and legitimacy of the political system. However, the existence of excessive fragmentation and short-term horizons have raised political transaction costs with a negative impact on a variety of policies. Most likely, the electoral reform will partially remedy the dysfunctionality of the party system. Hopefully, this will translate into more programmatic policy that reinforces political party labels instead of candidate-based agendas. Finally, reelection will consolidate the power of the president as the main agenda setter in the policymaking processes.

7

Veto Players, Fickle Institutions, and Low-Quality Policies: The Policymaking Process in Ecuador

Andrés Mejía Acosta, María Caridad Araujo,
Aníbal Pérez-Liñán, and Sebastián Saiegh

Introduction

Since Ecuador's return to democracy in 1979, Ecuadorian elected leaders have faced the twin challenge of dealing with fundamental ethnic, regional, and political differences while promoting major policy adjustments and structural reforms in the economic realm. The active participation of multiple actors whose consent is needed to approve policies, but who lack the institutional or temporal incentives to cooperate with one another, has produced low-quality policies in the social and economic realms. Attempts at reform, including a constitutional assembly in 1998, have consistently sought to increase the presidents' policymaking abilities—without improving incentives for cooperation. This reform pattern exacerbated existing political conflicts and brought greater policy deadlock, which at its extremes contributed to prematurely ending three presidential mandates in 1997, 2000, and 2005.

The process that led to democratization in Ecuador was characterized by a tremendous economic and social transformation of the state. The discovery of oil-rich fields in the Amazon during military rule boosted growth to unprecedented rates, increased public sector spending and investment, and encouraged rapid modernization of productive infrastructure (Araujo 1998). As a result, new social groups—mostly a stronger middle class, but also business, labor, and peasant organizations—demanded more participation and representation in the political arena (Hurtado 1990). The new generation of democratic reformers was determined to end more than five decades of personalistic politics, volatile coalitions, and regional conflicts. Since 1925, Ecuador has experienced more than 35 different administrations, including 13 caretaker governments, 11 administrations originating from a coup, 4 that were appointed by a constituent assembly; in all, only 7 resulted from elections (Hurtado 1990; Mejía Acosta 2002). Reformers turned to the Constitution to address structural problems of economic distribution, unequal development, and political fragmentation through economic planning and political reforms. Reforms included the adoption of a runoff system for presidential elections (1977), provisions to request party sponsorship of presidential candidates (1977), endowing presidents with strong agenda-setting powers (1983), adopting provisions to require nationwide participation of political parties (1977), a mandatory threshold for party registration (1977), and provisions for removing parties that had performed poorly in elections from the electoral registry (1978). While reforms sought to strengthen the executive power, they also reinforced the proliferation of opposition parties, thus reducing the likelihood that elected presidents would enjoy single-party majorities in congress. The adoption of midterm elections, coupled with the banning of immediate reelection for deputies (effective between 1983 and 1997), further weakened the legislative branch and created rent-seeking "amateur legislators" who left congress every two years (Mejía Acosta 2003). Table 7.1 illustrates the level of legislative fragmentation and weak political support facing most Ecuadorian presidents.

We argue that the policymaking process in Ecuador results from the interaction among three types of actors: a large number of veto players who translate their regional, ethnic, and political differences into the policymaking arena; a constitutionally strong president, endowed with significant agenda-setting and policymaking abilities but without partisan support; and a series of formal and informal "last-ditch" veto players, who may challenge or reverse policy decisions from outside conventional

Table 7.1. Ecuadorian Presidents and Congressional Support, 1979–2005

Years	President	Government party	Seats in congress	Largest party	Seats in congress
1979–81	Jaime Roldós[1]	CFP	44.9	CFP	44.9
1981–84	Osvaldo Hurtado	DP	0.0	CFP	17.4
1984–86	León Febres Cordero	PSC	12.7	ID	33.8
1986–88a	León Febres Cordero	PSC	19.7	ID	23.9
1988–90	Rodrigo Borja	ID	42.3	ID	42.3
1990–92[2]	Rodrigo Borja	ID	19.4	PSC	22.2
1992–94	Sixto Durán Ballén	PUR	15.6	PSC	27.3
1994–96[2]	Sixto Durán Ballén	PUR	3.9	PSC	33.8
1996–97	Abdalá Bucaram Ortiz[3]	PRE	23.2	PSC	32.9
1997–98	Fabián Alarcón Rivera	FRA	1.2	PSC	31.7
1998–00	Jamil Mahuad[4]	DP	28.1	DP	28.1
2000–03	Gustavo Noboa	(IND)	0.0	PSC	20.3
2003–05	Lucio Gutiérrez[4]	PSP	9.0	PSC	25.0
2005– Present	Alfredo Palacio	(IND)	0.0	PSC	25.0

Source: Mejía Acosta (2002).
[1] Died in a plane accident. Vice-president assumed mandate but lacked a congressional party contingent of his own.
[2] Mid-term elections.
[3] President ousted by congress. President of congress assumed mandate.
[4] President ousted by congress. Vice-president assumed mandate but lacked a congressional party contingent of his own.

policymaking arenas (whether this be through a constitutional court or street protests).

In the absence of political or material incentives that enable cooperation over time, the policymaking process in Ecuador adopts two possible—but competing—tracks. In the first scenario, presidents use their political and economic influence to distribute clientelistic payments to potential allies and to cement ad hoc policy coalitions in congress. These coalitions are short-lived, as political parties have diminishing incentives to cooperate with a minority government as new elections approach. The conflict between formal and informal veto players tends to reinforce policy deadlock and rigidity.

In the second scenario, presidents may accomplish intertemporal agreements by delegating authority to a specialized agency in policy areas where decision making requires enhanced technical expertise or a quick policy response. But increased delegation may produce policy volatility if the agency does not enjoy sufficient operational autonomy or technical capacity. Rather than generating a cooperative model of stable policies punctuated by adjustments when changes are needed, the Ecuadorian setup is more likely to produce a conflictive pattern of rigid policymaking punctuated by policy volatility.

Reforms adopted in the late 1990s have done little to improve this inefficient pattern of policymaking. A series of reforms allowed legislators to enjoy consecutive and longer terms in office by abolishing the non-reelection rule (1996) and eliminating midterm elections (1998). These reforms sought to promote a stronger "electoral connection" between legislators and their voters, as well as to extend the horizons for cooperation with the government. Ironically, the intended effects were offset, since a few years earlier legislators had lost the ability to bargain about budgetary allocations for their provinces.[1] Thus legislators could not access government allocations for their electoral districts and the government lost access to coalition building currencies (contrast the situation in Brazil, described in chapter 4, this volume). The adoption of dollarization in 2000 further stifled the policymaking process, partly because the central bank lost its influence in regulating monetary policy, and partly because this extreme form of exchange rate rigidity made fiscal policy the only instrument available for macroeconomic adjustment.

This chapter illustrates the workings of the policymaking process in the highly contentious Ecuadorian setting. The second section outlines the most relevant "outer features" of Ecuadorian policies in historical and comparative perspectives. The third section identifies the roles and incentives of three types of policy actors: decisive players, partisan

---

[1] In a national referendum held in 1995, Ecuadorian voters decided that legislators should no longer have the ability to access budgetary allocations for their provinces but instead be able to allocate spending based on budget sectors. The decision was influenced by the belief that legislators misspent provincial monies for their own political gain.

players, and "last-ditch" veto players. The fourth section describes the dynamics of the policymaking process in the context of severe political fragmentation and short time horizons. The section illustrates how policies tend to be quite rigid or inefficient in areas characterized by the presence of multiple veto players, whereas delegating policymaking authority to a strong "decisive" player may produce high policy volatility. These scenarios are further illustrated in the fifth section with a case study of fiscal policies. The sixth section summarizes the main arguments and concludes.

Public Policies in Ecuador

Ecuador's policymaking process is well described by Grindle and Thoumi's notion of "muddling through": a pattern by which conflicting political and economic views over policymaking alternatives do not always defeat policy proposals, but delay their implementation and limit their success (Grindle and Thoumi 1993, pp. 123–124). The proliferation of relevant veto players, the polarization of their policy preferences, and the lack of institutional mechanisms to facilitate, maintain, and enforce agreements over time are key elements that help explain poor policy performance in Ecuador. Ideally, public policies should be sustainable over time, respond to changing external conditions, be properly enforced, pursue the general welfare, and produce efficient outcomes. Taken in comparative perspective, Ecuadorian policies have the lowest rankings in the region, when such ideal attributes are taken into consideration (IDB 2005).

A first critical feature reflecting the quality of policies refers to the state's ability to maintain policy stability and continuity over time. This dimension is negatively affected if the survival of policies is contingent on political swings or idiosyncratic changes in policy preferences. Ideally, stable policies allow institutions to produce the expected results, since they build on previous agreements and tend to generate social consensus. Taken in comparative perspective, Ecuador ranks low in policy stability, mostly because Ecuadorian policymakers have faced institutional constraints to developing long-term cooperation. The combination of legislative term limits and midterm elections imposed de facto restrictions on legislators' political careers between 1983 and 1998. Executive and cabinet volatility contributed to additional policy instability and uncertainty. Since 1996, Ecuador has not had a president who has finished his four-year constitutional mandate. Economic cabinet ministers lasted less than a year in office between 1979 and 1998, on average, and this average dropped further after 1998. This chronic volatility affected the "investment-like" or intertemporal continuity of policies in Ecuador, and the lack of policy continuity has affected the country's commitment to long-term economic reform. For example, between 1979 and 1998, the Government of Ecuador negotiated nine letters of intent and signed seven loan agreements with the International Monetary Fund (IMF), but fulfilled only three of them.

A second critical dimension is the governments' ability to innovate policies in the presence of changing economic conditions or when current policies have ceased to work (policy adaptability). At the opposite end of this dimension, governments may get stuck with unsuitable policies for extended periods of time (policy rigidity). In Ecuador policies have not adequately changed to respond to substantial social, environmental, and economic shocks over the last two and a half decades. Some of the exogenous shocks that have affected macroeconomic performance include a high dependency on the international price of oil exports, the debt crisis of the 1980s, the international financial and banking crises in the mid- to late 1990s, and the presence of natural disasters such as floods, earthquakes, and armed conflicts with neighboring countries. As will be shown, the presence of multiple actors who are directly influential in the policymaking process (veto players) and their diverging policy preferences have hindered political cooperation and significantly increased the costs of policy change in Ecuador (Tsebelis 2002).[2] This is especially true with policy areas that are highly sensitive to the public domain, such as the oil sector. The government was unable

---

[2] Few veto players with converging policy preferences may also produce rigid results if there is a consensus to avoid reform (status quo- or SQ-bias) (Pérez-Liñán and Rodríguez-Raga 2003).

to provide a quick policy response and did not resume oil production for six months after an earthquake damaged the oil pipeline in 1987. Similarly controversial was the decision process for building a new oil pipeline between 1998 and 2000, with associated losses and increased uncertainty for this vital economic sector. Policy rigidities have also been present in the face of favorable shocks: the government has not been able to adopt and implement the necessary legislation to make efficient use of high oil prices since the year 2000.

A third, less prominent dimension is the state's ability to implement adopted reforms effectively. The quality of policy implementation depends in part on the existence of *enforcement technologies*, such as an independent judiciary and/or a professionalized bureaucracy. The presence of these bodies should reinforce the credibility of commitments and provide policymakers with incentives and resources to enhance their policy capabilities. The Ecuadorian state is characterized by a weak capacity to implement and enforce policy agreements over time. As will be illustrated in the next section, this weakness is mostly due to an ineffective government bureaucracy composed mainly of political appointees rather than career civil servants, a highly politicized judiciary, and the presence of "last-ditch" veto players, or street actors who have the ability to stop or reverse policy implementation. The lack of a merit-based civil service has disrupted policy implementation, especially in areas like economic reform, education, and social security. The implementation of economic reforms has been hindered by a constellation of last-ditch veto players, including indigenous and regional elites who have opposed changes to the status quo. Shifting legislative coalitions have also affected the continuity and stability of finance ministers and economic policy, and long-overdue education and social security reforms have been blocked by the active presence of well-organized but largely reactive unions. Land distribution in Ecuador is another example of poor implementation, since it has remained unequal and essentially unchanged in the last 25 years (World Bank, Ecuador Poverty Assessment, 2004c). Fiscal reforms, on the other hand, have improved significantly over the past few years, especially after President Mahuad delegated decision-making power to a new Internal Revenue Service (SRI). Part of the success of the SRI in collecting tax revenues and fighting tax evasion was due to its isolation from political pressures and the recruitment of technical staff.

The fourth dimension evaluates whether the state is capable of articulating policies that promote general welfare and represent the interests of the unorganized or geographically dispersed groups, or tends to systematically funnel benefits in favor of a privileged few (Cox and McCubbins 2001; IDB 2005). This is another dimension in which the Ecuadorian policymaking process scores a low regional ranking. In the highly fragmented and regionalized political context, the policy preferences and demands of well-organized and intense lobby groups tend to prevail over those of broader constituencies. This is especially true of intense groups who are in a position to provide short-term legislative support for a particular government agenda in exchange for selective rewards, policy concessions, and particularistic benefits. Sometimes these concessions are hard-wired in the form of earmarked allocations, some of which tend to benefit the military, specific charities, or others. Customs administration is another policy area in which private regarding interests prevail. The lack of an independent judiciary increases the possibility that private regarding benefits and concessions are also associated with acts of corruption.

Players and Institutional Incentives

Ecuador offers a unique setting for studying institutional theories of policymaking since the country has experimented with a wide range of institutional arrangements over time. Since the transition to democracy in 1978, the country has adopted two constitutions (1979 and 1998) and introduced a number of significant institutional reforms (in 1983–84, 1994–95 and 1997–98). We argue that the resulting institutional setup has created two different policymaking paths. When the government pushes the policymaking process through the legislative branch, this process is dominated by veto players (formal and informal) who tend to oppose policy reforms. Alternatively, when decision-making authority is delegated to a technical agency, the result could be policy stability or greater volatility, depending on the agencies' appointment procedures and institutional capabilities. The interaction between the two paths generates a rigid policymaking pattern punctuated by policy volatility, rather than a cooperative model of stable policies punctuated by adjustments. A series of formal and informal last-ditch veto players engage at the end, not only to oppose or stall policy decisions but in some cases to threaten regime stability altogether. This section explains these players' preferences and roles within the policymaking process.

Institutional Decisive Players

Decisive players are actors with formal proactive powers whose consent is individually sufficient but not necessary to approve policy changes. Examples include the president invoking decree powers, the monetary board, or "technocrats" in the cabinet. In a stylized situation, the presence of a decisive player would imply the absence of any other institutional veto player in the same policy area (Strom 1995). In practice, some policymakers tend to find ways to bypass other veto players, thus acquiring de facto powers. Decisive players include the executive, the cabinet, and the bureaucracy.

The Executive. Ecuadorian presidents embody a unique set of formal and informal attributes that make them "impotent dictators" in the policymaking process. On the one hand, they enjoy significant constitutional powers to set the policymaking agenda, promote and insist on proposed legislation, and use discretionary payoffs or selective incentives to reward cooperation from coalition partners. On the other hand, they never enjoy solid partisan support in the legislature, and existing currencies available to cement cooperation are rapidly depreciated in the eyes of election-driven politicians. As will be further discussed, Ecuadorian presidents cannot become effective formers of coalitions, despite their mighty constitutional and broad discretionary powers. Under the current constitution, the Ecuadorian president is elected every four years, and presidential reelection is allowed only after one period out of office. A runoff election takes place between the two top candidates if no contender obtains a majority of the popular vote, or 40 percent plus a

10-point distance from the runner-up. No president since 1979 has been elected in the first electoral round.

Shugart and Carey (1992) have described the Ecuadorian president as among the most powerful in terms of legislative powers, and as intermediate in terms of nonlegislative powers—the latter because congress can censure cabinet ministers (see also Payne and others 2002). The 1983 constitutional reform gave the president proactive powers in the form of fast-track economic lawmaking; an "urgent" economic bill introduced by the president becomes the reversionary policy if congress fails to act within 30 days (the original period of two weeks was doubled in 1998). The president has not been able to exploit emergency legislation powers as an effective lawmaking tool because the constitution limits the use of them to one per month.

The Ecuadorian president has strong reactive powers. A veto or partial veto must be overridden by congress within 30 days with a two-thirds supermajority, and the use of a package veto prevents congress from addressing the bill in question for one year. The strategic use of veto and decree power has given Ecuadorian presidents tremendous agenda-setting powers over the legislature, as will be illustrated throughout this chapter. This prerogative was further strengthened by the executive's exclusive power to initiate budgetary proposals. The other source of presidential power consists of almost exclusive control over the allocation of key political and economic assets, such as the ability to freely appoint and remove cabinet ministers and provincial governors, make discretionary use of off-budget spending accounts (*gastos reservados*), make policy concessions, grant judiciary pardons, and many other prerogatives for distributing pork and patronage.

The other side of the coin is characterized by the presidents' weak "partisan powers" (Mainwaring and Shugart 1997b). Presidential and legislative elections are concurrent (every four years) under the 1998 Constitution and were originally concurrent (every five years) under the 1979 Constitution, but the 1983 reform established midterm elections to renew more than 80 percent of congress every two years. Although the 1979 legislative election occurred simultaneously with the presidential runoff, in every subsequent general election the congressional race has coincided with the first round of the presidential contest (Mejía Acosta 2002).

The combination of runoff presidential elections (which encourage the proliferation of candidates in the first round), midterm congressional elections, and proportional representation (discussed below) allowed for a large number of legislative parties and condemned the president to have small legislative contingents (Conaghan 1994). On average, the president's party has controlled only 26 percent of the seats since 1979. As shown in table 7.1, no president has commanded a single-party majority in congress, and the ruling party has enjoyed a plurality of the seats during just 11 years over the last 25 years.

Cabinets. Cabinet positions in Ecuador are of relative importance for facilitating the formation of multiparty coalition governments. On the one hand, cabinet ministers are freely appointed and removed by the executive without congressional intervention. They enjoy significant policymaking influence over strategic areas, as well as access to a rich source of pork and patronage for their own constituencies (Mejía Acosta 2004). On the other hand, holding a cabinet position and formalizing a common agenda with the government is often considered an electoral liability from the perspective of other political parties. Furthermore, the value of holding a cabinet position decreases as new elections approach. Since the executive (and for a long time, legislators as well) could not seek reelection, there were no institutional incentives for long-term cooperation (Mershon 1996; Mejía Acosta 2004).

In the contentious Ecuadorian context, crafting government alliances poses a dilemma to potential partners: they want to reap the coalition benefits while avoiding the electoral liabilities of being associated with the government's agenda. Often, politicians opt to make ghost coalitions, or clandestine arrangements by which parties provided short-term support in exchange for government posts, policy concessions, and particularistic benefits while denying long-term alliances or programmatic support (Mejía Acosta 2004). Cabinet ministers often prefer to deny any party affiliation or formal links to political parties. This is the case for most "political" ministries like agriculture, communications, defense, education, environment, foreign relations, health, housing, interior, labor, public works, social welfare, and tourism, which could be used to reward legislative alliances in congress. Technical ministries—mostly concerned with economic issues—on the other hand, are explicitly shielded from political (congressional) pressure to ensure fast-track policymaking authority and increased decisiveness (Conaghan 1995). Taken together, evidence shows that "independent" politicians and technocrats with no explicit party affiliation make up 65 percent of cabinet positions (Amorim Neto 1998a; Burbano de Lara and Rowland García 1998).

Cabinet volatility in Ecuador is among the highest in Latin America (Martínez Gallardo 2005). On average, Ecuadorian ministers changed every 15 months between 1979 and 2002, with significant differences between the political cabinets (16.7) and the technical cabinets (12.3). Contrary to the common assumption of an openly belligerent legislature preying on cabinet ministers (Arteta and Hurtado 2002; Burbano de Lara and Rowland García 1998), presidential action—not congressional opposition—explains most of the cabinet removals during this period (156 of 292 cases). Congressional impeachments accounted for only 7 percent of all cabinet removals. Technocratic cabinet ministers lasted fewer months on average (11.5) than those who had some formal or informal congressional endorsement (18.0). High cabinet turnover rates reflect the failure of presidential strategies to isolate ministers' policymaking ability from the political realm, especially regarding economic matters. As the sixth section will illustrate, frequent cabinet reshuffling contributed to cementing ad hoc alliances with coalition partners, but hindered policy continuity in the long run.

The Bureaucracy. The president appoints the heads of most bureaucratic agencies, including the 15 ministries, the board of the central bank (with congressional approval since 1998), and the national oil company (PetroEcuador). In each of the 22 provinces, the president also appoints a governor, who acts as the head of the national civil service in the region. At the municipal level, the executive has some control only over local administrative courts (*juzgados de contravenciones and jueces de paz*), whose members are appointed by the minister of the interior. As explained in the following section, control over the bureaucracy sometimes allows the president to employ purely administrative policy instruments in order to bypass the legislature and achieve greater decisiveness.[3]

Although the top echelons of the bureaucracy generally have straight-forward political incentives to respond to the executive, the role of the middle ranks may vary according to the policy area. In complex technical areas (the finance ministry, PetroEcuador, and the central bank), as well as in the areas of defense and diplomacy, the bureaucracy is composed of seasoned public officials whose career prospects are based on merit-based evaluations. Other executive-run agencies are composed of highly qualified technical advisors, but they lack long-term career prospects, as they are often hired by development bodies as consultants on short-term assignments. A case in point is the National Council of Modernization (CONAM), in charge of planning.

Most of the public administration is made up of a mix of career officials with limited or outdated technical capacity and static ambitions. This is the case of administrative bureaucracies in the areas of education, health, and social security, among others. These large bureaucratic bodies are biased toward maintaining the status quo and therefore tend to oppose sector reforms. Finally, there are several government agencies whose personnel usually reflect political quotas given to coalition partners. These clientelistic bureaucracies, such as social welfare and labor, are dependent on shifting political coalitions and feature low levels of technical capacity, which undermines the agencies' policymaking capabilities.

The president has little control over the oversight agencies. Candidates for key positions, including those of the comptroller general, the solicitor general (*procurador*), the attorney general, and the superintendents of banking, public companies, and telecommunications, have been traditionally nominated by the president but ultimately appointed by congress.[4]

---

[3] On the use of rulemaking as a policymaking instrument ("para-constitutional" decree authority), see Carey and Shugart (1998a).

[4] The 1998 Constitution introduced two exceptions: the comptroller is now nominated by congress and appointed by the president, while the fiscal general is nominated by the Judicial Council and appointed by congress.

When those positions are politically sensitive, as in the cases of the fiscal general or the *procurador* (and lately the banking superintendent), the appointees tend to reflect the position of the pivotal legislator in congress (that is, the Social Christian Party).

Partisan Veto Players

Institutional veto players are actors with formal reactive powers whose consent is individually necessary but not sufficient to approve policy changes. Examples include the president and the parties necessary to form a congressional majority. Only when all institutional veto players agree on a policy proposal can the status quo be challenged (Tsebelis 2002). While this section focuses on legislative political parties, other veto players include parties in subnational governments, as well as different interest groups.

Political Parties. The Ecuadorian party system, the second most fragmented in Latin America after Brazil, is conventionally described as one of the least institutionalized in the region (Conaghan 1995; Mainwaring and Scully 1995a; Payne and others 2002; Jones 2005).[5] Party fragmentation and weak institutionalization in Ecuador are for the most part the combined result of ethnic and regional divisions in society enhanced by a permissive electoral system (Mejía Acosta 2004). Patterns of party competition reflect deeply rooted regional differences between the coastal and the Andean region. Although the 1979 Constitution set the rules for establishing a nationalized party system, Ecuadorian parties are also the most regionalized in Latin America (Jones and Mainwaring 2003). Until the late 1990s, the political space in Guayaquil and the coastal areas had been traditionally disputed between the rightist Social Christian Party (PSC) and the *caudillo*-based Ecuadorian Roldosista Party (PRE). In Quito and the Andean and Amazonic regions, the electoral space was disputed between the Christian Democratic Party (DP) and the Social Democratic

---

[5] Ecuador's mean institutionalization index is 1.43 out of a possible perfect score of 3.00, which falls below the regional average of 1.93.

Party (ID). The *Movimiento Pachakutik-Nuevo País* (MUPP) had entered the formal political arena, representing a highly mobilized sector of the indigenous population concentrated mostly in the jungle and mountain regions. Despite high levels of party fragmentation, four political parties (PSC, PRE, ID, and DP) "controlled" more than 65 percent of the legislative seats in the 1990s (Pachano 2004). These parties consolidated electoral bailiwicks, or *bastiones electorales*, meaning that such parties have prevented the entry of other parties in their arena, but in turn have not been able to leave their own territory to invade that of other parties (Pachano 2004). New populist and personalistic parties such as Lucio Gutiérrez' PSP and Alvaro Noboa's PRIAN increasingly challenged the space held by traditional parties after the 2002 presidential elections.

Institutional arrangements have constrained the power of party leaders to enforce unified voting among the rank and file (Mejía Acosta 2004). Party leaders had control over candidate selection, nomination, and allocation between 1979 and 1996, but legislative reelection was banned under the 1979 Constitution. Given the existence of term limits, party leaders could not directly influence the electoral future of party members. When reelection was allowed after 1996, the electoral system also changed to allow open list personalized voting, thus breaking the control of party leaders. A preliminary analysis indicates that since 1996, 27 percent of the legislators on average achieved immediate reelection and about 52 percent had some prior legislative experience—suggesting that Ecuador may be a case of "amateur legislators" progressively developing legislative careers (Jones and others 2002; Morgenstern 2002).

Based on patterns of electoral volatility and anecdotal evidence, Conaghan (1995) used the notion of "floating politicians and floating voters" to illustrate the loose connection between voters, politicians, and political parties. An alternative interpretation suggests that political parties and party leaders have played a greater role in the coalition-making process; parties can act as cartels that help solve collective action dilemmas in a highly competitive arena (Mejía Acosta 2004). Even if individual legislators were driven mainly by particularistic concerns, they were better off pledging some allegiance to a party leader empowered to advance the ambitions of the rank and file (Amorim Neto and Santos 2001; Mejía

Acosta 2004). Thus party leaders became key brokers during the coalition formation process. They bargained a set of clientelistic and particularistic payments from the president on behalf of their party members in exchange for delivering the party's votes to pass the president's agenda. From the presidential perspective, party leaders reduced transaction costs and offered a more efficient way of assembling coalitions rather than purchasing individual votes at retail prices. When party-switching occurred in Ecuador (an average of 10 percent of all congressional members between 1979 and 2002 changed parties each year), it was done by legislative "mavericks" who usually had short congressional careers, median or centrist party ideologies, and came from low-magnitude electoral districts. Empirical evidence indicates that party-switching incidents were associated with government tactics to "divide and conquer" the legislative opposition; nearly 80 percent of party-switching incidents between 1979 and 2002 came from opposition parties (Mejía Acosta 2004).[6] What is perhaps most interesting is that even after switching parties, most "independent" legislators often regrouped in proto-legislative organizations to empower an informal leader and collectively bargain new coalition payments with the executive. The formation of the Roldosista Group (GR) in 1982, the National Convergence Block in 1993, and the MIN in 2001 are relevant examples (Mejía Acosta 2004).

The Legislature. Ecuador has a unicameral congress formed by 100 deputies elected from 22 multimember districts. Until 1998, deputies were elected under a closed list system of proportional representation, but the 1998 Constitution adopted an open list procedure, encouraging candidates to compete against other parties as much as against other members of their own party (Pachano 1998).[7] The open list propor-

---

[6] Consistent with this argument, we find that higher party switching was associated with presidents who had minimal or no congressional support at the beginning of their mandates: Hurtado in 1982–83, Durán-Ballén in 1993–94, and Gustavo Noboa in 2000.

[7] Under the electoral law approved in March 2000, voters select individual members from party lists and each party pools the votes obtained by individual candidates. The total sum of votes obtained by the parties determines the distribution of seats according to the d'Hondt formula. In turn, seats are distributed within each party according to the number of votes obtained by the candidates.

Table 7.2. Bills Initiated and Approved, by Initiator and Type, Ecuador, August 1979–April 2004

Initiator period	Scope (percent)		Aim (percent)			
	National	Other[1]	Regulatory	Distributive	Other[2]	N
President, 1979–2002						
Bills initiated	64.8	35.2	83.5	13.8	2.6	491
Bills approved	62.4	37.6	84.1	13.4	2.5	157
Congress 1979–2002						
Bills initiated	45.0	55.0	73.5	24.7	1.8	5426
Bills approved	38.2	61.8	72.2	25.2	2.6	778
1979–96						
Bills initiated	40.7	59.3	67.2	29.5	3.3	3598
Bills approved	32.9	67.1	70.4	27.2	2.4	459
1996–98						
Bills initiated	45.8	54.2	74.8	22.8	2.4	663
Bills approved	40.5	59.5	74.8	23.9	1.2	163
1998–04						
Bills initiated	57.4	42.6	86.2	13.2	0.6	1165
Bills approved	51.3	48.7	81.4	17.9	0.6	156

Source: Authors, following Lowi (1964) and Taylor-Robinson and Diaz (1999).
[1] Regional, local, municipal, and individual
[2] Redistributive, foreign affairs, etc.

tional representation combined with relatively large districts (the average district magnitude is 4.5) would generally increase the incentives to cultivate the "personal vote" (Carey and Shugart 1995; Hallerberg and Marier 2004) in a system with a preexisting tradition of strong local and patronage politics (Conaghan 1995).[8] The fact that Ecuador has one of the most malapportioned legislatures in Latin America, with significant overrepresentation of rural vs. urban districts, should in theory reinforce the parochially oriented nature of its legislators (Cox and Morgenstern 2002; Snyder and Samuels 2001).

Table 7.2 shows the distribution of nearly 6,000 bills that were initiated by the president and congress between August 1979 and April 2004,

---

[8] Between 1979 and 1996, congressional seats were allocated using the largest remainders Hare system. Ecuador later adopted the d'Hondt procedure, but this technical change has not had any significant impact on the party system (Mejía Acosta 2002).

classified by initiator, outcome, policy scope, and the aim of the bill. Following Taylor-Robinson and Diaz (1999), we classify the scope of policies as nationwide or otherwise targeted at regions, sectors, municipalities, or individuals. Following Lowi (1964), we code the aim of each bill as regulatory, distributive, or other (redistributive, foreign affairs, and the like). Consistent with theoretical expectations, the presence of multiple partisan players has significantly obstructed the approval of legislation in Ecuador. Presidents obtained approval for 32 percent of the total number of bills they submitted to Congress (157 of 491), which is more than double the success rate of bills initiated by legislators: 14 percent (778 of 5,426).

Looking at the scope of bills, the data support the expectation that presidents are more likely to initiate nationally oriented legislation: 65 percent of the bills initiated by presidents between 1979 and 2002 had national implications, and so did 62 percent of the total number of bills initiated by the executive that were approved. In contrast, the share of legislation initiated by congress that sought to affect national constituencies represented 45 percent of bills, and 38 percent of the total number of congress-initiated approved bills. The seven-point gap can be explained as a position-taking strategy adopted by legislators who claim to initiate national legislation but are less willing to approve it. Despite this bias, the Ecuadorian congress does not fully conform to the expectation of being a locally oriented or parochial assembly. A brief comparison with the less-fragmented Paraguayan legislature illustrates this point more clearly: more than 60 percent of legislation initiated and approved by the Paraguayan congress between 1992 and 2003 sought to benefit individual, local, municipal, and regional constituencies, whereas less than 20 percent sought to affect national constituencies (see chapter 9, this volume).

Part of the explanation for the attention of Ecuadorian legislators to nationwide issues is that some legal reforms have limited their ability to initiate and distribute pork. A reform passed by plebiscite in 1996 banned legislators from handling budgetary allocations for provinces and limited discretionary spending. As a result, the percentage of nationwide bills initiated and passed by congress increased from 33 percent in 1979–96 to 41 percent in 1996–98, and the number of distributive bills declined from 27 to 24 percent. Further reforms approved after 1998 limited the legislators' ability to initiate spending laws that were not properly financed or budgeted. As a result, the percentage of nationwide bills increased to 51 percent in 1998–2002 and the percentage of distributive bills declined to 18 percent. An additional explanation for this pattern is that party leaders may have internalized the burden of obtaining resources for their rank-and-file's districts; thus particularistic concessions were not bargained for in a piecemeal form by individual legislators, but rather in wholesale agreements between the president and supporting party (see below).

A more refined interpretation of the data should explore the extent to which regulatory bills disguise legislators' attempts to seek patronage or ensure government spending for their constituencies. For example, some regulatory bills propose the creation of new municipalities or cantons (*cantones*) or state-sponsored institutions like universities, with the corresponding financial obligation (Araujo 1998). Others may seek direct subsidies or exemptions under generic titles that seek to promote better regulation of an industry or economic sector. From a political economy perspective, however, these regulatory bills are inefficient mechanisms for introducing or distributing pork to constituents since they increase the transaction costs of logrolling. Some conjectures about the political purpose of some regulatory bills are discussed in the next section.

Last-ditch Veto Players

"Last-ditch" veto players are actors with formal or informal reactive powers who are able to block the implementation of policy reforms. Institutional last-ditch veto players, such as the constitutional tribunal, have legal powers to stop the implementation of new policies. Noninstitutional players, such as unions or social movements, while lacking legal attributions, may have de facto capacity to block the execution and to force a reversion to the status quo. Some players, such as indigenous groups, may assume both roles. They act as a formal veto player in the national congress (Pachakutik), but may also be noninstitutional veto players if they choose to stage a street protest to oust an unpopular president (CONAIE). Noninstitutional veto players tend to be operationally "inefficient" because they typically need to shake up the whole policymaking process (even the constitutional order) in order to stop a particular policy from being adopted.

The Constitutional Tribunal. Until the late 1990s, judicial review was exercised by the supreme court (CSJ), which in turn was appointed by congress. But the constitutional reforms adopted by referendum in 1997 and by the 1998 national assembly aimed at giving the judiciary significant independence from political pressures. CSJ magistrates are now appointed for life by the CSJ itself. In theory, the new system was meant to reduce incentives for strategic behavior and politicization of the supreme court (Helmke 2002; Iaryczower, Spiller, and Tommasi 2002), while clearly separating constitutional issues from technical appeals (*casación*). The 1998 adoption of lifelong tenure for judges did not isolate the judiciary from political dynamics, but rather the opposite: it entrenched existing political alignments within the court. A severe institutional conflict was triggered in late 2004 when the PSC party (which had some influence in appointing existing supreme court judges), broke an implicit agreement with the government and launched a threat to impeach and investigate President Gutiérrez on allegations of corruption. In a sudden defensive alliance with the populist Roldosista Party (PRE) and the Alvaro Noboa Party (PRIAN), the government produced an unconstitutional "restructuring of the judiciary" that effectively dismissed 27 of 31 supreme court judges and replaced them with judges amenable to the new legislative coalition.[9] The congressional resolution violated the constitutional principle of judicial independence and triggered a political crisis that resulted in the ousting of President Gutiérrez four months later.

---

[9] The dismissal was made possible through an illegal interpretation of the twenty-fifth transitory provision in the 1998 Constitution. The constitution established that: "Government officials and other bureau members appointed by the National Congress since August 10, 1998 for a four-year term period, will remain in their offices until January 2003, by virtue of these constitutional provisions." However, this provision did not apply to the sitting judges, since they were elected in October 1997.

The constitutional tribunal (TC) was created in 1997 as the supreme entity of constitutional oversight and control independent of the three government branches.[10] Despite its formal creation in 1997, the TC became an effective mechanism of judicial review only in 2001, when an organic Law of Constitutional Control recognized its legal status.[11] According to the 1998 Constitution (Art. 275), the TC consists of nine members. While the nomination process allows for the participation of very diverse entities, it is congress that finally appoints TC members by simple majority. As expected, the election of TC magistrates reflects the contending political interests represented within the legislature. The prerogatives granted by the constitution strengthen the TC's roles of control and oversight in the political process, but also empower the TC as a last-ditch veto player with the capacity to stop and revert policy decisions.[12] The TC has the power to exercise judicial review over ordinary and organic laws, decrees, statutes, ordinances, regulations, and other resolutions issued by government institutions, and partially or completely suspend their effects (1998 Charter, Art. 276.1). The TC, however, does not have the authority to review the rulings of the judiciary in most cases.

The TC's crucial role in the policymaking process is also demonstrated by its capacity to rule on the constitutionality of bills during the legislative process (Art. 276.4 of the constitution and Art. 12.4 of the Constitutional Control Act). If the president justifies a veto arguing for the total or partial unconstitutionality of the bill, the bill is sent to the TC for a decisive ruling within 30 days. If the TC declares the full text of the bill unconstitutional, the bill is killed and congress cannot override the veto. If the TC upholds a partial unconstitutionality argument, the bill is returned to congress, which is forced to introduce amendments. If the

---

[10] The TC obtained constitutional status on February 13, 1997, but the law of constitutional control that specified the roles and prerogatives of the TC was enacted on July 2 of that same year.

[11] Legislative Resolution No. 22-050, published in the R.O. No. 280, March 8, 2001.

[12] The roles and attributions of the TC are contained in the Political Constitution, the Law of Constitutional Control, and indirectly in other municipal, provincial, and electoral legislation.

TC rejects the president's position, congress can directly publish the law in the Official Registry (Art. 154 of the 1998 Constitution).

Noninstitutional Veto Players. Levels of popular mobilization and protest have grown considerably since the early 1990s. According to a study conducted by the Centro Andino de Acción Popular (CAAP), the number of "social conflicts" (most of them corresponding to strikes and episodes of popular protest) grew progressively from 84 in 1985 to 118 in 1990, and from 371 in 1995 to 641 in 2000. The fall of the Bucaram, Mahuad, and Gutiérrez administrations in 1997, 2000, and 2005, respectively, illustrate the effects of increasing levels of popular mobilization; protests can significantly compromise government stability while reversing policy changes. That is, the probability of a government collapse grew in the 1990s, while the executive branch's ability to impose unilateral policy reforms declined considerably.

Part of this trend can be explained by the organization and expansion of the Confederation of Indigenous Nations of Ecuador, CONAIE (Yashar 1998). Yet, although CONAIE had a prominent role in organizing the protests that led to the demise of the Bucaram and Mahuad administrations, it would be misleading to attribute the increase in social unrest only to the indigenous movement. We compared the classification of social conflicts done by CAAP for four years: 1987 (a tense year for the Febres Cordero government), 1990 (a relatively quiet midterm year for the Borja administration), 1997 (the year of the fall of President Bucaram), and 2000 (the collapse of the Mahuad administration). Although the percentage of events coded as being strictly related to the indigenous movement has grown over time (0 percent in 1987, 2.5 percent in 1990, 4.0 percent in 1997, and 10.5 percent in 2000), those events still represented a minority of all conflicts. Even including other categories that may be indirectly related to CONAIE-led mobilizations (peasant, partisan, and civic-regional), these conflicts account for only about one-fourth to one-third of all protests during this period. It is clear that other factors have contributed to the patterns of popular protest, including a constantly high level of mobilization among state workers (representing one-fourth to one-third of all conflicts), increasing activation of labor conflict in the private sector (from less than 1 percent of all conflicts in 1987 to 15 percent in 2000), and a growing pattern of urban protest (from 9 percent of all conflicts in 1987 to 13 percent in 2000).

The Ecuadorian Policymaking Process (PMP)

The Ecuadorian PMP is best understood as a permanent conflict between decisive players with strong agenda-setting powers who seek to impose their policy preferences, and a large number of veto players who exert their ideological, regional, and ethnic interests into the policymaking progress. The interaction between the goals and ambitions of those actors has produced a conflictive pattern of rigid policymaking punctuated by policy volatility. This section illustrates each policy track in more detail. The pattern of policy rigidity is expected when the executive brings policy options to congress, but legislators' incentives to form policy coalitions with the government—usually cemented around clientelistic payments—rapidly erode as new elections approach. Deadlock results from the costly process of assembling multiparty coalitions. In policy areas where decision making requires enhanced technical expertise or a quick response from policymakers, the government may accomplish decisive action by delegating authority to a specialized agency, but the duration of resulting policies becomes contingent on the agencies' political survival. In Ecuador, "last-ditch" veto players may challenge or reverse policy decisions taken at the end of either path.

Policy Rigidity: Making Coalitions with Multiple Partisan Players

Making policy coalitions with multiple actors who pursue conflicting ambitions and act within short-term horizons requires exceptional bargaining skills. On the one hand, presidents control ample political and economic resources in a highly fragmented and competitive environment. Thus presidents become de facto agenda setters and coalition formers. On the other hand, this ample set of bargaining tools is insufficient to ensure long-term cooperation, for two main reasons. First, in the presence of presidential term limits, even attractive "currencies" quickly depreciate with the proximity of new elections. Second, the political liability of being associated with the government (which usually has declining levels of popularity) exceeds the expected benefits of cooperation. Political parties prefer to make short-lived and content-specific coalitions to preserve an image of political independence vis-à-vis their voters (Mejía Acosta 2006). The combined effect of multiple partisan players with generally short-term horizons helps explain the congressional bias toward deadlock or policy rigidity.

Coalition Incentives. Ecuadorian presidents enjoy a wide range of constitutional instruments and nonconstitutional mechanisms to entice legislative cooperation and promote their policy agendas. In addition to their previously discussed legislative powers, presidents can appoint and dismiss cabinet members, provincial governors, and some diplomatic postings; grant judiciary pardons; authorize government contracts; and (up until 1995) make discretionary use of off-budget allocations. The allocation of particularistic and discretionary currencies in the form of pork and patronage tends to prevail over the negotiation of programmatic and more transparent agreements around policy concessions or ministerial offices. In general, particularistic concessions are often used to craft "wholesale" agreements between the government and political parties (Mejía Acosta 2004). As explained earlier, party leaders—not individual legislators, as commonly believed—are the main protagonists in the coalition-making game. Party leaders significantly reduce transaction costs for the president since they have a better understanding of the policy preferences and demands of individual legislators. The third section also presented evidence to support the notion that legislative players, contrary to the conventional understanding of Ecuadorian politics, do not appear to initiate more distributive or pork-oriented legislation. In a context of strong party leaders, individual legislators do not need to initiate particularistic legislation since their leaders have a better chance to broker "wholesale" legislative agreements with the president and obtain concessions, jobs, and other patronage to reward the loyalty of legislators, their families, and political cronies. In exchange, individual legislators commit themselves to vote along party lines and thus, at least for a while, support the president's agenda.

Although leadership styles vary widely from one party to the next, the logic remains the same: party leaders are the providers of coalition benefits. Thus strong representatives with unchallenged party leadership, such as the case of the PSC, may impose tighter cooperation agreements on the president to protect or benefit their regional constituencies or supporting interest groups. For example, the PSC lent early support to narrow fiscal reforms during the early phase of the Mahuad administration in exchange for stalling customs reforms (a strong source of patronage for coastal bailiwicks) and stopping other banking reforms (which would have affected the PSC's business group supporters). Other parties, such as the center populist PRE, lent legislative support in exchange for a more assorted package of benefits that included cabinet positions, policy concessions, pork, and patronage. Parties on the left, such as Izquierda Democrática, or Democracia Popular, were willing to pass specific fiscal reforms (taxing luxury automobiles) as long as such revenues were earmarked in favor of municipal governments. More radical left parties such as Pachakutik or MPD may be more interested in trading legislative votes in exchange for pork and patronage for their highly visible constituencies: indigenous groups and some labor unions.

Coalition Duration. Party leaders broker agreements between the president and the rank and file, providing reliable votes for the president and distributing benefits for the rank and file. But party leaders in Ecuador are wary of being identified as *gobiernistas*, or supporters of the government agenda vis-à-vis the public and other political parties—especially if they feel that policy failure may become a liability for the party's ambitions in the next election. The eroding value of coalition currencies undermined the duration and credibility of policy agreements. Until 1996 legislators were not able to reap the electoral benefits of government collaboration because they were banned from immediate reelection. By the time term limits were lifted after 1996, an earlier reform prevented presidents and legislators from using budgetary allocations to secure political support, thus eliminating coalition currencies needed to enable policy change. The net result was the continued policy deadlock before and after these reforms.

The perception of policy immobility or deadlock is reflected in falling rates of presidential popularity, which in turn further diminish the incentives of political parties to be part of the government coalition in congress (Mejía Acosta 2004). Figure 7.1 compares the evolution of net presidential approval rates (monthly averages for Quito and Guayaquil) and the size of the formal presidential coalition in congress for the average administration between 1984 and 2002.[13] The formal coalition is defined as the legislative bloc that appoints the president of congress at the beginning of each legislative year (in the month of August) and it is assumed to be stable over the next twelve months.[14]

At the beginning of the period, opposition parties are likely to accept and acknowledge some form of government cooperation, while presidents still enjoy favorable or honeymoon popularity ratings, which occur on average during the first five to six months in office. When net popularity ratings are negative, the political liabilities of voting with the president exceed the expected benefits of government cooperation. At that point, party coalitions often adopt the form of clandestine alliances or ghost coalitions, where ad hoc agreements or "policy coincidences" take place between the government and parties from diverse affiliations, but any programmatic or long-term commitment is systematically denied (Mejía Acosta 2004). The absence of voting records in the Ecuadorian congress facilitated this informal mechanism of coalition formation. The resilience of ghost coalitions as a conventional legislative practice is the more remarkable since presidents and legislators from distinct political parties and tendencies have acknowledged their existence since the

---

[13] The boost in presidential approval rates observed during months 31 to 36 is partly an artifact of the idiosyncratic escalation of President Durán Ballén's approval rating to 76 percent in February 1995. But even excluding the Durán Ballén administration, typical approval rates rise from −27 percent in month 27 to +2 percent in month 36, and drop back to −46 percent by month 39.

[14] When the government party is not included among the parties that voted for the president of congress, the coding assumes that the president does not have formal legislative partners beyond his own party.

Figure 7.1. Evolution of Presidential Approval Rates and the President's Coalition in Congress over the Term, Ecuador, 1984–2002 (monthly averages)

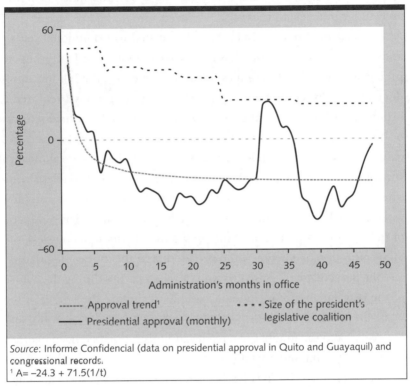

Source: Informe Confidencial (data on presidential approval in Quito and Guayaquil) and congressional records.
[1] A= –24.3 + 71.5(1/t)

early 1980s (Mills 1984; Grindle and Thoumi 1993; Burbano de Lara and Rowland García 1998). Often, legislative agreements were disguised under a cloud of heavy criticism against the president with the purpose of projecting an image of political chastity or independence vis-à-vis other parties and potential voters.

Coalition Formation and Legislative Success. To test some of our assumptions about the policymaking process in Ecuador, we developed a database with all the legislative bills initiated between 1979 (the inauguration of the Roldós administration) and 2003 (the end of the Noboa administration). The database contains 476 bills initiated by the executive, 5,161 bills initiated by the members of congress, 58 bills initiated by other institutions, and 209 bills of unknown origin, for a total of 5,904 bills. Although we suspect that most of the unidentified bills were initiated in congress, the latter 267 cases have been excluded from the analysis for practical purposes.

For each bill, we coded key variables related to institutional setting and the nature of the policy issue at stake. Among the first group of predictors was a set of dummies to capture whether: the bill was introduced by the executive as an "urgent" matter; the proposal required a two-thirds majority for its approval (in the case of constitutional reforms or organic laws); the bill was introduced after 1998 (when the executive gained additional constitutional powers); and legislators were allowed to run for reelection. In addition, we introduced a series of variables to capture the political environment during the legislative year (August–July) when the bill was introduced. These included the size (share of seats) of the president's party and of the president's coalition in congress, the ideological distance between the president and the average legislator,[15] and the percentage of legislators who switched parties during the course of the year. Finally, we included a variable to capture the length of the legislative term for the provincial deputies (anywhere between two and five years), and the number of days the administration had been in office at the time the bill was introduced.

For the characterization of policy issues, we employed a set of dummies to capture Lowi's (1964) typology of policy issues (distributive, redistributive, or regulatory) and Taylor-Robinson and Diaz's (1999) classification of policy levels (individual, municipal, public or private sectors, regional, national). In addition, we coded policy areas presumed to follow distinctive patterns: proposals to raise salaries, proposals to raise taxes, and proposals to create new municipalities or cantons—which Araujo identified as a disguised form of distributive politics (Araujo 1998).

Table 7.3 presents the results of the analysis. Equation 7.1 models the probability that a bill is initiated by the executive (as opposed to congress, the baseline category). The evidence suggests that the presi-

---

[15] Measured as the distance between the left-right location of the president and the mean left-right position of congress, using Coppedge's (1998) five-point scale.

Table 7.3. Initiation and Approval of Bills (Logistic Regression), Ecuador

Predictors	Equation 7.1. Initiation by the executive		Equation 7.2. Approval of bills initiated by the executive	
	Coeff.	S.E.	Coeff.	S.E.
Urgent bill			0.58**	–0.28
Post 1998	–0.09	–0.38	3.78***	–0.94
Bill requires 2/3	–0.6**	–0.25	–0.39	–0.57
Size president's party	–0.01	0	–0.02	–0.01
Size president's coalition	0.02***	0	–0.01	–0.01
Ideological distance	0	0	–0.03***	–0.01
Party switching (year)	0.05***	–0.01	–0.01	–0.02
Administration's days in office	0*	0	0	0
Length of legislative term	0	–0.08	–1.12***	–0.22
Legislative reelection	–0.23	–0.2	0.26	–0.43
N	5631		476	

Source: Authors
Note: Logistic regression coefficients (standard errors). DV in equation 7.1 is initiation by the executive (as opposed to congress). DV in equations 7.2 and 7.3 is bill was approved and signed into law. Baseline category is nationwide bills of regulatory intent (not seeking to raise taxes or salaries).
*Significant at .1 level **Significant at .05 level ***Significant at .01 level

dent is more likely to dominate the legislative agenda when his coalition is larger and when congressional parties break down (as switchers are likely to join the president's camp).[16] A 10 percent increase in the size of the president's coalition increases the odds of the president initiating a bill by 17 percent, while an additional 10 percent of party switchers expands the odds of presidential initiation by 73 percent. There is limited evidence that the president is more willing to initiate bills toward the end of his term, but this finding should be interpreted carefully. Because the size of the president's coalition tends to decline as the end of the term approaches, this finding reflects only the propensity of the

---

[16] The sign of the coefficient for party switching was unstable in different model specifications, and thus should be interpreted with caution.

executive to initiate proposals after controlling for the negative effects of a vanishing legislative coalition.[17] Regarding policy issues, the president is less likely to initiate distributive, individual, municipal, private sector, and regional bills than congress, but is more likely to propose policies related to salaries, taxes, and the public sector.

Equation 7.2 reflects the odds of executive-initiated bills ultimately becoming law. The results indicate that, in general, the formal agenda-setting powers of the president do play an important role at the approval stage, but legislative success rates overall remain low when compared to other countries. The president's ability to get bills passed is boosted by his urgency powers, which transform his proposal into the new reversionary point. Other things being equal, the odds of an urgent bill being approved increase by 78 percent.[18]

With regard to partisan powers, while a larger legislative coalition gives the president more confidence to initiate bills, the size of the coalition in and by itself is not sufficient to guarantee their approval. The main partisan factor driving the approval stage is the ideological distance between the president's program and the mean legislator in congress (see Table 7.4). In other terms, the formation of formal coalitions does not prevent the operation of veto players if the executive's proposals are too distant from the legislators' preferences.

The previous analysis of the policymaking process emphasizes that minority presidents in Ecuador sought policy changes by making significant policy concessions and distributing rewards (nonlegislative powers) to help cement congressional support, or using agenda-setting prerogatives (legislative powers) to bypass congressional demands and unilaterally imposing their preferred outcomes. In the first scenario, the high transaction costs of overcoming multiple players with short-term horizons outweighed the expected benefit of approved reforms, thus making the PMP highly inefficient. In the second scenario, the use of

---

[17] The correlation between days in office and size of the coalition is −.52 (significant at 0.001 level).

[18] The odds of presidential bills—urgent and ordinary—being approved after 1998 increased by 439 percent, but this figure should be interpreted with caution, since the actual probability depends on the values of other independent variables.

Table 7.4. Initiation and Approval of Bills (Logistic Regression), Ecuador

Predictors	Equation 7.1. Initiation by the executive		Approval of bills initiated by Equation 7.2. Executive		Equation 7.3. Congress	
	Coeff.	S.E.	Coeff.	S.E.	Coeff.	S.E.
Xs						
Urgent bill			0.58**	−0.28		
Post 1998	−0.09	−0.38	3.78***	−0.94	0.84**	−0.33
Bill requires 2/3	−0.6**	−0.25	−0.39	−0.57	−0.7***	−0.24
Size president's party	−0.01	0	−0.02	−0.01	−0.01**	0
Size president's coalition	0.02***	0	−0.01	−0.01	0	0
Ideological distance	0	0	−0.03***	−0.01	0	0
Party switching (year)	0.05***	−0.01	−0.01	−0.02	0	−0.01
Administration's days in office	0*	0	0	0	0***	0
Length of legislative term	0	−0.08	−1.12***	−0.22	−0.45***	−0.08
Legislative reelection	−0.23	−0.2	0.26	−0.43	0.95***	−0.15
Zs						
Distributive bill	−0.59***	−0.17	0.05	−0.37	−0.09	−0.11
Redistributive bill	−0.45	−0.53	6.37	−22.26	−0.6*	−0.35
Individual-level bill	−2.39***	−0.46	0.21	−0.95	0.73***	−0.14
Municipal-level bill	−1.67***	−0.31	0.19	−0.64	0.05	−0.15
Public sector bill	0.24*	−0.13	−0.18	−0.27	−0.15	−0.13
Private sector bill	−0.56***	−0.17	0.51	−0.42	−0.13	−0.14
Regional bill	−1.71***	−0.29	0.67	−0.59	0.28**	−0.13
Salary-raising bill	1.29**	−0.53	−5.85	−22.25	−0.13	−0.77
Tax-raising bill	1.71***	−0.33	0.49	−0.72	−1.91*	−1.01
Canton creation bill	−1.25	−0.77	6.64	−15.74	1.54***	−0.2
Constant	−2.92***	−0.31	2.83***	−0.79	−1.25***	−0.27
Nagelkerke R^2	0.162		0.292		0.112	
N	5631		476		5155	

Source: Authors

Note: Logistic regression coefficients (standard errors). DV in equation 7.1 is initiation by the executive (as opposed to congress). DV in equations 7.2 and 7.3 is bill was approved and signed into law. Baseline category for Zs is nationwide bills of regulatory intent (not seeking to raise taxes or salaries).

*Significant at .1 level **Significant at .05 level ***Significant at .01 level presidential decree authority to impose policy change (including stronger decree and veto powers after 1998) remained insufficient to alter the rigid nature of the legislative PMP because of the constitutional impediment to issuing more than one decree a month. The consequences of this observed rigidity are discussed in the case study on the workings of the fiscal PMP in the fourth section.

Policy Adaptability and Volatility: The Logic of Bureaucratic Delegation

In policy areas where decision making requires enhanced technical expertise or a quick response from policymakers, the policymaking process traditionally has delegated power to the technocracy. The transfer of decision-making authority to a bureaucratic agency solves the government's dilemma of collective action around complex or controversial regulatory processes and allows for policy decisiveness. Confronted with an unexpected shock, a technical bureaucracy has the authority to bypass veto players and adjust the existing policies accordingly. A critical factor to determine is who controls the agenda of the bureaucratic agent. The agency could be endowed with executive autonomy, or it could remain closely related to it. Legislators may also interfere with the agency so that they can preserve indirect control over the decision-making process. In the last two cases, the bureaucracy may be vulnerable to political shocks. For instance, the direction of the policy may change following the electoral cycle, or it may follow every change in the composition of the government. In this context, high decisiveness may ultimately lead to policy volatility. In the case of a highly independent agency that features high technical capacity, it may allow for a desirable pattern that combines some policy stability (nonresponsiveness to political shocks) with policy adaptability (responsiveness to economic shocks). If technical capacity is low, however, the result may be a new form of volatility, in which bureaucrats experiment with new policy instruments or policy fads every time the previous policy fails.

An example of delegation as a formal feature of the policymaking process can be found in the process by which monetary policy is adopted in Ecuador. Until 1998, the making of monetary policy in Ecuador had been the domain of the board of the central bank (called the monetary board), which consisted of seven members: a chairman appointed directly by the president (often an active commercial banker himself), two members appointed by private business associations, one member appointed by the association of bankers, two members appointed by the government, and the minister of finance. The direct involvement of private and technical actors was a deliberate attempt by the executive to isolate the decision-making process from political interference. But it also allowed for conflicts of interest, as there were no legal requirements that board members should quit their responsibilities in the private sector, or that they should sell their shares in the private banks (Jácome 2004). For more than a decade after the transition to democracy (1979–92), the exchange rate policies were characterized by a large amount of volatility, partly due to changes in government administrations and to adjustments for shocks. In this period, six different exchange rate regimes were implemented over three administrations. During this time, the average president of the monetary board lasted for 13 months.

The 1998 constitutional reform gave the central bank not only operational independence, but also political independence. The corporate representatives on the monetary board were replaced by a board of directors whose members were full-time technocrats, nominated by the president and appointed by congress, who could not hold shares in any financial institution in the private sector. The experiment of extreme delegation was short-lived. The 1999 fiscal and banking crisis undermined the trust and credibility of some regional business elites in the central bank's ability to remain autonomous from regional and political interests. In the eyes of Guayaquilean political and economic elites, the monetary authorities based in the Sierra (where Quito is located) had failed to aid the financial institutions on the coast—where the banking crisis was overwhelmingly focused—and were partly responsible for their collapse.[19] We argue that the process of eroding confidence in monetary

---

[19] The mayor of Guayaquil at the time (and former president), León Febres Cordero, repeatedly declared that he would "rise-up" the coast against the "centralism of Quito"

authorities accelerated the adoption of dollarization and the de facto termination of exchange rate regimes.

Dollarization, adopted in January 2000 and maintained by subsequent administrations since, is an extreme example of stabilizing the policy process. Its adoption was paradoxically supported by Guayaquil elites, contradicting at first sight the expected pro-exporter bias of the coastal region. According to Ms. Joyce de Ginatta—chairperson of the Guayas Chamber of Small Industries (*Cámara de la Pequeña Industria del Guayas*, CPIG)—dollarization helped reduce uncertainty and volatility by completely renouncing exchange rate policy because it relied less on strong, credible institutions than a fixed exchange-rate regime such as convertibility would have, and it required fewer legal reforms (in the fiscal sector and labor markets) for effective implementation. The stabilizing effects of dollarization extended to other spheres of the policymaking process. The tenure of the president of the board of the central bank decreased by about 25 percent, to an average duration of 16.5 months. And while the level of the exchange rate depreciated sharply during the crisis, it recovered after 2001 to pre-crisis levels.

Ecuador's experience with monetary policy illustrates how decisive players created an alternative policymaking track (the monetary board) to bypass institutional vetoes and produce swift policy changes. When decisive actors lose confidence in policy delegation (that is, they do not trust the autonomous agency), they may seek to redress the delegated powers and redefine the role of the agencies (through rigid responses such as dollarization).

Case Study: Fiscal Policy

The analysis of fiscal policies offers an exceptional opportunity to illustrate the two proposed policymaking paths in Ecuador. When policy

---

if those banks were closed. Although his threats effectively delayed intervention from the banking superintendence and corrective prudential measures were not implemented, eventually all the protected institutions failed anyway (Arteta and Hurtado 2002).

reforms are introduced to the legislative arena (as they were with the 2001 tax reform), this chapter shows a powerful executive who pushes reforms through decree and veto powers to compensate for the lack of congressional support. It also shows the difficulty of forming credible coalitions with legislators in the long run. Finally, it illustrates the role of the constitutional tribunal as a last-ditch veto player. The resulting outcome is a pattern of policy rigidity or inadequate responsiveness to proposed reforms. The alternative path of empowering a decisive player by means of bureaucratic delegation can produce decisive policy changes, but these are not stable over time (policy volatility). This is the case of revenue collection after the creation of a tax revenue agency (SRI) in 1997. The SRI's success in producing larger than expected tax collection for several years in a row is partly explained by the political isolation of its director, Elsa de Mena, and the bureaucracy's high technical capacity. Policy success occurred in this arena until the executive could no longer isolate the SRI from the political consequences of legislative coalitions. This section briefly outlines the main features of the fiscal policymaking process in Ecuador, and discusses resulting policy outcomes.

The Fiscal PMP

For the most part, fiscal policies are discussed in the congressional arena, where the conflicting interests and strengths of multiple veto players produce a strong bias in favor of the status quo. Although presidents have moderately high agenda-setting powers in the budget-making process, they had limited success in correcting fiscal imbalances. Presidents had a limited capacity to reduce government expenditures because nearly 85 percent of the spending budget was earmarked, and discretionary funds were used to secure political support from the opposition. In addition, reforms attempting to increase tax revenues were often blocked or downsized by congressional majorities who opposed systematic tax increases, and additional revenues generated by moderate tax reforms were insufficient, given the costs of cementing political coalitions.

The rigidity of the policymaking process became more evident in the presence of exogenous shocks that had a direct and severe impact on fiscal performance. Ecuador faced armed conflicts with Peru in 1981 and 1995, coastal floods in 1983 and 1997, droughts in 1995, earthquakes in 1987, and sudden changes in oil revenues (whether due to the breaking of oil pipelines in 1987 and 1999 or the sudden fall of international crude prices in 1986 and 1999).

Alternatively, presidents initiated fiscal reforms by concentrating decision-making authority and unilaterally adopting fiscal discipline measures (or *paquetazos*) to increase the prices of public goods and utilities or to reduce government subsidies and public spending. These reform initiatives were usually opposed and sometimes reversed following popular protests on the street, thus creating a cycle of policy volatility. It was not until the creation of an autonomous tax authority (SRI) in 1997 that presidents were able to break the status quo bias and effectively improve tax collection, especially after 2000.

The adoption of fiscal policies neatly illustrates how all the relevant features of the Ecuadorian PMP interact. A strong agenda-setting player lacks the congressional support to pass much-needed fiscal reforms; the resulting policy rigidity comes in the form of insufficient government revenues and earmarked expenditures. A decisive player (SRI) may be endowed with significant capacity to bypass veto players and introduce policy changes. In the end, however, last-ditch veto players retain the power to stall or revert unwanted outcomes.

Ecuadorian budget institutions were intentionally designed to prevent unbalanced public spending by giving greater decision-making authority to the president and the finance minister. In particular, the drafting process is mostly in the hands of the finance minister, whose authority on budgetary issues is considerably greater than that of the spending ministers. In terms of the interbranch bargaining process, the executive also has the upper hand. The constitution grants presidents the exclusive prerogative to initiate the budget process, and congress has 90 days to amend the budget proposal and approve it in a single debate (Article 258). In case of legislative inactivity, the president's budget enters into effect. Ecuadorian presidents also have executive decree authority (through economic urgency bills). Moreover, presidents can exert conditional agenda-setting power through the use of a line item veto (especially after 1998), which can be overridden only with a qualified majority of two-thirds of its members.

Moreover, Ecuador's budget-making framework includes legal provisions mandating that all new expenditures have proper financing: congress can pass only those amendments that do not increase the deficit or spending unless approved by the government. Finally, the executive is legally empowered to unilaterally cut spending after the budget has been approved when revenues are lower than projected. However, there are no borrowing constraints if there is a revenue shortfall, and the central government frequently assumes debt (and also nonguaranteed debt) originally contracted by other public agencies.

Despite these strong presidential powers, the fragmented nature of political representation in the Ecuadorian legislature has had the effect of giving these budget institutions a strong status quo bias. Presidents had the prerogative to propose legislation, but without being able to adopt their own policies, opposition forces would often reject those initiatives altogether. The extent of legislative opposition to fiscal adjustment can be explained by the electoral motivations of legislators. As discussed above, the permissive proportional representation electoral system favored the overrepresentation of rural areas. Moreover, the elimination of national deputies in 1998, coupled with the adoption of an open list proportional representation rule, reinforced the regional nature of the Ecuadorian congress. Therefore, election-minded party leaders had few incentives to adopt fiscal reforms, especially when they perceived that disaffected voters would punish their party in the next election. As a result, the combination of the particular features of the fiscal PMP and Ecuador's overall PMP often led to policy rigidity rather than more adaptable outcomes.

The Workings of the Fiscal PMP

Given the difficulty of enacting statutory policy changes, in order to cope with recurrent, adverse exogenous shocks, virtually every president since Ecuador's return to democracy—with the exception of President Roldós (1979–81)—has enacted austerity packages aiming at generating additional revenues and cutting government expenditures. As Jácome (2004, p. 7) points out, consecutive presidents since 1980 "brought in fiscal adjustment policies, but typically they were followed by periods of spending relaxation," plunging the country into a vicious cycle of insufficient reforms. This assessment is a good characterization of how the overall characteristics of Ecuador's political landscape affect the workings of the fiscal PMP and the nature of the country's fiscal policies: presidents' efforts to curtail expenditures encountered serious difficulties; meanwhile, generating new revenues by reforming taxing laws also seemed an elusive task.

On the spending side, earmarked expenditures, salaries (which are sort of an entitlement and thus very hard to reduce), pensions, and interest payments made fiscal adjustment very difficult. Moreover, the lack of change created a perverse inertia effect in which public expenditures tended to rise. In particular, increases in public sector wages and public-debt interest payments were responsible for the rapid increase in government expenditures (Araujo 1998; Jácome 2004). Between 1993 and 1996, for instance, current expenditures amounted to nearly 79 percent of total government expenditures; the wage bill accounted for 38 percent and debt interest payments represented 21 percent (Araujo 1998). Additionally, current expenditure was highly vulnerable to the performance of the exchange rate, given that most of the public debt was denominated in dollars.

The Ecuadorian congress played a key role in the rise of government expenditures by passing unfinanced spending laws—despite constitutional amendments designed to prevent this practice (Araujo 1998). According to Araujo, congressional intervention on the budgetary process increased the projected expenditures up to 10 percent of the original allocation. Even after the 1994 constitutional reform abolished congress's ability to alter budgetary allocations, legislators found alternative ways to introduce budget items that allowed for discretionary and clientelistic spending in the form of special transfers, off-budget items, and global allocations. Additionally, the legislative process reinforced the private regardedness of fiscal policies, as Araujo (1998) shows in a detailed description. Her study outlines the role of congress in passing bills intended to benefit specific interest groups, regions, and economic sectors. Focusing on the bills that passed through congress in the 1995–96 legislative period, Araujo found that 48 percent of bills generated new expenditures. These bills included the creation of new administrative units (*cantones*), lifetime pensions, creation of new projects and institutions, public works, forgiveness of debts, and government compensation.

Earmarking revenues was a common strategy devised to protect budgetary allocations from political pressures while granting intertemporal allocation of resources to coalition members. According to Jácome (2004), more than 50 percent of total revenues were earmarked in the 1990s. Most of the earmarking was established at the level of the constitution, such as the 1979 allocation of 30 percent of government revenues for education, or the allocation of 15 percent of revenues for local governments in the late 1990s. Not only did this practice curtail much of the executive's bargaining power, but the earmarked expenditures' constitutional status also shielded those items from political pressures, unless a political coalition could gather the required two-thirds majority for reform.

This mechanism, however, reinforced the rigidity of fiscal instruments. Earmarking reflected the powerful lobbying of interest groups such as the army, public sector unions, and local governments at a particular point in time. It was primarily focused on the redistribution of oil revenues. The strategy of hard-wiring budgetary allocations became counterproductive because, as was discussed above, legislative coalitions in Ecuador tend to be very ephemeral, so the use of long-term payments to secure "spot" support was highly inefficient. On the revenue side, the presence of multiple legislative players operating with short-term horizons also created significant obstacles to approving fiscal reforms and creating additional fiscal income. Ad hoc congressional majorities were often reluctant to pass reforms intended to affect broader political constituencies, such as income or consumption taxes.

For most of the 1980s and into the 1990s, Ecuador's revenue structure was heavily dependent on oil-related revenues from exports and local consumption. In some years, oil revenues accounted for 50 percent and even 70 percent of total government revenues. This dependence on the vagaries of international oil prices made for volatile revenue inflows

(Jácome 2004). Non-oil revenues, on the other hand, could not compensate for the mounting pressure of the slow decline of oil revenues on the fiscal balance, despite several attempts at reform. In fact, tax policies in Ecuador did not change a lot after 1991, despite the steady increase of fiscal deficits and falling oil prices in the early 1990s. The increase in non-oil revenues is mostly explained by a significant increase in "special" taxes. These taxes rose from 3.1 percent of GDP in 1992 to 4.4 percent of GDP in 1995, and included a special luxury tax approved during the 1995 armed conflict, and a 1 percent tax on financial transactions approved in 1998 with the support of the Social Christian Party (PSC).

These "quick fix" taxes were highly distortionary, and they may have generated perverse and destabilizing effects (Jácome 2004). The 1 percent tax on financial transactions imposed negative effects on the banking system's liquidity by discouraging the public's deposits/withdrawals and leading to the eventual closure of several small and medium banks. Taxing financial transactions also depressed the demand for money by heightening the public's preference for cash. Hence the tax reform contributed to the 1999 banking crisis (Jácome 2004).

There were other instances in which reforms were quite volatile, too. In most of these cases, presidents were able to make policy reforms that sought to enhance the government's revenues. However, because it was constrained by pressure from organized political groups and social organizations, the government repeatedly reversed fiscal adjustment decisions (Jacome 2004). The 2001 tax reform is a case in point. In the spring of that year, President Gustavo Noboa submitted a package of IMF-required fiscal reforms to congress to compensate for a $600 million deficit left by the year's unbalanced budget. The proposal—which was originally introduced as an economic urgency bill in the late 1990s—had two main components: to raise the VAT from 12 to 15 percent, eliminating a series of 40 smaller taxes and reducing the income tax; and to allow the Internal Revenue Service (SRI) to absorb the Customs Administration (CAE), in order to curb tax evasions from imports.

With the exception of a legislative group made up of independent legislators (MIN), the proposed bill stood little chance of success in a congress where President Noboa himself lacked party representation.

During the bargaining process, government officials considered granting some political incentives to pass the reform, including particularistic concessions, budgetary transfers to municipalities (2 points of VAT), tapping alternative sources of revenue, and making administrative reforms. However, negotiations proved fruitless as a congressional supermajority of 86 votes denied the government's proposed reform. On March 31, President Noboa used his veto powers to partially block congressional amendments, thus forcing congress to seek a two-thirds override majority if it wanted to prevail. A week later, the override motion fell short by six votes, thus turning the president's bill into law.

Press accounts accused government officials of buying votes from those pivotal players in exchange for particularistic rewards, including public works, fast-track government loans, and distribution of jobs to family and cronies (including both a governorship and the position of health minister for relatives of a PRE-El Oro deputy, Fulton Serrano). Angry party leaders presented a motion of unconstitutionality before the constitutional tribunal, which ruled in favor of the congressional majority a few weeks later, thus voiding the attempt at fiscal reform.

As this example illustrates, statutory implementation of tax reforms in Ecuador has proven to be very difficult. The adoption of other tax-related measures, though, has shown a greater degree of resoluteness. In particular, as argued earlier in this chapter, empowering a decisive player by means of bureaucratic delegation can enhance the player's policymaking capabilities. In the case of fiscal policy, delegating tax collection to a bureaucratic agency did improve fiscal performance. Even though the tax laws are still plagued by the problems discussed above, the existence of a competent tax collection agency ensures that whatever has to be collected is collected effectively (as opposed to no collection at all).

The creation of the Internal Revenue Service (SRI) in 1997 has contributed to an almost twofold increase in income from non-oil-related revenues. Since its operational restructuring in September 1998, the SRI increased revenue collection by 5.1 points of GDP, an 86 percent increase in revenue collection (Arteta 2003). For example, the increased revenues from VAT rose from 6.0 percent of GDP in the 1993–97 period to 11.1 percent of GDP in the 2000–04 period alone (110 percent), and exceeded the nominal increase in the VAT rate from 10 to 12 percent (20 percent). Enhanced tax collection certainly played a major role in bringing fiscal surpluses to Ecuador for four years in a row since 2000.

A key to the agency's success was the decisive role played by SRI's director Elsa de Mena, who enjoyed legal and actual independence from political influence. Acting in a contentious political environment, perhaps her most noteworthy political achievement is to have outlasted three Ecuadorian presidents between 1998 and 2004. Her committed nonpartisanship, coupled with the help of highly technical staff, helps explain her policy resoluteness. In 2004, she was fired. Her dismissal came as the result of the congressional interest in maintaining an inefficient tax authority, and the governments' need for continued political support in congress.

Beyond Delegation and Deadlock

What factors can explain the paradoxical coexistence of policy volatility and policy rigidity? The chapter has shown that the Ecuadorian policymaking process is the combined result of constitutionally strong, severely fragmented, and highly reactive policy actors. These actors pursue two alternative policy tracks, depending on whether the political agents (the executive, congress, or even an earlier constitutional assembly) have delegated policymaking power to the bureaucracy, and whether the president has the institutional power to control the agenda-setting process through the legislature. In the case of congressional policymaking, the president controls the agenda by initiating urgent bills that invert the logic of legislative deadlock: if congress is unable to act, the policy reverts to the president's preference. In contrast, in the case of bureaucratic delegation, the president controls the agenda by appointing technically decisive players.

Given the fragmentation of the Ecuadorian party system, the policymaking process has been generally slow and inefficient (or just unable) to respond to exogenous shocks in policy areas in which there is no delegation and the president is unable to exercise much agenda-setting power.

Ecuador's fiscal policy, with its rigidities in government spending and revenue collection, illustrates this pattern. In the absence of delegation, the policymaking process may become sensitive not only to exogenous shocks, but also to endogenous political shocks, if the president uses his legislative powers (particularly urgent bills and partial vetoes). In the short run, congress may simply let the president's policy "happen"; yet the policy may never be implemented because of the action of last-ditch veto players like the protest movements or the constitutional tribunal. Even if this is not the case, in the medium run a change in administration may easily bring a new change in policy.

A different set of problems emerges when legislators delegate policymaking power to the bureaucracy. When the president and corporate actors set the agenda for the bureaucracy by appointing the heads of the agencies, the result may be a different form of policy volatility. Our discussion of the workings of the early monetary board (1979–92) illustrates this issue. When, in contrast, agencies are relatively autonomous, they may create the conditions for policy adaptability—but only if they can mobilize technical resources and can be effectively shielded from political influence. The example of Internal Revenue Service (SRI) between 1998 and 2004 matched this description of effective and autonomous policymaking. Overall, the absence of a meritocratic civil service and an independent judiciary has consistently undermined effective policy delegation in Ecuador.

The large number of institutional reforms over the last two and a half decades suggest that long-term adjustments to the Ecuadorian policymaking process may not be—or at least are not entirely—a matter of legal reform. Changes in *informal* institutions and practices may be essential to address some of the deeply rooted causes of policy rigidity and volatility: the short time horizons of party leaders, the lack of policy congruence across regional actors, and the repeated activation of last-ditch veto players. But reforming informal institutions can be more difficult. This is an area in which academic knowledge is weaker, public information is obscured by stereotypes and frustration, and political consensus is, no doubt, much more difficult to achieve.

8

Policymaking in Mexico Under One-Party Hegemony and Divided Government

Fabrice Lehoucq, Gabriel Negretto, Francisco Aparicio, Benito Nacif, and Allyson Benton

Introduction

Though not rich, Mexico has the per capita GDP ranking of a middle-income developing country (it had a GDP per capita of approximately US$9,000 PPP as of 2005). Nonetheless, it ranks seventh (alongside Bolivia) out of eighteen countries in the region on a composite measure of a political system's ability to reach agreements in support of political and economic reforms, the Bertelsmann Transformation Index (BTI 2003; see Bertelsmann Foundation 2004). The Inter-American Development Bank's 2006 report on Economic and Social Progress in Latin America and the Caribbean, *The Politics of Policies*, rates public policies in Mexico (alongside Uruguay's) as the fifth best among 18 Latin American countries (IDB 2005). International and regional comparisons made even a decade earlier would have ranked Mexico (still) lower, when policymaking was more centralized, rigid, and substantially less transparent.

Mexico's economic performance and political system rankings merit reflection because its authoritarian system (1929–2000) was alleged to be suited for economic growth and policy effectiveness. In a region renowned for extra-constitutional changes in government, one-party stability in Mexico led analysts like Samuel P. Huntington to marvel that the Institutional Revolutionary Party (PRI) had found the coveted elixir for combining political stability and economic growth.

Until the early 1980s, the PRI had indeed squared the circle. Mexico's GDP grew at more than 6 percent a year between 1950 and 1981 (Maddison 2001). The PRI never lost an election. It could even claim to be inclusive: it had a place for industrial workers, small farmer (*campesino*) organizations, bureaucrats, and even for entrepreneurs (at least informally).

Regime continuity is consistent with Pablo Spiller's and Mariano Tommasi's (2003) theoretical claim that the existence of a few actors can lay the groundwork for the stable intertemporal agreements necessary for effective policymaking. Indeed, public policies were stable and coordinated during the heyday of one-party hegemonic rule. Nevertheless, as this chapter explains, Mexican policymaking also had several glaring weaknesses. Once growth began to falter in the 1970s, policymaking became rigid. Mexican presidents retained a fixed exchange rate and other closed economy policies, even when trade imbalances and public sector debt promoted severe recessions and major devaluations at the end of every six-year presidential term, or *sexenio* (Basáñez 1995). Policymaking was also much less public regarding than the regime's revolutionary rhetoric suggests. Unless a citizen belonged to one of several largely urban-based corporatist sectors, the state offered little in the way of public services until the 1990s. For much of the twentieth century, rural Mexicans (a majority until the 1960s) received little more than a piece of land on a government-controlled *ejido* (land collective) and several years of a (deficient) elementary school education.

This chapter suggests that a noncompetitive political system made for an opaque political system and thus prompted rigid, poor quality, and private regarding policies for much of the second half of the twentieth century. Because of centralization and secrecy, the policymaking process (PMP) resisted the delegation of complex policy tasks to an independent bureaucracy. One-party government also prevented the development of an independent judiciary.

We also argue that it would be a mistake to suggest that Mexican presidents were all-powerful during *presidencialismo* (the period of one-party hegemony). The corporatist organization of the economy endowed presidents with discretionary authority, but also enabled regime beneficiaries to limit the president's powers. Entrepreneurs could always export their capital if policymakers were capricious or failed to maintain macroeconomic health. Thus Mexican presidents almost always secured congressional approval of their bills (Casar 2002a), but they refrained from sending congress bills that redistributed power away from the corporatist pillars of the regime. When economic growth faltered, as Raymond Vernon (1965) noted four decades ago, Mexican *presidencialismo* was unable to adapt policies to reform a closed and highly regulated economy.

This chapter groups public policies and policymaking processes into two periods: the PRI era from the early 1950s to the mid-1990s, and the more recent period of divided government since 1997. Within the PRI era, it also refers to the heyday of Mexico's one-party regime between 1950 and 1982, as well as to a transitional period between 1983 and 1997 when technocratic presidents liberalized the economy and privatized many state companies (Centeno 1997). After a decade and a half of street protests and high-level negotiations to reform electoral institutions (Becerra, Salazar, and Woldenberg 2000; Eisenstadt 2003), the PRI lost its majority in the chamber of deputies, ushering in the current period of divided government. Three years later, the opposition National Action Party (PAN) candidate, Vicente Fox, won the presidential election, thus ending 70 years of PRI governments.

The chapter examines changes in Mexico's policymaking process as the country transitioned from single-party, hegemonic rule to divided government and the impact of these changes in the nature of public policies. The first of the seven following sections characterizes public policies in terms of the policy dimensions (or "outer features") discussed in the conceptual framework of chapter 1. The second characterizes the policymaking process (PMP), both during one-party hegemonic rule and divided government. The subsequent five sections examine the institutional foundations of the Mexican political system before and after democratization. They analyze the dynamics of the electoral system, congress, executive-legislative relations, the judiciary, and intergovernmental relations. The conclusion summarizes the findings and identifies several implications of the analysis for policymaking.

The Outer Features of Public Policy

Public policies during the PRI rule were stable and coordinated, if only because a centralized policymaking process allowed the president to steer policy around his preferences, and single-party rule gave some continuity to policies between *sexenios*. Policies also were clientelistic and private regarding because the PRI catered to corporatist interests. Despite single-party rule, however, public policies during the heyday of the PRI were less than adaptable. Changing tax or energy policies that negatively affected the corporatist sectors, for example, was difficult because these groups were pillars of the regime. This lack of adaptability was partly responsible for the recurrent macroeconomic crises associated with the end and beginning of *sexenios* between the 1970s and 1990s.

Democratization has changed some policy features, but not others. Policies continue to be fairly stable. In fact, some policies—such as macroeconomic policy and trade policy—have become more stable under divided government. Energy and tax policy, for example, remain inflexible, even as oil reserves are dwindling, and non-oil tax revenues remain among the lowest in the Western Hemisphere (approximately 10 percent of GDP, similar to Guatemala). In contrast, social spending, even in the context of an underfunded state, has made state policy more public regarding, as transfers have been better targeted to the poor and to the rural sectors that were underserved during the period of single-party rule. Social spending in this area has experienced the most change with changes in the PMP.

Table 8.1 summarizes key economic indicators and policy features in several relevant periods from 1950 to 2006. Mexico tripled its real GDP per capita from $2,365 to $7,137 (in 1990 U.S. dollars) and grew at an average rate of 2.1 percent between 1950 and 2003, which is 0.5 points higher than the average rate from the eight largest Latin American countries (Maddison 2007). This growth path has not been steady: the average GDP growth rate was 6.6 percent between 1950 and 1981, which suddenly fell to 0.1 during the crisis years of 1982 to 1988, and then recovered to a moderate rate of 3.2 between 1997 and 2006.

Table 8.1. Evolution of the Policymaking Process in Mexico, 1950–2006

Period / Variable	PRI era				Democratic era
	Desarrollo Estabilizador	Populism	Crisis, adjustment, and reform		Divided government
	1950–1970	1970–1981	1982–1988	1989–1997	1997–2006
GDP growth rate (percent)[1]	6.5	6.9	0.1	2.6	3.2
GDP growth (std. dev.) (percent)	2.7	2.2	3.1	3.9	2.2
Public deficit / GDP (percent)	< 2.0	7.2	12.5	0.7	0.7
Inflation rate (percent)	< 5%	17.6	88.4	21.2	7.4
Policy features	Stable, adaptable, and coordinated	Less stable, not coherent, rigid (reforms delayed)	Less stable, not coherent, rigid (reforms begin)	Increasingly stable, not coherent, less rigid (reforms continue)	Stable and adaptable (macro policies), less coordinated, more rigid (reforms stalled)
Social spending	Private regarding/clientelistic			Increasingly public regarding	
Macroeconomic policy	Disciplined	Deficitary	Volatile	Disciplined	
Exchange rate	Fixed rate		Controlled rate	Rate band	Floating rate
Trade policy	Closed economy		GATT entry	NAFTA	
Tax revenues			Low tax revenues		
Oil revenues	Increasing		Volatile	Stable	Decreasing
Pension policy	Pay as you go			Private sector reform only	
Energy policy	State-controlled monopolies in oil and electricity				
Labor policy	Dual regime for public and private sectors, no regulatory change				

Source: Authors' calculations based on INEGI and Banco de Mexico series.
[1] Average annual rates by period, except when indicated.

Public Policy during the PRI Era: 1950 to 1997

We distinguish between three stylized periods of the PRI era: stable development between 1950 and 1970, a populist period from 1970 to 1981, and a 15-year sequence of crisis, adjustment, and first-generation structural reforms between 1982 and 1997. In the so-called *desarrollo estabilizador* period between 1950 and 1970, policies were stable, coordinated, and coherent with a model of import substitution industrialization (ISI). Public policy fomented urban industrialization with fiscal discipline, low inflation, low interest rates, and a fixed and stable exchange rate. Worldwide growth and the absence of external shocks allowed the Mexican GDP to grow at an average annual rate of 6.5 with inflation rates below 5 percent during this period (Ortiz Mena 1998).

By the late 1960s, agricultural exports, the major source of foreign currency, diminished as their terms of trade became less favorable (Vernon 1965). Since diminishing currency inflows constrained the investments required by protected industries, trade restrictions and fixed exchange rate policy became unsustainable. By the early 1970s, the need for economic reform was clear and three policy options were available. First, policymakers could have moved to an export-led model to improve balance of payments problems. Second, they could have increased tax revenues, which represented only 12 percent of GDP in 1975 (Clavijo and Valdivieso 2000), to ease fiscal pressures. Either of these options would have entailed adapting public policies to changing economic conditions. Policy change, however, would have generated distributive conflicts with protected business groups and organized labor.

Unwilling to forge a political consensus to open up the economy and/or to raise taxes, Presidents Luis Echeverría (1970–76) and José López Portillo (1976–82) chose a third option: using foreign debt and deficit spending to sustain growth. Their governments financed deficit spending with inflation and foreign debt borrowing, readily available after the 1973 oil embargo. The pursuit of populist policies, however, wrecked macroeconomic stability. By 1976, when the public sector deficit exceeded 9 percent of GDP, the peso devaluated more than 70 percent after 22 years of stability (Bazdresch and Levy 1991). The discovery of large oil reserves in the mid-1970s made populist policies affordable since the expectation of oil revenues alleviated any financial constraints in the government. Between 1976 and 1981, public spending rose dramatically. When oil prices dropped in 1981, foreign debt doubled within a year. By 1982, the public deficit exceeded 16 percent of GDP amidst another severe peso devaluation and banking expropriation.

The 1981–82 crisis marked the end of the populist period and, not surprisingly, triggered radical economic adjustments and structural reforms. President Miguel de la Madrid (1982–88), who began to rely upon neoliberal technocrats (Centeno 1997), scaled down public spending to service mounting foreign debt payments, but was unable to control inflation, which reached an all-time peak in 1987. President Carlos Salinas (1988–94) continued his predecessor's economic reforms: taming inflation and deficits, divesting state enterprises, liberalizing trade and the financial sector, deregulation, renegotiating foreign debt, pursuing land tenure reform (*ejidos*), and granting limited central bank independence. Notably, the wage and stabilization pact to control inflation is evidence of President Salinas's ability to strike a credible intertemporal agreement with key actors and interests shortly after taking office. After Mexico joined the GATT (General Agreement on Tariffs and Trade) in 1985, the opening up of the economy became definitive when NAFTA (the North American Free Trade Agreement) came into effect in 1994.

The highly centralized policymaking process, despite its partial successes, was not flexible enough to innovate to cope with a run on the capital account and to adjust the exchange rate to avoid another end of *sexenio* crisis. Amid guerrilla uprisings and political assassinations, President Salinas was unwilling to adjust the peso before the 1994 elections. This led to an abrupt devaluation by more than 60 percent in December 1994, six months after the election was held and just three weeks after incoming President Ernesto Zedillo (1994–2000) took office (Gil-Diaz and Carstens 1996). As the GDP shrank by 6.9 percent in 1995, President Zedillo restored economic stability with an emergency tax increase and a floating exchange rate regime. Since then, macroeconomic and exchange rate policies have proven both stable and flexible.

The clientelistic organization of hegemonic one-party government meant that social spending benefited the urban-based, corporatist pillars of the regime. The economic growth between 1950 and the early 1980s did improve living standards across the country: Gini coefficients fell from 0.52 in 1950 to 0.42 in 1984, and the share of population under the poverty line fell from 73 to 30.2 in the same period (Székely 2005). However, it failed to help those who lived in the countryside: in 1984, 61.5 (28.5) percent of the rural (urban) population belonged to the four poorest income deciles (Lustig 1998). Rural Mexicans were forced either to settle for a collectively owned *ejido* that often took more than a decade to acquire from the president (Warman 2001), to leave the countryside for the city, or—like one in five Mexicans—to emigrate to the United States. This urban bias in policy is reflected in the fact that, in 1988, Mexico City area accounted for 70 percent of food subsidies (Scott 2004). And, when public policies proved incapable of adapting to changing economic conditions, economic volatility had dire social costs (Bazdresch and Levy 1991).

The reform period between 1982 and 1997 illustrates both the scope and limits of one-party hegemonic government. Major reforms occurred only after a crisis made them unavoidable, and some specific policies that lie close to the interests of key PRI constituencies proved to be difficult to reform even after such crises. Thus exports grew and diversified, but public revenues remained dependent on oil rents. While tax codes kept changing, revenues remained low. The private pension system was revamped, but public pensions did not change. Even though NAFTA encouraged investment and exports, the energy sector remained under state-controlled monopolies. As it turned out, liberalizing the economy proved to be easier to accomplish than reforming the public sector, and a number of second-generation reforms failed to pass even under unified PRI rule.

Public Policy under Divided Government: 1997 to 2006

Along with recurrent economic crises and economic and political reforms, the PRI gradually ceded ground in the chamber of deputies, losing its majority position in 1997. Mexico's macroeconomic outlook was robust and the 2000 presidential transition was crisis-free for the first time in 24 years. With the election of PAN's Vicente Fox in 2000 and Felipe Calderón in 2006, some policy areas remained stable. The budget remains balanced and monetary policy continues to be supportive of low inflation and a stable exchange rate. Public policies have become more public regarding, largely because of social spending programs like PROGRESA-Oportunidades, which started in 1997. However, other policy issues turned more rigid at the status quo levels: congress debated and failed to enact an overhaul of the tax system, energy reform, and legislative reelection.

The implementation of existing and new policies now is less coordinated because of the increased decentralization of the policymaking process and the number of its key actors. The budgetary process, which was previously oversimplified by single-party rule, turns out to be much more complex under divided government, as two legislative coalitions become necessary: one for the spending project and another for the revenue package (Casar 2001). Moreover, the 2003 budget led to a constitutional controversy regarding the veto powers of the president in budgetary matters vis-à-vis the chamber of deputies. On the other hand, increased subnational transfers reshaped the orientation of policy toward previously marginalized municipalities and states (Flammand 2007), as discussed in the next-to-last section of this chapter.

Macroeconomic and exchange rate policies are perhaps the most stable policies of the last twelve years in Mexico. After a period of volatility and recurring devaluations, monetary policy became stable and disciplined. Since 1995, the floating regime and a semi-independent central bank only seemed to have enhanced these features (Clavijo and Valdivieso 2000; Boyland 2001). Under divided government, the executive and legislature have continued supporting open economy policies.

Long-term policy rigidities are now exacerbated under divided government. Historically low tax revenues impose a critical limit on the Mexican state capabilities: excluding oil revenues, tax revenues as a share of GDP averaged only 9.7 percent between 1977 and 2002. While federal policymakers reformed tax codes and modernized tax revenue agencies, effective tax collection rates remain low because citizens and the state refuse to eliminate tax loopholes and regressive exemptions (Lehoucq 2006). Though President Zedillo reformed private pensions (Madrid 2003), he could not advance public pension reform, despite the enormous inequities that partial coverage implies (Scott 2005). Only in early 2007 did PAN President Felipe Calderón (2006–12) forge an agreement with corporatist leaders to privatize pensions for new public sector workers. There continues to be no reform of labor regulations, even though an antiquated labor code empowers old corporatist unions that, in 1997, included only 12.9 percent of the labor force (Bensusán 2004). PEMEX oil exports now represent less than 10 percent of total exports but oil revenues still account for about a third of total revenues, which in turn drains PEMEX's investment capabilities (Shields 2003). Since it requires constitutional changes, opening up the energy sector to private investors has proven much harder than other reforms (World Bank 2004b).

Divided government has become more public regarding, as rural/food policies and education spending illustrate. In the 1980s, for instance, price controls benefited mostly large producers and consumption subsidies were concentrated in urban areas (Friedmann, Lustig, and Legovini 1995). The focus of rural policy changed significantly in the 1990s, when targeted social programs that reallocate subsidies to rural and poor areas, such as PROGRESA-Oportunidades, substituted formerly biased subsidies. The share of these programs received by the lowest income decile rose from 8 to 33 percent between 1994 and 2002 (Scott 2004). With divided government, spending programs on agriculture, education, and health care for low-income groups have increased. Spending on social programs as a share of GDP has increased as a share of GDP, and the proportion of these resources going to rural residents has also increased (World Bank 2004b).

The Policymaking Process (PMP)

Unified government and corporatist control of the economy made a constitutionally weak president the linchpin of an intertemporal agreement that placed unwritten but nonetheless important limits on his authority. This PMP was responsive to changes in executive preferences, well coordinated among state institutions, and was beneficial (private regarding) for the corporatist pillars of the regime. Policymaking became less coordinated and less responsive to changes to the president's preferences after the PRI lost its congressional majority in 1997. It has also become less private regarding as poorer (and rural) Mexicans have become beneficiaries of several innovative public policies.

The Unified Government PMP

The first characteristic of *presidencialismo* was its narrowness. Key players were the president, his cabinet and advisors, and corporatist leaders. The most important cabinet members were the secretary of public finance and the secretary of the interior (*Gobernación*) (Ortiz Mena 1998). The finance secretary's importance stemmed from his control of revenues and expenditures. The secretary of the interior was responsible for domestic political management, and he ran the intelligence agencies that kept both supporters and opponents under surveillance (Aguayo Quesada 2001). He supervised state and municipal governments and orchestrated the deployment of resources that kept the PRI in control of the vast majority of elected posts in the country until the 1990s (Molinar Horcasitas 1991).

Leaders of the corporatist sectors, whose representatives sat in congress and colonized executive departments and agencies, were also key players during the heyday of *presidencialismo*. President Lázaro Cárdenas (1934–40) began the sectoral organization of Mexican society. Membership of the Party of the Mexican Revolution (PRM) was based on affiliation with the small farmer (*campesino*), labor, military, and popular sectors. In return for an *ejido*—common property bestowed on a group of *campesino* petitioners—landless farmers typically joined the National Confederation of *Campesinos* (CNC). Industrial workers and urban artisans became members of the Mexican Confederation of Workers, or CTM (Middlebrook 1995). The PRM also created a military sector, recognizing the threat posed by the large numbers of soldiers and officers who had fought during the Mexican Revolution (1910–20), in which one in ten Mexicans at the time had perished. In 1940, the regime disbanded the military sector (Camp 1992). Public sector employees, middle-class professionals, and anyone else not belonging to one of the aforementioned groups joined the National Confederation of Popular Sectors (CNOP).

Though the revolutionary family did not have an official place for capitalists, the PRI also created peak-level associations for factory owners, merchants, and bankers. Revolutionary nationalist ideology exalted public control of the economy, but economic realism led the PRI to incorporate the private sector into the regime outside the party and within officially recognized agencies (Purcell and Purcell 1977).

The canonical texts of the classic period of Mexican authoritarianism agree that the president, his cabinet, or the leaders of corporatist sectors did not represent the interests of most Mexicans. According to Pablo González Casanova's (1970) classic, *Democracy in Mexico*, the majority of Mexicans—most of whom lived in very poor rural areas or migrated to the United States or to urban areas (Eckstein 1977)—belonged to what he called the "marginal" sectors. Unlike members of the formal, urban sector—most of whom belonged to one of the corporations—the regime did not allow "marginals" to protest. Even members of the formal sector were allowed to seek redress for their demands only through officially sanctioned leaders, most of whom were more beholden to the regime than to their sector's membership. Fewer than 5 percent of rural residents and more than 70 percent of urban dwellers belonged to an officially sanctioned union or association, according to 1960 census data (González Casanova 1970), a circumstance that attests to the narrowness of the regime coalition and helps explain why its policies were so private regarding.

Secrecy was the second hallmark of the policymaking process under *presidencialismo*. Few were privy to the president's plans and calculations. Neither the courts nor congress oversaw the executive. State-controlled television stations trumpeted the regime's successes, discussed few of its failures, and offered little analysis of public affairs. Dependent on advertising fees paid by state agencies, the print media did not disseminate critical analysis of the regime's policies (Lawson 2002). The zenith of the regime's control of the press was in the late 1960s, when newspapers failed to report the 1968 student massacres (Scherer-García and Monsiváis 2003).

The reality of one-party, hegemonic rule meant that the chief executive consulted with his advisors, cabinet members, and corporatist leaders before sending a bill to congress. Legislative approval of most of his bills was automatic. The policymaking process for distributive measures, the kind that would impose a cost on an organized interest—entrepreneurs, large-scale commercial agriculturalists, or bankers, for example—became even more secretive. President López Mateos's (1964–70) decision to require entrepreneurs to share a portion of their profits with their workers was not even discussed with labor leaders, much less with the entrepreneurs, according to Susan Kaufman Purcell's (1975) classic account. The pertinent bill was sent to congress at the end of the legislative year to ensure that its measures would not be publicly debated. President Luis Echeverría's (1970–76) also secretly reformed CONASUPO, the state marketing board that bought staples and resold them at subsidized prices to urban and rural consumers, because officials concluded that their programs were doing little to stop rural out-migration and the increasing impoverishment of *ejido* members (Grindle 1977). In line with a statist economy philosophy, President Echeverría encouraged CONASUPO officials to redesign their programs by, among other things, shifting the purchase of staples from large-scale commercial farmers (whom the regime also rewarded with huge and expensive irrigation projects, loan guarantees and credits, and the like) to small-scale farmers. Again, the program was redesigned in secret to prevent well-organized interests from mobilizing against the shift in development priorities.

Only President López Portillo (1976–82) and his closest advisors knew that the *sexenio* would end with the nationalization of the banks. Once the president had gained legislative approval for the reform, entrepreneurs split in their response to this transgression of property rights (Elizondo Mayer-Serra 2001). The more radical—many based in the northern city of Monterrey—organized protests and filed a writ of *amparo* with the supreme court. Others accepted the change in the status quo and worked to secure bountiful compensation for their assets, many of which included bad loans that they were happy to foist onto the state. Judicial review proved fruitless because the supreme court declared that the writ was "superseded" by the constitutional amendments that congress had enacted after the expropriation of bank assets. Protest dissipated as bankers negotiated the terms of their compensation with new President Miguel de la Madrid (1976–82).

While members of the revolutionary family rarely challenged the president's supremacy in public, leaders of corporatist groups lent support to a regime because they used private channels to protect their positions (and rents) in Mexican society. And, despite the personalistic bonds linking regime leaders with one another, the PMP and policy-making remained stable. In line with classical constitutional theory, the executive organized elections and a PRI-dominated legislature certified their results (Lehoucq 2002). Supreme court justices served lifetime terms. Deputies and senators could not run for reelection, but the regime rewarded loyalty by placing them in other lucrative policy positions. Though the constitution also prevented the president from standing for reelection, he did hold power for a six-year term. More importantly, he could designate his successor (Castañeda 1999). *El dedazo*, in Mexican political parlance, maintained policy continuity and thus reassured members of the revolutionary family that defection was a worse strategy than cooperation with the PRI. The president, who had the longest time horizons, was the linchpin of the system.

The PMP Changes: Democratization and Divided Government

The PRI's survival is one of democratic theory's most intriguing puzzles. Modernization theory suggests that economic growth encourages societies to shed authoritarian governments beyond the threshold of a per capita GDP of $4,115 (Przeworski and others 2000). But by 1970 the Mexican economy had reached this plateau of $4,000 per capita GDP, yet unified government under the PRI remained in place.

Repeated economic and political crises corroded the bargains that sustained *presidencialismo*. Labor unionists and social movements shifted their support to left-wing parties in response to the PRI's abandonment of a state-dominated economic model (Bruhn 1997). Disaffection with the PRI also led urban voters to support left-wing parties or the right-of-center PAN. Similarly, entrepreneurs began to support the PAN in reaction to government arbitrariness (such as the 1982 bank nationalization) and because increasingly assertive exporters wanted free trade (Thacker 2000). Political protest and economic reform therefore led to the development of a multiparty system.

The PRI's share of the vote and of legislative seats declined steadily after the watershed and controversial elections of 1988 (see table 8.2). The official results indicate that Salinas won 50 percent of the votes to 32 percent for the leftist Cuauhtémoc Cárdenas (son of President Lázaro Cárdenas [1934–40]), and 17 percent for the right-of-center Manuel Clouthier. Castañeda (1999) suggests that the computer crash on the evening of election day allowed the regime to doctor tally sheets in favor of Salinas. Jorge Domínguez and James McCann (1997) compare surveys of voters and nonvoters to suggest that Salinas had won the elections, but by less than an absolute majority of the vote. Salinas's highly controversial election also triggered a decade-long period of institutional innovation that led to the establishment of an autonomous electoral court system (Becerra, Salazar, and Woldenberg 2000; Eisenstadt 2003) and competitive elections.

The 1997 midterm elections mark the shift from a closed, secretive policymaking process to one substantially more open and transparent. Democratization has strengthened the role of public opinion in political life (Moreno 2003). An increasingly assertive press generates previously unavailable information about politics and government policy (Lawson 2002). As the formal political process comes to life, citizens and state officials are building a new political system. New electoral laws are encouraging a multiparty system. This system—in the context of divided governments and federal arrangements—continues to advance corporatist interests, even as rural and regional interests are receiving increasingly larger shares of public spending. The activation of the separation of powers has also thrust the supreme court into the role of arbitrating the relations among the parts of government—and thus as the interpreter of a new and as of yet undefined intertemporal bargain among partisan and policy players.

Table 8.2. The Partisan Balance of Power between the President and Congress, Mexico, 1952–2003

Year of election	President	President's party	Vote percentage	Turnout[1]	Percentage of seats in Chamber of Deputies[2]	Percentage of seats in senate[3]
1952	Adolfo Ruiz Cortines	PRI	74.3	49.5	93.8	100
1955		—	—		94.4	—
1958	Adolfo López Mateos	PRI	90.4	50.1	94.4	100
1961		—	—		96.6	—
1964	Gustavo Díaz Ordaz	PRI	88.8	47.5	83.3	100
1967		—	—		83.5	—
1970	Luis Echeverría	PRI	85.9	59	83.6	100
1973		—	—		81.8	—
1976	José López Portillo	PRI	100	58.7	82.3	100
1979		—	—		74	—
1982	Miguel de la Madrid	PRI	72.5	60.7	74.8	100
1985		—	—		72.3	—
1988	Carlos Salinas	PRI	51.2	42.9	52	93.7
1991		—	—		64	95.3
1994	Ernesto Zedillo	PRI	50.2	66.8	60	74.2
1997		—	—		47.8	60.9
2000	Vicente Fox	PAN	42.5	64	44.6	39.8
2003		—	—		30.2	—
2006	Felipe Calderón	PAN	36.69	59	41.2	40.6

Sources: For data on the composition of the chamber of deputies between 1952 and 1994, see Nacif (2002). Except for the 2006 results, the source for the rest of the information is Schedler (2004). The source for the 2006 elections is the Federal Electoral Institute (IFE) (http://www.ife.org.mx/portal/site/ife/menuitem.918360bce8aa6a3e2b2e8170241000a0/, downloaded on May 7, 2007).

[1] Valid votes in presidential elections/registered votes.
[2] Seat percentages controlled by the party of the president in the chamber of deputies, which is totally renewed every three years.
[3] Seat percentages controlled by the party of the president in the senate. The senate is totally renewed every six years in concurrent elections with the presidency and the chamber of deputies. However, from 1988 to 1994 the senate experimented with partial renewal in staggered elections every three years.

The sections that follow examine the key institutional foundations of the PMP. They analyze institutional arenas—electoral rules and the party system, congress, the judiciary, and federalism—that shape the workings of the policymaking process. The discussion emphasizes both continuities and changes in the institutional dynamics associated with the transition from single-party, hegemonic rule to divided government.

Electoral Laws and Political Parties

Until the 1990s, noncompetitive elections, centralized nomination procedures, and the ban on legislative reelection made legislators dependent upon the president and the corporatist sectors within the PRI. Urbanization gradually created constituencies in favor of democratic change and in favor of economic liberalization (PAN) or opposed to it (PRD). Though the PRI's share of elected offices continues to decline, small farmer-sector organizations have increased their share of PRI seats because electoral formulas and district boundaries make the legislature more responsive to rural and regional interests. The median legislator is therefore increasingly at odds with a president elected from a national constituency, especially one representing the interests and views of the Mexican (urban-based) median voter.

Constituencies and Incentives

Along with Honduras, Panama, and Paraguay, Mexico is one of four countries that award the presidency to the winner of a simple majority. While the president is elected from a national district, individual legislators represent narrower constituencies. During the heyday of Mexican *presidencialismo*, the effects of these differences were muted because the corporatist representation also made deputies and senators responsive to the president and peak-level associations.

Until the 1960s, the median voter lived in a rural area. He was not well educated and his children did not always finish primary school. In all likelihood, he either was a member of an *ejido* or a landless agricultural worker. In either case, he received few benefits from the Mexican state. If he was a member of an *ejido*, he was beholden to PRI-sanctioned communal leaders. He had no access to health care or a retirement pension. Petitioning for land typically took up to a decade, during which time small farmers gave their votes to the PRI, and communal leaders were local PRI operatives (Warman 2001).

Since the 1970s, the Mexican population has gradually become urban, more educated, and thus less identified with the PRI. By the time of the 1988 general elections, less than half of survey respondents identified strongly or weakly with the PRI. Between 1989 and 2002, an average of 35.2 percent of survey respondents identified strongly or somewhat with the PRI. In the same period, identification with the PRD and the PAN gradually increased, such that these opposition parties came to hold the loyalties of an average of 11.5 percent and 19.8 percent of survey respondents, respectively. Throughout this period, slightly less than a third of respondents remained independent (Moreno 2003). In the 2006 general election, the share of *PRIístas* in the electorate had fallen to 23 percent. A fifth of survey respondents continue to identify with the PAN. The share of *PRDistas* has slightly increased to 15 percent of the electorate. On election day 2006, 37 percent of respondents identified themselves as independents.

By the 1990s, urbanization and political competition also created a new party system. Using the World Value Surveys, Alejandro Moreno (2003) shows that, for the two-thirds of respondents who can place themselves on a five-point left-right scale, electoral preferences are normally distributed and tilt toward the right. Between 1990 and 2000, the average placement of the Mexican citizen moved from 3.14 to 3.45 on a five-point scale, on which 1 is the left and 5 is the right. Though the PRI historically stood for a closed and nationalist economy, its supporters (perhaps out of deference to the party establishment) tended to favor market policies by the 1990s. PRD voters, in contrast, unabashedly favor social redistribution. PAN identifiers were more interested in social redistribution in the mid-1990s than were PRI voters. By the time of the 2000 election, however, both the PAN and the PRI had shifted to the left on economic policy. By 2006, citizens who identify with the PRI took more left positions on distributional issues than those of the PAN, even while *PRIístas* were slightly more conservative on moral or social issues than *PANístas* (Moreno 2006; Bruhn and Greene 2007).

Mexico's mixed system for electing congress is one of the least proportional of its kind and its key features date from 1977 (Molinar Horcasitas and Weldon 2001). Unlike the German mixed system, the partisan share of seats in congress does not have to equal proportional representation (PR) district seats. Since 1977, there have been 300 single-member plurality districts (SMPDs). In 1986, constitutional reformers doubled the number of PR legislators to 200. Since 1988, a citizen's single vote for the chamber of deputies simultaneously selects his or her SMPD and PR deputies. Electoral laws permit disproportionality of up to 8 percent between the popular vote and seat shares (Calvo and Escobar 2003). Since 1933, no legislator has been allowed to run for consecutive reelection.

Table 8.3 lists the sectoral composition of PRI deputies between 1943 and 2003. The data indicate that the popular sector has always had the largest number of representatives in the chamber of deputies. The popular sector includes members of the National Syndicate of Educational Workers (SNTE), FSTSE, and assorted professional groupings. The figures also indicate that workers have been losing their representation in congress. Labor unions experienced a decline in representation from a high of 29.6 percent of all PRI deputies in 1976 to a low of 7.6 percent in 2003. Representatives of the small farmer or agrarian sector rose from a low of 14.0 percent in 1991 to a high of 37.8 percent in 1997. The final column in table 8.3 shows the share of legislative seats the opposition won during these years, to help make the point that corporatist representation in congress has also undergone a secular decline.

Both the PRI and other parties are increasingly fielding candidates to suit state and local tastes. Growing numbers of deputies and senators have held state-level elected offices; legislators with only federal bureaucratic experience, or those coming directly from one of the PRI's corporations, account for a declining share of PRI deputies. Between 1985 and 1997, PRI deputy candidates who had been governors or members of state-level parties increased by 14.0 and 9.3 percent, respectively, Joy Langston (2002) estimates. Conversely, PRI candidates for the chamber coming from either the presidential cabinet or a corporatist sector fell by between 7 and 11 percent from 1985 to 1997. Between 1982 and 2000, PRI candidates for senate (nonlist) seats who came from one of the corporatist sectors dropped from 46 percent to 15 percent of all such candidates, Langston (2007) notes. Similarly, the number of candidates coming from a federal government post fell from 38 percent to 10 percent of the total.

As politics has become more competitive in Mexico, the PRI's share of a district's vote—like the Peronist party's in Argentina—has become positively associated with the rural share of the district's population (Gibson 1997). We calculate that, of the 25 percent of all SMPDs that

Table 8.3. Corporatist Affiliation of PRI Deputies, Mexico, 1964–2003

Legislative term	Number of deputies	PRI sectors, percent			Opposition deputies, percent[1]
		Peasant	Labor	Popular	
1964–66	N = 178	27.0	19.7	53.4	16.7
1967–69	N = 173	25.4	22.0	52.6	16.5
1970–72	N = 177	26.6	20.3	53.1	16.4
1973–75	N = 192	27.1	19.8	53.1	17.2
1976–78	N = 196	28.6	29.6	41.8	16.7
1979–81	N = 400	16.0	23.0	60.7	26.0
1982–84	N = 400	17.7	23.2	59.0	25.2
1985–87	N = 40	17.5	24.5	58.0	26.7
1988–90	N = 500	17.0	21.0	62.0	48.0
1991–93	N = 500	14.0	15.0	71.0	36.0
1994–96	N = 500				40.0
1997–99	N = 500	37.8	11.0	50.0	52.2
2000–02	N = 500				55.4
2003–05	N = 500	28.2	7.6	50.9	69.8
Average		23.4	19.8	55.4	32.2

Sources: For 1964–1976, see Smith (1979). For 1979, see Pacheco Méndez (2000). For 1988 and 1991, see Reyes del Campillo (1992). For 1982, 1985, and 1997, see Langston (2002). (Pacheco Méndez's estimates for 1985 and 1997 are within 1 or 2 percentage points of Langston's.) For 2003, see La Reforma, "Van partidos por voto rural," February 10, 2003, p. 8. The last column is from table 6.
[1] Until 2000, the opposition consisted of anti-PRI parties.

are predominately rural, the PRI won 90 percent of the vote in the 1997 election, and 81 percent in 2000 elections. In contrast, in the predominately urban SMPDs in those elections, the PRI won only 38 percent and 6 percent of the vote, respectively.[1] Using survey data from the 1997 CIDE post-election survey, Ulises Beltrán (2000) demonstrates that rural voters are more likely to support the incumbent party (or PRI), even if the respondent believes the economic situation has worsened. Loyalty to a party that championed land grants and particularistic goods in districts with poor, dispersed, and hard-to-reach voters may help explain why many voters remain *PRIístas*.

Dependence on rural districts helps explain why the Salinas (1988–94) and Zedillo administrations (1994–2000) each began major redistributive programs. President Salinas launched the National Solidarity Program, which delivered a panoply of social services to low-income communities throughout the country (Magaloni 2006), few of which had much effect on the urban bias of public policy. President Zedillo started the "PROGRESA" program, which provides income, nutritional, and educational services to the poorest households. This program, which the Fox administration has expanded and renamed "Oportunidades," has become an internationally recognized antipoverty program that, along with five other social programs (of a total of 20), favors rural over urban dwellers (Scott 2004).

Reliance on rural districts may account for the PRI's search for alternative antipoverty programs; uncertainty about their control encourages the PRI and its rivals to bid for the support of rural voters. In the 2003 midterm elections, the PRI's share of rural districts fell to 56.9 percent, even as it rebounded to win 30.8 percent of the majority urban districts. Increasingly up for grabs, rural voters are important

---

[1] A section is classified here as rural if the Federal Registry of Electors classifies as rural 50 percent or more of its sections, the highest-level jurisdiction within each district into which polling stations are grouped. This classification of electoral sections reflects the Federal Electoral Institute's (IFE) 1996 redistricting to correct for malapportionment. The authors' calculations suggest that 26 percent (or 79) of all SMPDs are rural and 59 percent (or 178) are urban. The Registry's classification of districts differs somewhat from the authors' and suggests that 115 are rural.

because 26 percent (79 out of 300) to 38.3 percent (115) of SMPDs are rural. Another 15 percent (43) to 22.6 percent (68) are mixed, that is, districts with large numbers of rural voters.[2] Depending on the measure used, therefore, 41 percent to 60 percent of SMPDs are packed with rural voters, although only slightly more than a quarter of the population lives in rural areas and agriculture contributes less than 5 percent of GDP. Districting, along with divided government, therefore makes legislators from rural constituencies and senators from economically marginal states pivotal players in the PRI and therefore within congress.

From One-Party Hegemony to the Separation of Powers

With the demise of one-party government, the president lost the ability to direct policy change. The absence of a partial or line item veto and other agenda-setting powers—such as executive decree authority or the ability to impose deadlines for congress to deal with executive-initiated legislation—makes the Mexican presidency a potential "reactive" player in the PMP. His veto power, however, means that he can do more than initiate legislation and wait for congress to enact it. A recent classification suggests that the Mexican executive has the fifth weakest set of legislative powers among 18 Latin American countries (IDB 2005).

Unified (and Authoritarian) Government

Weldon (1997a) suggests that three factors made *presidencialismo* possible (see also Casar 2002b). The first condition was *PRIísta* unified government. The second was party discipline. The final condition was the

---

[2] The Federal Electoral Registry catalogues the remaining 39.1 percent of districts as either "urban concentrated" (62) or urban (55) (La Reforma, February 10, 2003, "Van partidos por voto rural," p. 8). Before the 1996 reapportionment, rural areas were even more overrepresented in congress, since district boundaries date from 1977 and are based on demographic projections from the 1970 population census (Pacheco Méndez 2000). For a classification of districts until 1988, see Pacheco Méndez (2000).

president's ability to set the party's agenda and sanction uncooperative behavior among the members of the PRI's legislative contingent.

Table 8.4 includes data on the legislative process from the fifty-sixth (1991–93) to the sixtieth legislatures (2003–06): the last two in which the PRI led unified governments and the first three in which no single party has had the majority in congress. For each legislature, table 8.4 shows the number of legislative bills passed by and initiated in the chamber of deputies according to source, as well as the percentage that each source contributes to the total volume of legislation enacted. The data include only bills originating in the chamber of deputies, for which the senate plays the role of revising chamber. Standing committees are formally the agenda-setters in congress; what is debated and voted upon on the floor are committee reports, not the bills themselves. As the volume of legislation initiated in the chamber of deputies has grown dramatically since 1997, the probability for a bill to die at committee stage has increased from .39 to .82 between 1991 and 2006.

During one-party hegemonic government, the president had the highest success rate: executive-initiated bills represented 81.9 percent and 79.9 percent of the legislation that congress enacted. Table 8.4 also indicates that the president was virtually assured of legislative approval of his bills during the heyday of the PRI. The executive's share of all legislation far surpassed that of the other sources taken together, including PRI legislators.

Although the opposition initiated a significant amount of legislation, opposition bills rarely survived the committee stage. Opposition legislative bills ranged from 31.7 percent to 54.3 percent, but their contribution to the total volume of the chamber's legislation was only 4.7 percent to 14.8 percent, respectively. PRI congressional majorities themselves delegated substantial lawmaking authority to the executive. They were responsible for only between 7.4 percent and 6.5 percent of all legislation between 1991 and 1997. Moreover, the fact that only 37 percent of PRI initiatives (and about 10 percent of enacted legislation) came from its legislators suggests that they played a minor role in lawmaking. The president was not only the chief executive but also the chief legislator.

Table 8.4. Legislative Bills Introduced in and Passed by the Chamber of Deputies, Mexico, 1991–2006

	Unified government				Divided government					
	1991–94		1994–97		1997–2000		2000–03		2003–06	
Source	Passed/ introduced	Percent contribution	Passed/ introduced	Percent contribution	Passed/ introduced	Percent contribution	Passed/ introduced	Percent contribution	Passed/ introduced	Percent contribution
Executive	122/124	81.9	83/84	76.9	28/32	20.4	50/61	18.2	18/34	3.7
Deputies	26/117	17.4	24/165	22.2	108/549	78.8	210/1060	76.4	432/2496	89.1
PRI	11/30	7.4	7/19	6.5	15/86	10.9	54/306	19.6	170/900	35.1
PAN	4/26	2.7	8/1	7.4	31/168	22.6	65/265	23.6	95/490	19.6
PRD	2/1	1.3	3/1	2.8	20/157	14.6	45/294	16.4	69/438	14.2
Other	1/19	0.7	5/20	4.6	17/77	12.4	21/153	7.6	92/608	19
Joint	8/10	5.4	1/2	0.9	25/61	18.2	25/42	9.1	6/1	1.2
Opposition	7/1	4.7	16/144	14.8	68/408	49.6	120/753	43.6	331/1946	68.2
Senators	0/0	0	0/0	0	0/0	0.7	0/0	0	19/69	3.9
State legislatures	1/2	0.7	1/2	0.9	1/25	0.7	15/86	5.5	16/94	3.3
Total	149/243	100	108/251	100	137/606	100	275/1207	100	485/2693	100

Sources: Sistema Integral de Información y Documentación de la Cámara de Diputados for 1991 to 2000 and Gaceta Parlamentaria (http://gaceta.cdhcu.org.mx) for 2000–2006.

The data include legislative bills originating in the chamber of deputies; permits, symbolic legislation, and senate minutes were omitted.

Divided Government

Divided government has transformed the role of the Mexican president. Deprived of any constitutional means of setting the congressional agenda, the president faced the prospect of turning into a merely reactive force. His veto power enables him only to maintain the status quo, not change it. Certainly, opposition parties cannot form a minimum winning coalition without the support of the president and his party. However, minority presidents need the backing of at least one of the two main opposition parties to obtain legislative approval of their bills.

Table 8.4 shows that there has been a substantial increase in the number of non-PRI bills and a notable decline in the number of executive-initiated proposals since the mid-1990s. President Zedillo (1994–2000) reduced the number of bills he sent congress after the PRI lost its legislative majority in 1997. The number of executive-initiated bills fell from an average of 83 to 32 per year. By limiting his legislative program, President Zedillo was able to maintain a success rate in Congress of 87.5 percent. The legislative agenda of the administration increased quite notably when President Fox took office in 2000. The total number of executive-initiated bills rose to 61 during the first half of his administration. After Fox lost the 2003 midterm elections, his administration sponsored only 34 bills. In fact, during the second half of his administration, President Fox had the lowest success rate—53 percent—of any Mexican chief executive since the formation of the PRI.

The most important indicator of the impact of divided government on the constitutional balance of power is the decline in congressional approval of executive-initiated legislation. In the last two legislatures in which the PRI had a majority, the president initiated from 81.9 to 76.9 percent of the volume of legislation. In contrast, from 1997 to 2000, executive-initiated legislation amounted to only 20.4 percent of the total number of bills passed by the chamber of deputies. During the first half of the Fox administration, government bills represented just 18.2 percent of all bills. After losing the 2003 midterm elections, the influence of President Fox on the congressional agenda collapsed. His administration was responsible for only 3.7 percent of all bills congress enacted between 2003 and 2006. At the same time, the importance of opposition-sponsored legislation increased, accounting for a larger share of bills than that of the president and his party taken together. With the advent of divided government, the president saw his role as chief legislator vanish.

Another significant aspect of the legislative process reported in table 8.4 is that divided government has not involved any reduction in total legislative output, even if it has made it harder to enact second-generation structural reforms. Table 8.4 shows that the total volume of legislation, measured by the number of bills passed by the chamber of deputies, has been higher during the period of divided government than during the last two legislatures in which the PRI controlled both congress and the presidency. The total legislative output rose from 104 and 98 bills in the fifty-fifth and fifty-sixth legislatures to 275 in the fifty-eighth legislature, and 485 in the fifty-ninth legislature.

Congress: From Single-Party to Multiparty Government

González Casanova (1970) describes congress in the heyday of the PRI as a powerless institution that merely played a symbolic role. Extensive delegation to the executive responded to the career incentives of PRI legislators, for whom political survival ran counter to promoting congressional authority. Under divided government, legislators have reformed congressional procedures and have taken a more active role in the PMP. The constitutional ban on consecutive reelection limits the policymaking capabilities of congress.

Congress under Presidencialismo

During the heyday of the PRI, most legislation was actually drafted in the executive departments. Table 8.4 shows that deputy-initiated bills fluctuated between 19.1 percent and 20.1 percent of the total volume of legislation from 1991 to 1997, the last two legislatures in which the PRI had a majority in the chamber of deputies. This pattern of the lawmaking process was similar a decade earlier, when the PRI majority in the chamber was even larger. In the 1982 and 1988 legislatures, deputy-initiated bills amounted to 14.3 percent and 22.6 percent of all laws that the deputies passed (Nacif 1995). Weldon (1997b) tracks the origin of this pattern back to the early 1930s, shortly after the foundation of the PRI.

The marginal contribution of the PRI majority in the chamber of deputies to the volume of legislation (less than 10 percent) confirms that its regular strategy was to delegate the drafting of legislative initiatives to executive departments. PRI legislators used to justify this practice on the grounds that the technical capabilities of the congress were quite limited in comparison with those of executive departments. However, extensive delegation to the executive branch and a failure to develop the necessary technical capabilities was a function of the career incentives that legislators, particularly PRI legislators, faced (Ugalde 2000).

The ban on consecutive reelection made legislative service a mere stepping-stone to other political positions. Data on legislative careers show the lack of professionalization among politicians serving in the Mexican congress (Campos 2003). Between 1934 and 1997, an average of 86 percent of the members of the chamber of deputies served only one term. Only 11 percent on average served a second term. This figure fell to practically zero for those serving a third term or more. A period in the chamber of deputies was a very important experience for politicians seeking a seat in the senate. From 1982 to 1994, 67.7 percent of the members of the senate had served in the chamber of deputies for at least one term. The chamber of deputies was the previous experience of political office for one-third of the senators during that period (Nacif 1996).

PRI politicians considered not only the benefits of holding a seat in either house of congress, but also the sequence of offices related to congressional service. For aspiring state governors, congressional service was the most significant political experience. After the presidency of the republic, state governorships were the most valuable positions for ambitious politicians. In several respects, a governorship was more attractive than a senate seat. Governors' ability to organize teams and reward loyalty placed them at the center of the promotional structure at the state and municipal levels. Between 1976 and 1995, 45.2 percent of elected governors had previously served in congress (Nacif 1996).

The system of congressional governance under presidencialismo was highly centralized (Martínez-Gallardo Prieto 1998). It revolved around the *Gran Comisión*, a committee comprising representatives of state delegations to the chamber of deputies and the senate. In practice, the PRI legislative leader chaired the *Gran Comisión*. Its powers included staffing committees, assigning committee chairs, appointing administrative officials, allocating financial resources, and staffing the *Mesa Directiva*—the legislative body governing plenary meetings. Under PRI rule, standing committees did little more than review executive-initiated legislation. They typically ignored bills from different sources, especially from opposition legislators—a practice known in the parliamentary jargon as the "freezer." The chair of the *Gran Comisión* could expedite the passage of executive legislation and, when necessary, circumvent committee chairmen.

Congress under Divided Government

As opposition parties grew in size during the 1980s, they gained the ability to force the PRI majority to reform congressional procedures. The 1991 reform of the chamber of deputies brought an end to the old system of government based on the *Gran Comisión* and gave the opposition parties access to committee chairs and secretaryships. The real change in the role of congress, however, came about only after 1997, when the PRI lost its majority in the chamber of deputies.

Opposition parties have been responsible for a disproportionate share of legislative activity since 1997. Under PRI unified governments, as the data in table 8.4 show, opposition-initiated bills accounted for between 4.6 percent and 13.1 percent of all bills. This indicator soared to 48.2 percent and 43.2 percent during the first two legislatures under divided government. During the second half of the Fox administration, the opposition sponsored 68.2 percent of all bills. The significance of this change can hardly be exaggerated: the contribution of opposition parties to the total volume of legislation has been greater than that of the president and his party taken together since 1997.

Divided government also transformed congressional governance. Building on the precedent established by the 1991 reform of the chamber of deputies, in 1999 Congress passed a new Organic Law of Congress that introduced power-sharing arrangements in both houses of the legislature. The allocation of committee chairs and secretaryships on the basis of proportional representation, already in operation in the chamber of deputies, was extended to the senate. A committee comprising all legislative party leaders—the *Junta de Coordinación Política* in the chamber of deputies and the *Junta de Gobierno* in the senate—replaced the *Gran Comisión* as the governing body.

Though divided government makes the committees central players in the policymaking process, the ban on consecutive reelection and existing legislative arrangements weaken the role of standing committees. The practice of multiple committee assignments (all deputies must belong to at least three committees) inhibits specialization. Also, the system of open rules that prevails in floor proceedings leaves committee reports unprotected against unfriendly amendments. Finally, the 1999 Organic Law of Congress gave leaders of legislative factions the power to remove committee members at any time without consulting the plenary, thereby undermining the independence of standing committees. The weakness of the committee system prevents congress from gathering information, assessing policy alternatives, and overseeing the implementation of legislative change.

Unlike their counterparts in the United States, the national leaderships of Mexican parties, called the National Executive Committees (CEN), are very powerful. Their leverage stems from their influence on the nomination of candidates and their control of lavish campaign finance subsidies. The CEN's control over party factions begins with the nomination of candidates. The CEN reserves safe seats—top positions on the party list or safe districts—for those politicians who will play leading roles within the legislative faction. The PRD and the PRI recently introduced the practice of holding elections for the coordinators of their legislative factions (in other parties, including the PAN, the CEN appoints the coordinator of the legislative faction), but the CEN has ultimate control over the process of selecting the parliamentary faction leadership.

Indicators of party unity confirm that parliamentary factions usually vote as a bloc. The average Rice index (an indicator of party unity, which consists of the difference between the percentage of party members voting against and for a bill) has been greater than 90 percent for every party since 1997, with the president's party typically displaying the most discipline (Casar 2000; Díaz-Iturbe 2006).

The Judiciary: The Supreme Court

Between the late 1920s and 1994, presidents manipulated constitutional rules for designating high court justices. A highly centralized PMP also deprived the supreme court of the means and motives to rule against the PRI. Since 1994, the creation of impartial rules of appointment, the establishment of a more extensive judicial review, and the opening up of the PMP has permitted the emergence of a more independent supreme court. The available evidence suggests that the Court's short-term strategy has been to act as a veto player. Nevertheless, a more experienced and professional high court might be able to take a proactive role in defining and enforcing intertemporal agreements among partisan and policy players.

The Supreme Court under Presidencialismo

Since the late 1920s, constitutional rules and political centralization have prevented the high court from acting as a collective actor with its own policy preferences. The party in power secured the loyalty of supreme court judges through the rules on their appointment, tenure, and impeachment. Under these conditions, the Court reserved for itself a sphere of relative independence in protecting citizens from some irregular procedures but never attempted to defy the party in power in fundamental political decisions, even when the PRI violated the constitution.

The 1917 constitution sought to guarantee the formal independence of the supreme court by empowering state legislatures to nominate members to the high court, who then needed to be approved by a two-thirds majority in a joint session of congress. It also granted judges lifetime appointments after a trial period of six years. In 1928, President Calles

(1924–28) secured a constitutional amendment that allowed presidents to nominate judges, subject to the approval of a simple senate majority. A presidential nominee, however, was automatically approved if the senate did not act upon his nomination or if the senate rejected two successive presidential nominees. In 1934, President Cárdenas (1934–40) passed a new constitutional amendment that replaced the lifetime tenure of judges with a six-year term concurrent with that of the president.

Judicial careers were already politicized when, in 1944, a new constitutional reform restored the lifetime tenure of supreme court justices. Between 1933 and 1995, 47 percent of all justices had a political position at the federal or local level before being appointed. Between 1940 and 1994, 20 percent of the members of the supreme court ended their terms prematurely to occupy similar political positions (Domingo 2000). Another indicator of politicization is that, since 1946, most presidents had an opportunity to renew *at least* 40 percent of the members of the supreme court (Fix-Fierro 1999).

Limited powers of judicial review also weakened the supreme court's position. Between 1917 and the early 1990s, the *amparo* suit was the supreme court's most powerful means of reviewing the constitutionality of norms and laws. As in the rest of Latin America, any citizen could invoke an *amparo* against a law or administrative act that he believed arbitrarily violated a constitutional right or guarantee. While the *amparo* (particularly the *amparo contra leyes*) provided the Court with the opportunity to decide whether a law or a government act breached the constitution, it limited the ability of judges to act as independent guardians of the constitution for two reasons (Baker 1971; Taylor 1997; Fix-Fierro 1999). First, writs of *amparo* usually involve establishing the facts of a case rather than the meaning of the constitutional text, as in most types of judicial review (Baker 1971; Taylor 1997). Second, both the constitution and the law of *amparo* establish that a successful writ of *amparo* only has *inter partes* (between the parties) effects: that is, it only exempts the plaintiff, not anyone else. Writs of *amparo* only acquire general effects—benefit all individuals in similar circumstances—in Mexico if the supreme court grants comparable writs of *amparo* in favor of five plaintiffs. The absence of an authority responsible for determining the similarity of writs of *am-*

paro, however, has weakened the practical implementation of this rule (Garro 1990; Schwarz 1990). The constitution and the law of *amparo* also prevented the supreme court from ruling on certain matters, such as religious freedom, education, voting rights and the implementation of electoral rules, the deportation of foreigners, decisions taken by decentralized public entities, and the right to challenge presidential decisions on the expropriation of land (Schwarz 1977).

The available evidence confirms that the Court, while not completely null as an enforcer of individual rights, was neither a veto player in the PMP nor an impartial enforcer of an intertemporal agreement. In a study of 3,700 *amparo* suits between 1917 and 1960 in which the president is mentioned as the responsible authority, González Casanova (1970) finds that the supreme court decided in favor of the plaintiff in 34 percent of the cases. The Court either denied the merits of the rest of the *amparo* suits or dismissed them on procedural grounds. In a more detailed analysis of supreme court rulings in *amparo* suits, Schwarz (1977) observes that the Court appeared to be relatively independent when deciding on the legality of administrative procedures, particularly in the areas of expropriations and taxes. More than 50 percent of these cases were decided in favor of the plaintiff between 1954 and 1968. In other areas, however, such as labor regulations, economic policies, or political dissent, the court ruled in favor of the executive.

Both González Casanova (1970) and Schwarz (1977) conclude that in politically sensitive areas, the supreme court rarely defied the PRI. In these cases, the Court either ruled against the plaintiff, dismissed the case on procedural grounds, or declared that the matter was beyond the competence of the courts (Fix-Fierro 1999). In 1982, for example, the Court decided against hundreds of *amparos* that challenged the constitutionality of the 1982 bank nationalization, even though the measure violated constitutionally defined property rights. During the 1960s, the Court dismissed, on procedural grounds, *amparos* invoked against the so-called crime of "social dissolution," a fairly broad legal category that basically penalized actions of political dissent. In other cases, the Court declined its jurisdiction to decide on potentially conflictive issues by invoking the doctrine of "political questions." While the constitution and the law of *amparo* excluded the jurisdiction of the courts on some electoral matters (such as the decisions made by electoral boards and legislatures on the legality of electoral procedures), the Court interpreted this doctrine broadly enough to refuse to hear any case that touched upon matters of voting rights (Schwarz 1977).

The Supreme Court since 1994

The 1994 constitutional reform, passed with the support of the main opposition party, the PAN, gave the supreme court the power to play a more active role in the PMP. While the president retained the power to nominate candidates to the Court, the threshold for their appointment in the senate was increased from simple majority to a qualified majority of two-thirds. To lessen the politicization of supreme court nominations, the reform required that candidates should not have been secretaries of state, prosecutors, federal deputies, senators, or state governors during the year before their nomination.

The reform also created a new type of judicial review: the "action of unconstitutionality" (AU). Wholly independent of the *amparo* suit, the AU allows the Court to declare laws or administrative acts unconstitutional if such a decision is supported by eight of the eleven supreme court justices (unlike the *inter partes* effect of *amparo* rulings). A second important reform in 1996 extended the judicial review under AUs to include the adjudication of electoral disputes. AUs differ from *amparo* suits in that citizens cannot initiate them. Only a limited number of political authorities have the authority to invoke them, such as a percentage of federal deputies and senators, or the attorney general.

Another important change was the strengthening of the Court's power to act on constitutional controversies (CC). Before 1994, constitutional controversies were limited to conflicts among states and between them and the federation. Since 1994, constitutional controversies have included conflicts between the federal branches of government. The reform also established that whenever local laws are involved, supreme court rulings in constitutional controversies might invalidate those laws if no fewer than eight of the eleven justices agree on the decision.

With formal guarantees of independence, more effective powers of judicial review, and divided government, several deductive models of judicial decisions in separation-of-powers systems predict the development of a more proactive Court (Ramseyer 1994; Epstein and Knight 1997; Iaryczower, Spiller, and Tommasi 2002). In a study of constitutional controversies between 1994 and 2000, Magoloni and Sánchez (2001) find that the supreme court still ruled in favor of the PRI, either by ruling against the merits of the claim or by dismissing the case on procedural grounds. However, in a time-series analysis of both constitutional controversies and actions of unconstitutionality from 1994 to 2003, Tapia Palacios (2003) concludes that the percentage of the Court's rulings in favor of the PRI falls as the PRI's hold on elected offices declines. The probability of the Court ruling in favor of the PRI was 85 percent between 1995 and 1997, when the PRI was a defendant in both constitutional controversies and actions of unconstitutionality (Tapia Palacios 2003). Between 1997 and 2000—that is, when the PRI lost its majority in the chamber of deputies for the first time since the 1930s—the probability fell to 34 percent. After 2000, when the PRI lost the presidency, the probability of a decision in favor of the PRI declined to 31 percent.

Selected case studies also show that between 1997 and 2000, the supreme court ruled against the PRI in politically sensitive matters. In September 1998 it ruled in favor of the PRD, which had challenged the constitutionality of an electoral law in the state of Quintana Roo that granted the plurality vote-winner an automatic majority of seats in the legislature. In 1999, all the main opposition parties won a constitutional controversy that forced President Zedillo to disclose secret financial information that potentially involved the illegal funding of his electoral campaign.[3]

These rulings can be interpreted as a reputation-building strategy. By ruling against the PRI between 1997 and 2000, the supreme court asserted its independence as the PRI was losing its grip on Mexican politics. As to the PAN—the party of President Vicente Fox (2000–06)—between 1997 and 2000, the percentage of cases decided in favor and against the party

---

[3] *El Universal*, March 20, 2000.

was almost the same as in the previous three-year period (Tapia Palacios 2003). Nonetheless, the percentage of cases decided in favor of the PAN fell from 37 percent between 1997 and 2000 to 7 percent between 2000 and 2003. In the latter period, the supreme court did not seem to have been ruling either for or against the PRI, since the percentage of cases decided in favor and against the PRI was almost identical.

These recent trends suggest that the Court might be shifting its strategy from being just a veto player in the PMP. During Fox's presidency, for instance, the Court invalidated one executive decree that allowed private companies to generate electricity and another that exempted from taxes the users of fructose in industrial production. At the same time, however, the Court did not appear to be ruling disproportionately in favor or against the government. In mid-2005, the supreme court ruled in favor of a presidential CC that made it clear that the executive could veto the expenditures portion of the annual budget bill. It has also become very active in the interpretation of the Mexican state's international obligations and the protection of human rights. In June 2004, for instance, the Court decided that the forced disappearance of persons is a crime not subject to a statute of limitations, thus permitting the prosecution of former public officials for human rights abuses committed during the 1960s and 1970s. These cases suggest that, if divided government persists and control over the presidency rotates among parties, a more experienced supreme court could change from being a veto player to being an impartial enforcer of intertemporal agreements among policy and partisan players.

Federalism and Intergovernmental Relations

During the PRI's heyday, tight federal control over tax collection helped create and then reinforce a highly centralized PMP—one that enabled presidents to pursue policies that favored national over regional interests. As the PRI's hegemony declined, the president's discretionary authority in the assignment of federal resources ended. Decentralization has also led states and municipalities to become veto players in the PMP. While subnational governments are responsible for more than a third of total

public sector expenditures, they do not collect enough taxes to cover the
money they spend.

The Centralization of Intergovernmental Relations

The centralization of tax authority in the federal government was the
driving force behind the loss of local autonomy in Mexico. Beginning
in 1947, local governments began to relinquish more and more tax authority to the federal government in exchange for guaranteed shares
of federal tax revenues and exclusive authority over some small taxes
(Courchene, Diaz-Cayeros, and Webb 2000). The centralization of tax
collection was possible because local politicians surrendered tax authority in exchange for fiscal compensation from the federal government
(Diaz-Cayeros 1997b). This process culminated in 1979 with the creation
of the *Sistema Nacional de Coordinación Fiscal* (SNCF). Local politicians
found it expedient, as it guaranteed shares of growing national VAT
(value added tax) collections and access to rising federal oil revenues
(Diaz-Cayeros 1995). Though states could, and still can, legally opt out
of the system and recover local tax authority, the SNCF equilibrium has
proven quite stable. Few politicians have been willing to risk a loss of
guaranteed fiscal revenues in exchange for fiscal freedom. Indeed, on
only one occasion has a governor—that of Baja California Sur—threatened to leave the system (Diaz-Cayeros 1997a).

The regional distribution of federal transfers reflected presidential
priorities, not regional ones. States received revenue shares in line with
former revenue collected from their own state-level taxes and the national sales tax, which perpetuated interregional disparities (Diaz-Cayeros
1995). As late as 1991, the formula used to allocate state transfer shares
heavily weighted their current share in overall tax revenues, with 72.29
percent of these transfers being based on tax collection. As a result, the
Federal District (DF) and wealthier states like Nuevo León and Baja
California have consistently received more resources from the federal
government than poorer states, located predominately in the south. The
GDP per capita in 2000 was US$22,816 (PPP) in the Federal District (a
figure comparable to Spain's), $15,837 in Nuevo León, and $12,434 in

Baja California. In contrast, the national GDP per capita rate was $8,831, indicating that federal transfers magnified already stark differences in wealth among Mexico's 32 states (PNUD 2003).

The lack of a regional voice in the PMP was also reflected in federal public investment spending (*inversión pública federal*, IPF), which is an important source of public investment for economic and social development projects. Rather than being awarded to states on the basis of economic and social need, however, IPF funds fostered economic growth in the country's most productive economic sectors (such as the petroleum industry in the states of Veracruz and Tabasco, and the industrial and manufacturing sectors in the DF) (Diaz-Cayeros 1997b). Until the 1980s, most presidents favored industrial over agricultural, social, and regional development programs, and thus chose to target regional (state) industrial centers that were critical to national economic prosperity and growth. Indeed, between 1965 and 1982, 61 percent of IPF resources were directed to industrial development (42 percent) and infrastructure (19 percent) projects that tended to benefit wealthier states, compared to 13 percent directed toward agriculture, and 21 percent toward social welfare projects targeted toward more rural and less-developed regions. Regardless, the division of IPF funds also varied from term to term, reflecting variation in presidential policy priorities, and the secretiveness and centralization of the PMP.

Regional favoritism was possible because local leaders abdicated electoral, fiscal, and policy authority to the federal government (Ayala Espino 1988). Although the lack of a regional voice in the PMP aggravated regional inequalities, the equilibrium bargain between federal and local leaders remained robust. Local leaders from both poor and wealthier areas exchanged partisan loyalty for guaranteed political careers and for predictable shares of government resources. Economic favoritism, however, also helped reward the most important PRI followers—including public utilities workers, workers in private industry, and business groups—because it delivered jobs and prosperity to states that already had strong corporatist representation in the national government. Leaders from poorer areas, though their careers were guaranteed, were marginalized from most policy programs, while the federal government used its control over the PMP to support the most economically influential areas of the country.

Decentralization and the New Federal Pact

The economic crisis of the 1980s pressured the federal government to cede some political, fiscal, and policymaking authority to local governments (Cornelius and Craig 1991; Rodríguez and Ward 1994; Rodríguez 1997; Cornelius, Eisenstadt and Hindley 1999). Such decentralization involved changing the formulas used to calculate state shares of fiscal transfers, the policy responsibilities allocated to state governments, and the way that federal public investment projects are undertaken. Congress has since placed additional taxes within the SNCF system and increased total tax revenues allocated to state governments. By 1998, in addition to fiscal resources, the federal government had transferred education, health care, and public security responsibilities to state and municipal governments. Before the 1983 decentralizing reforms, states accounted for about 11 percent of total public expenditures, and municipalities, for 2 percent. By 2005, states and municipalities accounted for 40 percent of total public expenditures, even though states raise no more than 11 percent of their spending from local taxes (INEGI 2007).

Local political interests have begun to find a voice in the policymaking process. They have demanded more transparent resource allocation that reflects their economic and fiscal interests. As a result, the distribution of federal tax-sharing revenues has begun to reflect more than just annual tax collections; it now includes funds based on population size and economic and social needs (Diaz-Cayeros 1995; Rodríguez 1997; Ward, Rodríguez, and Cabrero Mendoza 1999). Gone too are the days of extreme favoritism toward those areas most likely to contribute to economic growth. Poor states have benefited most from this change. States with the highest levels of poverty experienced, on average, 33 percent growth in the per capita transfer of *participaciones* in the 1990s alone.[4] Wealthier states, by contrast, have seen negative growth in per capita

---

[4] *Participaciones* are revenues collected from a state's own taxes and their share of VAT.

revenue shares (Rodríguez 1997). More developed states also have experienced a decline in per capita public investment, while poorer areas received a higher amount of federal funds for development projects. These trends have created a federal arrangement whereby states free ride on the national government because no state taxes its citizens to cover its expenditures. This is a situation that is placing increasing pressure on the federal government because of the narrowness of the tax base in Mexican society. It is also polarizing states between a larger number of poorer states entirely dependent on federal largess and a smaller number of wealthier states that are not.

The decentralization of resources, along with the rise of competitive party politics in state and municipal elections, has increased the role of subnational politicians and politics in national policymaking. Most of Mexico's most important presidential contenders in recent years have all served as governors. Though President Calderón (2006–12) never served as a state executive, former President Fox (2000–06) was governor of Guanajuato. The PRD's 2006 presidential candidate, Andrés Manuel López Obrador, served as mayor of Mexico City (2000–06). This is a major change from prior years when presidential contenders tended to come from bureaucratic careers rather than elected ones, as the section above on electoral and party systems shows.

State leaders can also affect voting outcomes in the federal congress. Recent research shows that, when their interests collide with those of the federal government or party leaders, governors can exert considerable sway over federal legislators from their state, causing important party splits on key issues, particularly fiscal and budgetary ones (Langston 2007). Though much of the political clout of governors stems from their important role in helping legislators get on ballots and win seats, it also is due to the fact that many politicians hope to return to local political careers after serving in the national congress. Governors have also begun to rethink the ways that they can cooperate to affect the federal PMP. To this end, they formed the National Conference of Governors (CONAGO) in 1999 to help coordinate their interests and present a common front to the national government. Though having only limited success thus far, scholars have noted that governors from small states that had until recently been all but overlooked by national leaders now can expect to have their complaints and suggestions heard by cabinet members and even the president (Flammand 2007).

Conclusion

Policymaking in Mexico is consistent with the argument that political cooperation among a small number of political actors leads to the development of stable intertemporal linkages. Though the presidency is constitutionally weak, unified government and the corporatist organization of the economy transformed the president into a national agenda setter. One-party hegemonic government gave rise to a political system that benefited organized urban interest groups and ignored the majority of Mexicans living in (and fleeing) rural poverty. It was a less than solid arrangement—one that the president made credible by consulting with corporatist leaders, letting them share in the spoils of office, and loading the constitution with promises to each of these sectors. As a result, public policies were stable, coordinated, and coherent until the 1970s.

Without competitive elections, however, most partisan and policy decisions were made in secret. Authoritarianism prevented the development of a professional and high-quality bureaucracy. It kept an independent judiciary from enforcing a stable and modern agreement that transcended the personalistic relations among the president, the members of the cabinet, and corporatist leaders. By exchanging particularistic policies for support from narrowly based corporatist sectors, *presidencialismo* relinquished the right to tax society and thus to build a modern, professional state with the rule of law.

When policy reform might have caused losses for one or more urban-based groups, however, PRI presidents typically postponed dealing with thorny issues. Hence during the 1970s and early 1980s, Mexican presidents did little to solve balance of payments crises and the increase in the public (foreign) debt, given the rigidity of tax collection and expenditure policies. The costs of reforming an economy that had become macroeconomically unstable by the 1970s helps to explain why economic volatility did not force change in the policies of a highly centralized PMP. After massive devaluations and periodic negative growth rates—both of which recurred with the end of the six-year presidential term and the start of a new one—several presidents adapted a centralized PMP to new economic and political circumstances. Presidents De la Madrid (1982–88), Salinas (1988–94), and Zedillo (1994–2000) opened up the economy to international competition, deregulated it, and privatized many state companies.

Democratization has created a decentralized and more open policymaking process that benefits a wider set of interests. The proportional aspects of a mixed electoral system fuel the growth of a three-party system. The majoritarian components of the electoral system, along with the boundaries among SMPDs, now favor parties occupying the median position in congress (typically, the PRI) and rural voters, who comprise a quarter of the electorate and contribute less than 5 percent to national GDP. Intergovernmental relations magnify this outcome and actually encourage states to abdicate responsibility for collecting their own taxes and instead to free ride on federal revenues. Divided government and decentralization therefore fragment power in a political system once famous for one-party, hegemonic rule.

This chapter suggests several implications for policymaking in and outside Mexico. First, *presidencialismo* was more powerful in appearance than in reality. Almost universal congressional support for executive-based initiatives conceals the fact that Mexican presidents, unless faced with a serious crisis, could not secure approval of any measures that redistributed significant resources away from the corporatist groups on which it based its support. Only when lawmaking touched on non-controversial issues could the president win the consent of corporatist sectors—which held legislative seats commensurate with their economic importance—and organized business to enact or change laws. This outcome suggests that the centralization of political power does not substitute for the construction of a political consensus necessary for effective public policies.

Second, there has been as much continuity as change in policymaking during the last fifty years in Mexico. Though Mexico has been macroeconomically stable since the mid-1990s, policymakers took more than two decades to shift from a fixed exchange rate and closed economy policies to a floating exchange rate regime and open economy policies. The rigidity of policymaking contributed to macroeconomic turbulence during the 1970s and 1980s, an outcome that worsened the public regardedness of policies during these decades. Though political and economic reforms of the 1990s benefited rural and poor citizens, the underlying rigidities of public policies has contributed to unimpressive growth rates (approximately 3.2 percent a year since 1997); rates unable to transform the living standards of many Mexicans.

Third, increasing rates of growth to lift the half of Mexicans living in poverty and reduce income equality requires addressing a multiplicity of policy rigidities. Raising historically low rates of taxation—little more than 10 percent of GDP—requires ridding the tax code of a large number of loopholes. Reform of the energy sector remains captive to inefficiencies at PEMEX, its union, and the demands of a central state that relies upon dwindling oil exports for more than a third of total public sector expenditures. Education reform demands confronting the largest union in Latin America, one whose leadership has shown little interest in improving the quality of public education, but that has extracted generous salary increases during the Fox administration. Until Mexico's policymaking process forges a consensus to address these and related rigidities, the living standards of Mexicans will not improve dramatically.

9

Political Institutions, Policymaking Processes, and Policy Outcomes in Paraguay

José Molinas, Anibal Pérez-Liñán, Sebastián Saiegh, and Marcela Montero

Introduction

Paraguay has experienced one of the lowest growth rates in Latin America over the last 25 years, with economic growth well below the population growth, and a resulting decrease of per capita income. Meanwhile, since 1947, Paraguay has been under the rule of the Colorado party. No political party currently in power anywhere in the world has governed longer than the Colorado party. In spite of both the stability of the Colorado party's control of the government and the country's deteriorating macroeconomic conditions, no major reforms have been implemented in Paraguay in recent years.

Economic reforms intended to stabilize the economy have usually come to a standstill in the legislative stage. For example, in 2002, while Paraguay was experiencing one of its most severe economic crises, the minister of finance resigned in protest over congressional delays in authorizing a stand-by agreement with the International Monetary Fund (IMF). One year later, after his election as Paraguay's new president, Nicanor Duarte-Frutos adopted some of the reforms suggested by the IMF. In 2004 the situation improved; the economy grew 4 percent—the highest rate since the mid-1990s. However, the economy suffered from a variety of external shocks in 2005 and growth fell to 3 percent. Against this background, the authorities sought to implement an ambitious program of structural reforms. However, in 2006 the president was incapable of mustering enough legislative support for these measures. The economic results at the end of the year were certainly disappointing. Persistent inflationary pressures and a large and underfinanced budget approved by the Paraguayan congress negatively affected economic growth.

The fact that most reform attempts were stalled rather than implemented, and were then either overturned or implemented very inefficiently, reveals that the country's levels of policy adaptability are very low. Why has it been so difficult to modify public policies in Paraguay? Is this rigidity a problem for all policy areas or only for some contested policy dimensions? This chapter sets out to answer these questions. It characterizes the Paraguayan policymaking process (PMP) between 1954 and 2003. It identifies four distinctive periods in the evolution of the Paraguayan PMP: the "golden age" of the Stroessner dictatorship (1954–81), the late Stronismo period (1982–89), the transitional Rodríguez regime (1989–93), and the current period marked by democratic institutions (1993–present).

The rest of this chapter proceeds as follows. The second section presents a stylized model of the PMP under the rule of Alfredo Stroessner (1954–89). The third section provides an overview of the 1989–93 transitional regime, discussing how the dictatorship's policymaking rules, which initially remained in place, allowed for an initial period of rapid policy change. In the years that followed, however, these rules changed in order to allow for the democratization process and the emergence of new players. The fourth section characterizes the distinctive patterns of the policymaking process that emerged after the adoption of the 1992 Constitution. The fifth section discusses the workings of the post-1993 policymaking process, using evidence from executive-legislative relations. The sixth section examines the characteristics of the public policies under the new PMP. Finally, the seventh section offers some concluding remarks. Our conclusions suggest that the current Paraguayan PMP may be flexible for the provision of particularistic benefits, but is rigid for the approval of broad regulatory or redistributive policies.

The study of the Paraguayan case offers valuable theoretical insights regarding two issues. First, in recent years an emerging literature has emphasized that the presence of multiple veto players (political actors whose consent is necessary but not sufficient to alter the policy status quo) reinforces policy rigidities and prevents policy change (Tsebelis 2002). We show that, to some extent, this has been the case in Paraguay: the democratization process begun in 1989 multiplied the number of potential veto players and thus made policy change more difficult. However, we also show that concentration of power in a policy dictator (a single player whose consent is necessary and sufficient to alter policies) does not guarantee policy adaptability: when the dictator is able to transfer the costs of failure to somebody else (as the Stroessner regime did in the 1980s), he has little incentive to correct inefficient policies.

Second, there is uncertainty in the political economy literature with regard to the relationship between the dimensions of policy adaptability-rigidity and public-private regardedness. Public regarding policies tend to generate public goods, while private regarding policies tend to generate private goods or benefits for narrowly targeted sectors (Cox and McCubbins 2001). While Cox and McCubbins suggest that less decisive and adaptable policymaking tends to generate more private regardedness as a way to get things done, the Paraguayan case suggests that these two dimensions may in fact be orthogonal: while levels of policy adaptability in Paraguay varied considerably over time, private regardedness has been constant, as the system has been historically marked by patronage and clientelism.

The Policymaking Process under Stroessner

On May 4, 1954, after seven years of unstable one-party rule, a military coup removed President Federico Chaves from office. The leader of the coup, Gen. Alfredo Stroessner, soon gained control over the executive branch, the Colorado party, and the army, establishing a regime that would last for almost 35 years—a regime characterized by fear, repression, and cooptation. Stroessner held office longer than any other ruler in Paraguayan history, and by 1989 approximately 75 percent of the population had grown up under the Stroessner regime, and therefore had no experience with democratic rule (Lambert and Nickson 1997).

Throughout this period, the basic structure of the policymaking process (PMP) remained quite constant. The chief executive was a dictator not only in the political sense of the term, but also in the technical sense because his approval was both necessary and sufficient to implement policy change. This concentration of power also fostered policy adaptability during the 1960s and the 1970s. However, when several conditions changed in the 1980s, they were not successfully addressed by the Stroessner regime and policy rigidity ensued.

Gen. Alfredo Stroessner's grip on power rested on a "cooperative" arrangement among state officials in all three branches of government and the bureaucracy, the Colorado party, and the armed forces, the so-called "triumvirate" of power (state-party-military). This arrangement was based on a single premise: that Stroessner would remain in office for the foreseeable future.[1] Stroessner's reelection was secured through several mechanisms. First, repression against political dissidents was backed up by a "permanent" state of siege (renewed every 90 days) and by ambiguous regulations, such as Law 209, which penalized "fostering hatred among Paraguayans" as a criminal offense. Second, the system established a culture of fear due to the arrest, torture, and death or exile of selected opposition leaders. This selective repression, combined with a widespread informal network of political spies, was internalized by the population, with the result that repression on a large scale was not always necessary, given the distrust and suspicion that dominated the country. Third, the Colorado party was strengthened nationwide, rewarding membership with economic and political incentives under the patronage system that tied people to the regime at all social levels. Fourth, after two elections with Stroessner as the only candidate (in 1954 and 1958), there was a tightly controlled multiparty system with limited political activity granted to selected opposition parties (1962–89).

Under this system, the so-called *stronato*, Gen. Stroessner was elected to office eight times, with 98.4 percent of the vote in 1954, 97.3 percent

---

[1] Originally, the 1967 Constitution established reelection for only one more period, but after the 1977 reform the president could be reelected indefinitely.

in 1958, 90.6 percent in 1963, 70.9 percent in 1968, 83.6 percent in 1973, 90.0 percent in 1978, 90.1 percent in 1983, and 88.6 percent in 1988 (Lambert 1997). According to the electoral law in place since the late 1950s, the winning party in a "competitive election" was granted 67 percent of the seats in congress. Congressional representatives could be re-elected indefinitely. Following the legal precedent of previous charters, the 1967 Constitution gave Stroessner great powers over congress and the judiciary. The president was able to dissolve congress without restrictions, and congress had no ability to convene itself. Congress was not an important arena of policymaking because the initiative for all major policymaking was expected to come from the executive, and legislators had no real veto power. The role of congress—as well as the judiciary—was merely to provide a democratic façade, and it was therefore expected to be supportive of the executive's policy initiatives.

Therefore, Stroessner and key collaborators from the Colorado party and the armed forces that surrounded him made all policymaking decisions. For the most part during this period, the bureaucracy remained a secondary player. Although "threatening" ministers like Edgar L. Ynsfrán were eventually purged, Stroessner preserved a rather stable cast of characters in the cabinet. In the early 1980s, Paul Lewis (1982, p. 73) noted:

> There has been a tendency for the *stronato's* governing elite to become a gerontocracy. General Marcial Samaniego, the defense minister, and General César Barrientos, the finance minister, are old army friends of Stroessner's who have served in his government from the beginning. Raúl Peña, the education minister, Tomás Romero Pereira, the minister without portfolio, and Raúl Sapena Pastor, who recently retired as foreign minister, have also served more than 20 years in their posts. Sabino Montanaro, the minister of interior, is a 15-year veteran on the cabinet. Saúl González (justice), Hernando Bertoni (agriculture), and Adán Godoy Giménez (health) have all served more than 10 years. So did Ynsfrán, who for 11 years at the Ministry of Interior was reputed to be the second most powerful man in the country.

The presence of a stable ministerial team was more consistent with the private regarding policymaking process (and ultimately with the emergence of policy rigidities) than with the development of a highly trained and stable bureaucracy. Although some "islands of excellence" were attempted (for instance, the *Secretaría Técnica de Planificación* was created in 1962 under the aegis of the Alliance for Progress), their impact on the overall PMP was limited.

With respect to the Colorado party, Stroessner was able to transform it from a party deeply divided along factional lines into a highly united and vertically organized political instrument (Lambert 1997). He purged the party of opposition, converted it into an instrument that legitimized his regime, and used this mass-based, agrarian party to mobilize support and repress opposition. Between 1954 and 1966, Stroessner consolidated his own control over the party by selectively purging internal party opponents (Lambert 1997). As a result, Stroessner imposed a "granitic unity" on the party through repression and expulsion of internal opposition and through the promotion of politicians loyal to him (Lambert 1997). In addition, the Colorado party progressively became a mass-based party with extensive control of the media, patronage resources, and extensive grassroots support. Its leaders developed a nationwide network of *seccionales* (local party offices) that mobilized support for the regime and represented the "eyes and ears" of the government, employing thousands of spies to report antigovernment sentiment among the population (Lambert 1997). Unopposed elections of centrally nominated candidates at the local party offices guaranteed tight control over the party. Moreover, the *seccionales* administered the political patronage system. Membership in the party was mandatory for all state employees, including teachers, members of the armed forces, and judges. Patronage, dispersed mainly through the party, tied people of all social levels to the regime (Nickson 1997). In exchange for public employment, public employees attended meetings and parades, and donated part of their income—which was automatically deducted from their paychecks—to the party (Arditi 1993). Senior party members received lucrative contracts for state projects, holdings in public companies, and other opportunities to become successful businessmen (Lambert 1997).

The third key component of the PMP was the role of the armed forces. The alliance between them and the Colorado party was consolidated in 1947 (seven years before Stroessner took over). After a short but brutal civil war that depleted the military of 90 percent of its officer corps, the armed forces were reorganized under the supervision of the Colorado party (Lambert 1997). Stroessner strengthened this alliance through the mandatory membership of military officers in the Colorado party, and by unifying his command as president, commander in chief of the armed forces, and honorary president of the Colorado party. Throughout the 1950s, Stroessner brought the military under his own control. While disloyalty was punished, loyalty was rewarded with promotion and economic privileges. Military officials had access to land and lucrative positions in state monopolies, as well as a free hand in illicit businesses such as widespread contraband.

Given this consolidation of power, the government, the Colorado party, and the armed forces had long time horizons during the 1960s and the 1970s. The incentive structure was stable and the partnership remained cohesive and strong. The main enforcer of the intertemporal deals was Stroessner himself, and the main deterrent to defection from Stroessner's policymaking game was punishment for disloyal behavior. In other words, the Paraguayan policymaking process during this period was based on four simple rules. First, the executive branch was to be the source of any changes to the status quo. Congress was not expected to be the locus of policy innovation, and responsibility for policy performance was exclusively the president's. Second, a cohesive ruling party was expected to support the president's proposals in congress (Lewis 1982). A legislative career was essentially the reward for politicians loyal to the president, and the Colorado party was always guaranteed a majority (and even a two-thirds supermajority) under the "incomplete list" electoral system in force until 1992. Third, the judiciary was expected to shield the president's policies from external challenges. Fourth, it was assumed that disgruntled social actors could be coopted, bribed, or repressed to accept new policies.

This system generated a dictator whose acquiescence was both necessary and sufficient to alter the policy status quo. To sustain this arrangement, two lasting deals were enforced: the first allowed major military leaders to control illegal rent-seeking activities (smuggling operations, drug trafficking), and the second allowed the Colorado politicians to control the distribution of patronage positions in the public administration.

Within this general framework, specific intertemporal policy agreements were viable but for the most part irrelevant, because politicians and military officers had delegated the policymaking function to the executive. This delegation of authority allowed Stroessner to adopt a host of policy changes. For example, in the first years of the regime, Stroessner reversed some of the nationalistic policies of the 1940s (for instance, the monopoly on the internal beef trade controlled by the Paraguayan Meat Corporation, Copacar). In 1957, the government adopted a major IMF-sponsored stabilization program. It included the deregulation of trade, the reduction of the monetary base, cuts in public expenditures, and a wage freeze. The ensuing stand-by loan in 1957–61 and the recovery of foreign credit allowed for an extensive road construction program (Campos and Canese 1987).

The alliance of the armed forces, the Colorado party, and the government also reinforced the expectations of a long time horizon for the regime. Therefore, the Stroessner regime showed a significant ability to reap the benefits offered by long-term economic opportunities. For instance, development toward the Brazilian border in order to diversify a dependent pattern of economic relationships with Argentina required large investments and an active and stable foreign policy. This large-scale movement toward the eastern border required coordination of land distribution, internal rural migration, and massive construction, among other initiatives, and was possible because of the intertemporal "cooperation" of the key actors (the government, the party, and the armed forces). The adaptation of the development model to allow for increasing integration with Brazil would have been unlikely under short-lived governments like the ones characterizing the post-Chaco war period (1936–54). During that 18-year period, there were 12 different presidents, and political volatility prevented an adaptation to changing economic environments.

The long time horizon also made it possible for the regime to undertake deeper economic reforms. During the 1956–81 period, the government distributed more than 88,000 farms covering 7.4 million hectares in 48 colonies (Lynn Ground 1984). This land distribution represented 59 percent of the existing farms in 1956 and 35 percent of the existing farms in 1981. These policies promoted the emergence of a local agricultural business sector related to the regime. This sector took advantage of the boom in soybean and cotton production during the following decade. During this period, the government also built roads, silos, and most importantly, the biggest dam in the world, the Itaipú hydroelectric dam, built jointly with Brazil. This large-scale project encouraged the emergence of a large construction sector. This industry grew from fewer than 22 family-owned construction companies in the early 1970s to some 250 corporations after the Itaipú period (Borda 1993).

The long-term growth strategy turned out to be very effective. During the 1960s, real GDP growth was 4.2 percent. In the ensuing decade, Paraguay had one of the highest growth rates in the region, with real GDP increasing at 8 percent.

In stark contrast with the 1954–81 period when the Paraguayan PMP fostered adaptable policies, between 1982 and 1989 the regime tended toward much more rigid ones. As the "shadow of the future" became increasingly shorter, cooperative arrangements among key stakeholders of the Stroessner regime became harder to sustain. The main reason was the dictator's age and his (perceived) deterioration in health, particularly after 1987 (Abente Brun 1993). Since the enforcer of the intertemporal agreements was Stroessner himself, the problem of succession was a big one. In contrast to less institutionalized neo-patrimonial regimes in which power was easily transferred to the dictator's son after his death (Nicaragua in 1956, Haiti in 1971), the *Militantes* (the faction that sought a dynastic solution to the succession problem) confronted a diverse set of groups within the Colorado party and the armed forces. Consistent with the prediction of the folk theorem in game theory, this intertemporal cooperation was more difficult to sustain when the end of the game was approaching with more certainty.[2] In fact, the end of the Stroessner

---

[2] In game theory, folk theorems are a class of theorems that imply that in repeated games, any outcome is a feasible solution concept, if under that outcome the players will minimize the maximum possible loss that they could face in the game.

regime was ultimately the consequence of a struggle for succession (Martini and Lezcano 1997).

The twilight of Stroessner's regime also coincided with increasingly harsh economic conditions. Following the conclusion of the Itaipú dam project, the Paraguayan economy entered a deep recession that lasted well into the 1980s. At the same time, the debt crisis hurt two of Paraguay's main trade partners, Brazil and Argentina. Paraguay's GDP declined for two consecutive years, leaving production 4 percent lower in 1983 than in 1981. Growth resumed in 1984, but the average rate during 1984–86 was well below population growth (World Bank 1992).

The sectors that suffered most after 1982—construction, commerce, and finance—were those that had grown most rapidly in the 1970s boom. By now, the support of these sectors had become very important for the Stroessner regime. Instead of forcing the domestic economy into conformity with the external conditions, the government tried to avert the post-Itaipú recession by continuing with its investment and spending programs. These policies only piled a financial disequilibrium on top of the recession. The economy still stagnated and inflation accelerated. To finance its increased spending, the government sharply increased its external borrowing. Medium- and long-term debt (including arrears) rose from 15 percent of GDP in 1981 to 62 percent in 1987. Moreover, the external funds were largely used on unprofitable projects, which added to macroeconomic instability and eventually led to the suspension of disbursements from several creditors (World Bank 1992).

In terms of its "welfare" effects, the *Stronismo's* PMP (1982–89) provides a good example of the independence between policy adaptability and public regardedness. Throughout the entire 1954–89 period, policies in Paraguay were characterized by their low public regardedness. Their purpose was to benefit mainly the loyal members of the Colorado party and the armed forces. Even during its "golden" years, membership in the Colorado party was a requirement for conducting business with the government, and an extensive patronage system was administered by a nationwide network of *seccionales*. According to Ramon

Fogel (1993, p. 16), the resources invested in the hydroelectric dams (76 percent to Itaipú and 24 percent to Yasyretá) were "channelled by a reduced group of civilian and military followers of the dictator nucleated in few companies ... and ultimately devoted to speculation, the development of financial enterprises, and the acquisition of ranches; therefore the powerful economic groups integrated themselves to new economic sectors."

Campos and Canese (1987) identify a series of "inconvenient" public investments that began in the second half of the 1970s. The authors claim that these projects shared a common pattern characterized by a dubious need for the venture, an oversized plan, the impossibility of recovering the investment, the evaluation of the proposal by interested parties, a resort to foreign loans, the avoidance of public bidding, and a systematic recourse to foreign suppliers. Among them were the ACEPAR steel plant, the airport near President Stroessner City (today Ciudad del Este), the bridge over the Paraguay River at Concepción City, the purchase of military helicopters and vessels, the construction of large hospitals, and the Chaco telecommunications program. In trying to explain these "white elephants," the authors concluded that "the large magnitude of the public sector expenditures ... leads to the conclusion that this is one of the most important ways to generate a surplus that is concentrated by a small number of people" (Campos and Canese 1987, p. 82).

The lack of public regardedness also reinforced the policy rigidities of the 1980s. As an example of this problem, the recession of the 1980s did not lead to a reduction in clientelism or patronage politics. On the contrary, public employment—which had grown at an average 4.5 percent per year in 1975–80—grew at a 4.8 percent rate in 1980–84, and at a 5.6 percent rate in 1984–87 (Campos and Canese 1990). The total number of public jobs expanded from 82,000 in 1980 to 119,000 in 1989 (Campos and Canese 1990, table 4). In 1982, before the 1983 general election, the total wage bill in the public sector (excluding state enterprises) grew by 19 percent, just at a time when the economy was decelerating. As a result, the share of public wages on total public consumption grew from 58 percent in 1981 to 68 percent in the following years.

The Post-Dictatorial Period

On February 3, 1989, a coup led by General Andrés Rodríguez drove Alfredo Stroessner out of power and initiated the transition to democracy. Following the "standard procedure" in place since 1954, Gen. Rodríguez was nominated as the Colorado party candidate for the May 1989 presidential election and won with 74 percent of the vote.

The collapse of the old regime had three consequences. In the short run, the arrival of a new coalition, combined with a PMP that remained centered on the executive, allowed for a new period of rapid policy change. In the medium run, the internal struggles within the new coalition progressively eroded the president's control over the Colorado party and planted the seed of factionalism discussed below. In the long run, increasing respect for civil liberties and the adoption of a new constitution in 1992 facilitated the incorporation of new players into the policymaking process—and thus multiplied the number of veto points.

An interesting aspect of this brief "transitional" period is that the policymaking process initially operated under the existing rules—but now under a new leadership. Between 1989 and 1993, the transitional regime preserved the executive-centered policymaking process under the command of Andrés Rodríguez. Therefore, it provides almost a "quasi-experimental" setting to further evaluate the opportunities and constraints afforded by the old PMP. We would expect to observe a continuation of previous public policies (that is, policy stability) along the dimensions in which the policy preferences of the old and the new regime coincided. Similarly, we would expect to observe rapid policy change along the dimensions in which the preferences of the old and new regimes diverged.

The analysis of some of the main policies adopted in this transitional period lends support for these expectations. One area in which Rodríguez shared the same preferences as his predecessor was land tenure policies. After the overthrow of the Stroessner regime, the most pressing issue coming from the Paraguayan countryside was the small farmers' (*campesinos*) struggle for land. The end of public lands in the 1980s, coupled with the difficulties the *campesinos* had in obtaining land through market mechanisms because of poverty and the low profitability of *campesino* crops, created a massive number of landless *campesinos*. There were more than 110,000 landless families in 1989. In that year, the Paraguayan congress sought to address this problem with a new land reform program intended to target landless families (Servicio de Consultoría Informativa, December 1989). However, the Rodríguez administration did not implement these changes effectively. While congress passed laws authorizing the expropriation of more than half a million hectares, the effective implementation of those expropriations only affected 47,134 hectares (9 percent of the affected area) (Servicio de Consultoría Informativa, October 1995). In addition to the very slow implementation of the expropriation procedures, the government did not have the political will to recover much of the land that had been acquired dishonestly by high-ranked officers under the dictatorial regime (Servicio de Consultoría Informativa, December 1989).

In some key aspects, the respective policy preferences of the Stroessner and Rodríguez administrations diverged. As a result, an initial flurry of policy reform took place in the early 1990s. After a long period of post-Itaipú rigidity, economic policies during the transitional period (1989–93) targeted the deregulation of the economy. This process included exchange rate liberalization, substantial tariff reductions, deregulation of agricultural prices, and deregulation of interest rates (Servicio de Consultoría Informativa, December 1989, 1990, 1991). The first year of the Rodríguez administration was marked by the elimination of the multiple, fixed exchange rate system, a reduction of tariffs, and the liberalization of agricultural prices. In 1990, the administration liberalized interest rates and signed Law 60/90, promoting foreign investment. A year later, Paraguay joined Mercosur (with Argentina, Brazil, and Uruguay), reducing by 47 percent all tariffs for member products not included in the exceptions list. A goal of zero tariffs was set for 1996. That same year, the government reduced the required reserves in the central bank for bank deposits and signed Law 117/91, establishing equal treatment for national and foreign investors (who became eligible to receive investment promotion incentives). Paraguay also joined the Multilateral Investment Guarantee Agency (MIGA), part of the World Bank Group, for coverage against losses due to noncommercial risks. In

1992, the government again reduced tariffs and enacted a tax reform that involved the creation of a value added tax and a simplification of the tax structure.

While some public policies moved from rigidity to adaptability in the early 1990s, low public regardedness remained a constant outer feature. In 1991 government resources were still used to finance the Colorado party in elections (Servicio de Consultoría Informativa, December 1991) and corruption was not seriously addressed. For example, in 1990 the executive vetoed a law to create a National Commission of Investigation of Corruption against the Public Sector.

The New Policymaking Process

The 1989–92 transitional period initiated slow but steady processes of democratization and decentralization. Freedom of speech and association were granted to the people; elections became progressively cleaner; advances were made toward the renovation of the judiciary system and many judges appointed for political reasons under the dictatorial regime were removed. Nonetheless, it was not until 1992 that the adoption of a new constitution restructured the underlying rules of the game. In particular, the "triumvirate" of the Colorado party, the government, and the military that had characterized the Stroessner regime was significantly weakened under the new constitutional framework.

On December 10, 1991, Paraguayans cast ballots for a 198-member constituent assembly. Three weeks later, a national constitutional assembly was formally established. It included 122 members from the ruling Colorado party and 55 from the Authentic Radical Liberal Party (PLRA). The assembly's main purpose was to replace the existing constitution, which was adopted in 1967 under Stroessner. Specifically, it sought to establish a system of checks and balances and proclaim the illegality of dictatorship and tyranny. On March 10, the assembly's draft committee approved articles calling for the separation and balance of powers (executive, legislative, and judicial). In addition, on May 27, it also approved articles prohibiting presidential reelection, creating the office of vice president, and establishing civilian control over the armed forces. These provisions, as discussed below, proved to be crucial for the particular unfolding of the new Paraguayan PMP. The constitutional assembly approved the new constitution on June 20. Two days later, President Gen. Andrés Rodríguez swore an oath to uphold the new constitution, despite the fact that in his opinion the article banning him and members of his family from the 1993 elections was "an affront" to his honor.

On May 9, 1993, a new president, legislators, and departmental governors were elected simultaneously in national elections. Juan Carlos Wasmosy, the Colorado party candidate, received 40 percent of the vote, and became the first civilian president of Paraguay in 39 years. Wasmosy's victory ensured the continued grip of the Colorado party on the country's political power. However, unlike Rodríguez, the newly elected president had to operate under the new institutional framework established in the 1992 Constitution.

Among the most important changes introduced in the 1992 Constitution were those affecting the powers of the presidency. The new institutional framework deprived the president of the power to dissolve congress. It endowed the executive branch with relatively weak "proactive" and "reactive" powers.[3] The 1992 Constitution (article 210) constrains the president's proactive powers in three ways. First, the president is not allowed to issue unilateral decrees and must instead introduce "urgent" bills in congress (which he can legally enforce if congress fails to act in 60 days). Second, the president is not allowed to introduce more than three urgent bills per year. Third, congress can lift the urgency character of a bill with two-thirds of the votes, reverting to the normal policymaking process. For this reason, the proactive powers of the executive branch are generally considered to be "toothless." In addition, the president's line item veto can be overridden by an absolute majority of congress.

---

[3] Consistent with Shugart and Carey (1992), Payne and others (2002) characterize the reactive powers of the Paraguayan president as "moderate" vis-à-vis the "weak" reactive powers of the Costa Rican and Honduran presidents who presumably lack partial veto powers. However, articles 126–127 of the Costa Rican constitution allow the president to "amend" bills passed by congress and return them to the assembly for reconsideration, and article 220 of the Honduran constitution is ambiguous about the possibility of a partial veto.

Furthermore, the provisions regarding the election of the president also affected the subsequent capacity of the officeholders to make an appeal to their "legitimacy" and "go public" when needed. The constitutional assembly established that the president and vice president would be elected by plurality for five-year terms by a simple majority of the electorate. The simple majority rule obviated runoff elections in the event that no one candidate received an absolute majority. Therefore, the system allowed for "minority" presidents to be elected. The article banning presidential reelection also created the potential for a lame duck president after a few years in office.

With respect to the legislative branch, deputies and senators are elected in concurrent elections every five years and can be reelected indefinitely—in contrast to the president. The 1992 Constitution instituted a chamber of deputies with 80 members to be elected from 18 districts for five-year terms. The deputies are elected from closed party lists using the d'Hondt divisor form of proportional representation in relatively small districts (the average district magnitude is 4.4). In theory, the closed list system creates few incentives to cultivate the "personal vote" (Carey and Shugart 1995; Hallerberg and Marier 2004) but, as shown below, legally mandated party primaries and relatively small districts have encouraged particularistic politics in the lower chamber. The senate consists of 45 members elected from closed party lists in a nationwide electoral district. Thus in contrast to the deputies, who have clear incentives to promote departmental interests, senators do not represent local elites but rather constitute visible party figures at the national level. In other respects, the Paraguayan bicameral system is highly congruent—meaning that the partisan composition of the house and the senate is usually quite similar (Lijphart 1999; Llanos 2002).

Most importantly, the 1992 Constitution granted congress more "proactive" and "reactive" powers than it had under Stroessner. It was now in charge of appointing members of the supreme court and the judiciary. Moreover, with an effective two-thirds opposition majority, it could not only block government legislation but also overrule presidential decrees. Finally, the legislature was also now able to initiate investigations into past cases of military corruption and human rights violations (Nickson 1997).

The 1992 Constitution also included several provisions intended to reform the judicial system. The new charter included a broad definition of human rights and established a new framework for the court system, and also sought to promote judicial independence: the constitution mandated that 3 percent of public expenditures be allocated to the judiciary and decreed that judges were not allowed to hold partisan posts. In addition, a jury to prosecute judges (independent from the supreme court's control) and a *Consejo de la Magistratura* to select judges were established. However, many of these initiatives were never fully implemented (or implemented at all). The result was a somewhat more autonomous, but hardly competent judiciary.

Another important aspect of the new policymaking process was the emergence of important civil society organizations with the capacity to act as "last-ditch" veto players and thus to exercise a check on the government's authority. In particular, the greater freedom of association experienced since 1989 has allowed a considerable organizational strengthening of autonomous *campesinos* organizations. The strengthening of these organizations was characterized not only by the widening of their membership, but also by a much better articulation of local organizations into regional and national small farmer federations. In the 1989–92 period alone, more than 12,500 new families were organized into more than 550 new committees (Ocampos and Rodríguez 1999). The organized *campesinos* also became actively engaged in scaling up their organizational networks in wider instances of coordination. A first attempt at widening coordination among the organized *campesinos* was the *Federación Nacional Campesina* (FNC). The FNC was born in July 1991 and initially included 15 organizations and approximately 7,000 members (Servicio de Consultoría Informativa, December 1991). The organizations associated with CONAPA took the initiative of creating the FNC (Ocampos and Rodríguez 1999). In 1992, with the newly created FNC, there were four national small farmer federations with at least 15,000 members (Ocampos and Rodríguez 1999).

Against the backdrop of these institutional provisions and the emergence of these new veto players, the factor that arguably contributed more to shape a new PMP was the realignment of Paraguay's political forces.

Historically, partisan politics in Paraguay have centered on the competition between two nineteenth-century organizations: the Colorados (or the National Republican Association, ANR) and the Liberals (nowadays called the Authentic Radical Liberals, PLRA). The recovery of political rights by Paraguayan citizens was reflected in the electoral participation of new political forces. During the transitional period, the emergence of independent candidates and new political forces challenged this two-party system. Independent candidates ran for positions in the national assembly in late 1991. A new political party, the middle-class *Partido Encuentro Nacional* (PEN), achieved 23 percent of the total presidential votes in the 1993 election. Additional parties (Oviedo's *Unace, the Movimiento Patria Querida, and País Solidario*) emerged in the early 2000s.

As the democratic transition process has unfolded, the opposition represented by the Liberal party and the new political forces has increasingly gained access to the policymaking process. Although the ANR is still the largest party (winning 67 percent of the seats in the lower chamber in 1989, 50 percent in 1993, 56 percent in 1998, and 46 percent in 2003), the Liberals were able to capture the vice presidency in the 2000 election (which was scheduled to fill the vacant position after the vice president was killed in 1999). Smaller middle-class parties (*Encuentro Nacional, País Solidario*, and *Patria Querida*) and a Colorado splinter (*Unace*) have been able to capture a few seats in congress.

The executive branch for the most part has remained under Colorado control (exceptions to this rule have been the capture of the vice president's office by the Liberals in the 2000 election, and the incorporation of the PEN into the cabinet in 1999–2003), but the adoption of proportional representation has made the congressional arena increasingly pluralistic. Figure 9.1 depicts the transformation of Paraguay from a hegemonic party system into a multiparty system, using the effective number of parties index (Laakso and Taagepera 1979).[4] Before 1963,

---

[4] The Effective Number of Parties is an index akin to the Hirschman-Herfindahl index of market concentration (HHI) that weights the distribution of legislative seats among political parties. The formula for the index is $ENP = 1/\sum \left(p^2 \right)$, where p represents the proportion of seats controlled by each party in the lower chamber.

Figure 9.1. Effective Number of Parties in the Chamber of Deputies, Paraguay, 1954–2004 (Laasko-Taagepara index)

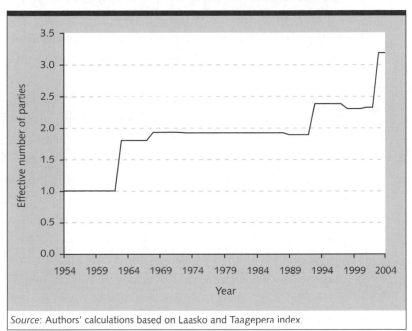

Source: Authors' calculations based on Laasko and Taagepera index.

when Stroessner allowed token opposition into congress, the effective number of parties was 1.0. Between 1963 and 1992, the average effective number of parties was 1.9. During the last decade, however, multiparty-ism has emerged in the Paraguayan congress, with 3.2 effective parties currently in the chamber of deputies.

Alongside these "party system" transformations, the Colorado party itself was also experiencing very important changes. Specifically, the "granitic unity" of the ruling party during the Stroessner era gave way to increasing factionalism. The atomization of the party took place in five stages, starting with the election of the constituent assembly and leading to the ANR splinter in 2003:

1. Although the Colorado party won a majority of the seats in the 1992 constituent assembly, the presence of internal factions created room for the formation of strategic coalitions with op-

position forces. For instance, the Colorado leaders from the hinterland (the "*Bancada Campesina*") managed to establish the constitutional bases for the decentralization process (Barreda and Costafreda 2002), and the faction led by Luis M. Argaña was able to impose a constitutional ban on Rodríguez's presidential reelection.

2. In response to this move, the commander of the cavalry and President Rodríguez's right-hand man, Gen. Lino Oviedo, blocked Argaña's presidential ambitions. In late 1992, when Luis M. Argaña and Juan Carlos Wasmosy confronted each other in the presidential primary, Oviedo intervened in the vote counting process to ensure the defeat of Argaña. This move placed Gen. Oviedo in a highly influential position during the new Wasmosy administration after 1993.

3. In 1996, the conflicts within the Colorado party entered a new phase. The insistence of Gen. Oviedo on encroaching in the political process eventually led to a showdown with President Wasmosy. In April 1996, Wasmosy ordered the retirement of his military ally and Oviedo responded with a failed insurrection (Ayala Bogarín and Costa 1996). This action ultimately led to Oviedo's arrest and justified his proscription from the 1998 general election, even though the general had emerged as the favorite candidate in the Colorado primary, defeating Luis M. Argaña.

4. Because Oviedo was under arrest, his running mate Raúl Cubas Grau was named the official Colorado candidate for 1998. For legal reasons, Luis M. Argaña became his vice president. President Cubas's decision to release Oviedo from prison immediately after he took office in August 1998 created a new confrontation with the Argaña faction and an impeachment threat from congress. There was some speculation that congress would remove President Cubas and install Argaña as the new chief executive until the vice president was shot and killed in March 1999. Argaña's killing triggered a wave of protests (known as the "Paraguayan March") that ended with the resignation of Cubas and the installation of Luis González Macchi as interim president.

5. Over the next three years, the Oviedista faction reciprocated by attempting to unseat President González Macchi several times. A failed military coup took place in May 2000 and, in the midst of several corruption scandals, the Oviedistas and the Liberal party attempted to impeach González Macchi at least three times.[5] Still in exile and banned from running in the presidential election, Gen. Oviedo ordered the transformation of his Colorado faction into a new party, Unace (*Unión Nacional de Colorados Eticos*), for the 2003 race.[6]

The events illustrate how the internal factionalism became the norm in the party, and the extent to which traditional Colorado-military relations deteriorated. In this context, new regulations instituted (legally mandated) primary elections to define the candidacies and the composition of party conventions. The new regulations also banned the practice of deducting contributions to the Colorado party from public sector paychecks and prevented party affiliation among military officers.

The Workings of the New PMP

As a result of the historical background described above and the institutional structure created by the 1992 Constitution, the workings of the Paraguayan policymaking process are very different from the mechanisms in place during the *Stronato*. This section seeks to characterize this new PMP from 1993 to the present day. This period includes the Wasmosy (1993–98), Cubas Grau (1998–99), González Macchi (1999–2003), and Duarte Frutos (2003–06) administrations.

Because the rules governing the PMP are still in flux, it is difficult to establish them with precision. This section presents an interpretation of how the post-1993 policymaking process works, and then confronts

---

[5] An impeachment finally took place in early 2003, but the senate acquitted González Macchi.

[6] Gen. Lino Oviedo returned to Paraguay in late June 2004. At the time of this writing, he was facing a sentence of 10 years in prison.

these conjectures with evidence from executive-legislative relations. Our main conclusion is that in the post-1993 period, Paraguayan presidents have been much weaker in terms of their ability to pass their agendas. Consequently, most presidents have had a hard time passing national policies, and have had to resort mostly to particularistic ones (which in some cases were needed to help pass the others).

Given the tradition of strong presidentialism, Paraguayan presidents have continued to be the initiators of all "relevant" policies. However, the executive branch's ability to impose the policy agenda has been crippled by three factors. First, as discussed above, the 1992 charter deprived presidents of their immense constitutional powers (such as the power to dissolve congress). Second, the reelection ban on the executive transforms every president into a lame duck. The third important factor that has to be taken into account is the fragmentation of the ANR since 1993.

Regarding this last issue, figure 9.2 shows the evolution of the Rice index of party unity for the Colorado and the Liberal parties in the chamber of deputies from 1994 to 2004. The Rice index ranges from 0, when the party is evenly split on any legislative vote, to 100, when all the members of the party vote together (Rice 1925).[7] Because the chamber of deputies, in contrast to the senate, collects roll call votes on a regular basis, it was possible to estimate the cohesion scores using 1,409 controversial votes since 1995.[8] Figure 9.2 suggests that the cohesion of Paraguayan parties at present is quite low. At the peak of the factional confrontation in 1999, the Colorado party reached an abysmal unity score of just 30 points. The average ANR score during the González Macchi administration was 43 points. In contrast to the ANR, the PLRA has shown increasing cohesion over time, but its Rice scores are not particularly high (75 on average for all years and 81 during the best year). In a comparative study, John Carey found average Rice scores of 91 points for Mexican parties, 81 for Chilean parties, 79 for Peruvian and Uruguayan parties, 75 for Brazilian parties, and 88 for Argentine parties (Carey 2002b). In his study of

---

[7] The formula for the index is $R = |Ayes - Nays|/(Ayes + Nays)*100$

[8] Controversial votes were defined as decisions in which at least 25 percent of the legislators voted against the winning side (Mainwaring and Pérez-Liñán 1997). The focus

Figure 9.2. Party Unity, Paraguay, 1994–2004 (Rice index)

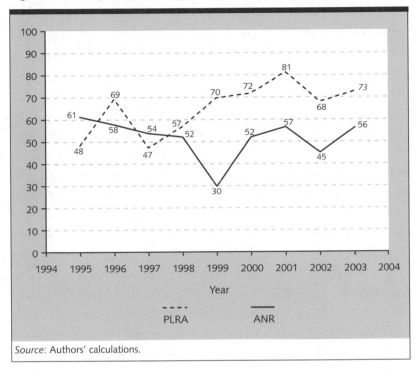

Source: Authors' calculations.

the Argentine chamber of deputies, Mark Jones (2002) found that the two largest parties (PJ and UCR) consistently had scores above 90 points between 1989 and 1997.[9]

As the "granitic unity" of the ruling party during the Stroessner era gave way to factionalism, the Colorado party's ability to play the role of a "legislative dictator" has eroded. In practical terms, this means that a Paraguayan president moved from controlling a "granitic" Colorado

---

on controversial votes guarantees that minor legislative decisions, which are normally consensual and thus inflate party unity scores, are not given undue influence.

[9] Comparison of unity scores is always difficult because roll call votes are not equally frequent in all legislatures and researchers select votes using slightly different criteria. Instead of dropping all noncontroversial votes, Carey weighted votes according to their closeness and the number of legislators absent. Jones provided "relative" unity scores, ignoring absent legislators and abstentions.

party with 67 percent of the seats in congress in 1963 to bargaining with a factionalized party with 46 percent of the seats in 2003. As a result, we would expect that the capacity of successive presidents to enforce policy change in congress using their partisan powers would decline monotonically following the Rodríguez administration.

At the same time, a tradition of clientelism has encouraged factional party leaders to build their own private clienteles in order to compete for the control of their parties. The legally mandated primaries have compounded the problem, triggering a competitive drive for enrolling new party members under the banner of each faction. Although congressional reelection is not banned by the constitution, the electoral context has created greater uncertainty about the political survival of legislators. In 1998, 54 percent of the deputies were reelected—a figure comparable to Chile's lower house (Morgenstern 2002). Five years later, only 21 percent of the deputies remained in their seats, a situation that resembled the turnover of Argentina's "amateur" legislators (Jones and others 2002).[10] The decline was consistent across all major parties. Voters often enroll to participate in the primaries because of selective incentives provided by party bosses, but they are far from being committed party members. Therefore, legislators confronted with legally mandated primaries and with more competitive general elections are inclined to initiate particularistic bills for credit-claiming purposes and major bills for position-taking purposes. In other words, given the declining reelection rates and the tradition of a weak legislature, it is unlikely those legislators will be interested in grand policymaking.

The decline in presidential powers, the multiplication of opposition parties, and the emergence of autonomous factions within the ruling party points to the increasing propensity of congress to operate as a veto player. In fact, the number of controversial bills has grown over time. Bill-related controversy (reflecting the greater role of factional veto players) tends to arise over comprehensive (nationwide, regionwide, or sector-wide) policies with regulatory or redistributive intent. In contrast, particularistic

---

[10] These figures are estimates of unconditional reelection, based on roll call data. We do not know how many deputies were actually placed in the lists.

policies with low visibility and low marginal cost are less likely to generate friction within the legislature or in executive-legislative relations.

In this context, presidents eager to pass broad legislative agendas are forced to build legislative coalitions using selective incentives. Four resources stand out for this purpose. First, presidents can use patronage positions (particularly in administrative areas of wide regional coverage such as education or public health) to benefit the constituents of loyal legislators. Second, they can accelerate or delay the disbursement of funds for legislators' particularistic projects. Third, they can grant limited voice and visibility to small middle class parties, always eager to convince their urban constituents that they have leverage in the PMP. Fourth, in extreme circumstances they can blackmail their fellow ANR leaders, arguing that in the absence of cooperation, policy failures will end the era of Colorado rule in the near future.

Although there is little empirical evidence available on the use of these coalition instruments, recent historical events suggest that they may have some intrinsic limitations. Take, for example, Nickson's (1997, pp. 187–88) account of Wasmosy's attempts to build a "governability pact" after he won the presidency in 1993:

> The fragile alliance inside the Colorado Party that had brought Wasmosy to the presidency began to break down within months of his taking office. Few party leaders were committed to the scaling-down of the public sector announced in his inaugural address, fearing that it would destroy the political power base of the Colorado Party ... In order to counter his lack of support within the Colorado Party, Wasmosy made concessions to the PLRA in order to obtain a working majority in Congress. In his inaugural address, he floated the idea of a "governability pact" so as to ensure the passage of legislation ... The governability pact assisted the passage of legislation originating from the executive ... however, it did little to forge an agreement over the fundamental structural reforms still needed to strengthen the overall democratization process. The political agenda soon became dominated by bitter opposition from the executive to new legislation originating in Congress.

Alternatively, patronage and pork seem to be an effective way to attract peripheral factions in the ruling party and in the PLRA, both of which are groups with limited resources that need to consolidate their electorates in order to survive in the primaries or eventually challenge the mainstream leaders in the party. At the same time, those resources may be less effective in dealing with stronger factions both within the ANR (like the Oviedistas) or the PLRA. To the extent that the leaders of these factions perform for a national audience and are eyeing the major prize (the presidency) in the coming election, they may be more reluctant to enter into agreements or they may demand excessive retribution for their support. Similarly, the argument about the need to preserve Colorado dominance in future elections can easily be turned on its head. When unions and *campesino* mobilizations oppose a policy initiative, Colorado leaders will invoke this argument in order to block policy change.

These conditions suggest that the Paraguayan system will provide relative flexibility for the provision of particularistic (private regarding) policies, but relative rigidity for the provision of comprehensive regulatory or redistributive policies. Particularistic policies refer to policies that are limited in scope (focusing on individuals or towns) and are distributive in nature (transferring public funds to those beneficiaries). In contrast, policies aimed at regulating broad economic sectors or nationwide activities and those intended to redistribute income and opportunities across social groups are expected to be more controversial and thus more likely to be stalled.

An examination of all the legislative bills (4,576 *proyectos de ley*) that received final treatment in congress between 1993 and 2003 supports these conjectures.[11] First, there seems to be a clear division of labor in terms of the scope of the policies initiated by different branches. The executive branch dominates the formulation of nationwide policies and

---

[11] Final treatment means that: the bill was approved and signed by the president; the bill was rejected by congress or vetoed by the executive; or the bill was treated for the last time at some point between 1993 and 2003 but the legislators made no final decision (that is, the bill was withdrawn, archived, or is pending).

policies related to the public sector (constitutionally, the executive has gatekeeping power over the initiation of the budget). In contrast, the legislature dominates the production of individual-level and local bills, and more surprisingly, the production of bills targeted to the private sector. In addition, members of congress have a greater propensity to initiate bills that have a distributive purpose and a limited scope (that is, that are particularistic). Under this definition, we find that only 7 percent of all the bills initiated by the executive during the period under study can be classified as particularistic, as opposed to 50 percent of all the bills initiated by the chamber of deputies, and 55 percent of all the bills initiated by the senate.

Second, and more importantly, the evidence suggests that in contrast to the 1954–89 period—which was characterized by the virtual absence of any significant veto players—the "old" pattern of policymaking was progressively dismantled in the early 1990s. To assess the impact of the process of legislative fragmentation on the PMP, we classified all bills according to their fate. Policy initiatives were coded as: approved (signed into law); rejected; or stalled (archived, withdrawn, or pending).[12] Figure 9.3 shows the passage rates of executive and legislative initiatives for each administration. The passage rates of executive-initiated bills declined from 96 percent during the last 16 months of the Rodríguez administration (a significant figure considering the lame duck position of the president) to 65 percent during the González Macchi administration. González Macchi's passage rate is comparable to the average found in a study of 11 presidential countries (63 percent) but is clearly lower than the rate of 72 percent enjoyed by other presidents with majority parties in congress (Cheibub, Przeworksi, and Saiegh 2004). Figures for the Duarte administration could not be interpreted, given the truncated sample (80 percent of the bills initiated by the executive and 93 percent of the bills initiated by congress were still pending resolution by the end of 2003, when our dataset ends).

---

[12] Some bills are archived when their content is incorporated into a larger initiative. So in a few cases, archived bills may have not been really stalled. Unfortunately, there is no practical way of identifying those bills.

Figure 9.3. Success Rate of Legislative Bills, by Administration and Initiator, Paraguay, 1992–2003 (percent of bills approved)

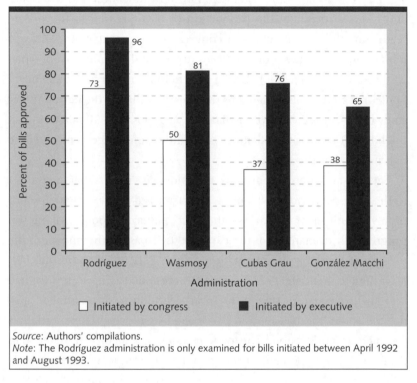

Source: Authors' compilations.
Note: The Rodríguez administration is only examined for bills initiated between April 1992 and August 1993.

It is clear from figure 9.3, though, that the model of executive-dominated policymaking has been increasingly challenged by the process of political fragmentation. But it is also true that fragmentation has hurt the ability of legislators to pass their preferred policies. The rate of congress-initiated bills that were approved has declined from 73 percent during the last months of the Rodríguez administration to about 38 percent as of 2003.

Figure 9.4 presents information on the passage rates of bills initiated by the executive and the legislature by type of policy (particularistic versus nonparticularistic) under four different administrations. The data show that for nonparticularistic policies, the passage rates tend to decline from presidency to presidency both for the executive and the leg-

Figure 9.4. Success Rate of Bills, by Initiator, Administration, and
Type of Policy, Paraguay, 1992–2003
(percent of bills approved)

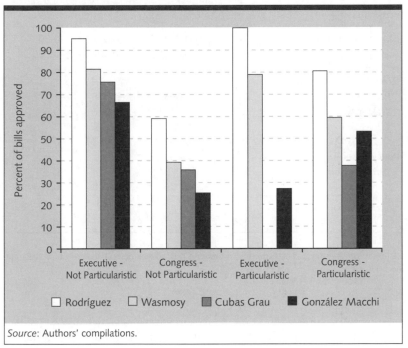

Source: Authors' compilations.

islature. In addition, in the case of legislative initiative, the figure shows that particularistic policies, being the least controversial initiatives, were the most likely to pass throughout the whole period. This pattern is less clear in the case of executive initiative, particularly under Presidents Cubas and González Macchi, who initiated very few particularistic policies (in fact, Cubas did not send a single piece of legislation of this type to congress). It should be noted, though, that even when nonparticularistic policies clear the legislative hurdle and become laws, their probability of being challenged by other "veto players" is significantly higher (see the discussion of the workings of the PMP below).

Based on this information, table 9.1 presents a logistic regression that models the simultaneous effects of institutional factors and policy types on the probability of policy change (as measured by policy approval and

Table 9.1. Passage Rate and Presidential Veto of Legislative Bills, by Initiator and Policy Area, Paraguay

Predictor	Model 9.1 Approval		Model 9.2 Presidential Veto	
Months to next election	0.004	–0.003	0.009	–0.008
Administration's months in office	–0.013	–0.002***	0.002	–0.006
Executive Initiation by				
Rodríguez	3.887	–0.593***	–1.378	–1.022
Wasmosy	1.952	–0.113***	–2.476	–0.589***
Cubas Grau	1.29	–0.373***	(a)	
González Macchi	1.185	–0.103***	–2.047	–0.515***
Policy Type				
Particularistic	0.918	–0.073***	–2.324	–0.352***
Constant	–0.261	–0.096***	–3.038	–0.264***
Nagelkerke R	0.162		0.122	
N	4446		4446	

Source: Authors.
a Dummy omitted for Cubas from model because it produces perfect separation of the data (no bill initiated by Cubas was ever vetoed).
***Significant at the 1% level.

presidential vetoes). The dependent variable in model 9.1 indicates whether a bill was ultimately approved (as opposed to rejected or stalled). The baseline category corresponds to nonparticularistic bills. The results of model 9.1 suggest the following conclusions. First, executive-initiated bills are more likely to be successful than congressional bills, but this advantage has eroded with successive administrations since they faced increasing levels of political fragmentation. Second, particularistic initiatives are more likely to pass than the bills in the baseline category. Third, although there is no clear evidence of an electoral policy cycle, the results suggest that the capacity of the system to promote policy change declines as the president approaches the end of the term.[13]

---

[13] The inclusion of two time variables, one reflecting the number of months elapsed in office and the other indicating the months pending to the next election (whether national or municipal contests) is intended to separate the effects of the electoral calendar from the "lame duck" effect.

In order to provide a more substantive interpretation of these results, we also simulated the expected probability of policy change (given the coefficients in model 9.1) under a particular set of initial conditions. These conditions are the following: the legislature initiates the bill; the administration is in the middle of the term; and there are no intermediate elections. The results show that the Paraguayan policymaking process is well equipped to deliver particularistic policies. These types of bills have the highest passage rates, ranging between 55 and 61 percent. In contrast, the ability of the legislative process to produce regulatory policies seems much weaker (16 to 35 percent). This general pattern holds even if one assumes that the executive branch and not the legislators initiate the proposals. A "contemporary" president (someone with leverage in between Cubas Grau and González Macchi), initiating a bill in the thirtieth month in office, would face an expected probability of passage ranging between 84 percent (for particularistic bills) and 55 percent (for nonparticularistic bills).

Finally, to complement these findings, we selected the occurrence of presidential vetoes as an alternative measure of controversy in the policy areas (model 9.2 in table 9.1). This measure is somewhat orthogonal to approval (a vetoed bill may still become law if congress overrides a package veto or accepts the president's partial veto) and it is intended to measure the controversy surrounding a bill rather than its success. Our dataset contains 104 episodes of partial or total vetoes. Our results confirm the idea that particularistic policies are less controversial (and therefore less likely to be vetoed by the executive), while redistributive and regulatory policies are more likely to generate friction in the policymaking process.

The Characteristics of Policies under the New PMP

The evidence presented in the previous section supports the notion that important changes have occurred in the Paraguayan PMP. Acknowledging that a new policymaking process is in place leads to the following questions: what are the features of public policies under this new PMP? How do they compare to the outer features of policies in previous historical periods? The patterns described in the last section suggest that the new policymaking process has generated policies that display both traditional and novel characteristics. On the one hand, Paraguayan public policies still show a conventional feature: low public regardedness. On the other hand, the current period contrasts with the "golden age" of *Stronismo* and with the Rodríguez transitional regime because during these two periods executive concentration of power allowed for fast policy change. In the democratic context, however, the multiplication of factional veto players has imposed low decisiveness on the PMP.

As noted above, the Stroessner model initially generated significant levels of policy adaptability, followed by increasing rigidity in the 1980s as the private regarding policies ossified. In part, these levels of adaptability resulted from the ability of the regime to marshal resources around long-term strategic projects like the "March towards the East." (This capacity to marshal resources also generated perverse side effects, such as inefficient patterns of public investment.) It is clear that for the most part, the current policymaking process lacks the same ability. Low decisiveness is in part the result of a weakened executive—with regard to both constitutional and partisan powers—but also of legislators with little incentive to engage in policymaking beyond particularistic projects.

These changes can be observed by looking at the pace and scope of economic reforms. During the Rodríguez administration, a set of reforms focusing on tax reforms, the balance of payments liberalization, financial liberalization, and price deregulation were implemented. Following this impulse, in 1993 the incoming Wasmosy administration allowed public companies and the Social Security Institute (IPS) to transfer their deposits to the private banking system. The Rodríguez and Wasmosy administrations also privatized a few medium-sized public companies: LAPSA airlines (*Líneas Aéras Paraguayas*), the merchant fleet (*Flota Mercante del Estado*), the ACEPAR steel company (*Aceros del Paraguay*), and the Paraguayan Administration of Sugar-Cane Spirits (APAL). However, only marginal changes have occurred after this initial period of reforms.

For example, on August 16, 1999, a day after taking office, President Cubas announced drastic measures to respond to the "critical" economic situation, citing the urgent need to cut the nation's US$200 million budget deficit. However, only a week later, congress warned it would not give him a "blank check" to confront the economic problems. The legislature's resistance was mostly driven by the internecine wrangling in the Colorado party. In particular, it had nothing to do with the economic reforms themselves, but it was related to political unrest generated by Cubas's commutation of Oviedo's sentence. Congressional leaders argued that the political crisis was likely to drive away foreign investors and thus should be addressed before any economic reforms were considered. Similarly, in 2000, the González Macchi administration was unable to implement policies to address Paraguay's fiscal deficit, which had surpassed 2.4 percent of GDP. Among those measures was a long-delayed privatization program that faced strong opposition from both the legislature and mobilized groups in the population (we discuss some episodes related to the privatization process below).

Three years later, when Nicanor Duarte-Frutos took office as Paraguay's president on August 15, 2003, this tendency toward policy rigidity seemed to be ripe for a change. Soon after his election, he sent a delegation to Washington to talk with representatives of the international financial institutions and explain the details of his "100-day plan" which gave priority to seven legislative initiatives. Despite not having a majority in the senate and the fact that the chamber of deputies was evenly split between the Colorado plurality and the opposition, the political environment for reform had improved. A small party, the emergent party *Patria Querida*, initially served as a pivotal player, negotiating with the president the approval of critical bills. For example, in 2004, the Duarte administration was able to secure passage of a tax reorganization law with the support of legislators from the *Patria Querida* party. The approval process involved several compromises with members of this party, and therefore, the resulting law was significantly amended to reflect the interests of their constituencies. Nonetheless, the new law (*Ley de Reordenamiento Administrativo y de Adecuación Fiscal*) proved to be an important accomplishment for the Duarte administration not only because it allowed the government to increase tax revenue, but also because the passage of the law was a condition for the IMF to give Paraguay a loan of US$70 million.

However, this cooperative situation soon proved to be a transitory one, and the main features of the PMP discussed above reemerged. While the legislature has been too fragmented to exercise power on its own, since 2005 it has persistently blocked major reforms. For example, during 2006, the general banking law was not approved (or considered) by the legislature.

Unsurprisingly, the *internismo* (infighting) within the Colorado party has been the main obstacle that Duarte faced throughout his presidency. In February 2006, after a failed censure vote against him promoted by *Patria Querida* and the Liberal party with the support of some Colorado deputies, Duarte sought to seize control of the party by competing for its presidency. Despite having obtained an overwhelming majority of votes, he did not take over the party's presidency in the wake of a controversy as to whether he could legally exercise it while being president of the Republic. This negative reaction to his decision to assume the presidency of the party is yet another sign of the extreme factionalization of the Colorados.

As these examples clearly illustrate, the current Paraguayan PMP has a limited ability to modify major policies. Many areas of reform identified as crucial by key stakeholders have been stalled. Among those delayed reforms are the privatization of public enterprises in the telecommunications, safe water, and railroad sectors; reform of social security; reform of the health system; a civil service reform; the reform of state-owned banks; the implementation of policies to promote rural land markets; and the modernization of public sector management, including the strengthening of the regulatory system in the financial sector.

This is not to say that Paraguayan presidents are completely unable to foster policy change—they still control important partisan and patronage resources—or that the ability to impose unilateral policy agendas would be always desirable; veto players perform a major function in any democratic PMP. The executive still controls important patronage resources that can be used to build policy coalitions, but such resources may be less effective when competing factions aspire to publicly distance themselves from the officials in López Palace. Thus the potential for policy adaptability may be low in the areas of regulatory and redistributive policy, where controversial issues are more likely to arise.

The quality of implementation of regulatory policies has also been hindered by the lack of a professionalized bureaucracy. In spite of the democratic process initiated in 1993, but consistent with an inability to introduce important policy reforms, post-Stroessner Paraguay has not been able to develop an effective, relatively independent, yet accountable bureaucracy. In 2000, Law 1626/00 sought to modernize the public service career by establishing a clearer system of selection, training, promotion, and retirement. Among its key features was the creation of the *Secretaría de la Función Pública*, in charge of increasing rationalization, transparency, and efficiency in human resource management, with the rank of a ministry. However, the law has been challenged as unconstitutional, substantially delaying its full application (World Bank 2003). Thus, Paraguay does not have clear descriptions of public positions, an effective training system, procedures manuals, a consistent scale of public salaries or any performance evaluation of public employees (World Bank 2003). Moreover, the factionalization that has characterized Paraguayan politics in the post-Stroessner period has permeated the public bureaucracy. Public hiring practices are characterized by a high degree of arbitrariness. These hiring practices are based principally on political favors and the support of political parties. At lower levels, its main consequence is that the Paraguayan bureaucracy is plagued by patronage.

With respect to policy stability, as noted, the Stroessner dictatorship was able to impose intertemporal policy deals until the succession crisis loomed on the political horizon. In contrast, the current PMP seems to have little ability to enforce long-term transactions, given the ban on presidential reelection, the discord and the political realignments within the ANR, and the focus of the opposition on removing the ANR from power in the medium run.

This conclusion, however, must be qualified on four grounds. First, the current players seem to agree on the overall rules for the production and distribution of particularistic policies. Second, the increasing number of veto players may ultimately impose a low rate of policy change in the years to come. These two conditions, however, seem to have added rigidity (rather than stability) to existing policies. Third, it must be noted that a direct comparison between the stability of the Stroessner policies and the uncertainty of the current policy regime may be deceiving. At the core of the Stroessner model was the elimination of policy controversies—and these are precisely the instances in which the PMP must generate either short-term policy volatility or stable intertemporal transactions.

Despite all the changes in the post-1993 PMP, there is a feature of public policies that has remained constant since the Stroessner period, the low level of public regardedness. This problem has taken two forms, corruption and particularistic policy (including the distribution of public jobs and pork). Corruption is the "classic" manifestation of the problem. In 2002, Paraguay ranked 98 out of 102 countries in the Transparency International Corruption Perceptions Index—the lowest score in Latin America. In addition, Paraguay occupied position 140 (out of 155 ranked countries) in the World Bank governance index (Kaufmann, Kraay, and Zoido-Lobatón 1999).

Although less visible in the media, particularistic policymaking may be a more relevant dimension of this issue. Particularism is the legal manifestation of the low public regardedness that permeates the system. About 55 percent of all the bills initiated by Paraguayan legislators are distributive in nature and 64 percent are narrow in scope (individual or municipal). In contrast, only a quarter of the bills initiated by the Ecuadorian congress are distributive, and barely one-fifth are targeted at the municipal or individual levels (Araujo and others 2004). The data presented above indicate that particularistic policies occupy most of the efforts of Paraguayan legislators; they are noncontroversial and are less likely to be vetoed by the executive.

Patronage is another manifestation of private regarding policymaking. As discussed above, public hiring practices are characterized by a high degree of arbitrariness and are based principally on political favors and clientelism. Moreover, positions in the public bureaucracy are an attractive resource in the hands of politicians. Ugo Panizza (1999) has estimated that the average public employee in Paraguay earns 17 percent more than a worker with similar characteristics in the private sector, while the equivalent public sector premium in the average Latin American country is about 4 percent.

Compared to the Stroessner system, the democratic PMP displays greater inclusiveness, lower coordination, and higher decentralization of the distributive process. Therefore, the system seems to be quite flexible for the production and distribution of particularistic policies (individual pensions, public jobs, and the like). At the same time, the initiation of such bills seems to be driven by clearly electoral considerations, and the combination of legally mandated primary races and contested general elections may increase competition for pork among legislators in the future.

The relationship between two of these outer features (low public regardedness and low adaptability) is complex and deserves further exploration. We hypothesize that two opposite effects may be taking place. On one hand, in a context of declining formal and partisan powers, particularistic policy may be one of the few resources left to the executive branch in order to negotiate with congress. An expansion of pork barrel politics may be consistent with a strategic attempt by the executive to overcome its increasing weaknesses. In the current context, the president may have a limited ability to adopt new regulatory or redistributive schemes, but he could be even weaker in the absence of distributive policy. On the other hand, exposés of corruption delegitimize the policymaking process, ignite social mobilization, and discourage the formation of a legislative consensus—thus increasing policy rigidity.

Two organizations that can effectively act as "last-ditch" veto players in the Paraguayan PMP are the public employees union and the campesino movement. For example, in 1993, the *campesino* movement launched a campaign demanding that the government forgive cumulative interest on agricultural credits. This campaign brought together 22 national and local *campesino* organizations into the Coordinación Interdepartamental de Organizaciones Campesinas (CIOC). Congress passed a bill addressing the CIOC's demands, but the bill was vetoed by the executive (Servicio de Consultoría Informativa, December 1993).

Following this episode, *campesino* protests escalated in 1994. The protests included a march of 20,000 *campesinos* in Asunción, roadblocks, and demonstrations all over the country. Unionized workers organized a successful national strike in support of the *campesinos'* demands. As a result of these mobilizations, an expanded Mesa Coordinadora Nacional de

Organizaciones Campesinas (MCNOC) was created. The MCNOC has led regular *campesino* protests and negotiations since 1995. In 1999, the *campesinos* unexpectedly played a key role in the opposition to President Cubas Grau, allowing for González Macchi's rise to power.

Though the MCNOC emerged as a visible political actor at that point, its potential to act as a last-ditch veto player became clear only three years later, when *campesino* mobilizations blocked González Macchi's privatization program. Confronted with mounting deficits, the administration embarked upon a program to privatize the public telecommunications company (Antelco, later renamed Copaco), the water supply (*Corposana*, later renamed ESSAP), and the Carlos Antonio López railroad. In May 2000, the senate passed a bill delegating powers to the executive for this purpose. The chamber of deputies approved the bill in October and the government intervened in the three companies a few days later. By mid-2001, Copaco, the leading case in the process, was already entering the final stage of its privatization.

However, in April 2002 the press disclosed that the administration had paid $600,000 to a private notary in order to register the transfer of assets from Antelco (the public company) to Copaco (the renamed firm to be privatized), even though the registration should have been handled by the attorney general at no cost to taxpayers. The People's Democratic Congress, an alliance of *campesino* and union leaders, mobilized against the "corrupt privatization" of Copaco. In June, thousands of campesinos marched to Asunción. The Central Nacional de Trabajadores (CNT) called for a general strike and the congressional opposition initiated impeachment proceedings against González Macchi. Worried about the 2003 presidential race, Colorado legislators negotiated the repeal of the privatizations with union and *campesino* leaders in exchange for the dismantling of the protest movement. In the afternoon of June 6, the senate approved by a 32 to 7 vote a new bill suspending the sale of Copaco, ESSAP, and the railroads. To the horror of the IMF and the minister of finance, the president signed the bill immediately, deactivating the protests and thus the impeachment charges.

This shows that public regardedness can be a double-edged sword. Although particularistic policy may facilitate policymaking by giving the executive additional instruments of negotiation with congress, corruption may erode the credibility of the PMP in the long run, activate the mobilization of "last-ditch" veto players, and ultimately make the problem of policy rigidity even more acute.

Conclusion

This chapter highlights the differences between Paraguay's policymaking process under the rule of Alfredo Stroessner with the policymaking process that emerged after the adoption of the 1992 Constitution. This exercise allowed us to identify the distinctive patterns of the country's current PMP, to examine its workings and to characterize the outer features of public policies.

For each of the four periods (Stroessner I, Stroessner II, transition, and current), table 9.2 summarizes the key players, the point of policy initiation, the effective number of parties, the veto players, the ability to enforce intertemporal agreements, the policy adaptability, the level of public regardedness, and the capacity to enforce rules in the long run.

Table 9.2 underscores two of our main conclusions. First, the presence of multiple veto players may be neither necessary nor sufficient to create policy rigidities. True, the current period contrasts with the "golden age" of *Stronismo* and with the Rodríguez transitional regime because during these two periods the executive concentration of power facilitated fast policy change. But when partisan factions converge in their policy preferences (as in the case of particularistic policies), policy change is easily achieved. At the same time, the presence of a policy dictator did not prevent policy rigidity in 1982–89. Overall, though, the democratization process that started in 1989 multiplied the number of potential veto players and, as a result, made policy change more difficult.

Second, the historical evidence supports the idea that policy adaptability and public regardedness are independent dimensions of the policymaking process. While levels of policy adaptability in Paraguay have varied considerably over time (even during the *Stronato*), private regardedness has been constant, as the system has been historically marked by the extensive use of patronage and clientelism.

Table 9.2. Comparison of the Policymaking Process in Different Historical Periods, Paraguay, 1954–2003

	Stroessner I 1954–1981	Stroessner II 1982–1989	Transition 1989–1992	Current 1993–2003
PMP				
Key players	Dictator, military ANR	Dictator, military, ANR	President, military factions within ANR	President, congress ANR's factions, new parties
Policy initiation	President	President	President	President *and* congress
Effective number parties (period mean)	1.6	1.92	1.89	2.42
Veto players	Virtually none	Virtually none	Increasing role of factions	Increasing role of opposition in congress
Policy features				
Capacity to enforce intertemporal transactions	High (assuming stability in dictator's preferences)	Low (succession problem)	Low (reelection problem)	Low (assuming controversial issues)
Policy adaptability	High	Declined as private regarding policies ossified	High	Low capacity to adopt new regulatory or redistributive policies
Public regardedness	Low	Low	Low	Low

Source: Authors.

These conclusions notwithstanding, we think that the most important contrast between the current period and the Stroessner years is probably the greater potential for incremental changes to the policymaking process. The conditions under which the current policymaking process emerged were clearly marked by the fragmentation and instability that characterized Paraguayan politics in the post-Stroessner years. In that period, the political system experienced a coup attempt, the assassination of a vice president, the resignation of a president, and a subsequent administration led by a nonelected interim president. In no small part, these events were triggered by unresolved struggles within the Colorado party. And these tensions can certainly be traced back to some of the decisions adopted in the 1992 constitutional assembly, most notably the ban on reelection for incumbent presidents. The presence of a "succession problem" looming on the horizon did not create a propitious context for developing a learning process about how to build intertemporal policy agreements.

This succession problem, though, has become more apparent in recent years, and thus it seems possible that Paraguay's political leaders are ready to tackle it in more explicit and institutionalized ways. Even though it is unlikely that President Duarte will secure enough support to make a constitutional amendment that would enable him to stand for reelection, everything indicates that the next presidential election will be a close one. And, as long as the leaders of the Colorado party understand that the chances of holding on to power are smaller, they may realize that they may benefit from abandoning their excessive *internismo*.

Of course, this is just a matter of speculation. However, the fact that the Colorado party may face a serious electoral challenge in the April 2008 election can generate expectations for more stable rules of the game in the long run, and thus the opportunity to introduce changes in the workings of the policy making process that will allow Paraguyan leaders to make and enforce intertemporal policy agreements.

10

Political Institutions and Policymaking in Venezuela: The Rise and Collapse of Political Cooperation

*Francisco Monaldi, Rosa Amelia González, Richard Obuchi, and Michael Penfold**

Introduction

Venezuela's democratic history, from 1958 to 2006, offers a striking case study of political institutions and policymaking processes. Venezuela used to be the model stable democracy in the troubled Latin American region, but in the last decade it has become one of the least stable and most polarized. It used to have one of the best economic performances in the region, but it has had one of the worst performances in the last three decades. Recent studies have attributed a major part of Venezuela's economic decline to the (largely exogenous) dramatic reduction in per capita oil income, which occurred in the 1980s and 1990s, and to the increasing volatility of oil prices.[1] Institutional and policymaking

* The authors are grateful to Elisa Trujillo and Angel Cárdenas for research assistance and acknowledge the comments, data, and advice of Mariano Tommasi, Ernesto Stein, Pablo Spiller, Eduardo Zambrano, Ricardo Hausmann, James Robinson, Juan C. Echeverry, Miriam Kornblith, Gustavo Tarre, Francisco Rodríguez, Moisés Naím, Ricardo Villasmil, Thad Dunning, Javier Corrales, Mercedes Briceño, Javier Santiso, Mark Payne, and participants at the following seminars: IDB, Harvard, CAF, IESA, UCAB, ISNIE 2005, and 2004 LACEA Political Economy Group. For a more detailed discussion of the arguments in this chapter, see the longer working paper version in Monaldi and others (2005).

[1] See, for example, Rodríguez and Sachs (1999) and Hausmann and Rigobón (2002).

factors cannot significantly explain the size of the initial decline in performance; however, they seem crucial to understand the incapacity of the Venezuelan polity to return to a sustainable development path.

This study shows that the political institutions that established Venezuela's democracy in the 1960s were deliberately set up to generate a cooperative equilibrium whereby the winners would have limited powers, and to a significant extent share the benefits of power and spoils of office with the losers. Thus the stakes of power were low. Constitutionally weak presidents, strong centralized political parties, and corporatist policymaking arrangements characterized this institutional framework. Cooperation induced a relatively effective policymaking process and good policy outcomes.

However, an oil boom and its aftermath unraveled the cooperative framework and induced rapid economic decay. The political reforms implemented in the late 1980s to improve governance further weakened the party system and induced a highly uncooperative and volatile policymaking process. The recent institutional transformation led by President Hugo Chávez, which concentrated power in the presidency and weakened the constitutional checks and balances, increased the stakes of power: what is at stake in elections has become much more important because the winner will take all, in effect. These changes have induced a complete breakdown in cooperation and a highly polarized political system.

The institutional framework that prevailed from 1958 to 1988, based on the Pact of Punto Fijo and the 1961 Constitution, was designed to support consensus building among a small set of national party leaders and corporatist groups. The electoral system and the centralized structure promoted strong, disciplined parties, ruled by the national leadership. The significant constraints to presidential prerogatives limited the spoils of office and thus the stakes of power, increasing the incentives for cooperation (and accordingly, reducing the incentives for deviating from cooperation). The existence of centralized corporatist groups and their formal incorporation into the policymaking process provided permanence across different party administrations.

The resulting policymaking process was highly cooperative, with significant stability and coherence, although at the expense of some flexibility and efficiency. The general guidelines were brokered between the national party and corporatist leaders, including prominently the presidents, which then ordered the legislature to seal the deals in the form of laws. The parties delegated a lot of the policymaking to the executive, but within the restrictive limits provided by the constitution. The typical vehicle for the formulation of specific laws were presidential consultative commissions, with the participation of party and corporatist group representatives. Similarly, in the implementation phase, the key actors were represented through the boards of the executing agencies.

The policymaking process in general generated bipartisan *state* policies (*políticas de estado*), rather than governmental policies that changed with each administration. Despite the alternation of the two main parties in power, policies such as foreign relations, oil, industry, education, and health had significant stability. Also, during the first three administrations, fiscal policy was conservative, guided by an implicit balanced budget rule.

The oil booms and busts of the 1970s and 1980s significantly distorted the policymaking process, promoting presidential unilateralism, fiscal deficits, rent-seeking, and corruption. The negative effects on economic performance followed. Moreover, the dramatic decline in per capita oil income contributed to the increasing unpopularity of the leading political parties.

To improve governance, some major political reforms were implemented at the proposal of a presidential Commission for State Reform, created in 1984. Key national political leaders were opposed to these reforms, but the economic crisis and political events, including the riots of 1989, prompted them to pass the reforms in congress. The main reforms were the direct election of governors and mayors, and the transformation of the electoral system from proportional representation into a mixed system with a plurality component.

These institutional reforms, combined with the market reforms that weakened the patronage system, contributed to the deconsolidation of the party system and a significant decline in cooperation in the policymaking process. The federalization of politics, jointly with the decline in voter support for the leading parties produced by economic underperformance, led to an increasing fragmentation of the party system, high political volatility, and weakening party discipline. By dramatically reducing the entry barriers to the political system and providing an electoral connection between regional political leaders and voters, political decentralization and electoral reform inadvertently contributed to democratic deconsolidation. Regional leaders became relevant players in the national legislature. Transaction costs increased as the volatility and number of key players increased.

As a result, during the 1990s, policies were highly unstable and incoherent. Economic reforms, such as tax reform, were difficult to pass in the legislature, and those that were implemented were generally reversed. Moreover, during the last decade Venezuela has systematically ranked among the last places—both in the region and the world—in the indicators of institutional and policy quality collected by different international institutions, including the World Bank, the Inter-American Development Bank, Transparency International, and the World Economic Forum.

The institutional transformations introduced by President Hugo Chávez have dramatically changed the policymaking process. The 1999 Constitution and the more recent institutional changes have significantly increased presidential supremacy and political centralization. The concentration of authority that has resulted has no parallel in Venezuela's democratic history. This radical escalation in the stakes of holding power has made political cooperation very difficult; as a result, cooperation has completely broken down, resulting in high polarization and instability.

This study is structured as follows. The second section presents the characteristics of the policymaking process during the first period (1958–88) and its institutional foundations. The third section presents the characteristics of the policymaking process in the second period (1989–2006) and its institutional foundations, including the subperiod of Chávez's revolution (1999–2006). The fourth section describes the evolution of the features of Venezuela's public policies and their link to the changing policymaking framework. The fifth section concludes.

The First Period: The Consolidation of Democracy—Cooperation and Stability, 1958 to 1988

Two major periods can be identified during Venezuela's democratic experience in which the explanatory variables—political institutions and policymaking processes—have notably different characteristics. The first period of democratic consolidation (1958–88) was characterized by cooperation, low political volatility, low fragmentation, and limited political competition. In contrast, the second period (1989–2006) was characterized by a significant decline in cooperation, high political volatility, and high political fragmentation.

The transition to democracy in 1958–61 was consolidated under a set of institutional arrangements based on a multiparty elite agreement called the Pact of Punto Fijo. The pact was agreed upon by the leaders of the three main political parties.[2] The contents of the pact included arrangements for power sharing, such as the distribution of cabinet positions among competing parties, and the implementation of basic common social and economic policies regardless of the presidential and legislative electoral outcomes. In addition, the pact stipulated the need to create corporatist mechanisms that guaranteed that labor unions and business interests, through umbrella organizations such as the *Confederación de Trabajadores de Venezuela* (CTV) and Fedecamaras, respectively, would be consulted and incorporated into the policymaking process. The Catholic Church also supported the pact by signing an ecclesiastic agreement with the state in which it committed itself to help moderate conflicts and was guaranteed public financing.[3]

---

[2] Rómulo Betancourt of the Social Democratic AD, Rafael Caldera of the Christian Democratic COPEI, and Jóvito Villalba of the center-left-nationalist URD.

[3] The nature and consequences of the two democratic constitutional moments of 1947 and 1961 clearly reveal the different correlation of forces that prevailed and the learning process that occurred between them. In 1947, the AD took advantage of its overwhelming popular majority to call for an elected constitutional assembly. It received 78 percent of the vote and 86 percent of the seats and used its absolute dominance to impose a constitution very close to its preferences, alienating many relevant actors. But by 1958, the AD's dominance had declined. Rómulo Betancourt (AD) won the presidency, but this time the party received 49 percent of the votes and 55 percent of

The pact had an enduring impact on the type of presidential system adopted by the 1961 Constitution, which was aimed at limiting presidential powers, diminishing political polarization, restricting electoral competition, and creating political institutions that would foster consensus for conflict resolution. The learning experience from the breakdown of Venezuela's democracy in 1948 allowed political parties to understand the importance of designing institutions to mitigate the concentration of authority and thus the stakes of holding power (Rey 1972, 1989).

The Policymaking Process in the First Period

Under the theoretical framework of Spiller, Stein, and Tommasi (2003), the first period can be generally characterized as having conditions highly conducive to political cooperation: few key political actors, repeated play, and low stakes of power. This cooperation seems to have been positively reflected in some features of the public policies of the period: they were relatively less volatile than the ones in the second period, and some were relatively more effective (including the autonomy and efficiency of the state-owned oil company PDVSA, the high growth rate of the 1958–78 period, expansion of health care and education, and a stable international policy).

There were four leading characteristics of the policymaking process in this period. First, there were few key players and repeated play (stable actors). Second, parties and national party leaders played a significant role, while legislators played a marginal role. Third, presidents played a prominent role, given that political parties and congress delegated powers to the executive. Fourth, corporatist arrangements formally incorpo-

---

the seats in congress (chamber of deputies). Based on the spirit of pact making, the 1961 Constitution was crafted by a special congressional committee co-chaired by Raúl Leoni (AD) and Rafael Caldera (COPEI). Party leaders decided that regardless of the electoral outcome of the congressional elections, the committee would be balanced. It included eight representatives from the AD (36 percent), four from the COPEI, four from the URD, three from the communist party (PCV), and three independents (Kornblith 1991). AD leaders agreed that the composition of the constitutional committee would overrepresent the opposition. As Corrales (2003, p. 19) has argued, the result of this decision was "a constitution designed to prevent single party hegemony."

rated labor and business groups into the policymaking process, with a crucial role for distributing oil rent to maintain political stability.

Few and Stable Key Political Actors. The policymaking process included relatively few key players, primarily the presidents, the national leaders of the two major parties (the AD and COPEI), and the leaders of the two peak corporatist interest groups (the CTV and Fedecamaras). The existence of a highly centralized, disciplined, and nonfragmented party system, and the fact that the concerns of interest groups were channeled through corporatist arrangements with the peak labor and business associations, allowed the president to conduct policy consultation with a very limited number of actors. Compared to the Latin American region and to most of the second period, the policymaking process in this first period can be characterized as one in which the policy process was concentrated in very few and stable players.

The six presidential administrations in this 30-year period were represented by only two parties: the AD (four times) and COPEI (two times). The same parties generally controlled the leadership of congress. With a few exceptions, the two parties controlled or heavily influenced the leading corporatist groups and were influenced by them. Parties were typically governed by a president, a secretary general, and a national committee. Party leaders were very stable. In the AD, six fundamental leaders, four of whom became president, led the party from 1958–88. In the COPEI, three fundamental leaders, two of whom became president, led the party. National party leaders had relatively long tenures and almost all were members of congress with long legislative careers. Party leaders decided how the party voted in congress and had significant control over congressional nominations.

Intertemporal linkages among key political actors were strong. Policymaking was a repeated game with stable actors. It was very costly for an individual politician to deviate from the cooperative equilibrium of the two-party rule. Minority parties such as the MAS did not have a major policymaking role but were guaranteed access to small prerogatives in order to keep them "inside" the system (such as large autonomous budgets for universities and cultural projects controlled by the left).

Figure 10.1. Effective Number of Parties in Venezuela, 1958–2005 (seats in the lower house)

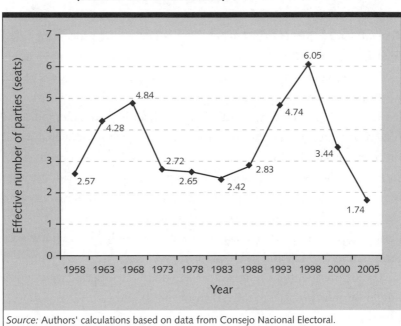

Source: Authors' calculations based on data from Consejo Nacional Electoral.

The party system had relatively low fragmentation, as can be seen in figure 10.1. In the first elections of 1958, the effective number of parties (ENP) represented in the chamber of deputies was 2.6.[4] In the next two elections the ENP rose, as a result of two significant splits in the AD. However, the system consolidated again into a two-party system in the next four elections from 1973 to 1988. The ENP in that period was on average 2.6, lower than the Latin American regional average (3.1), and much lower than the country's average during the 1990s (5.4).[5]

---

[4] The effective number of parties is computed by taking the inverse of the sum of the square of all parties' seat shares. It reflects the number of "relevant" parties (weighted by their relative size).

[5] Regional average calculated with data available, 1978–2001. Calculations based on data from Consejo Nacional Electoral (CNE) and regional data from Payne and others (2002).

Figure 10.2. Volatility in the Lower Chamber of the Legislature in Venezuela, 1963–2005

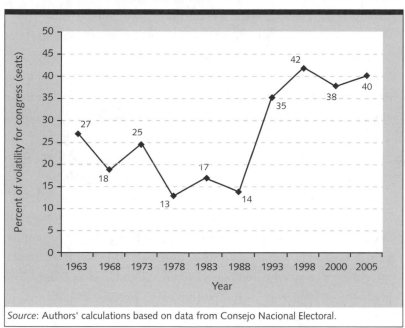

Source: Authors' calculations based on data from Consejo Nacional Electoral.

Party volatility in congress was also relatively low. In the chamber of deputies the Volatility Index was 19 percent in 1958–88, below the Latin American average of 22 percent. Moreover, volatility tended to decline until 1988 (to 14 percent), as can be seen in figure 10.2. The average volatility increased dramatically from 1989 to 2000 to an average of 38 percent, compared to a regional average of 23 percent. Volatility in the presidential vote was even lower in the first period (14 percent), close to half the regional average of 24 percent. It increased dramatically from 1989 to 2000 (to 52 percent), compared to a regional average of 28 percent. From 1989 to 2006, Venezuela had the largest volatility in the presidential vote in the region.

Predominant Role of National Party Leaders and Marginal Role of Legislators. Policy agreements were negotiated between the presidents, the national party leaders (the *cogollos*, in Venezuelan popular jargon), and the peak corporatist groups. Then, if required, they were rubber-stamped into law by the disciplined party delegations in the legislature. The party leaders were also the leaders in the legislature.

Even though the use of informal arenas meant that agreements were less formal than they would have been if made in the legislature, the existence of disciplined parties provided a structure that enabled inter-temporal cooperation. In addition, when the president's coalition had a majority in the legislature, the president was typically given an enabling law to legislate by decree, under limits set by the parties. Finally, as will be shown below, the executive often created policy-advising commissions with the involvement of the CTV and Fedecamaras (Crisp 2000).

The relatively marginal role played by the legislature in Venezuela's policymaking can be illustrated by the low number of laws annually approved, compared to other countries in the region, such as Argentina, Brazil, or Colombia (Coppedge 1994). Moreover, there was also a low annual output of laws in the first period compared to the second one.[6] The marginality of legislators in the policymaking process is confirmed by the data on initiation of laws. From 1959 to 1989, the executive initiated 66 percent of the ordinary laws approved and legislators initiated just 34 percent. In contrast, from 1990 to 2001, the percentage of ordinary laws initiated by legislators increased to 61 percent.[7]

In the seven legislative terms included in the first period (1958–88), a majority of the legislators (60 percent) lasted only one term in congress, and only a small minority (8 percent) lasted four terms or more. However, of those who lasted four terms or more, about 80 percent belonged to the parties' national leadership, confirming that leaders did have long tenures.[8] From 1989 to 2006, legislators lasted even fewer terms than in

---

[6] From 1959–89, an annual average of 8 ordinary laws was approved. From 1989–2001 the annual average output of ordinary laws increased to 12. Of course, the quality of laws is not captured in these figures.

[7] Authors' calculations based on data from Servicio Autónomo de Información Legislativa (SAIL).

[8] Legislators lasted an average of 1.8 terms. Given the relatively low volatility, the most plausible hypothesis is that the turnover rate of legislators is the result of not being renominated.

the first period. Some 82 percent of legislators lasted just one term, 17 percent lasted two terms, and only 1 percent remained in the legislature in all three terms.[9]

The percentage of new legislators (legislator turnover) tended to decline during the first period. In the first three terms from 1963 to 1973 it was 71 percent on average, whereas from 1963 to 1973 it declined significantly to 55 percent as the two-party system consolidated. In the second period, the percentage of new legislators rose again to an average of 78 percent. Compared to other Latin American countries for which there are turnover data, Venezuela's average figure for the first period (63 percent) is not particularly high. In Argentina about 80 percent of the legislators are not reelected. In Brazil the figure is 57 percent, in Ecuador 73 percent, in Chile 41 percent, and in the United States, 17 percent.[10] In contrast, in the second period, turnover reached Argentinean levels.

Party discipline was extremely high during the first period. Virtually all votes were counted with raised hands since perfect discipline was assumed (roll calls were almost never used). In the few instances in which a party member did not want to follow the party line, his alternate member replaced him and voted according to the party line. The lack of individual member initiative, combined with the high turnover of members of congress, meant that there were very few incentives to specialize or gain expertise. Committees were not very relevant, since they did not have agenda-setting or gatekeeping powers. In general, it can be said that Venezuelan legislators have always been amateurs, with the exception of the national party leaders in the first period.

Predominant Role of Presidents, Delegation by Parties and the Legislature. The 1961 Constitution did not give presidents significant legislative prerogatives. However, despite being constitutionally weak, presidents

---

[9] Calculations based on data from CNE.

[10] The figure for Venezuela is not perfectly comparable with the other countries. It refers to the percentage of new members in congress, whereas the figure for the other countries refers to the percentage reelected of those who were candidates (Araujo and others 2004).

dominated the policymaking process. They were often delegated legislative powers and initiated most of the legislation approved by congress. The lack of expertise and experience in the legislature was often compensated by delegation to the executive. However, party leaders maintained veto power over legislation, setting significant limits on the exercise of presidential power. The cooperative equilibrium made presidents look quite powerful, but their powers were actually constrained by the institutional framework—as became evident once cooperation declined.

In the case of enabling laws, presidents were delegated specific authority to legislate for a period of less than a year on economic and financial matters. The enabling law established limits to the delegated authority and congress could modify the decree-laws if it desired to do so. Still, the delegated authority gave the president significant agenda-setting power to establish the status quo. All three presidents with a majority in congress in the first period exercised this prerogative. In contrast, minority presidents were not given enabling laws. The president could also decree the suspension of some constitutional rights; as long as congress did not reestablish the rights (by simple majority), the president would have decree authority in that area. However, whenever the constitutional rights were reestablished, the decrees ceased to be effective.

President Pérez (1974–78), who had a majority in congress and received an oil windfall, dramatically expanded the use of presidential decrees and represented an exceptional case of presidential unilateralism, with few apparent restraints. However, with this exception, the presidential legislative powers were exercised inside the limits imposed by party leaders. The windfall of oil resources dramatically increased the informal powers of the president in a way for which the political system was not prepared. In addition, the decline of the threat presented by the guerrillas in the 1960s made unilateral presidential behavior more viable.

Corporatist Arrangements in the Policymaking Process. In terms of the participation of interest groups in the policymaking process, very few democracies in the region had so few (and stable) players participating. In Venezuela, single peak dominant associations of labor and business existed, and were incorporated formally into the policy process.[11] Only Chile and Mexico had similar single peak associations, and only in Mexico were they formally incorporated as often as in Venezuela (Crisp 2000). From 1958 to 1988, these types of corporatist arrangements were used more frequently and were given more importance than from 1989 to 1998. During Chávez's presidency, they have completely broken down.

Pressure groups were not interested in lobbying individual legislators because the legislator's job was to rubber-stamp decisions already negotiated by the party leaders and the executive. As a result, lobbying at the policy design phase occurred basically through two formal channels: corporatist representation inside parties and presidential consultative commissions. At the implementation phase, lobbying had a formal role through the presence of corporatist members in the boards of the decentralized public administration agencies (see discussion below).

All presidents in the period made extensive use of consultative commissions for the design of policy. Between 1959 and 1989, Venezuelan presidents created 330 advisory commissions to formulate public policy (Crisp 2000). These commissions institutionalized corporatist consultation. According to Crisp (2000, p. 119): "Umbrella groups for capital and organized labor were considered partners in decision making who had every right to make their voices heard on virtually every issue." A significant amount of the legislation initiated by the executive had its genesis in these commissions. Four groups clearly dominated the commissions: the AD, the COPEI, the CTV, and Fedecamaras. Most commissions were dominated by national representatives, with little participation from the regions. The composition of commissions was very similar across administrations; as a result, a change in the governing party did little to alter the access of interest groups to the policymaking process (Crisp 2000). Crisp concludes (2000, p. 116): "This (stability of compo-

---

[11] The Confederation of Venezuelan Workers (CTV) was dominated by members of the AD, while COPEI had a minority representation on its board. In the case of the business umbrella group, Fedecamaras, party involvement was subtler. Nevertheless, many presidents of Fedecamaras were tied to a particular party, and some of the board members were tied to the parties.

sition) calls into question the ideological differences between the major two parties and the impact of elections in Venezuela." One explanation for this apparent puzzle is the high degree of cooperation that existed. In a cooperative environment, parties would not significantly change policies as a result of transfers of power. In the case of Venezuela, the bipartisan distribution of oil rents through formal corporatist arrangements, combined with the institutional framework in place, which encouraged the sharing of benefits, reduced the stakes of power, and made cooperation possible.

The Venezuelan state created a large number of governmental agencies and state-owned companies, known collectively as the decentralized public administration (DPA). A significant proportion of policies in the first period were implemented through these agencies. The representation of corporatist groups in the DPA was also institutionalized. Again, the AD, the COPEI, the CTV, and Fedecamaras had the most significant roles.[12] The corporatist composition of the boards of the DPA also remained relatively stable across administrations.[13]

Examples of corporatist participation in DPA agencies included the following. The Agricultural Bank had three members representing producer and small farmer (*campesino*) groups on its five-member board. The governing body of the Venezuelan Investment Fund (FIV) included the presidents of the CTV, Fedecamaras, and the Banking Association. The Industrial Credit Fund had representatives from the CTV, the Industrial Council (an affiliate of Fedecamaras), and the Federation of Small Industrials (Combellas 1999). Even the central bank (BCV) had representatives from the CTV and Fedecamaras on its board until the early 1990s. The DPA served as one of the main channels for distributing oil wealth. Even though it was highly politicized and inefficient, it was also highly cooperative and relatively stable. In this case, cooperation did not necessarily imply efficiency.

---

[12] From 1959 to 1989, 362 bureaucratic agencies were created. The creation of DPA agencies peaked in the first Pérez administration, when 159 agencies were created (Crisp 2000).

[13] The agencies created by the AD and the COPEI had a very similar composition, according to the figures provided by Crisp (2000).

Institutional Foundations of the First Period

Most characteristics of the political system and the policymaking process in the first period can be partially attributed to the institutional framework set up by the Pact of Punto Fijo and the Constitution of 1961. Their key objective was to attain political stability in light of imminent threats from the plotters of military coups and the leftist guerrillas supported by Cuba. The memory of the failed democratic experience of 1945–48, when the AD exercised hegemonic power, also weighed heavily on the founders when they designed the institutional foundations of the political system. To a significant extent, the outcomes of that system—the strong disciplined parties, the relatively low fragmentation despite the pure proportional representation system, the centralization of decision making at the national level, the significant delegation of policymaking to the president, the marginal role of congress, the lack of expertise of the legislators, and the low volatility and low polarization of the party system—were all a result of the institutional framework. The key institutional features were:

1. A constitutionally weak president, with significant delegation of informal powers. The limitations on presidential power reduced the stakes of power and provided the party leaders with veto over major policy changes. Given the high degree of cooperation among the parties and the strong and disciplined parties induced by the institutional setting, having a weak president did not generate high obstructionism among branches of the government.

2. A relatively concentrated party system. This outcome was induced by the plurality presidential election held concurrently with all legislative elections, the lack of elections for regional executive offices, and the ballot structure engineered to maximize presidential coattails. The pure proportional representation system, which tends to produce fragmentation and rarely produces a two-party system, was significantly compensated by the factors mentioned above. The proportionality guaranteed a contained political space for minority groups.

3. Strong powers of national party leaders over the party legislators. This outcome was induced by the proportional representation system, with single closed and blocked party lists and with only one ballot for all legislative bodies. The lack of regional elected offices did not provide alternative opportunities for regional leaders and increased the costs of defecting from the large parties (those with probability of obtaining the presidency).

4. Few incentives for individual legislators to specialize or acquire legislative expertise. The control exerted by party leaders over their congressional delegations, a byproduct of the electoral system, discouraged such incentives. Moreover, decision making was centralized in the national party leadership. As a result, the legislature was relatively marginalized from the policymaking process. Most legislators did not stay in congress for long periods; only the party leaders did.

5. Delegation of policymaking to the executive. The lack of expertise and marginality of legislators in the decision-making process and the limits set to presidential powers might explain why party leaders were willing to delegate powers. The corporatist arrangements, such as the presidential commissions and decentralized public administration, allowed for party involvement and "alarms" at lower levels of the policymaking process.

The Executive Branch. The literature on the Venezuelan presidency appears to present a remarkable contradiction. Comparative studies, such as those by Shugart and Carey (1992) and Payne and others (2002), show that the Venezuelan president (before the 1999 Constitution) had the weakest legislative powers of any president in the Latin American region (and among the weakest in all other world presidential systems). In contrast, most of the literature focused on the Venezuelan political system contends that Venezuela suffered from a significant degree of hyper-presidentialism, following the tradition of powerful *caudillos* (strongmen) that historically prevailed in the region (Coppedge 1994; Crisp 1997; Corrales 2002).

This chapter argues that even though in equilibrium the Venezuelan president seemed very powerful since he had the leading policy role, his powers were in fact significantly restricted by the 1961 Constitution. As explained, the framers, who were the leaders of the parties, set those restrictions deliberately to limit potential deviations. To a large extent, the behavioral appearance of power was the result of the limited delegation by the national party leaders of strong and disciplined parties in a cooperative environment. However, the Venezuelan president had some relevant formal and informal powers that have not been generally acknowledged in the comparative literature and that varied between the two periods in study. In the 1990s, once the president's partisan powers and other informal powers declined, the president began to be perceived as weak. Eventually, the 1999 Constitution increased the presidential powers dramatically, further changing the policymaking process, concentrating authority and the spoils of office in the presidency, and thus increasing the stakes of power.

The literature classifies the constitutional powers into legislative powers (lawmaking authority, reactive and proactive) and nonlegislative powers (power to appoint and remove cabinet officials) (Shugart and Carey 1992; Payne and others 2002). Under the 1961 Constitution, the Venezuelan president had very limited legislative powers, especially if compared with the Latin American region (which on average had stronger powers than the other presidential systems in the world). In the index of legislative powers developed by Shugart and Carey (1992), Venezuela had the lowest score (zero). The Latin American regional average in the period 1958–88 was 4.6 [14]

Legislative powers include reactive powers such as the power to veto legislation (partially or entirely). Most presidents can use their veto as a negotiation tool with the legislature, but in Venezuela the veto served only to delay the approval of legislation, since the same simple majority

---

[14] This index is calculated using the simple addition of a point value ranging from zero (low) to four (high) assigned in six categories of legislative power. The maximum possible value was 24. The highest value in Latin America was 12 for Chile's 1969 Constitution.

that could approve a law could also override the president's veto. The authority to legislate by presidential decree is one of the most significant proactive powers. The Venezuelan president did not have autonomous decree power, unless enabled or allowed by congress. Another proactive power is the exclusive initiative for legislation in specific areas. Here again, the Venezuelan president had no prerogatives.[15] An additional presidential legislative prerogative is the power to call for a popular referendum to pass certain legislation, without the need of congressional approval. In Venezuela, this option was not provided by the 1961 Constitution. The presidential prerogatives in the approval of the budget were also below the regional average.

The Venezuelan president did have nonlegislative powers of cabinet formation and dismissal, in line with most Latin American countries (Shugart and Carey 1992; Payne and others 2002). However, one crucial element that has not been developed by the comparative literature on presidential powers is the authority to appoint and dismiss governors. Before 1989, the Venezuelan president could freely appoint and dismiss all governors. In practice, this meant that the president had control over the constitutional allotment of the national budget to the regions (15 percent). The power to appoint governors makes a significant difference, especially in a country that is formally federal.[16]

The literature has also identified an alternative indirect source of presidential authority: the partisan powers in the legislature. The number of significant parties and the discipline and cohesion of parties can all affect partisan support for the president. However, it is important to differentiate this type of power from powers that are constitutionally provided. The constitution provides the formal rules of the game. In contrast, the partisan powers are an equilibrium result derived from the interaction of political institutions and other social and political factors.

---

[15] The only exception was the budget law. The lack of this type of prerogative in Venezuela contrasts with other countries such as Brazil and Chile, where this power is extensive in many areas (Payne and others 2002).

[16] For example, imagine that in Argentina or Brazil the president appointed all regional and local authorities; it would imply a significant increase in the presidential powers in other areas of the policymaking process.

In practice, the real ability to use formal constitutional powers is constrained and expanded by these other factors.

Yet again, the argument advanced here is that the constitutionally weak Venezuelan president seemed in equilibrium to be quite powerful, but such powers were contingent on other factors such as the strong party system, the right to appoint governors, and the control of significant oil rents. Once these factors changed, the weak formal powers became evident, as occurred in the 1990s.

Presidents enjoyed relatively high partisan powers in the first period. They never faced a majority opposition and had very strong disciplined parties backing them. Between 1958 and 1988, three of the six presidents (50 percent) had a partisan majority in the lower house. Four out of six (67 percent) had majorities in coalition with other parties. In contrast, of the five presidential administrations between 1988 and 2006, only one (Chávez since 2005) has had a single party majority in congress. The Latin American regional average, for 1978 to 2002, was 30 percent (when the presidential administration had a presidential party majority in the lower house) and 54 percent (when the president's party had a majority in coalition with other parties) (Payne and others 2002).

Presidential Elections, Concurrency, and Its Consequences. Presidents were elected by plurality for five-year terms in elections concurrent with the legislative elections (for all seats). Until 1993, the voter had just one ballot (*tarjetón*) to vote for both the president and the legislature. One card with the color and symbol of the party (and since the 1970s, the photo of the presidential candidate) had to be marked to vote for the president, and next to it a smaller identical card had to be marked to vote for both chambers of the legislature. Voters could not split their vote between chambers. The combination of plurality (as opposed to runoff) with concurrency, and the structure of the ballot maximized presidential coattails. The presidential election—because of its winner-take-all nature—tends to produce a strategically concentrated vote, and combined with high coattails, produces high party concentration. An additional element promoting concentration was the lack of regional elections.

The evidence seems to point to the significance of presidential coat-tails and vote concentration. The difference between the vote for the top two presidential candidates and the vote for their parties (from 1958 to 1988) was always below 10 percentage points, with the exception of the 1988 election, when dissatisfaction with the AD and COPEI started to increase.

Until 1999, Venezuelan presidents could run again only ten years af-ter the end of their first term (non-immediate reelection). This feature made all presidents "lame ducks," reducing their influence as their term began to elapse. The lack of immediate presidential reelection, com-bined with the absence of term limits for legislators, provided another advantage for national party leaders.

The Legislative Branch and the Party System. As noted, the legislature was characterized by low party fragmentation. Parties were highly dis-ciplined and the national party leadership decided the vote of their congressional delegation. Legislators played a marginal role and most were amateurs. However, party leaders were very stable and remained in congress for longer periods. To a large extent, these characteristics of the party system can also be derived from the institutional foundations. In particular, the type of electoral system, and the lack of regional elec-tions for executive officials, provided national party leaders with power-ful tools with which to discipline and control their party's rank and file. The institutional restrictions on political competition and the control of oil rents allowed the AD and COPEI to create a two-party alternation of power that enjoyed a high degree of stability.

Between 1958 and 1988, legislative elections were done using a pure proportional representation (PR) system with single closed and blocked lists. There were 23 districts, equivalent to the states. The average district magnitude was 6.1—medium-sized, by Latin American standards—mak-ing it relatively proportional.[17] The low fragmentation of the party system

---

[17] Five countries in the region have larger average district magnitude and ten countries have lower. The Venezuelan PR system had an index of disproportionality of 4.4 (on average); the regional mean was 5.4 (Payne and others 2002).

in the first period was not engineered by the proportional representation system. Instead, the PR system guaranteed that all minorities were represented in the legislature. As explained, the low fragmentation had other institutional foundations: the concurrency with plurality presidential elections, the ballot structure, and the lack of regional elections.

The single closed and blocked list electoral system constituted a powerful disciplinarian tool in the hands of the party leadership. It allowed the party leadership to control the nominations (who gets in the list) and the order of election (who gets elected first), pooled the votes of party candidates (avoiding intraparty rivalry), and limited internal competition.[18] Shugart and Carey's (1992) index of party leadership strength, resulting from the electoral system, gave Venezuela a value of 8, above the regional average of 6.

The Federal System. Before 1989, even though the country was formally federal, no regional executive authorities were elected. Governors were freely appointed and removed by the president. The lack of regional elections had significant consequences for the party system under a federal structure. Governors did not have any incentive to cultivate their personal vote. On the contrary, they had to be completely loyal to the president. Governors were often personally connected to the president or the national party leaders, and on occasion did not come from the region they governed. Governors had almost no influence in the approval of the national budget, and those who did not follow the orders of the president could be dismissed immediately.

The Judiciary. Congress elected the supreme court by simple majority in a joint session. Magistrates (and their alternates) were appointed for nine-year periods, in a staggered process in which one-third of the justices were

---

[18] For example, in the AD, the National Executive Council (CEN) had significant control over the nomination process. Regional party authorities sent a list with three times more names than the magnitude of their district. The CEN reserved the right to pick one-third of the candidates from outside the list and had free reign in establishing the order of the list. In practice, this meant that the CEN decided who could get elected (Crisp 2001).

elected every three years. To increase the number of magistrates, a two-thirds majority in a joint session of congress was required. Justices could be reelected. Since the legislative term lasted five years, no congressional majority could elect more than two-thirds of the magistrates. As a result, the composition of the supreme court did not completely follow the legislative majorities. Evidence of the independence of the Court seems mixed. Magistrates were generally selected in a negotiation between the leadership of the AD and COPEI. However, the Court did serve as an enforcer of constitutional limits to presidential power, and presidents generally did not control the Court. Nevertheless, it is unclear whether the supreme court could enforce rules against the wishes of the party leadership.

The Second Period: The Deconsolidation of Democracy— Decline and Breakdown of Cooperation, 1989–2006

This section describes the changes in the policymaking process that have resulted from the profound transformation in political institutions in the last two decades. In contrast to the first period, which was characterized by few and stable actors, resulting in cooperative agreements, the second period, until recently, was characterized by multiple actors, high electoral volatility, and institutional instability. As a consequence, it has been more difficult to generate cooperative agreements among politicians or to create an adequate environment for sustainable reforms and long-term policy commitments. For example, during this period there was a dramatic decline in the autonomy and capacity of the few pockets of professional bureaucracy that had been created in the past, and cabinet instability increased significantly. Moreover, after the election of Hugo Chávez in December 1998 and the draft of a new constitution in 1999, political cooperation experienced a complete breakdown. The new constitutional framework—which increased the stakes of power— has fostered political instability and polarization.

Two distinct subperiods can be distinguished in this period of democratic deconsolidation: the decline of the party system from 1989 to 1998, and the rise of Chávez's revolution after 1999. Although both subperiods have some commonalities—including the deconsolidation of democracy, and the increase in political instability and polarization—it is important to acknowledge some very important differences. For example, after a period of dramatic increase in party fragmentation in the legislature, by 2006 only supporters of President Chávez remained in the national assembly. Similarly, in the 1990s presidents were relatively weak, whereas after the 1999 Constitution, the president became significantly more powerful. Therefore, most characteristics described in this section apply primarily to the 1989–98 period. Some other elements refer mainly to the Chávez administration (1999–present), to which a separate subsection is dedicated.

The most significant institutional changes that occurred at the beginning of this period were the introduction of direct elections for governors and mayors in 1989 and the modification of the legislature's electoral system from pure proportional representation to a mixed-member system of personalized proportional representation in 1993. These changes helped significantly weaken the power of traditional parties and national party leaders. Also, in the context of a significant change in electoral preferences, these institutional transformations contributed to increase party fragmentation, volatility, and legislator turnover.

In general, the policymaking process in the second period was characterized by many key players, who were volatile; a more prominent role for the legislature and the judiciary, and a declining role of parties; a less predominant role of presidents (until 1999); a decline in the influence of corporatist groups; an increased role of the military; a key role for regional authorities (until 2004); and increased stakes of power, starting with the 1999 Constitution.

The effective number of parties (ENP) in the chamber of deputies increased dramatically. In the period of two-party dominance (1973–88), the ENP was just 2.6, on average. As shown in figure 10.1, it surged to 4.7 in 1993, and in 1998 it rose again to a maximum 6.05. In 2000, it declined to 3.4 because of the significant share of Chávez's party (MVR); however, among the opposition parties, fragmentation was even higher than in 1998. In 2005 the opposition withdrew from congressional elections, arguing fraudulent electoral conditions. As a result, there is only one party in the legislature. Thus Chávez supporters are the only ones represented in the national assembly.[19] The average ENP from 1989 to 2000 (4.7) was significantly higher than the regional average in the same period (3.5).[20] Venezuela went from being one of the least fragmented party systems to being the third most fragmented in Latin America; by 2006 it was again the least fragmented.

Volatility also dramatically increased during the second period. In terms of lower chamber seats, the average volatility from 1990 to 2006 was 39 percent, well above the Latin American average of 23 percent. Venezuela again moved from being one of the least volatile countries in the region to the second most volatile.[21] Compared to the first period, average volatility more than doubled (see figure 10.2). In terms of volatility in presidential party vote, the increase was even more dramatic. It reached 53 percent and 60 percent in the 1993 and 1998 elections, respectively. On average, Venezuela has had the highest volatility in presidential voting in the region in the last ten years.

In addition, during this period, civilian control over the military dramatically weakened, resulting in a higher risk of democratic breakdown. During this period, different factions within the armed forces attempted three failed military coups (two in 1992 and one in 2002). This situation contrasts with the previous 20 years, in which political parties managed to exercise significant control over the armed forces, helping to consolidate democratic rule. The increasing influence of the armed forces on civilian affairs has become even more salient since the election of President Chávez.

The Legislature

During the 1990s, the transformation of the policymaking process, along with the multiplication of relevant policy actors at the national and regional levels, increased transaction costs substantially, making it more

---

[19] Support for Chávez's candidates at the time of the election ranged from 55 to 65 percent.

[20] Calculations based on CNE data and regional data from Payne and others (2002).

[21] It was surpassed only by Peru. Data from CNE and regional data based on Payne and others (2002).

difficult for political players to credibly commit. Unlike the first period, in which political exchanges were conducted at low transaction costs in small and stable groups, in the 1990s transactions were negotiated among a larger number of shifting players in more open and conflictive arenas. Paradoxically, as a result of the decline of party elite agreements, the legislature played a much more significant role. National party leaders could not easily broker deals outside of congress, as had been the practice. While in the first period legislators initiated just 34 percent of all the ordinary laws approved on average, from 1989 to 2001 the figure almost doubled to 62 percent.

Between 1989 and 2004, legislators became less disciplined and more specialized. Factions within parties and individual representatives were able to undermine the power of party barons on specific policy issues. Key legislation approved at the national level (either by congress or by executive decree), had to be negotiated with regional actors. Proponents had to introduce regional considerations to gain the support of governors and mayors. For example, legislators were able to push reforms to deepen fiscal transfers to the regions despite the opposition from national party authorities and the national executive. Regional leaders have powerful incentives to extract more resources from the center, especially since Venezuela has the largest vertical fiscal imbalance in Latin America and the rules of the distribution of fiscal resources have become more discretionary. The lack of discipline among legislators was expressed not only in their increasing independence on policy issues with respect to the party leaders, but also by their splitting off from the parties that had nominated them. Factions within consolidated political parties such as the AD, COPEI, MAS (and even Chávez's MVR) split off from 1989 to 2004, creating their own independent legislative groups.

Electoral Reforms

Institutional instability created weaker intertemporal linkages among politicians and policymakers. These linkages were weakened by continuous changes in the institutional rules, as well as increased political uncertainty stemming from the risk of breakdown of the democratic regime. The rules of the political game have been in constant flux during the past 15 years. After decades without significant modifications, electoral rules were changed five times and the constitution was rewritten, considerably modifying the incentives of political actors. Different versions of the mixed electoral system were used for the legislative elections of 1993, 1998, 2000, and 2005.[22] In addition, moving from a closed-list pure proportional representation system to a mixed system, with some members elected by plurality, weakened the incentives for party discipline and the power of national party leaders—especially when combined with regional elections.

In 1998, congress approved the separation of legislative and presidential elections for the first time, with the elections to be held that year. Congressional elections were set to coincide instead with regional and local elections, held a few weeks before the presidential elections. This modification was designed by the traditional parties to reduce the coattail effects that a potential landslide victory by Chávez might produce on the legislature. Instead, the parties attempted to build their support in congress based on the strength of their regional governments (and the regional authorities' coattails). As a result, these legislative elections generated the largest political fragmentation in Venezuela's history (more than six effective parties). Moreover, the separation of legislative and presidential elections would be the norm in the future, since the 1999 Constitution set a five-year legislative term and a six-year presidential term.

These institutional reforms contributed to the erosion of the strict control that party leaders exercised over nomination procedures. This in turn weakened party discipline in the legislature. In addition, the lack of a stable electoral system did not help to consolidate electoral incentives, increasing the levels of uncertainty that politicians faced when building their careers.

---

[22] In 1993, 60 percent of the deputies were elected by closed and blocked lists, while the remaining 40 percent were elected in single-member plurality districts. In 1998, the rules were changed again to elect 50 percent of the deputies in multimember plurality districts. In 1999, in the elections of the constituent assembly, the constitutional mandate to use a proportional formula was completely abandoned in favor of a majoritarian system. In the 2000 legislative elections, the mixed system was readopted, but this time with 65 percent elected in multimember plurality districts. In 2005, the mixed system was implemented without global proportionality, dramatically increasing its disproportionality.

The Executive Branch

In terms of presidential powers, there were two distinct subperiods from 1989 to 2006. From 1989 to 1998, presidents were relatively weak. In contrast, since 1999, when the new Constitution was approved, the presidency has gained extensive powers. In 1989, presidential powers were substantially reduced with the introduction of the direct election of governors and mayors. Presidents lost control over part of the budget (the constitutional allotment to the regions) and over the discretionary appointment and dismissal of governors, which had been a potent negotiation tool. In addition, the decline in oil fiscal income and the market-oriented reforms, which limited discretionary subsidies and reduced rent-seeking opportunities, also reduced the political currency of presidents (Villasmil and others 2004).

Changes in the party system, particularly the fragmentation and emergence of less cohesive and disciplined parties, undermined the partisan powers of the president. During the first period, three of the six presidents (50 percent) had a partisan majority in the lower house. Four out of six had majorities in coalition with other parties. In contrast, since 1988, only one president has had a majority of his own party (Chávez, since 2005).[23] The existence of divided government increased the confrontations between the legislature and the executive branch. Because of the decline in presidential power, the executive branch had less influence in the legislative process in the 1990s. From 1959 to 1989, the executive initiated two-thirds of the ordinary legislation; from 1989 to 2001, this figure declined to 39 percent.

In the second period, from 1989 to 2006, cabinet stability also declined significantly. From 1958 to 1988, cabinet members lasted 2.13 years in their positions, on average (over a five-year term). In contrast, from 1989 to 1993, ministers lasted only 1.4 years. Their tenure increased to 1.8 years from 1994 to 1999, and declined again to 1.3 years from 1999 to 2004. That dramatic decline in cabinet stability contributed to a significant increase in policy volatility, as shown below (see also Monaldi and others 2005).

---

[23] Chávez had a coalition majority from 2000 to 2005 and was in minority in 1999.

In contrast to the previous constitution, the 1999 Constitution significantly increased the presidential legislative prerogatives. As discussed below, since 1999, a systematic concentration of power in the executive branch has occurred.

The Rise of Federalism

Although Venezuela was formally federal for more than a century, it was only in 1989 that the dormant federal system was activated, after the initiation of the direct elections of governors and mayors. There are two elements of Venezuela's political decentralization that transformed its party politics: the increasing competition and higher number of electoral arenas at the subnational level; and the possibility of reelection for governors and mayors, as well as the nonconcurrency between regional and presidential elections. These institutional features provided new regional political actors with an opportunity to gain independence vis-à-vis the national authorities. Since 2004 the influence of governors has lessened as power has become more centralized.

Increasing Competition and Higher Number of Electoral Arenas. From 1958 to 1988, entry barriers for political parties were relatively high, since presidential and congressional elections were held concurrently, maximizing presidential coattails. Moreover, entry into congress was decided by national party leaders, who had control over the nominations. With the introduction of the direct election of governors and mayors, traditional political parties characterized by hierarchical and inflexible organizations had to present individual candidates in more than 20 states and 300 municipalities. To compete effectively in these contests, party leaders gradually had to loosen centralized control over the nomination of candidates. Increasing the number of electoral arenas implied reducing the entry barriers to competition. Minority parties attempting to win elections at the national level could now compete more effectively at the regional and local levels. These parties could build their organization at the national level, based on their success at the regional level (Penfold 2004a, 2004b).

During this period, several new political parties, such as *CausaR*, *Proyecto Venezuela*, *Convergencia*-LAPI, MVR, PPT, and *Primero Justicia* used federalism as a springboard to enter into the political system and build a national party organization. In the first election for governors in 1989, the AD and COPEI dominated the electoral market, with 90 percent of the governorships. However, during the following elections their dominance waned as new political organizations emerged and decentralized parties such as MAS obtained significant power for the first time. By 1998, the AD won only 35 percent of the governorships and COPEI won 22 percent; meanwhile, MVR won 17 percent, MAS won 13 percent, and regional parties won 13 percent.[24]

The multiplication of electoral arenas not only provided an incentive for some political parties to pursue an electoral strategy aligned with regional interests, but also forced national parties to use alliances with other political organizations to compete effectively in these different arenas. National political parties became increasingly dependent on party alliances between 1989 and 2000.

Reelection and Nonconcurrent Elections. The immediate reelection of governors and mayors in contests that were organized separately from national elections also increased the independence of these political actors. Governors and mayors running for reelection had greater opportunity to distance themselves from national party leaders and even disassociate themselves from the party structure. The fact that their reelection depended to a great extent on their performance—and not on coattails from presidential candidates backed by centralized parties—created incentives for governors to behave more independently.

---

[24] One example of how political careers were built in this period is the rise of Andrés Velásquez and his party, *Causa R*, which had been a marginal party in the previous period. He was able to build the party starting with his victory as governor of the state of Bolivar in 1989. His effective performance allowed Velásquez to compete in the presidential elections of 1993 and receive 22 percent of the vote. *Causa R* continued its success by later winning the mayoralty of Caracas in 1992 and the governorship of Zulia in 1996 (Penfold 2004a, 2004b).

The federalization of Venezuelan politics also implied that these governors, in the context of a decaying party system and the deepening of the decentralization process, could build their own political organizations to support their careers. The reelection rule also fostered internal conflicts between party authorities at the national level and new party leaders at the regional and local levels. These tensions remained unresolved and on occasion forced regional players to separate themselves from their parties. In this sense, federalism enacted a dual dynamic: the formation of new regional political parties, and the split from hierarchical political parties such as the AD, COPEI, and MVR (Penfold 2004a, 2004b).

The Judiciary

The fragmentation of the party system and the decline in party discipline from 1989 to 2000 undermined the strong grasp that national party barons exercised over the judicial system. Increasing demands from civil society for expanded access to justice and judicial independence received support from the supreme court. With the assistance of the World Bank, the modernization of the Court was initiated. The Court assumed a more politically autonomous and activist role. The increasing judicial independence of the Court can be illustrated by its leading role in the impeachment of President Pérez in 1992 and by its many rulings—to resolve conflicts over elections—that negatively affected the largest parties (the AD and COPEI).

Despite the changes that occurred in the early 1990s in the judicial system, the perception of judicial independence today is extremely low. During the Chávez presidency, the government took full control of the supreme court, effectively ending the independence of the judicial system.

Chávez's Revolution:
Institutional Sources of the Breakdown in Cooperation

In 1998, Hugo Chávez was elected president of Venezuela as an outsider, under an electoral platform to radically dismantle what was perceived to be a corrupt and dysfunctional political system. In 1999, President Chávez, with the support of the supreme court, summoned a constitutional assembly to craft a new constitution, violating the reform process established in the 1961 Constitution. With 56 percent of the vote, the president's supporters obtained 95 percent of the seats in the constitutional assembly. These disproportional results were the result of the adoption of a majoritarian system, contradicting the proportional representation electoral system prescribed by the prevailing constitution.

The constitutional assembly created the political conditions to modify key institutional rules and substantially increase presidential powers (Monaldi and others 2005). Among the most relevant new elements in the 1999 Constitution are the following: First, the presidential term was expanded from five to six years with one immediate reelection. As a result, a Venezuelan president may rule for a longer continuous period (12 years) than any other Latin American president (the regional median is five years). Second, the president was provided complete control over the promotions within the armed forces, without need for approval from the national assembly. Third, the new constitution eliminated the senate and therefore the equal representation of the states in the legislature. Fourth, it allows the president to activate any kind of referendum without any support in the legislature (including one to summon a constitutional assembly with full powers). As a by-product, the constitution is now extremely easy to change if the executive is willing to do so and has the necessary popular support. Fifth, it eliminated any public financing for the political parties. Finally, the constitution introduced the possibility of recalling the mandate of mayors, governors, and the president, contingent upon the approval of a stringent set of conditions.

As a result of the constitutional reforms, presidentialism was reinforced and federalism was weakened. The political regime that emerged was radically different from the Punto Fijo system and also from the one prevailing from 1989 to 1998. During the Punto Fijo period, the democratic system revolved around the political parties. In the *chavista* era, the center of gravity is in the presidency. Given the constitutional powers obtained by the president, most political actors have no choice but to subordinate their political careers to the executive branch. In addition, President Chávez's control over the legislature has allowed the executive to pack the supreme tribunal and the electoral council with his supporters, as well as to appoint loyalists in the attorney general and comptroller's offices. The concentration of power that has resulted dramatically increased the stakes of power, contrasting with the institutional framework that prevailed from 1958 to 1998.

Under Chávez, Venezuela has experienced yet another transformation of its policymaking process. This era is characterized by very few key actors, a declining role of political parties, a more prevalent presence of the armed forces, and a significant dominance of the president over the policymaking process. The degree of political polarization and conflict in the country between the *chavismo* and the opposition is so deep that discount rates are high and policies are rarely negotiated in institutionalized arenas. Policies are usually crafted as an attempt to maximize political power, rather than designed on efficiency grounds. Cooperation has completely broken down. The "winner-takes-all" dynamic embedded in the 1999 Constitution can help to explain why Venezuela has experienced three general strikes, a failed coup, and massive street protests in the last five years.

In early 2007, at the beginning of his new presidential term, Chávez proposed a new modification of the constitution. Among the proposals are unlimited presidential reelection and a significant decline in the powers granted to regional governments. These constitutional changes would further concentrate power in the hands of the president, weaken federalism, and increase the stakes of power.

Characterization of Public Policies in Venezuela, 1958–2006: From Cooperative Distribution of Oil Rents to Crisis and Instability

The outer features of Venezuela's public policies have undergone significant transformations that can be directly attributed to the combined effect of changes in the policymaking process and changes in exogenous conditions (primarily oil income). The first fifteen years (1958–73) were characterized by cooperation, stability, and effective performance. The next 15 years of oil boom and bust (1974–88) were characterized by less cooperation, ineffectiveness, and some inflexibility. The last period (1989–2006) has been characterized by the marked decline and final breakdown of cooperation, high policy instability, and reversal of reform.

1958–73: Cooperation with a Relatively Stable Oil Market

From 1958 to 1973, there were features of public policies that suggested effective intertemporal cooperation among policy actors. Economic and social policies were relatively stable and bipartisan. Health and education coverage were rapidly expanded. Import substitution industrialization advanced with government financing. Oil policy was consensual and macroeconomic performance was quite good.

Venezuela's economic management during this period was characterized by three simple, stable, and coherent rules geared toward inducing economic growth and minimizing political conflicts, according to Hausmann (1990): the fixed nominal exchange rate rule, allowing a significant degree of real exchange rate stability and reducing uncertainty; the fixed nominal interest rate rule; and the fiscal rule—spend what you earn (in oil revenues).[25] These rules were effectively maintained through the first three presidential terms. The stability of the rules reflected cooperation rather than stringent legal or constitutional commitment mechanisms. However, they benefited from a favorable external environment.[26] The executive did not incur significant deficits or engage in other forms of fiscal opportunism. Inflation was kept

---

[25] Hausmann (1995, p. 99) explained the conservative fiscal rule of the period as follows: "(the rules) granted the State a license to spend according to the oil income. There was no license to increase internal taxation or to monetize the fiscal deficit."

[26] The remarkable stability of theses policies was clearly related to the workings of the policymaking process, which induced a long-term cooperative agreement geared to minimizing political conflicts, and to the special characteristics of the economy and the external environment, which provided the favorable conditions necessary for the policies' longevity. However, the rules were set on the assumption that oil income was going to be a relatively stable and increasing source of revenue for the government, as it generally was until the 1970s. The gold-dollar stability also helped the policies work.

strictly under control, averaging 2.6 percent per year, and the exchange rate remained fixed until 1983. In addition, public expenditures were systematically geared toward improving health and education services and infrastructure, which was consistent with the long-term goal of providing the political system and the economy with a sound basis.[27] The internal coherence of the policies adopted during this period resulted in a good economic performance. From 1958 to 1973, per capita GDP grew at a relatively high rate, averaging 2.1 percent per year. The unemployment rate decreased from 10.8 percent to 4.9 percent from 1959 to 1973 (Valecillos 1993).

1973–88: Cooperation in the Midst of Oil Booms and Busts

The increase in oil prices in the 1970s marked a change from the previous period because it allowed a significant increase in the expenditure possibilities of the government, which in turn dramatically distorted the policy choices available. During the first Pérez administration (1974–79), oil revenues were used to finance an ambitious plan of development based on the nationalization of mineral industries, the creation of state-owned enterprises, investments in public infrastructure, and generalized subsidies. The increase in fiscal revenue promoted a departure from the previous fiscal conservatism, according to which government expenditure was limited to the revenues obtained. The administration not only spent the extraordinary fiscal revenue, but also used its favorable position in the international financial system to increase the external debt and finance the fiscal deficits (from $600 million in 1973 to $11 billion by 1978).

During the two presidential terms that followed, even though the decline of oil revenue in the late 1970s underscored the economic vulnerabilities of this set of policies, some factors induced politicians to avoid

---

[27] For instance, from 1957 to 1973, the average enrollment per year in primary, secondary, and university education increased 6.4 percent, 14.2 percent, and 18.2 percent, respectively. Analogously, education expenditure (as a share of the total budget of the government) increased from 4.5 percent in 1957 to 18.6 percent in 1973 (Echevarría 1995).

economic reforms. First, political actors expected that the decline in oil revenue was transitory. Second, the main political actors considered that structural adjustment would undermine the foundations of the political system, given that expenditure policies were directly geared toward benefiting the main constituencies of the political parties. As a consequence, the balanced budget rule was abandoned; instead, external debt was used to finance the negative external shocks. Although during the Herrera (1979–83) and Lusinchi (1984–88) administrations some policies were changed because of the deterioration of economic conditions, both administrations systematically tried to avoid any short-term negative distributive impacts on their key constituencies. The fundamental and common feature of policies during this period was a clear aversion to political conflict, which translated into the use of oil income as an instrument to decrease social tensions, as Naim and Piñango (1988) have noted. The side effect of this approach was the multiplication of fragmented policies, resulting in a lack of coordination and long-term sustainability, as well as ineffectiveness.

From 1982 until 2003, per capita oil fiscal income tended to decline and was highly volatile. In contrast with its previous performance, Venezuela became one of the most striking cases of economic underperformance in Latin America after 1978. Between 1978 and 1988, the growth rate of the GDP per capita became very volatile and decreased an average of 1.8 percent per year.

1989–Present: Decline and Breakdown of Cooperation

From 1988 to the present, there has been a significant decline in cooperation, and policy goals have been contradictory and highly volatile. The second Pérez administration (1989–93) tried to implement a systematic market reform program. The reforms were geared toward promoting the development of a market economy by correcting the distortions accumulated during the previous decade. The drastic change in the orientation of public polices was a clear departure from those of the previous three decades. The administration faced the open rejection of its policy proposals by the most important political actors (including the governing party, AD). Public disputes between the executive and the legislature were common, and some crucial reforms were not allowed to pass in congress (such as tax reform). Venezuela was one of the few Latin American countries in which the initial reformer was politically defeated and reforms were reversed (Villasmil and others 2004). Fiscal policy lacked cooperative features. The only fiscal reform proposal of Pérez's administration that was finally approved was the value added tax law (VAT), which was accepted under extremely exceptional political circumstances.[28] In order to pass it, transfers to regional governments had to be increased to get the governors' support in congress.

The electoral campaign of President Caldera (1994–99) was based on an open rejection of the market reforms. He transformed and reduced the VAT, but had to keep the higher level of transfers. The advent of a massive banking crisis in 1995 prompted the legislature to grant special decree powers to President Caldera. He used them to reestablish economic controls. By 1996, the deterioration in economic conditions forced Caldera to reverse course and undertake some reforms. The main policy measures included an opening of the oil sector to private investment, an increase in gasoline prices, and an increase in the VAT. In order to obtain support for these reforms, public sector wages were increased 117 percent. In addition, total transfers to local and regional governments increased by 2.25 percentage points of the GDP, through an increase in revenue earmarking. The influence of the governors in congress again proved significant in obtaining a sizeable increase in decentralization in expenditures.[29]

During this entire period, effective fiscal reform has been elusive, while tax policy has been very volatile. Since 1992, the income tax law has been reformed six times, the value added tax has been reformed ten times, and the tax on banking transactions has been "temporarily" established five

---

[28] It passed into law during the 1992–93 interim presidency of Velásquez, after two coup attempts and the impeachment of Pérez.

[29] In particular, in late 1996, new legislation established a minimum level of transfers (about 15–20 percent) from the VAT revenue and, at the beginning of 1998 the legislature approved a law in which a share of oil royalties had to be transferred to the states.

times (Briceño 2002). The changes to the president's budget introduced by congress increased substantially (Puente 2003).[30]

Policies have undergone a radical change once again throughout the Chávez administration (1999–present). Policies have become more volatile partially as a result of political instability. Many reforms implemented during the previous administrations have been reversed, including trade policy, privatization, the liberalization of the interest rate and the exchange rate. Cabinet turnover has significantly increased. Governance and institutional quality have declined notoriously (see figure 10.3).

Overall Quality of Public Policies

An abundant body of evidence suggests deterioration in the quality of public policies from 1989 to 2006, not only compared to the previous periods, but also compared to the performance of other Latin American countries during the same period. For example, the relative position of Venezuela in the different components of the Global Competitiveness Report (GCR) reveals that the country is one of the worst performers in the world in areas related to public policy outcomes (World Economic Forum, various years). Moreover, its ranking has worsened throughout the last decade.

The Governance Indicators of the World Bank Institute (2004) also reflect the low and declining quality of Venezuela's policies and institutions. In all six indicators, Venezuela is significantly below the regional average and declined between 1996 and 2004. As can be seen in figure 10.3, in the political instability index, Venezuela's percentile rank is 14, while the

---

[30] As measured by the average absolute difference of congressional changes to the executive's budget for each year. Puente (2003) finds that two patterns of congressional activity have characterized the last three decades: one with a low level of congressional involvement in the budget process (1973–85) and another with a high level of involvement (1986–99). From 1973 to 1985, congress usually approved the budget presented by the government with relatively few changes. However, from 1986 to 1998, only three annual appropriations involved a change of less than 5 percent, six involved a change of more than 26 percent, and one involved a change of more than 36 percent.

Figure 10.3. Governance Indicators, Selected Countries, 2004 (percentile rank)

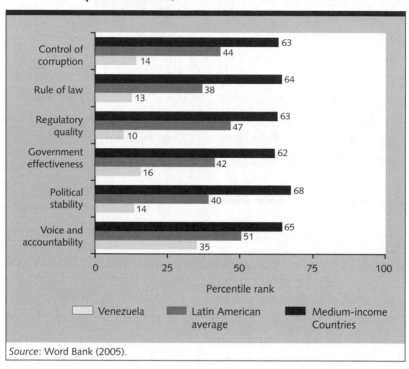

Source: Word Bank (2005).

Latin American average is 40.[31] In the index of government effectiveness, Venezuela has declined from 24 percent to 16 percent, while the regional average has been above 40 percent. In regulatory quality, the indicator has fallen from 45 percent to 10 percent, while the regional average has been around 50 percent. In the rule of law index, Venezuela has fallen from the 29 percent percentile to 13 percent, while the regional average has been around 40 percent. Finally, in the control of corruption index, Venezuela has declined from 28 percent to 14 percent. Moreover, as shown in figure 10.3, Venezuela fares even worse if compared to the average of the countries with similar levels of per capita GDP. Similarly, in the

---

[31] The last indicators available are from 2004. There are almost 200 countries in the database. The percentile rank reflects the percentage of countries that did worse in the indicator than the case studied.

public policy indicators produced by the Inter-American Development Bank (2005), Venezuela fared significantly below the regional average in efficiency, coordination and coherence, enforcement and implementation, stability and adaptability, and overall policy quality. In addition, Lora's structural reform index (Lora 2001) indicates that Venezuela has had one of the poorest and more volatile performances in the region in terms of the advancement of market reform.

To illustrate the features of Venezuela's public policies, the discussion that follows briefly discusses some characteristics of three crucial policy areas: public administration, decentralization, and oil.

Public Administration. Even though there has never been an effective civil service system in Venezuela, the evidence seems to point to the fact that, during the first three administrations of the democratic era, the quality of the bureaucracy was significantly better than it has been in the last two decades. From 1958 to 1973, although there was not significant political commitment to create a professional civil service, the bureaucracy worked relatively well in terms of its capacity to respond to or cope with the population's needs. The coverage of the public services was considerably expanded and the foundations of some model organizations were established, including the central bank and the national library.

In 1960, during the Betancourt administration, the Public Administration Commission (CAP) was created with the assistance of the United Nations. The CAP recommended the enactment of the administrative career law and the creation of the central personnel office, both reforms aimed at creating the institutional basis for the professionalization of the civil service. However, during the first two democratic administrations, national party leaders blocked attempts to pass these reforms in congress. Still, Presidents Betancourt and Leoni implemented some limited reforms by executive decree.[32] In 1968, Rafael Caldera (COPEI)

---

[32] During the coalition governments of Betancourt and Leoni, all political parties in the Punto Fijo Pact wanted to carry out their own bureaucratic recruitment and thus were reluctant to delegate entry into the public administration to an autonomous civil service (COPRE 1990). President Betancourt used executive decree powers in 1960

won the presidential election, with a minority in congress. Finally, the AD, now out of power but with a large presence in congress, decided to approve the administrative career law to create a civil service and limit the executive's power over the bureaucracy.

Even with the civil service law, the bureaucracy began a process of progressive decline during the oil booms (1973–83). The goals of the law were distorted and it was mostly reduced to being a guarantee of job stability.[33] Moreover, during Pérez's first administration, the central government grew dramatically. In 1989, the Presidential Commission for State Reform (COPRE) presented a proposal for public administration reform. It was based on a diagnosis of two general dysfunctions: the existence of patronage and excessive centralization.[34] However, there still were some very significant exceptions to the rule. These "pockets of efficiency" included the oil company PDVSA, the central bank, the electric power producer Edelca, and the Metro de Caracas. They relied on a totally different human resources notion based on merit, continued assessment, and education. Politics had little or nothing to do with the selection and compensation of an employee.

From 1989 to the present, public administration performance declined significantly, even though, during the early 1990s, some significant reforms were implemented to try to reverse its progressive deterioration. Those reforms included better pay for the top positions, structural reforms in key agencies such as the tax authority (SENIAT) and the ministry of industry and commerce (MIC), the creation of independent tech-

---

to pass a regulation on government personnel. Although this regulation provided a minimum legal framework to govern public servants, it still reflected some lack of long-term commitment to a civil service policy. In 1965, President Leoni passed some guidelines that would regulate the human resources system on some issues, such as hiring, dismissals, promotions, and salary raises.

[33] Political party affiliation was the principal criterion used to determine entry, and for the first time salaries were not adequate enough to attract qualified people into the civil service. There was virtually no performance evaluation for civil servants, and the process of training was totally set aside.

[34] The patronage system was based on the use of oil revenues to distribute particular benefits. These benefits also included entry into a stable job within the public administration. Loyalty and submission to party authority were the criteria used, rather than meritocracy.

nical advisory offices in congress and the ministry of finance, and a new law for the Central Bank of Venezuela that strengthened its autonomy. However, by 2006 almost all those reforms had been completely reversed and even the previous successes were upturned. The MIC displayed the same features as the rest of the bureaucracy. The technical advisory offices have been disbanded. The pockets of efficiency mentioned before suffered a dramatic decline in meritocracy and autonomy. Only the SENIAT shows a significant level of effectiveness. Moreover, by 2002, the wage ratio of top salaries to minimum salaries had declined to 6 (from 16 in the early 1990s). As a result, it was difficult to recruit qualified personnel. During the first three administrations, some of the best professionals in the country were civil servants. At the time, salaries were competitive (Gónzalez 2002).[35]

According to the appointment strategy index developed by Barbara Geddes (1994), Venezuelan governments from Betancourt to Lusinchi undertook a compartmentalization strategy that was characterized by political selection of top administrative personnel, informal meritocratic recruitment and promotion based on performance in agencies the president deems most critical, and recruitment of the rest of the bureaucracy through customary patronage channels. Geddes (1994) gave the first three democratic presidential administrations an index of 5 (where zero represents pure patronage and 10 pure meritocracy). In contrast, the index declined to an average of 3.66 for the next three administrations and increased during Pérez's reforms (the last period studied). Taking into account the low scores obtained by the Venezuelan bureaucracy in the World Bank indicators of government effectiveness (in the sixteenth

---

[35] One of the most important reasons for the decline of the bureaucracy was the significant decline of public servant salaries relative to private sector salaries. In 1965, public sector salaries were on average more than 2.3 times higher than the average private sector salary. In the 1970s this ratio declined to less than two and became very volatile. By the mid-1990s, the ratio was less than one (Baptista 2001). Part of the explanation for the dramatic erosion of public sector salaries has to do with the huge expansion in public sector employment that occurred during the oil booms. After oil revenues declined it was difficult to cut back personnel or nominal wages. However, real wages in the public sector suffered a dramatic decline.

percentile) as well as others (such as the Global Competitiveness Report), the last two administrations would probably be given a very low score in Geddes' index.[36] The Chávez administration has had the most openly partisan selection strategy of any administration in Venezuela's democratic history.

Decentralization Policy. Decentralization in Venezuela began belatedly in comparison with other Latin American countries. Until the late 1980s, federalism in Venezuela was a legal formality. It was only in 1989 with the direct election of governors and mayors that a decentralization policy became a reality. The process has remained structurally fragile, especially in terms of its financial side, and has been vulnerable to attempts to reverse it, given the region's dependence on vertical intergovernmental transfers.

Once it began, decentralization policy came to be an illustrative case of high volatility. The fate of the process has depended largely on the preferences of politicians in charge of the government. There was significant progress during Pérez's second administration. In 1989, several laws were enacted providing a legal base for decentralization, and many competencies and resources were transferred. The provisional government of President Velazquez (1993–94) gave a greater push to decentralization. The FIDES, a fund for regional investment, was created with earmarked tax funds, and the ministry of decentralization was formed. During President Caldera's administration, decentralization slowed down. However, governors obtained additional fiscal resources through their influence in congress. Finally, with President Chávez, decentralization has been severely affected. The process leading to the transfer of concurrent competencies to the states has been blocked. Health and education decentralization have been partially reversed, and expenditure decentralization has declined, breaking the increasing trend.

---

[36] In Geddes' index (1994), Venezuela was either at the regional average or above it in terms of meritocracy. However, today Venezuela is clearly below the average in the region.

Oil Policy. Oil policy epitomized the stability and cooperation in Venezuela's public policies. However, such cooperation did not always bring welfare-enhancing policies. From 1958 to 1975, all governments systematically increased the taxation of the foreign-owned oil companies working in the country. Governments also provided incentives for rapidly increasing production, but at the same time did not renew oil concessions, setting the companies' horizon in 1983. As a result, companies began to disinvest and exploited the oil fields already in production more intensively. A decade later, as could be expected, the lack of investment produced a decline in production. The cooperation of all the parties involved in the policy process to extract more resources from the oil companies was remarkably effective. However, its long-term effects were negative. The specific nature of this sector—its high level of sunk costs—provides part of the explanation for this shortsighted behavior. It allowed politicians to postpone the costs of a predatory strategy for more than a decade.

The decline of the oil industry was eventually reversed with nationalization in 1976. The creation of the state-owned oil company, PDVSA, offers a remarkable example of a high degree of cooperation, this time with positive consequences. The company was structured so as to minimize politicization and maintain operational and financial autonomy. As a result, it became the most efficient institution of the Venezuelan state.

Oil policy continued being remarkably cooperative until the 1990s. The opening of the oil sector to foreign investment was supported by the AD and COPEI, but opposed by Chávez. After winning the election, he eliminated PDVSA's financial and operational autonomy. A conflict ensued, which led to a dramatic decline in the company's capacities. The opening of the oil sector has been significantly reversed. The breakdown in cooperation is highly visible.

Conclusion

The analysis of the outer features of public policies in Venezuela tends to support the general hypothesis of the theoretical framework proposed by this project; namely that under conditions favorable for cooperation, such as those that prevailed in the first period (1958–88), policies generally had some desirable outer features, such as stability and coherence. This conclusion is particularly evident if one compares the first period with the noncooperative policymaking process that has prevailed in Venezuela during the last two decades, characterized by increasingly unstable, incoherent, and shortsighted public policies.

In the first period, policies were relatively coherent, stable, and bipartisan. Despite the alternation of two parties in power, in many areas policies could be characterized as *state* policies rather than *governmental* policies. Leading examples were foreign relations, oil policy, industrialization policy, education policy, and health policy. Fiscal policy was relatively well managed until the oil shocks of the 1970s significantly distorted the policy process. The bureaucracy was relatively effective, well paid, and stable in the first two decades, and even after the oil booms and busts, pockets of efficiency were preserved, such as the oil company PDVSA and the central bank. Oil policy was stable and coherent but shortsighted in the first two decades, although the creation of the PDVSA in 1976 reflected a high level of cooperation and long-term commitment among the political actors.

In contrast, the second period has been characterized by high policy volatility and the lack of long-term policy commitments. Fiscal and tax policies have been erratic and high inflation has persisted. Bureaucratic autonomy has dramatically eroded. The pockets of efficiency have been almost fully disbanded. Oil policy has been unstable and often shortsighted, and decentralization of public services has been volatile and incoherent.

In the Venezuelan case it is clear that the cooperative policymaking process that prevailed in the first three decades of democracy was to a large extent the result of the institutional foundations that were deliberately put into place by the Pact of Punto Fijo. The constitution significantly limited the benefits of power. This was especially relevant in a country where considerable stakes were involved in the control over oil revenues. In particular, presidential powers were significantly constrained relative to regional standards. The institutional framework also stimulated the existence of strong, centralized, and disciplined political parties. In addition, some features reduced the fragmentation induced by a proportional electoral system. All these elements contributed to generating a remarkably cooperative policymaking process.

The dramatic decline in cooperation that has occurred in the last decade and a half can be partially attributed to the popular discontent generated by the poor economic performance of the 1980s, which was largely due to the exogenous fall in oil fiscal revenue. Nevertheless, the institutional reforms of the late 1980s also contributed to changing the incentive structure of the polity, weakening the party system, and making the policymaking process less cooperative. The election of regional authorities and the change in the electoral system weakened party discipline and promoted political fragmentation. Combined with the decline in oil fiscal revenues, these reforms also engendered a relatively weak executive branch.

From a partial equilibrium perspective, these institutional reforms should have produced positive results—and from the perspective of the quality of public services and democratic accountability, they seem to have been quite effective (De la Cruz 1998). A closed and centralized political system became more open, decentralized, and competitive. However, these reforms contributed to unravel the cooperative equilibrium that had prevailed, without providing an alternative incentive structure to induce cooperation. In that sense, the general equilibrium perspective used in this book allows for a different take on the Venezuelan institutional reforms.

Although during the first period the policymaking process showed remarkably cooperative features, in the end it failed to deliver policies that promoted long-term growth or dealt effectively with external shocks. This apparent puzzle might have two possible explanations. The optimal strategy for cooperative politicians might not entail implementing public policies that foster economic growth if those policies are detrimental to their political survival. In some contexts, cooperation might support the maintenance of power. Moreover, in the case of governments financed by oil rents, whose magnitude does not depend on the general quality of public policies, political cooperation might not necessarily imply efficiency. In the case of Venezuela, under the resource abundance provided by oil, the favorable conditions for cooperation seem to have fostered the creation of a political cartel devoted to distributing oil rents among political clients. The oil resources, and some of the institutions that fostered cooperation, also undermined the ability of new political competitors to enter into democratic contestation, representing high entry barriers. In other words, cooperation was collusive, limiting democratic competition. As a result, the cartel implemented policies that were unsustainable once oil rents declined. Morever, because of its closed nature, the cartel was slow to adapt to changes in the political environment, leading to its demise. An alternative explanation is that the size of the positive and negative external shocks was so significant that it would have been extremely difficult to manage under any institutional framework. The poor economic performance caused by the shocks, combined with the reform attempts, led to the deconsolidation of democracy.

In addition to the literature arguing that the poor economic performance in the last two decades in Venezuela and in other oil-exporting countries can be largely attributed to oil income decline and volatility, there exists a growing literature proposing that the dependence on oil rents produces a tendency toward authoritarianism and institutional decay.[37] This literature suggests a complementary explanation for the decline of the Punto Fijo democracy. One simplified version would be that the elite Punto Fijo pact allowed for the creation of a limited democracy by significantly reducing the stakes of power, avoiding the authoritarian fate of other oil exporters and failed democracies in the region. However, the oil boom and bust induced economic decline and institutional decay. The efforts to reform the economy and the political institutions

---

[37] See Ross (2001); Sala-i-Martin and Subramanian (2003); Isham and others (2003). At least six causal channels are proposed. First, the stakes of power are very high in oil-dependent societies, and control of the oil revenue generates a high prime for holding onto power. Second, oil dependence allows for low levels of non-oil taxation, which leads to a lack of accountability and weakens the state's administrative capacity. Third, oil resources can be spent on patronage. Fourth, oil revenue can be used for repression. Fifth, since the state controls most resources, civil society and private entrepreneurs are less autonomous. Sixth, oil rents generate a tendency toward corruption.

contributed to the collapse of the political system by weakening the bases of the cooperative equilibrium that was in place.

Finally, some authors have pointed out that the Venezuelan institutional framework of Punto Fijo lacked representativeness, accountability, and transparency. For example, Karl (1986) argues that the transition to democracy based on elite pacts can be successful in stabilizing democracy, but tends to produce exclusionary political systems.[38] The restrictive nature of the political system was exacerbated after the oil boom and a two-party system emerged. According to this perspective, the "deficit of democracy" eventually led to the demise of the political system.[39]

---

[38] In Punto Fijo, the radical left was deliberately left out of the elite pact. In the 1960s, these groups formed a significant guerrilla movement supported by Cuba. By the end of the decade the insurgency was defeated and most of its leaders became involved in parties that got a small share of the vote.

[39] From the perspective of theoretical framework developed by Spiller, Stein, and Tommasi (2003), it is interesting to note that in Latin America, with the exception of Costa Rica, the only three civilian regimes (Colombia, Mexico, and Venezuela) and two democracies (Colombia and Venezuela) that survived uninterruptedly since the 1950s have been regimes with limited competition. The three regimes generated policymaking systems that were rather cooperative and achieved good performance for a while. Eventually, however, all faced problems of legitimacy and performance that led to institutional reforms that reduced the cooperative nature of the system. One interesting line of further research would be studying the relationship between the competitive characteristics of the political regime, the cooperation it induces in the policymaking process, and its long-run sustainability.

References

Abente Brun, Diego. 1993. "Las etapas de la transición y el camino por recorrer." In *Paraguay en Transición*, edited by D. Abente Brun, 147–159. Caracas: Editorial Nueva Sociedad.

Abreu, Dilip. 1988. "On the Theory of Infinitely Repeated Games with Discounting." *Econometrica* 56 (2): 383–396.

Abuelafia, Emmanuel, Sergio Berensztein, Miguel Braun, and Luciano Di Gresia. 2005. "Who Decides on Public Expenditures? A Political Economy Analysis of the Budget Process: The Case of Argentina." Washington, DC: CIPPEC/Inter-American Development Bank. Mimeo.

Acosta, Olga Lucia, and Richard Bird. 2003. "Evaluación de las recomendaciones sobre impuestos locales en la reforma estructural del sistema tributario colombiano y estudio y recomendaciones sobre la situación de los ingresos tributarios de los departamentos." Estudios para la Misión del Ingreso Público. Toronto, Canada: University of Toronto. Mimeo.

Acuña, Carlos. 1991. "La relativa ausencia de exportaciones industriales en la Argentina. Determinantes políticos y sus consecuencias sobre la estabilidad y el tipo de democracia esperables." *Realidad Economica* 100: 9–38.

Acuña, Carlos. 1995. *La nueva matriz política argentina*. Buenos Aires, Argentina: Editorial Nueva Visión.

Acuña, Carlos, Sebastián Galiani, and Mariano Tommasi. 2007. "Understanding Reform: The Case of Argentina." In *Understanding Market Reforms in Latin America*, edited by Josè M. Fanelli. Basingstoke, UK: Macmillan.

Aguayo Quesada, S. 2001. *La charola: una historia de los servicios de inteligencia en México*. Mexico, D.F., Mexico: Editorial Grijalbo.

Aldrich, John. 1995. *Why Parties? The Origin and Transformation of Political Parties in America.* Chicago: The University of Chicago Press.

Alemán, Eduardo. 2003. "Legislative Rules and the Amending Process: Theory and Evidence from Argentina, Chile and México." Paper presented at the American Political Science Association Annual Meeting, Philadelphia, PA.

Alemán, Eduardo. 2006. "Policy Gatekeepers in Latin American Legislatures." *Latin American Politics & Society* 48 (3): 125–155.

Alesina, Alberto. 2004. *Institutional Reforms in Colombia.* Cambridge, MA: MIT Press.

Alesina, Alberto, Ricardo Hausmann, Rudolf Hommes, and Ernesto Stein. 1999. "Budget Institutions and Fiscal Performance in Latin America." *Journal of Development Economics* 59 (2): 253–273.

Alston, Lee, and Bernardo Mueller. 2003. "Democratization and Exploiting the Gains from Trade: Executive and Legislative Exchange in Brazil." *Journal of Law, Economics and Organization* (submitted).

Alston, Lee, Gary D. Libecap, and Bernardo Mueller. 2000. "Property Rights to Land and Land Reform: Legal Inconsistencies and the Sources of Violent Conflict in the Brazilian Amazon." *Journal of Environmental Economics and Management* 39: 162–188.

Alston Lee, and Bernardo Mueller. 2006. "Pork for Policy: Executive and Legislative Exchange in Brazil." *Journal of Law Economics and Organization* 22 (1): 87–114.

Alston, Lee, Marcus Melo, Bernardo Mueller, and Carlos Pereira. 2007. *On the Brazilian Road to Good Governance: Recovering from Economic and Political Shocks.* Working Paper, University of Colorado (August).

Ames, Barry. 1995a. "Electoral Rules, Constituency Pressures, and Pork Barrel: Bases of Voting in the Brazilian Congress." *Journal of Politics* 57 (2): 324–343.

Ames, Barry. 1995b. "Electoral Strategy Under Open-List Proportional Representation." *American Journal of Political Science* 39 (2): 406–433.

Ames, Barry. 2001. *The Deadlock of Democracy in Brazil.* Ann Arbor: University of Michigan Press.

Amorim Neto, Octavio. 1998a. "Cabinet Formation in Presidential Regimes: An Analysis of 10 Latin American Countries." Presented at the Latin American Studies Association, Chicago, IL.

Amorim-Neto, Octavio. 1998b. "Of Presidents, Parties, and Ministers: Cabinet Formation and Legislative Decision-Making under Separation of Powers." Doctoral dissertation, University of California, San Diego.

Amorim Neto, Octavio. 2002. "Presidential Cabinets, Electoral Cycles, and Coalition Discipline in Brazil." In *Legislative Politics in Latin America*, edited by Scott Morgenstern and Benito Nacif. New York: Cambridge University Press.

Amorim-Neto, Octavio, and Hugo Borsani. 2004. "Presidents and Cabinets: The Political Determinants of Fiscal Behavior in Latin America." *Studies in Comparative International Development* 39 (1): 3–27.

Amorim Neto, Octavio, Gary Cox, and Matthew McCubbins. 2003. "Agenda Power in Brazil's Camara dos Deputados, 1998–98." *World Politics* 55 (4): 550–578.

Amorim Neto, Octavio, and Fabiano Santos. 2001. "The Executive Connection: Presidentially Defined Factions and Party Discipline in Brazil." *Party Politics* 7 (2): 213–234.

Aninat, Cristóbal. 2006. "El Proceso Legislativo Chileno: Análisis del Proyecto de Ley de Rentas Vitalicias 1994-2004". Documento de trabajo Departamento de Estudios de Superintendencia de Administradoras de Fondos de Pensiones de Chile. Por publicarse.

Aninat, Cristóbal. 2007. "Balance de Poderes Legislativos en Chile: ¿Presidencialismo exagerado o bases para un sistema político cooperativo?" *Revista Política no. 47*, Universidad de Chile, Santiago, Chile, forthcoming.

Aninat, Cristóbal, and John Londregan. 2004. "Non-Pigouvian Payoffs and the Politics of Agricultural Trade Liberalization in Chile." Paper presented at the Midwest Political Science Association 62nd Annual Meeting, Chicago, IL.

Aninat, Cristóbal, and Joaquín Vial. 2005. *Who Decides on Public Expenditures? A Political Economy Analysis of the Budget Process in Chile.*

Research Department, Inter-American Development Bank, Washington, DC. Unpublished.

Aninat, Cristóbal, John Londregan, Patricio Navia, and Joaquín Vial. 2006. *Political Institutions, Policymaking Processes, and Policy Outcomes in Chile.* Research Network Working Paper R-521, Inter-American Development Bank, Washington, DC.

Ansolabehere, Stephen, James M. Snyder, and Michael M. Ting. 2002. "Bargaining in Bicameral Legislatures: When and Why does Malapportionment Matter?" *American Political Science Review* 97 (3): 471–481.

Araujo, María Caridad. 1998. "Gobernabilidad durante la crisis y políticas de ajuste." Proyecto CORDES-Gobernabilidad, Quito, Ecuador.

Araujo, María Caridad, Andrés Mejía, Aníbal Pérez-Liñán, and Sebastian Saeigh. 2004. "Political Institutions, Policymaking Processes, and Policy Outcomes in Ecuador." Latin American Research Network, Inter-American Development Bank, Washington, DC.

Archer, Ronald P., and Matthew S. Shugart. 1997. "The Unrealized Potential of Presidential Dominance in Colombia." *In Presidentialism and Democracy in Latin America,* edited by Scott Mainwaring and Matthew S. Shugart. New York: Cambridge University Press.

Ardanaz, M., M. Leiras, and Mariano Tommasi. 2007. "Beyond Plaza de Mayo. Provincial Party Bosses in Argentina." Universidad de San Andrés. Buenos Aires, Argentina. Mimeo.

Arditi, Benjamín. 1993. "Del granito al archipiélago: el Partido Colorado sin Stroessner." In *Paraguay en Transición,* edited by Diego Abente-Brun, 161–172. Caracas: Editorial Nueva Sociedad.

Arretche, Marta. 2003. "Financiamento federal e gestão local de políticas sociais: o difícil equilíbrio entre regulação, responsabilidade e autonomia." *Ciência e Saúde Coletiva* 8 (2): L 331–345.

Arteta, Gustavo. 2003. "Antes y Después del SRI." *Carta Económica* 5.

Arteta, Gustavo, and Osvaldo Hurtado Larrea. 2002. "Political Economy of Ecuador: The Quandary of Governance and Economic Development." Quito: CORDES. Unpublished.

Ayala Espino, José. 1988. *Estado y desarrollo: La formación de la economía mixta mexicana (1920–1982)*. Mexico, D.F., Mexico: Fondo de Cultura Económica.

Ayala, Ulpiano. 1998. "La regulación de los fondos de pensiones en América Latina: Reseña y lecciones de la experiencia." *Coyuntura Económica* 28 (4): 189–209.

Ayala Bogarín, Oscar, and José María Costa. 1996. *Operación Gedeón: Los secretos de un golpe frustrado*. Asunción: Editorial Don Bosco.

Baker, Richard D. 1971. *Judicial Review in Mexico: A Study of the Amparo Suit*. Austin: University of Texas Press.

Baldrich, Jorge. 2003. "The Political Economy of Short Run Fiscal Policy. Some Evidence from Argentina, 1994–2001." Universidad de San Andrés, Buenos Aires, Argentina. Mimeo.

Bambaci, Juliana, Pablo T. Spiller, and Mariano Tommasi. 2007. "The Bureaucracy." In *The Institutional Foundations of Public Policy: A Transactions Theory and an Application to Argentina*, edited by Pablo Spiller and Mariano Tommasi. Cambridge, UK: Cambridge University Press.

Baptista, Asdrubal. 2001. *Bases Cuantitativas de la Economía Venezolana: 1830–2000*. Caracas, Venezuela: Ediciones IESA.

Barreda, Mikel, and Andrea Costafreda. 2002. "La Transición Democrática y el Sistema Político-Institucional." In *Diagnóstico Institucional de la República del Paraguay*, edited by J. Prats i Català. Barcelona: IIG-PNUD.

Basáñez, Miguel 1995. *El pulso de los sexenios: 20 años de crisis en México*. Mexico, D.F., Mexico: Siglo XXI.

Bates, Robert. 1997. "Open-Economy Politics: The Political Economy of the World Coffee Trade." Princeton University, Princeton, NJ. Mimeo.

Bawn, Kathleen, and Frances Rosenbluth. 2006. "Short vs. Long Coalitions: Electoral Accountability and the Size of the Public Sector." *American Journal of Political Science* 50 (2): 251–265.

Bazdresch, Carlos, and Santiago Levy. 1991. "Populism and Economic Policy in Mexico, 1970–1982." In *The Macroeconomics of Populism in Latin America,* edited by Roger Dornbusch and Sebastian Edwards. Chicago: University of Chicago Press.

Becerra, R., P. Salazar, and J. Woldenberg. 2000. *La mecánica del cambio político: elecciones, partidos y reformas.* Mexico, D.F., Mexico: Cal y Arena.

Beltrán, Ulises. 2000. "Factores de ponderación del voto retrospectivo." *Política y Gobierno* 7 (2): 425–442.

Bensusán, G. 2004. "A New Scenario for Mexican Trade Unions: Changes in the Structure of Political and Economic Opportunities." In *Dilemmas of Political Change in Mexico,* edited by K. J. Middlebrook. London: Institute for Latin American Studies, University of London.

Bercoff, José, and Osvaldo Meloni. 2007. "Federal Budget Allocation in an Emerging Democracy. Evidence from Argentina." Universidad Nacional de Tucumán, Buenos Aires, Argentina. Mimeo.

Bergara, Mario, Andrés Pereyra, Ruben Tansini, Adolfo Garcé, Daniel Chasquetti, Daniel Buquet, and Juan Andrés Moraes. 2006. *Political Institutions, Policymaking Processes, and Policy Outcomes: The Case of Uruguay.* Research Network Working Paper #R-510. Research Department, Inter-American Development Bank, Washington, DC.

Berkman, Heather, Carlos Scartascini, Ernesto Stein, and Mariano Tommasi. 2007. "Political Institutions and Policy Outcomes around the World." Inter-American Development Bank, Washington, DC. Mimeo.

Bertelsmann Foundation. 2004. *Bertelsmann Transformation Index 2003: Political Management in International Comparison (BTI).* Gütersloh, Germany: Bertelsmann Stiftung.

Bill Chavez, Rebecca. 2003. "The Construction of the Rule of Law in Argentina: A Tale of Two Provinces." *Comparative Politics* 35 (4): 417–437.

Blondel, Jean. 1982. *The Organization of Governments: A Comparative Analysis of Governmental Structures.* London: Sage Publications.

Blondel, Jean. 1985. *Government Ministers in the Contemporary World.* London: Sage Publications.

Bouzas, Roberto, and Emiliano Pagnotta. 2003. *Dilemas de la Política Comercial Externa Argentina.* Buenos Aires, Argentina: Fundación OSDE/Universidad de San Andrés.

Boyland, Delia M. 2001. *Defusing Democracy: Central Bank Autonomy and the Transition from Authoritarian Rule.* Ann Arbor: University of Michigan Press.

Braguinsky, Eugenia, and María Fernanda Araujo. 2006. "Base de datos de Decretos de Necesidad y Urgencia: análisis cuanti-cualitativos de las disposiciones presidenciales de carácter legislativo (2003–2006)." Documento de Políticas Públicas. Buenos Aires, Argentina: CIPPEC.

Braun, Miguel, and Mariano Tommasi. 2004. *Fiscal Rules for Subnational Governments: Some Organizing Principles and Latin American Experiences.* Working Paper 78. Inter-American Development Bank/Center of Studies for Institutional Development (CEDI, Fundacion Gobierno y Sociedad), Washington, DC.

Briceño, Mercedes. 2002. "Costo Tributario." In *Costo Venezuela: Opciones de Política para Mejorar la Competitividad,* edited by Michael Penfold. Caracas, Venezuela: CONAPRI.

Bruhn, Kathleen. 1997. *Taking on Goliath: The Emergence of a New Left Party and the Struggle for Democracy in Mexico.* University Park: Pennsylvania State University Press.

Bruhn, Kathleen, and Kenneth F. Greene. 2007. "Elite Polarization Meets Mass Moderation in Mexico's 2006 Elections." *Political Science and Politics* 49 (January): 33–38.

Buchanan, James, and Gordon Tullock. 1962. *The Calculus of Consent: Logical Foundations of Constitutional Democracy.* Ann Arbor: University of Michigan.

Burbano de Lara, Felipe, and Michel Rowland García. 1998. *Pugna de Poderes: Presidencialismo y Partidos en el Ecuador, 1979–1997.* Quito, Ecuador: Corporación de Estudios para el Desarrollo-Fundación Konrad Adenauer.

Calvo, Guillermo. 1996. *Money, Exchange Rates, and Output.* Cambridge, MA: MIT Press.

Calvo, Guillermo, and Allen Drazen. 1998. "Uncertain Duration of Reform: Dynamic Implications." *Macroeconomic Dynamics* 2 (4): 443–455.

Calvo, Ernesto, and Marcelo Escolar. 2003. "La implementación de sistemas electorales mixtos en legislaturas de magnitud fija: teorías y soluciones." *Política y Gobierno* 10: 359–399.

Calvo, Ernesto, and Juan Pablo Micozzi. 2005. "The Governors' Backyard: A Seat-Vote Model of Electoral Reform for Subnational Multiparty Races." *Journal of Politics* 67 (4): 1050–1074.

Calvo, Ernesto, and Maria Victoria Murillo. 2003. "Who Delivers? Partisan Clients in the Argentine Electoral Market." Paper presented at the Harvard University Conference Rethinking Dual Transitions: Argentine Politics in the 1990s in Comparative Perspective, Boston, MA.

Calvo, Ernesto, and Maria Victoria Murillo. 2004. "Who Delivers? Partisan Clients in the Argentine Electoral Market." *American Journal of Political Science* 48 (4): 742–758.

Calvo, Ernesto, and Maria Victoria Murillo. 2005. "A New Law of Argentine Politics? Partisanship, Clientelism, and Governability in Contemporary Argentina." In *Argentine Democracy: The Politics of Institutional Weakness,* edited by Steven Levitsky and María Victoria Murillo. University Park: Pennsylvania State University Press.

Camp, Roderic Ai. 1992. *Generals in the Palacio: The Military in Modern Mexico.* New York: Oxford University Press.

Campos, Emma Rosa. 2003. "Un Congreso sin congresistas: la no reelección consecutiva en el poder legislativo mexicano, 1934–1997." In *El legislador a examen: el debate sobre la reelección legislativa en México,* edited by Fernando Dworak. Mexico, D.F., Mexico: Fondo de Cultura Económica.

Campos, Luis A., and Ricardo Canese. 1987. *El Sector Público en Paraguay: Análisis de sus Inversiones y Empresas.* Asunción: Centro Interdisciplinario de Derecho Social y Economía Políticas.

Campos, Luis A., and Ricardo Canese. 1990. *La Reestructuración Democrática del Sector Público.* Asunción: CEDES-BASE.

Cárdenas, Mauricio. 2007. "Economic Growth in Colombia: A Reversal of 'Fortune'?" *Ensayos sobre política económica* 25(53).

Cárdenas, Mauricio, and Zeinab Partow. 1998. *Oil, Coffee and the Dynamic Commons Problems in Colombia*. Research Network Working Paper R-335. Inter-American Development Bank, Washington, DC.

Cárdenas, Mauricio, Roberto Junguitom, and Mónica Pachón. 2004. *Political Institutions, Policymaking Processes, and Policy Outcomes: The Case of Colombia*. Latin American Research Network, Inter-American Development Bank, Washington, DC.

Cárdenas, Mauricio, Carolina Mejía, and Mauricio Olivera. 2006. *La economía política del proceso presupuestal colombiano*. Working Paper No. 31. Inter-American Development Bank, Washington, DC.

Carey, John M. 1996. *Term Limits and Legislative Representation*. New York: Cambridge University Press.

Carey, John M. 2002a. "Parties, Coalitions, and the Chilean Congress in the 1990s." In *Legislative Politics in Latin America*, edited by Scott Morgerstern and Benito Nacif. Boston, MA: Cambridge University Press.

Carey, John M. 2002b. "Getting Their Way, or Getting in the Way? Presidents and Party Unity in Legislative Voting." Presented at the American Political Science Association, Boston, August.

Carey, John M. 2003. "The Reelection Debate in Latin America." *Latin American Politics and Society* 45 (1): 119–133.

Carey, John M. 2006. Legislative Organization (or, What We Want from Legislatures and What Comparative Legislative Studies Tells Us About Whether We Get it). In *The Oxford Handbook of Political Institutions*, edited by Sarah Binder, Rod Rhodes, and Bert Rockman. Oxford: Oxford University Press.

Carey, John M., and Peter Siavelis. 2003. *El Seguro para los Subcampeones Electorales y la sobrevivencia de la Concertación*. Centro de Estudios Públicos, *Estudios Públicos* 90 (Fall), 5–27.

Carey, John M., and Matthew S. Shugart. 1995. "Incentives to Cultivate a Personal Vote: A Rank Ordering of Electoral Formulas." *Electoral Studies* 14 (4): 417–439.

Carey, John M., and Matthew Soberg Shugart. 1998a. "Calling out the Tanks or Filling Out the Forms?" In *Executive Decree Authority*, edited by John M. Carey and Matthew Soberg Shugart. New York: Cambridge University Press.

Carrasquilla, Alberto. 2003. "La sostenibilidad de la deuda pública." Ministerio de Hacienda y Crédito Público, Bogota, Colombia.

Casar, María Amparo. 2000. "Coaliciones y cohesión partidista en un congreso sin mayoria: la Camara de Diputados de Mexico." *Politica y Gobierno* 7 (1): 101–144.

Casar, María Amparo. 2001. "El proceso de negociación presupuestal en el primer gobierno sin mayoría: un estudio de caso." In *Impuestos y Gasto Público en México desde una Perspectiva Multidisciplinaria,* edited by Juan Palbo Guerrero. Mexico, D.F.: CIDE/Miguel Angel Porrúa.

Casar, María Amparo. 2002a. "Executive-Legislative Relations: The Case of Mexico." In *Legislative Politics in Latin America,* edited by Scott Morgenstern and Benito Nacif. New York: Cambridge University Press.

Casar, María Amparo. 2002b. "Las bases político-institucionales del poder presidencial en México." In *Lecturas Sobre el Cambio Político en México,* edited by Carlos Elizondo Mayer-Serra and Benito Nacif. México, D.F., Mexico: Fondo de Cultura Económica.

Caselli, Francesco, and Massimo Morelli. 2004. "Bad Politicians." *Journal of Public Economics* 88 (3–4): 759–782.

Casteñeda, Jorge. 1999. *La herencia: arqueología de la sucesión presidencial en México.* Mexico, D.F., Mexico: Editorial Alfaguara.

Castro, Marcus Faro de. 1997. "O Supremo Tribunal Federal e a Judicialização da Política." *Revista Brasileira de Ciências Sociais* 12 (34): 147–155.

Cepeda, Manuel José. 2004. "La defensa judicial de la Constitución: Una tradición centenaria e ininterrumpida." In *Fortalezas de Colombia,* edited by Fernando Cepeda. Washington, DC: Inter-American Development Bank.

Centeno, Miguel Ángel. 1997. *Democracy Within Reason: Technocratic Revolution in Mexico,* 2nd edition. University Park: Pennsylvania State University Press.

Chasquetti, Daniel. 2004. "Democracia, Multipartidismo y Coaliciones en América Latina: evaluando la difícil combinación." In *Tipos de Presidencialismo y Coaliciones Políticas en América Latina*, edited by Jorge Lanzaro. Buenos Aires, Argentina: CLACSO.

Cheibub, José Antonio. 2002. "Minority Governments, Deadlock Situations, and the Survival of Presidential Democracies." *Comparative Political Studies* 35 (3): 284–312.

Cheibub, José Antonio, Argenlina Figueiredo, and Fernando Limongi. 2002. "Presidential Agenda Power and Decision-Making in Presidential Regimes: Governors and Political Parties in the Brazilian Congress." Prepared for delivery at the Annual Meeting of the American Political Science Association, Boston, MA.

Cheibub, José Antonio, Adam Przeworski, and Sebastian Saiegh. 2004. "Government Coalitions and Legislative Success under Presidentialism and Parliamentarism." *British Journal of Political Science* 34 (4): 565–587.

Cheibub, José Antonio, and Fernando Limongi. 2002. "Democratic Institutions and Regime Survival: Parliamentary and Presidential Democracies Reconsidered." *Annual Review of Political Science.*

Clavijo, Fernando, and Susana Valdivieso. 2000. "Reformas estructurales y política macroeconómica." In *Reformas económicas en México, 1982–1999*, edited by F. Clavijo. Mexico, D.F., Mexico: Fondo de Cultura Económica.

Clavijo, Sergio. 1998. "Pension Reform in Colombia: Macroeconomic and Fiscal Effects." Documento CEDE 98-01. Bogota, Colombia, Centro de Estudios sobre Desarrollo Económico.

Cleary, Matthew, and Susan Stokes. 2006. *Democracy and the Culture of Skepticism. Political Trust in Argentina and Mexico.* New York: Russell Sage Foundation.

Combellas, Ricardo. 1999. "La inserción de los grupos de intereses en el estado venezolano." In *Doce textos fundamentales de la ciencia política venezolana.* Caracas, Venezuela: Instituto de Estudios Políticos, Universidad Central de Venezuela.

Comisión de Racionalización del Gasto y de las Finanzas Públicas. 1997. *El saneamiento fiscal, un compromiso de la sociedad.* Bogota, Colombia: Ministerio de Hacienda y Crédito Público.

COPRE (Comisión Presidencial para la Reforma del Estado). 1990. *Antecedentes de la Reforma del Estado.* Caracas, Venezuela: COPRE.

Conaghan, Catherine M. 1994. "Loose Parties, 'Floating' Politicians, and Institutional Stress: Presidentialism in Ecuador, 1979–1988." In *The Failure of Presidential Democracy, Vol. 2, The Case of Latin America,* edited by Juan Linz and Arturo Valenzuela. Baltimore, MD: Johns Hopkins University Press.

Conaghan, Catherine M. 1995. "Politicians Against Parties: Discord and Disconnection in Ecuador's Party System." In *Building Democratic Institutions: Party Systems in Latin America,* edited by Scott Mainwaring and Timothy Scully. Stanford, CA: Stanford University Press.

Coppedge, Michael. 1994. *Strong Parties and Lame Ducks: Presidential Patriarchy and Factionalism in Venezuela.* Stanford, CA: Stanford University Press.

Coppedge, Michael. 1998. "The Dynamic Diversity of Latin American Party Systems." *Party Politics* 4 (4): 547–568.

Cornelius, Wayne, and Ann L. Craig. 1991. *The Mexican Political System in Transition.* La Jolla, CA: Center for U.S.-Mexican Studies, University of California.

Cornelius, Wayne, Todd A. Eisenstadt, and Jane Hindley, eds. 1999. *Subnational Politics and Democratization in Mexico.* La Jolla, CA: Center for U.S.-Mexican Studies, University of California, San Diego.

Corrales, Javier. 2002. *Presidents without Parties: the Politics of Economic Reform in Argentina and Venezuela in the 1990's.* University Park: Pennsylvania State University Press.

Corrales, Javier. 2003. "Power Asymmetries and Post-Pact Stability: Revisiting and Updating the Venezuelan Case." Paper presented at the 2003 American Political Science Association meeting in Philadelphia, PA.

Courchene, Thomas, Alberto Diaz-Cayeros, and Steven B. Webb. 2000. "Historical Forces: Geographical and Political." In *Achievements and Challenges of Fiscal Decentralization: Lessons from Mexico*, edited by Marcelo M. Giugale and Steven B. Webb. Washington, DC: World Bank.

Cowan, K., Micco, A., Mizala et al. 2003. *Un diagnóstico del desempleo en Chile*. Santiago: Inter-American Development Bank/Universidad de Chile.

Cowhey, Peter, and Matthew McCubbins, eds. 1995. *Structure and Policy in Japan and the United States: An Institutionalist Approach*. New York: Cambridge University Press

Cox, Gary. 1997. *Making Votes Count: Strategic Coordination in the World's Electoral Systems*. Cambridge, UK: Cambridge University Press.

Cox, Gary. 2006. "The Organization of Democratic Legislatures." In *The Oxford Handbook of Political Economy*, edited by Barry Weingast and Donald Wittman. Oxford: Oxford University Press.

Cox, Gary, and Octavio Amorim Neto. 1997. "Electoral Institutions, Cleavage Structures, and the Number of Parties." *American Journal of Political Science* 41 (1): 149–174.

Cox, Gary, and Matthew McCubbins. 1994. "Bonding, Structure, and the Stability of Political Parties: Party Government in the House." *Legislative Studies Quarterly* 19 (2): 215–231.

Cox, Gary, and Matthew McCubbins. 2001. "The Institutional Determinants of Economic Policy." In *Presidents, Parliaments, and Policy: Political Economy of Institutions and Decisions*, edited by Stephen Haggard and Matthew McCubbins. Cambridge, UK: Cambridge University Press.

Cox, Gary, and Matthew McCubbins. 2005. *Setting the Agenda: Responsible Party Government in the U.S. House of Representatives*. New York: Cambridge University Press.

Cox, Gary, and Scott Morgenstern. 2001. "Latin America's Reactive Assemblies and Proactive Presidents." *Comparative Politics* 33 (2): 171–190.

Cox, Gary, and Scott Morgenstern. 2002. "Epilogue: Latin America's Reactive Assemblies and Proactive Presidents." In *Legislative Politics in Latin America*, edited by Scott Morgenstern and Benito Nacif. Cambridge, UK: Cambridge University Press.

Crain, Mark. 2001. "Institutions, Durability, and the Value of Political Transactions." In *The Elgar Companion to Public Choice*, edited by William F. Shughart II and Laura Razzolini. Cheltenham, UK: Edward Elgar.

Crain, Mark, and Robert Tollison. 1979. "Constitutional Change in the Interest-Group Theory of the Government." *Journal of Legal Studies* 8 (1): 165–175.

Crisp, Brian. 1997. "Presidential Behavior in Systems with Strong Parties." In *Presidentialism and Democracy in Latin America*, edited by Scott Mainwaring and Matthew Shugart. Cambridge, UK: Cambridge University Press.

Crisp, Brian. 2000. *Democratic Institutional Design: The Powers and Incentives of Venezuelan Politicians and Interest Groups*. Stanford, CA: Stanford University Press.

Crisp, Brian. 2001. "Candidate Selection in Venezuela." Paper presented at the Latin American Studies Association (LASA) Congress Washington, DC.

Danesi, Silvina. 2004. "A Dieciocho Años de Democracia, la Gestión en la Honorable Cámara de Diputados de la Nación." Tesis de Maestría. Maestría en Administración y Políticas Públicas, Universidad de San Andrés.

Daughters, Robert, and Leslie Harper. 2006. "Fiscal and Political Decentralization." In *The State of the Reforms of the State in Latin America*, edited by Eduardo Lora. Washington, DC: Inter-American Development Bank.

De la Cruz, Rafael. 1998. *Descentralización en perspectiva*. Caracas, Venezuela: Ediciones IESA/Fundación Escuela de Gerencia Social.

De Luca, Miguel. 2004. "Political Recruitment of Presidents and Governors in the Argentine Party-Centered System." Prepared for the symposium Pathways to Power: Political Recruitment and Democracy in Latin America. Graylyn International Conference Center, Wake Forest University, Winston-Salem, NC.

De Riz, Liliana. 1986. "Dilemas del parlamento actual." In *El parlamento hoy*, edited by Liliana De Riz, Ana M. Mustapic, Mateo Goretti, and Monica Panosyan. Buenos Aires, Argentina: Estudios CEDES.

Díaz-Cayeros, Alberto. 1995. *Desarrollo Económico e Inequidad Regional: Hacia un Nuevo Pacto Federal en México*. México, D.F., Mexico: Editorial Porrúa.

Díaz-Cayeros, Alberto. 1997a. "Federalism and Veto Players: Equilibrium in Local Political Ambition in Mexico." Paper presented at the American Political Science Association, Washington, DC.

Díaz-Cayeros, Alberto. 1997b. "Political Responses to Regional Inequality: Taxation and Distribution in Mexico." Ph.D. dissertation. Department of Political Science, Duke University, Durham, NC.

Díaz Iturbe, Diego. 2006. "Disciplina de partido: estudio comparado del Senado de la República y la Cámara de Diputados de México en la LIX Legislatura." Unpublished Licentiate Thesis, Centro de Investigación y Docencias Económicas, Mexico, D.F.

Diermeier, Daniel, and Keith Krehbiel. 2003. "Institutionalism as a Methodology." *Journal of Theoretical Politics* 15 (2): 123–144.

Diermeier, Daniel, Michael Keane, and Antonio Merlo. 2005. "A Political Economy Model of Congressional Careers." *American Economic Review* 95 (1): 347–373.

DIPRES (Dirección de Presupuesto). 2004. *Estadísticas de las Finanzas Publicas: 1987–2003*. Santiago, Chile: DIPRES.

Dixit, Avinash. 1996. *The Making of Economic Policy. A Transaction-Cost Politics Perspective*. Cambridge, MA: MIT Press.

Domingo, Pilar. 2000. "Judicial Independence: The Politics of the Supreme Court in Mexico." *Journal of Latin American Studies* 32 (3): 705–735.

Domínguez, J. I. and McCann, J. 1997. *Democratizing Mexico: Public Opinion and Electoral Choice*. Baltimore, MD: Johns Hopkins University Press.

Dornbusch, Roger, and Sebastian Edwards, eds. 1991. *The Macroeconomics of Populism in Latin America*. Chicago: University of Chicago Press.

Dugas, John C. 2001. "The Origin, Impact and Demise of the 1989–1990 Colombian Student Movement: Insights from Social Movement Theory." *Journal of Latin American Studies* 33 (4): 807–837.

Eaton, Kent. 2005. "Menem and the Governors: Intergovernmental Relations in the 1990s." In *Argentine Democracy: The Politics of Institutional*

Weakness, edited by Steven Levitsky and María Victoria Murillo. University Park: Pennsylvania State University Press.

Echavarría, Juan José, Carlina Rentaría, and Roberto Steiner. 2003. "Descentralización y salvamentos (bailouts) en Colombia." *Coyuntura Social,* Bogotá, Fedesarrollo, no. 28, June.

Echeverría, Oscar. 1995. *La Economía Venezolana 1944–1994.* Tercera Edición Actualizada. Caracas, Venezuela: FEDECAMARAS.

Echeverry, Juan Carlos, Leopoldo Fergusson, and Pablo Querubín. 2004. *La batalla política por el presupuesto de la Nación: Inflexibilidades o supervivencia fiscal.* Bogota, Colombia: Centre de Estudios sobre el Desarrollo Económico.

Eckstein, Susan. 1977. *The Poverty of Revolution: The State and the Urban Poor in Mexico.* Princeton, NJ: Princeton University Press.

Eggertsson, Thráinn. 2005. *Imperfect Institutions.* Ann Arbor: University of Michigan Press.

Eisenstadt, Todd A. 2003. *Courting Democracy: Party Strategies and Electoral Institutions.* New York: Cambridge University Press.

Elizondo Mayer-Serra, Carlos. 2001. *La importancia de las reglas: gobierno y empresario después de la nacionalización bancaria.* Mexico, D.F., Mexico: Fondo de Cultura Económica.

Epstein, Lee, and Jack Knight. 1997. *The Choices Justices Make.* Washington, DC: Congressional Quarterly Press.

Escobar, Andrés. 1996. "Ciclos Políticos y Ciclos Económicos en Colombia: 1935–1994." *Coyuntura Económica* (June).

Etchemendy, Sebastián. 2002. "Constructing Reform Coalitions: The Politics of Compensations in the Argentine Path to Economic Liberalization." *Latin American Politics and Society* 43 (3): 1–35.

Evans, Peter. 2001. "Beyond 'Institutional Monocropping': Institutions, Capabilities, and Deliberative Development." Berkeley University, Berkeley, CA. Mimeo.

Evans, Peter. 2004. "Development as Institutional Change: The Pitfalls of Monocropping and Potentials of Deliberation." *Studies in Comparative International Development* 38 (4): 30–53.

Fearon, James D. 2006. "Self-Enforcing Democracy." Stanford University, Stanford, CA. Mimeo.

Ferreira Rubio, Delia, and Matteo Goretti. 1998. "When the President Governs Alone: The Decretazo in Argentina, 1989–93." In *Executive Decree Authority*, edited by John M.Carey and Matthew S. Shugart. Cambridge, UK: Cambridge University Press.

Figueiredo, Argelina Cheibub, and Fernando Limongi. 1995. "Mudança Constitucional, Desempenho Legislativo e Consolidação Institucional." *Revista Brasileira de Ciências Sociais* 29: 175–200.

Figueiredo, Argelina Cheibub, and Fernando Limongi. 1997. "Presidential Power and Party Behavior in the Legislature." Paper presented at the Meeting of the Latin American Studies Association (LASA), Mexico, D.F., Mexico.

Figueiredo, Argelina Cheibub, and Fernando Limongi 1999. *Executivo e Legislativo na Nova Ordem Constitucional*. São Paulo, Brazil: Editora Fundação Getúlio Vargas.

Figueiredo, Argelina Cheibub, and Fernando Limongi. 2000. "Presidential Power, Legislative Organization, and Party Behavior in Brazil." *Comparative Politics* 32 (2): 151–170.

Fix-Fierro, Héctor. 1999. "Poder Judicial." In *Transiciones y Diseños Institucionales*, edited by Sergio López Ayllón and María del Refugio González. Mexico, D.F., Mexico: Universidad Nacional Autónoma de México.

Flammand, Laura. 2007. "Collective Action through Association: The Mexican National Conference of Governors." Paper presented at the Midwest Political Science Association's Annual Meetings, Chicago, IL.

Fogel, Ramón. 1993. "La estructura social paraguaya y su incidencia en la transición a la democracia." In *Paraguay en Transición*, edited by Diego Abente Brun, 13–30. Caracas: Editorial Nueva Sociedad.

Friedman, James W. 1971. "A Noncooperative Equilibrium for Supergames." *Review of Economic Studies* 38 (1): 1–12.

Friedmann, Santiago, Nora Lustig, and Arianna Legovini. 1995. "Mexico: Social Spending and Food Subsidies During Adjustment in the 1980s." In *Coping with Austerity*, edited by Nora Lustig. Washington, DC: Brookings Institution.

Fudenberg, Drew, and Eric Maskin. 1986. "The Folk-Theorem in Repeated Games with Discounting and with Incomplete Information." *Econometrica* 54 (3): 533–556.

Fudenberg, Drew, and Jean Tirole. 1991. *Game Theory.* Cambridge, MA: MIT Press.

Fukuyama, Francis. 2006. "Do Defective Institutions Explain the Gap Between the United States and Latin America?" *The American Interest* 2 (2) Nov-Dec.

Galetovic, A. 2001. "Banda del Azúcar: quién pagó y quien se benefició." Santiago, Chile: Departamento de Ingeniería Industrial, Universidad de Chile.

Galiani, S., Heymann, D., and Tommasi, M. 2003. "Expectativas frustradas: el ciclo de la Convertibilidad." *Desarrollo Económico* 43 (169): 3–44.

Gallagher, Michael, Michael Laver, and Peter Mair. 1992. *Representative Government in Western Europe.* New York: McGraw-Hill.

Garro, Alejandro M. 1990. "Eficacia y Autoridad del Precedente Constitucional en América Latina: Las Lecciones del Derecho Comparado." In *Derecho Constitucional Comparado México-Estados Unidos,* edited by James F. Smith. Mexico, D.F., Mexico: Universidad Nacional Autónoma de México.

Geddes, Barbara. 1991. "A Game Theoretic Model of Reform in Latin American Democracies." *American Political Science Review* 85 (2): 371–392.

Geddes, Barbara. 1994. *Politician's Dilemma: Building State Capacity in Latin America.* Berkeley: University of California Press.

Geddes, Barbara. 1995. "Uses and Limitations of Rational Choice Theory." In *Latin America in Comparative Perspective: New Approaches to Methods and Analysis,* edited by P. Smith. Boulder, CO: Westview Press.

Geddes, Barbara.. 2002. "The Great Transformation in the Study of Politics in Developing Countries." In *Political Science: The State of the Discipline, Centennial Edition,* edited by Ira Katznelson and Helen V. New York: W. W. Norton & Company.

Gerring, John, Strom C. Thacker, and Carola Moreno. 2005. "Centripetal Democratic Governance: A Theory and Global Inquiry." *American Political Science Review* 99 (4): 567–581.

Gibson, Edward L. 1997. "The Populist Road to Market Reform: Policy and Electoral Coalitions in Mexico and Argentina." *World Politics* 49 (3): 339–370.

Gibson, Edward L. 2004. "Federalism and Democracy in Latin America: Theoretical Connections and Cautionary Insights." In *Federalism and Democracy in Latin America,* edited by Edward Gibson. Baltimore, MD: Johns Hopkins University Press.

Gibson, Edward L., and Ernesto Calvo. 2000. "Federalism and Low-Maintenance Constituencies: Territorial Dimensions of Economic Reform in Argentina." *Studies in Comparative International Development* 35 (3): 32–55.

Gil-Diaz, Francisco, and Augsutin Carstens. 1996. "One Year of Solitude: Some Pilgrim Tales About Mexico's 1994–1995 Crisis." *American Economic Review* 86 (2): 164–169.

González Casanova, Pablo. 1970. *Democracy in Mexico.* New York: Oxford University Press.

González, R. A. 2002. "Diagnóstico Institucional del Sistema de Servicio Civil en Venezuela." Paper prepared for the Regional Policy Dialogue at the Inter-American Development Bank, Washington, DC.

Green, Edward, and Robert Porter, R. 1984. "Non-cooperative Collusion Under Imperfect Price Information." *Econometrica* 52 (1): 87–100.

Grindle, Merilee. 1977. *Bureaucrats, Politicians and Peasants in Mexico: A Case Study in Public Policy.* Berkeley: University of California Press.

Grindle, Merilee, and Francisco Thoumi. 1993. "Muddling Toward Adjustment: The Political Economy of Economic Policy Change in Ecuador." In *Political and Economic Interactions in Economic Policy Reform: Evidence from Eight Countries,* edited by R. H. Bates and A. O. Krueger. Oxford, UK: Blackwell.

Grofman, Bernard, and Andrew Reynolds. 2001. "Electoral Systems and the Art of Constitutional Engineering: An Inventory of the Main Findings." In *Rules and Reasons: Perspectives on Constitutional Political Economy,* edited by Ram Mudambi, Giuseppi Sobbrio, and Pietro Navarra. Cambridge: Cambridge University Press.

Gutiérrez Sanín, Francisco. 1999. "La reforma política: Una evaluación crítica." Pensamiento Jurídico. *Revista de Teoría del Derecho y Análisis Jurídico* 11. Bogota, Colombia: Universidad Nacional de Colombia, Facultad de Derecho, Ciencias Políticas y Sociales.

Gutiérrez Sanín, Francisco. 2001. "¿Se ha abierto el sistema político colombiano? Una evaluación de los procesos de cambio (1970–1998)." *América Latina Hoy* 27: 189–215.

Haggard, Stephen. 1995. "The Reform of the State in Latin America." Paper prepared for the Annual World Bank Conference on Development in Latin America and Caribbean, Rio de Janeiro, Brazil.

Haggard, Stephen. 2000. "Interests, Institutions and Policy Reforms." In *Economic Policy Reforms: The Second Stage*, edited by Anne Krueger. Chicago: University of Chicago Press.

Haggard, Stephen, and Robert Kaufman. 1992. *The Politics of Economic Adjustment: International Shocks, Distributive Conflicts and the State.* Princeton, NJ: Princeton University Press.

Haggard, Stephen, and Matthew McCubbins. 2001. *Presidents, Parliaments and Policy.* New York: Cambridge University Press.

Haggard, Stephen, and Steven Webb. 2000. "What Do We Know About the Political Economy of Economic Policy Reform?" In *Modern Political Economy and Latin America,* edited by Jeffrey Frieden, Manuel Pastor, and Michael Toms. Boulder, CO: Westview Press.

Hallerberg, Mark, and Patrik Marier. 2004. "Executive Authority, the Personal Vote, and Budget Discipline in Latin American and Caribbean Countries." *American Journal of Political Science* 48 (3): 571–587.

Hartlyn, Jonathan. 1993. *La Política del Régimen de Coalición.* Bogotá, Colombia: Tercer Mundo Editores, UniAndes-CEI.

Hausmann, Ricardo. 1990. *Shocks Externos y Ajuste Macroeconómico.* Caracas, Venezuela: Banco Central de Venezuela.

Hausmann, Ricardo, Dani Rodrick, and Andrés Velasco. 2005. *Growth Diagnostics.* Working Paper. Cambridge, MA: Harvard University.

Helmke, Gretchen. 2002. "The Logic of Strategic Defection: Court-Executive Relations in Argentina under Dictatorship and Democracy." *American Political Science Review* 96 (2): 291–304.

Henisz, Witold. 2000. "The Institutional Environment for Economic Growth." *Economics and Politics* 12 (1): 1–31.

Hopenhayn, Hugo A., and Pablo A. Neumeyer. 2003. "The Argentine Great Depression, 1975–1990." Universidad di Tella, Buenos Aires, Argentina. Mimeo.

Hoskin, Gary, Francisco Leal, and Harvey Kline. 2004. "Descentralización fiscal en Colombia." http://www.georgetown.edu/pdba/Comp/Control/Publico/designacion.html. January 15, 2004.

Huber, John, and Nolan McCarty. 2001. "Legislative Organization, Bureaucratic Capacity and Delegation in Latin American Democracies." Mimeo.

Hurtado, Osvaldo. 1990. *Política Democrática: los últimos veinte y cinco años.* Quito, Ecuador: Fundación Ecuatoriana de Estudios Sociales y Corporación Editora Nacional.

Iaryczower, Matias, Pablo Spiller, and Mariano Tommasi. 2002. "Judicial Independence in Unstable Environments, Argentina 1935–1998." *American Journal of Political Science* 46 (4): 699–716.

Iaryczower, Matias, Pablo Spiller, and Mariano Tommasi. 2006. "Judicial Lobbying: The Politics of Labor Law Constitutional Interpretation." *American Political Science Review* 100 (1), February.

Iaryczower, Matias, Pablo Spiller, and Mariano Tommasi. 2007. "The Supreme Court." In *The Institutional Foundations of Public Policy: A Transactions Theory and an Application to Argentina*, edited by Pablo Spiller and Mariano Tommasi. Cambridge: Cambridge University Press.

Iaryczower, Matias, Sebastian Saiegh, and Mariano Tommasi. 1999. *Coming Together: The Industrial Organization of Federalism.* Working Paper 30. Buenos Aires, Argentina: Center of Studies for Institutional Development, Fundación Gobierno y Sociedad.

IDB (Inter-American Development Bank). 2005. *The Politics of Policies. The Role of Political Process in Successful Public Policies.* Economic and Social Progress in Latin America and the Caribbean 2006 Report. Washington, DC: IDB.

INEGI. 2007. Instituto Nacional Estadística Geografía y Informática, Sistemas Nacionales Estadístico y de Información Geográfica. http://www.inegi.gob.mx (accessed August 2007).

International Monetary Fund. 2001. *Brazil: Report on Observance of Standards and Codes (ROSC)—Fiscal Transparency.* IMF Country Report 01/217. Washington, DC: International Monetary Fund.

Isham, Jonathan, Michael Woolcock, Lant Pritchett, and Gwen Busby. 2003. "The Varieties of Resource Experience: How Natural Resources Export Structures Affect the Political Economy of Growth." Middlebury College Economics Discussion Paper 03-08. Middlebury, VT: Middlebury College.

Jácome, Luis. 1996. *Tipo de cambio nominal y real en el Ecuador. Una mirada a la experiencia con regímenes de minidevaluaciones y de flotación dirigida.* Nota Técnica del Banco Central del Ecuador no. 32. Quito, Ecuador: Banco Central del Ecuador.

Jácome, Luis. 2004. *The Late 1990s Financial Crisis in Ecuador: Institutional Weaknesses, Fiscal Rigidities, and Financial Dollarization at Work.* International Monetary Fund Working Paper no. 04/12. Washington, DC: International Monetary Fund.

John, Paul, and Martin Saiz. 1999. "Local Political Parties in Comparative Perspective." In *Local Parties in Political and Organisational Perspective,* edited by Martin Saiz and Hans Geser. Boulder, CO: Westview Press.

Johnson, Joel, and Jessica Wallack. 2006. "Electoral Systems and the Personal Vote: Update of Database of Particularism." University of California, San Diego. Mimeo.

Jones, Mark. 1997. "Federalism and the Number of Parties in Argentine Congressional Elections." *Journal of Politics* 59 (2): 538–549.

Jones, Mark. 2001. "Political Institutions, Political Cleavages, and Candidate Competition in Presidential Elections." Michigan State University. Mimeo.

Jones, Mark. 2002. "Explaining the High Level of Party Discipline in the Argentine Congress." In *Legislative Politics in Latin America,* edited by Scott Morgenstern and Benito Nacif. Cambridge, UK: Cambridge University Press.

Jones, Mark. 2004. "The Recruitment and Selection of Legislative Candidates in Argentina." In *Pathways to Power: Political Recruitment and Candidate Selection in Latin America,* edited by Peter Siavelis and Scott Morgenstern.

Jones, Mark. 2005. "The Role of Parties and Party Systems in the Policymaking Process." Paper prepared for the Inter-American Development Bank's Workshop on State Reform, Public Policies and Policymaking Processes. Washington, DC: IDB.

Jones, Mark, and Wonjae Hwang. 2005. "Party Government in Presidential Democracies: Extending Cartel Theory Beyond the U.S. Congress." *American Journal of Political Science* 49 (2): 67–82.

Jones, Mark, and Scott Mainwaring. 2003. "The Nationalization of Parties and Party Systems: An Empirical Measure and an Application to the Americas." *Party Politics* 9 (2): 139–166.

Jones, Mark, Osvaldo Meloni, and Mariano Tommasi. 2007. "Voters as Fiscal Liberals." Universidad de San Andrés. Mimeo.

Jones, Mark, Sebastian Saiegh, Pablo Spiller, and Mariano Tommasi. 2002. "Amateur Legislators-Professional Politicians: The Consequences of Party-Centered Electoral Rules in a Federal System." *American Journal of Political Science* 46 (3): 656–669.

Jones, Mark, Sebastian Saiegh, Pablo Spiller, and Mariano Tommasi. 2006. "Congress, Political Careers, and the Provincial Connection." In *The Institutional Foundations of Public Policy: A Transactions Theory and an Application to Argentina,* edited by Pablo Spiller and Mariano Tommasi. Cambridge, UK: Cambridge University Press.

Junguito, Roberto, and Hernán Rincon. 2007. "Política Fiscal." In *Economía Colombiana del Siglo XX: Un Análisis Cuantitativo,* edited by James A. Robinson and Miguel Urrutia. Bogotá, Colombia: Fondo de Cultura Económica.

Karl, Terry Lynn. 1986. "Petroleum and Political Pacts: The Transition to Democracy in Venezuela." In *Transitions from Authoritarian Rule,* edited by Guillermo O'Donnell, Phillipe Schmitter, and Laurence Whitehead. Baltimore, MD: Johns Hopkins University Press.

Katz, Richard. 1997. *Democracy and Elections*. Oxford, UK: Oxford University Press.

Kaufmann, D., A. Kraay, and M. Mastruzzi. 2003. *Governance Matters. III. Governance Indicators for 1996–2002*. World Bank Policy Research Department Working Paper. Washington, DC: World Bank.

Kaufmann, Daniel, Aart Kraay, and Pablo Zoido-Lobatón. 1999. *Aggregating Governance Indicators*. Policy Research Working Paper no. 2195. Washington, DC: World Bank.

Kay, Stephen J. 2003. "Pension Reform and Political Risk." Paper prepared for the Latin American Studies Association (LASA) XXIV International Congress, Dallas, TX.

Kitschelt, Herbert. 2000. "Linkages between Citizens and Politicians in Democratic Polities." *Comparative Political Studies* 33 (6/7): 845–879.

Kornblith, Miriam. 1991. "The Politics of Constitution Making: Constitutions and Democracy in Venezuela." *Journal of Latin American Studies* 23 (1): 61–89.

Krehbiel, Keith. 1991. *Information and Legislative Organization*. Ann Arbor: University of Michigan Press.

Laakso, Markku, and Rein Taagepera. 1979. "The Effective Number of Parties: A Measure with Application to Western Europe." *Comparative Political Studies* 12 (1): 3–27.

Lambert, Peter. 1997. "The Regime of Alfredo Stroessner." In *The Transition to Democracy in Paraguay*, edited by Peter A. Lambert and Andrew Nickson. New York: St. Martin's Press.

Lambert, Peter, and Andrew Nickson, eds. 1997. *The Transition to Democracy in Paraguay*. New York: St. Martin's Press.

Landes, William, and R. Posner. 1975. "The Independent Judiciary in an Interest Group Perspective." *Journal of Law and Economics* 18 (3): 875–901.

Langston, Joy. 2002. "Los efectos de la competencia política en la selección de candidatos del PRI a la Cámara de Diputados." In *Lecturas Sobre el Cambio Político en México*, edited by Carlos Elizondo Mayer-Serra and Benito Nacif. Mexico, D.F., Mexico: Fondo de Cultura Económica.

Langston, Joy. 2007. "Complementary Principals in Mexico's Chamber of Deputies." Unpublished manuscript. CIDE, Mexico.

Lawson, Chappell. 2002. *Building the Fourth Estate: Democratization and the Rise of a Free Press in Mexico.* Berkeley: University of California Press.

Lehoucq, Fabrice E. 2002. "Can Parties Police Themselves? Electoral Governance and Democratization." *International Political Science Review* 23 (1): 29–46.

Lehoucq, Fabrice. 2006. "Why Is Structural Reform Stagnating in Mexico? Policy Reform Episodes from Salinas to Fox." Background Paper for the Institutional and Governance Review for Mexico, World Bank, May.

Lehouq, Fabrice. 2007. "Proceso de políticas, partidos e instituciones en la Costa Rica democrática." In *Democracia Estable: alcanza? Análisis de la Gobernabilidad en Costa Rica,* edited by Fernando Straface and Miguel Gutiérrez. Washington, DC: Inter-American Development Bank.

Levitsky, Steven. 2007. "From Populism to Clientelism? The Transformation of Party-Labor Linkages in Latin America." In *Patrons or Policies? Citizen-Politician Linkages in Democratic Politics,* edited by Herbert Kitschelt and Steven Wilkerson. New York: Cambridge University Press.

Levitt, Steven, and Mauricio Rubio. 2005. "Understanding Crime in Colombia and What Can Be Done About It." In *Institutional Reforms: The Case of Colombia,* edited by Alberto Alesina. Cambridge, MA: MIT Press.

Lewis, Paul. 1982. *Socialism, Liberalism and Dictatorship in Paraguay.* New York: Praeger.

Lijphart, Arend. 1991. "Constitutional Choices for New Democracies." *Journal of Democracy* 2 (1): 72–84.

Lijphart, Arend. 1994. *Electoral Systems and Party Systems. A Study of Twenty-Seven Democracies, 1945–1990.* Oxford, UK: Oxford University Press.

Lijphart, Arend. 1999. *Patterns of Democracy: Government Forms and Performance in Thirty-Six Countries.* New Haven, CT: Yale University Press.

Lima, Edilberto Carlos Pontes. 2004. "Algumas observações sobre orçamento impositivo no Brasil." Brasilia, Brazil, Consultoria Legislativa da Camara dos Deputados. Mimeo.

Lindauer, David, and Lant Pritchett. 2002. "What Is the Big Idea? The Third Generation of Development Advice." *Economia: Journal of the Latin American and Caribbean Economic Association* 3 (1): 1–39.

Linz, Juan. 1990. "The Perils of Presidentialism." *Journal of Democracy* 1 (1): 51–69.

Linz, Juan. 1994. "Presidential or Parliamentary Democracy: Does It Make a Difference?" In *The Failure of Presidential Democracy*, edited by Juan Linz and Arturo Valenzuela. Baltimore, MD: Johns Hopkins University Press.

Linz, Juan, and Arturo Valenzuela, eds. 1994. *The Failure of Presidential Democracy*. Baltimore, MD: Johns Hopkins University Press.

Llanos, Mariana. 2002a. *Privatization and Democracy in Argentina. An Analysis of President Congress-Relations*. New York: Palgrave.

Llanos, Mariana. 2002b. "El Bicameralismo en América Latina." Presented at the Tercer Congreso Internacional de Latinoamericanistas en Europa (CEISAL), Amsterdam, July 3–6.

Llanos, Mariana. 2003a. "Bicameralism in the Americas: Around the Extremes of Symmetry and Incongruence." *Journal of Legislative Studies* (9) 3:54–86.

Llanos, Mariana. 2003b. *Los Senadores y el Senado en Argentina y Brasil: Informe de una encuesta*. Working Paper 10. Institute für Iberoamerika-Kunde, Hamburg, Germany.

Lleras, Carlos, and Marcel Tangarife. 1996. *Constitución Política de Colombia Origen: Evolución y Vigencia*. Bogota, Colombia: Biblioteca Jurídica Diké.

Londregan, John. 2000. *Legislative Institutions and Ideology in Chile*. New York: Cambridge University Press.

Lora, Eduardo. 2001. *Las Reformas Estructurales en América Latina: Qué se ha reformado y cómo medirlo*. Working Paper 462. Research Department, Inter-American Development Bank, Washington, DC.

Lora, Eduardo, Ugo Panizza, and Myriam Quispe-Agnoli. 2004. *Reform Fatigue: Symptoms, Reasons, and Implications.* RES Working Paper 1005, Inter-American Development Bank, Washington, DC.

Loureiro, Maria Rita, and Fernando Abrucio. 1999. "Política e Burocracia no presidencialismo brasileiro: o papel do ministério da fazenda no primeiro governo Fernando Henrique Cardoso." *Revista Brasileira de Ciências Sociais* 14 (41): 69–89.

Lowi, Theodore. 1964. "American Business, Public Policy, Case-Studies, and Political Theory." *World Politics* 16 (4): 677–715.

Lustig, Nora. 1998. *Mexico: The Restructuring of the Economy,* 2nd edition. Washington, DC: Brookings Institution.

Lynn Ground, Richard. 1984. "El auge y la recesión de la economía paraguaya, 1972–1983. El papel de la política económica interna." In *Economía del Paraguay Contemporáneo,* Vol. 2. Asuncion: CPES.

Madison, James, John Jay, and Alexander Hamilton. 1961 [1787]. *The Federalist Papers.* New York: New American Library.

Maddison, Angus. 2001. *The World Economy: A Millennial Perspective.* Paris, France: OECD.

Maddison, Angus. 2007. *The World Economy, 1–2030 AD: Essays in Macroeconomic History.* Oxford: Oxford University Press. (Historical data available at http://www.ggdc.nct/maddison/)

Madrid, Raúl. 2003. *Retiring the State: The Politics of Pension Privatization in Latin America and Beyond.* Stanford, CA: Stanford University Press.

Magaloni, Beatriz. 2006. *Voting for Autocracy: Hegemonic Party Survival and its Demise in Mexico.* New York: Cambridge University Press.

Magaloni, Beatriz, and Arianna Sánchez. 2001. "Empowering the Courts as Constitutional Veto Players: Presidential Delegation and the New Mexican Supreme Court." Paper presented at the Annual Meeting of the American Political Science Association, San Francisco, CA.

Mainwaring, Scott, and Matthew Shugart. 1997a. *Presidentialism and Democracy in Latin America.* Cambridge, MA: Cambridge University Press.

Mainwaring, Scott, and Matthew Shugart. 1997b. "Conclusion: Presidentialism and the Party System." In *Presidentialism and Democracy in Latin America,* edited by Scott Mainwaring and Matthew Shugart. Cambridge: Cambridge University Press.

Mainwaring, Scott, and Aníbal Pérez-Liñán. 1997. "Party Discipline in the Brazilian Constitutional Congress." *Legislative Studies Quarterly* 22 (4): 453–483.

Mainwaring, Scott, and Timothy Scully, eds. 1995a. *Building Democratic Institutions: Party Systems in Latin America.* Stanford, CA: Stanford University Press.

Mainwaring, Scott, and Timothy Scully. 1995b. "Introduction: Party Systems in Latin America." In *Building Democratic Institutions: Party Systems in Latin America,* edited by Scott Mainwaring and Timothy Scully. Stanford, CA: Stanford University Press.

Marcel, Mario, Marcelo Tokman, Rodrigo Valdés, and Paula Benavides. 2001. "Balance Estructural del Gobierno Central: Metodología y Estimaciones para Chile 1987–2000." Dirección de Presupuesto, Estudios de Finanzas Públicas no. 1, Santiago, Chile.

Martínez Gallardo, Cecilia. 2005. "The Role of Latin American Cabinets in the Policymaking Process." Inter-American Development Bank, Washington, DC. Mimeo.

Martínez Gallardo-Prieto, Cecilia. 1998. "Las legislaturas pequeñas: la evolución del sistema de comisiones en la cámara de diputados de México, 1824–2000." Licenciatura thesis. Instituto Tecnológico Autónomo de México, Mexico, D.F., Mexico.

Martini, Carlos and Carlos Maria Lezcano. 1997. "The Armed Forces." In *The Transition to Democracy in Paraguay,* edited by Peter Lambert and Andrew Nickson. New York: St. Martin's Press.

Mejía-Acosta, Andrés. 1998. "Partidos Políticos: El Eslabón Perdido de la Respresentación." In *La Ruta de la Gobernabilidad*, edited by Fernando Pachano. Quito, Ecuador: Corporación de Estudios para el Desarrollo.

Mejía Acosta, Andrés. 2002. *Gobernabilidad Democrática-Sistema Electoral, Partidos Políticos y Pugna de Poderes en Ecuador, 1978–1998.* Quito: Fundación Konrad Adenauer.

Mejía Acosta, Andrés. 2003. "La Reelección Legislativa en Ecuador: Conexión Electoral, Carreras Legislativas y Partidos Políticos (1979–2003)." In *El Legislador a Examen. El Debate Sobre la Reelección Legislativa en México: Una Perspectiva Histórica e Institucional,* edited by Fernando F. Dworak. México, D.F.: Fondo de Cultura Económica.

Mejía Acosta, Andrés. 2004. "Ghost Coalitions: Economic Reforms, Fragmented Legislatures and Informal Institutions in Ecuador." Ph.D. Dissertation. Department of Political Science, University of Notre Dame, Notre Dame, Indiana.

Mejía Acosta, Andrés. 2006. "Crafting Legislative Ghost Coalitions in Ecuador: Informal Institutions and Economic Reform in an Unlikely Case." In *Informal Institutions and Democracy: Lessons from Latin America,* edited by Gretchen Helmke and Steven Levistky. Baltimore, MD: Johns Hopkins University Press.

Melo, Marcus André. 1998. "Constitucionalismo e Escolha Racional." *Lua Nova* 43: 53–80.

Melo, Marcus André. 2002. *Reformas Constitucionais no Brasil. Instituições Políticas e Processo Decisório.* Rio de Janeiro, Brazil: Revan.

Melo, Marcus André. 2004. "Explaining the Capacity to Tax and to Reform: The Divergent Paths of Argentina and Brazil." Paper prepared for the Taxation and Development workshop, Danish Institute for Development Studies, Copenhagen: Denmark.

Meneguello, Rachel. 1998. *Partidos e Governo no Brasil Contemporâneo (1985–1997).* São Paulo, Brazil: Paz e Terra.

Mershon, Carol. 1996. "The Costs of Coalition. Coalition Theories and Italian Governments." *American Political Science Review* 90 (3): 534–554.

Middlebrook, Kevin J. 1995. *The Paradox of Revolution: Labor, the State and Authoritarianism in Mexico.* Baltimore, MD: Johns Hopkins University Press.

MIDEPLAN (Ministerio de Planificación). 2000. *Encuesta de caracterización socio-económica nacional (CASEN).* Santiago, Chile.

Miles, Marc, Edwin Feulner, and Mary Anastasia O'Grady. 2003. *2004 Index of Economic Freedom: Establishing the Link Between Economic*

Freedom and Prosperity. Washington, DC: Heritage Foundation/ Wall Street Journal.

Miller, Jonathan M. 1997. "Judicial Review and Constitutional Stability: A Sociology of the U.S. Model and Its Collapse in Argentina." *Hastings International and Comparative Law Review* 77: 151–162.

Mills, Nick D. 1984. *Crisis, Conflicto y Consenso. Ecuador: 1979–1984*. Quito: Corporación Editora Nacional.

Mizala, Alejandra and Pilar Romaguera. 2001. "La Legislación Laboral y el Mercado del Trabajo en Chile: 1975–2000." In *Reformas, crecimiento y políticas sociales en Chile desde 1973*, edited by Ricardo French-Davis and Barbara Stallings. Santiago, Chile: CEPAL.

Mody, Ashoka, and Martin Schindler. 2004. "Argentina's Growth: A Puzzle?" International Monetary Fund, Washington, DC. Mimeo.

Molinar Horcasitas, Juan. 1991. *El tiempo de la legitimidad: elecciones, autoritarismo y democracia en México*. Mexico, D.F., Mexico: Editorial Cal y Arena.

Molinar Horcasitas, Juan, and Weldon, Jeffrey A. 2001. "Reforming Electoral Systems in Mexico." In *Mixed-Member Electoral Systems: The Best of Both Worlds?* edited by Mathew Shugart and Martin Wattenberg. New York: Oxford University Press.

Molinelli, N. Guillermo, M. Valerie Palanza, and Gisela Sin. 1999. *Congreso, Presidencia y Justicia en Argentina: Materiales para su Estudio*. Buenos Aires, Argentina: Temas/Fundación Gobierno y Sociedad.

Monaldi, Francisco. 2005. "The role of Regional Political Authorities in the National Policymaking Process: A Comparative Perspective of Latin American Cases." Inter-American Development Bank, Washington, DC. Mimeo.

Monaldi, Francisco, Rosa Amelia González, Richard Obuchi, and Michael Penfold. 2005. *Political Institutions, Policymaking Processes, and Policy Outcomes in Venezuela*. Research Network Working Paper R-507. Washington, DC: Inter-American Bank Development Bank.

Montes, J. Esteban, Scott Mainwaring, and Eugenia Ortega. 2000. "Rethinking the Chilean Party System." *Journal of Latin American Studies* 32 (3): 795–824.

MOPTT (Ministerio de Obras Públicas, Transportes y Telecomunicaciones). 2003. *Sistema de Concesiones en Chile: 1990–2003.* Santiago, Chile.

Mora, Monica. 2002. "Federalismo e Dívida Estadual no Brasil." Texto para Discussão 866. Rio de Janeiro, Brazil: IPEA.

Moreno, Alejandro. 2003. *El votante mexicano: democratización, actitudes políticas y conducta electoral.* Mexico, D.F., Mexico: Fondo de Cultura Económica.

Moreno, Alejandro. 2004. "Issues and Parties in the Mexican Congress: Is Ideological Differentiation a Cause of Gridlock?" Paper presented at the conference "Reforming the State in Mexico: The Challenge After Fox and NAFTA," Kellogg Institute, University of Notre Dame.

Moreno, Alejandro. 2006. "Ideologías, estilos de vida y votos." *Foreign Affairs in Español,* April–June 6(2): 53–65.

Morgenstern, Scott. 1998. "The U.S. Model and Latin American Legislatures." Duke University, Durham, NC. Mimeo.

Morgenstern, Scott. 2002. "Explaining Legislative Politics in Latin America." In *Legislative Politics in Latin America,* edited by Scott Morgenstern and Benito Nacif. Cambridge, UK: Cambridge University Press.

Morgenstern, Scott, and Benito Nacif, eds. 2002. *Legislative Politics in Latin America.* Cambridge, UK: Cambridge University Press.

Morgenstern, Scott, and Peter Siavelis. 2004. "Political Recruitment and Candidate Selection in Latin America: A Framework for Analysis." Working paper for the symposium Pathways to Power: Political Recruitment and Democracy in Latin America. Wake Forest University, Winston-Salem, NC.

Morón, Eduardo, and Cynthia Sanborn. 2006. *The Pitfalls of Policymaking in Peru: Actors, Institutions and Rules of the Game.* Research Network Working Paper no. R-511. Research Department, Inter-American Development Bank, Washington, DC.

Mueller, Bernardo. 2001. "Institutions for Commitment in the Brazilian Regulatory System." *Quarterly Review of Economics and Finance* 41 (5): 621–643.

Mueller, Dennis. 1996a. *Perspectives on Public Choice*. Cambridge, UK: Cambridge University Press.

Mueller, Dennis. 1996b. *Constitutional Democracy*. Oxford, UK: Oxford University Press.

Mueller, Dennis. 2003. *Public Choice III*. Cambridge, UK: Cambridge University Press.

Murillo, María Victoria. 1997. "Union Politics, Market-Oriented Reforms and the Reshaping of Argentine Corporatism." In *The New Politics of Inequality in Latin America: Rethinking Participation and Representation,* edited by Douglas Chalmers et al. Oxford, UK: Oxford University Press.

Murillo, María Victoria. 2001. *Labor Unions, Partisan Coalitions, and Market Reforms in Latin America*. New York: Cambridge University Press.

Mustapic, Ana M. 2002. "Oscillating Relations: President and Congress in Argentina." In *Legislative Politics in Latin America,* edited by Scott Morgenstern and Benito Nacif. Cambridge, UK: Cambridge University Press.

Nacif, Benito. 1995. "The Mexican Chamber of Deputies: The Political Significance of Non-Consecutive Reelection." D.Phil. thesis. Oxford University, Oxford, UK.

Nacif, Benito. 1996. *Political Careers, Career Ambitions and Career Goals.* Working Paper 51. Mexico, D.F., Mexico: CIDE-Division de Estudios Politicos.

Nacif, Benito. 2002. "Understanding Party Discipline in the Mexican Chambers of Deputies: The Centralized Party Model." In *Legislative Politics in Latin America,* edited by Scott Morgenstern and Benito Nacif. Cambridge, UK: Cambridge University Press.

Naim, Moisés, and Ramón Piñango. 1988. *El Caso Venezuela: Una ilusión de armonía*. Caracas: Ediciones IESA.

Nascimento, Edson Ronaldo, and Ilvo Debus. n.d. *Lei Complementar 101: Entendendo a Lei de Responsabilidade Fiscal,* 2nd edition. Brasília, Brazil: Tesouro Nacional.

Navia, Patricio, and Andrés Velasco. 2003. "The Politics of Second Generation Reforms in Latin America." In *After the Washington*

Consensus: Restarting Growth and Reform in Latin America, edited by Pedro-Pablo Kuczynski and John Williamson. Washington, DC: Institute for International Economics.

Nickson, Andrew. 1997. "Corruption and the Transition." In *The Transition to Democracy in Paraguay,* edited by Peter A. Lambert and Nickson. New York: St. Martin's Press

Nicolau, Jairo. 2000. "Disciplina Partidária e Base Parlamentar na Câmara dos Deputados no Primeiro Governo Fernando Henrique Cardoso (1995–1998)." *Dados* 34 (4): 1–23.

Nielson, D. L., and M. S. Shugart. 1999. "Constitutional Change in Colombia: Policy Adjustment Through Institutional Reform." *Comparative Political Studies* 33 (3): 313–341.

North, D. 1994. "Economic Performance Through Time." *American Economic Review* 84 (3): 359–368.

Nunes, E. 1997. *A Gramática Política do Brasil.* Rio de Janeiro, Brazil: Jorge Zahar.

Ocampo, José Antonio. 2004. "Entre las Reformas y el Conflicto: Economía y Política en Colombia." United Nations, New York. Mimeo.

Ocampos, Genoveva, and José Carlos Rodríguez. 1999. *Hacia el Fortalecimiento de la Sociedad Civil en Paraguay: Un Desafío Pendiente.* Asunción: Centro de Documentación y Estudios.

Orstein, Norman, Thomas Mann, and Michael Malbin. 1998. *Vital Statistics in Congress, 1997–1998.* Washington, DC: American Enterprise Institute.

Ortiz Mena, A. L. 1998. *El desarrollo estabilizador: reflexiones sobre una época.* Mexico D.F., Mexico: El Colegio de México/Fondo de Cultura Económica

Pachano, Simón. 1998. *La Representación Caótica.* Quito, Ecuador: FLACSO-Konrad Adenauer.

Pachano, Simón. 2004. "El Territorio de los Partidos. " In *Partidos Políticos en la Región Andina: entre la crisis y el cambio,* edited by Miriam Kornblith, Simón Pachano, Martín Tanaka, Elisabeth Ungar Bleier, and Carlos Arturo Arévalo. Lima: IDEA-Ágora Democrática.

Pacheco Méndez, G. 2000. *Caleidoscopio electoral: elecciones en México, 1979–1997.* Mexico, D.F., Mexico: Fondo de Cultura Económica.

Pachón Buitrago, Mónica. 2003. "Explaining the Performance of the Colombian Congress: Electoral and Legislature Rules, and Interactions with the Executive." Paper prepared for the 2003 Meeting of the Latin American Studies Association, Dallas, TX.

Panizza, Ugo. 1999. *Why Do Lazy People Make More Money? The Strange Case of the Public Sector Wage Premium.* Working Paper no. 403. Washington, DC: Inter-American Development Bank.

Payne, James L. 1968. *Patterns of Conflict in Colombia.* New Haven, CT: Yale University Press.

Payne, Mark, Daniel Zovatto, Fernando Carrillo, and Andrés Allamand. 2002. *Democracies in Development: Politics and Reform in Latin America.* Washington, DC: Inter-American Development Bank.

Payne, Mark, Alisia Adsera, and Charles Boix. 2003. "Are You Being Served? Political Accountability and Quality of Government." *Journal of Law, Economics and Organization* 19 (2): 445–490.

Penfold, Michael. 2004a. "Electoral Dynamics and Decentralization in Venezuela." In *Decentralization and Democracy in Latin America,* edited by Alfred Montero and David Samuels. Notre Dame, IN: University of Notre Dame Press.

Penfold, Michael. 2004b. "Federalism and Institutional Change in Venezuela." In *Federalism and Democracy in Latin America,* edited by Edward L. Gibson. Baltimore, MD: Johns Hopkins University Press.

Pereira, Carlos. 2000. "Why Have Brazilian Legislators Decided to Clean Up Their Sidewalks? The Influence of the Brazilian Political Institutions on the Process of State Reform." In *Handbook of Global Political Policy,* edited by Stuart Nagel. New York: Marcel Dekker.

Pereira, Carlos, and Bernardo Mueller. 2000. "Uma Teoria da Preponderância do Executivo: O Sistema de Comissões no Legislativo Brasileiro." *Revista Brasileira de Ciências Sociais* 15: 45–67.

Pereira, Carlos, and Bernardo Mueller. 2002. "Comportamento Estratégico em Coalizões Presidencialistas: as Relações entre Executivo e Legislativo na Elaboração do Orçamento Brasileiro." *Dados* 45 (2): 265–302.

Pereira, Carlos, and Bernardo Mueller. 2003. "The Cost of Governing: Strategic Behavior in Brazil's Budgetary Process." *Comparative Political Studies* 37 (7): 781–815.

Pereira, Carlos, and Bernardo Mueller. 2004. "The Cost of Governing: Strategic Behavior of the President and Legislators in Brazil's Budgetary Process." *Comparative Political Studies* 20 (1): 1–32.

Pereira, Carlos, and Timothy J. Power. 2005. "Coalition Management Matters." Presented at the Workshop on Corruption and Accountability in Latin America, Michigan State University.

Pereira, Carlos, and Lucio Renno. 2003. "Successful Re-election Strategies in Brazil: The Electoral Impact of Distinct Institutional Incentives." *Electoral Studies* 22 (3): 425–448.

Pereira, Carlos, Timothy Power, and Lucio Renno. 2005. "Under What Conditions Do Presidents Resort to Decree Power? Theory and Evidence from the Brazilian Case." *Journal of Politics* 67 (1): 178–200.

Pérez Liñán, Anibal. 2006. *Presidential Impeachment and the New Political Instability in Latin America.* Cambridge, UK: Cambridge University Press.

Pérez Liñán, Aníbal, and Juan Carlos Rodríguez Raga. 2003. "Veto Players in Presidential Regimes: Institutional Variables and Policy Change." Prepared for delivery at the 2003 Annual Meeting of the American Political Science Association, San Francisco, CA.

Perotti, Roberto. 2005. "Public Spending on Social Protection in Colombia: Analysis and Proposals." In *Institutional Reforms: The Case of Colombia,* edited by Alberto Alesina. Cambridge, MA: MIT Press.

Persson, Torsten, and Guido Tabellini. 2000. "Comparative Politics and Public Finance." *Journal of Political Economy* 108 (6): 1121–1161.

Persson, Torsten, and Guido Tabellini. 2003. *The Economic Effect of Constitutions. What Do the Data Say?* Cambridge, MA: MIT Press.

Pinheiro, A. C. 1997. *Judicial System Performance and Economic Development.* São Paulo, Brazil: Universidade de São Paulo.

Pinheiro, Armando Castelar. 2000. *Judiciário e Economia no Brasil.* São Paulo: Sumaré Press.

Pinheiro, Armando Castelar, and Célia Cabral. 1998. "Mercado de Crédito no Brasil: O Papel do Judicário e de Outras Instituições." *Ensaios BNDES 87.*

Pistor, Katharina. 2000. *The Standardization of Law and Its Effect on Developing Economies.* G-24 Discussion Paper 4, July.

Pizarro, Eduardo. 1995. "La Comisión para la Reforma de los Partidos: Cortina de hurno o necesidad histórica." *Análisis Político* 26: 72–87.

Pizarro, Eduardo. 2002. La Atomización Partidista en Colombia: El Fenómeno de las Microempresas Electorales. Working Paper No. 292, Kellog Institute, University of Notre Dame, Indiana.

Posada-Carbó, Eduardo. 2001. "La Reformulación De La Paz." Bogota, Colombia. Mimeo. http://www.ideaspaz.org/articulos/download/31lareformulaciondelapaz.pdf

Posner, Richard. 1993. *What Do Judges Maximize? (The Same that Everybody Else Does).* Chicago Working Paper in Law and Economics 15. Chicago: University of Chicago.

Przeworski, Adam. 2005. "Democracy as an Equilibrium." *Public Choice* 123 (3-4): 253–273.

Przeworski, Adam., Michael Alvarez, José Antonio Cheibub, and Fernando Limongi. 2000. *Democracy and Development.* New York: Cambridge University Press.

Puente, José Manuel. 2003. "The Political Economy of Budget Allocation in Venezuela." Unpublished manuscript.

Purcell, John F. H., and Susan Kaufmann Purcell. 1977. "Mexican Business and Public Policy." In *Authoritarianism and Corporatism in Latin America,* edited by James M. Malloy. Pittsburgh, PA: University of Pittsburgh Press.

Purcell, Susan Kaufmann. 1975. *The Mexican Profit-Sharing Decision: Politics in an Authoritarian Regime.* Berkeley: University of California Press.

Rae, Douglas. 1967. *The Political Consequences of Electoral Laws.* New Haven, CT: Yale University Press.

Ramseyer, Mark J. 1994. "The Puzzling Independence of Courts: A Comparative Approach." *Journal of Legal Studies* 23 (2): 721–745.

Ramseyer, Mark J., and Frances McCall Rosenbluth. 1993. *Japan's Political Marketplace*. Cambridge, MA: Harvard University Press.

Rasch, Bjorn. 1999. "Electoral Systems, Parliamentary Committees, and Party Discipline: The Norwegian Storting in a Comparative Perspective." In *Party Discipline and Parliamentary Government*, edited by Bowler, Farrel and Katz. Columbus, OH: Ohio State University Press.

Rauch, James E., and Peter B. Evans. 2000. "Bureaucratic Structure and Bureaucratic Performance in Less Developed Countries." *Journal of Public Economics* 75 (1): 49–71.

Resende, L. F. 2000. "Comunidade Solidária—Uma Alternativa aos Fundos Sociais." Texto para Discussão 725. Brasília, Brazil: IPEA.

Rey, Juan Carlos. 1989. *El Futuro de la Democracia en Venezuela*. Caracas: IDEA.

Rey, Juan Carlos. 1972. "El Sistema de Partidos Venezolano." *Politeia* 1. Caracas: Instituto de Estudios Politicos.

Reyes del Campillo, Juan. 1992. "Candidatos y campañas en la elección federal de 1991." In *Las elecciones federales de 1991*, edited by Alberto Aziz Nassif and Jacqueline Peschard. Mexico, D.F., Mexico: Editorial Porrúa / CIIH-UNAM.

Rice, Stuart A. 1925. "The Behavior of Legislative Groups: A Method of Measurement." *Political Science Quarterly* 40 (1): 60–72.

Rocha, Ricardo. 1999. *La economía colombiana tras 25 años de narcotráfico*. Bogota, Colombia: United Nations Drug Control Programme.

Rodden, Jonathan. 2003. "Federalism and Bailouts in Brazil." In *Fiscal Decentralization and the Challenge of Hard Budget Constraints*, edited by J. Rodden, G. Eskeland, and J. Litvack. Cambridge, MA: MIT Press.

Rodden, Jonathan, and Erik Wibbels. 2002. "Beyond the Fiction of Federalism: Macroeconomic Management in Multi-tiered Systems." *World Politics* 54 (4): 494–531.

Rodríguez, Francisco, and Jeffrey Sachs. 1999. "Why Do Resource-Rich Economies Have Slower Growth Rates? A New Explanation and an Application to Venezuela." *Journal of Economic Growth* 4(3).

Rodríguez, Victoria E. 1997. *Decentralization in Mexico: From Reforma Municipal to Solidaridad to Nuevo Federalismo.* Boulder, CO: Westview Press.

Rodríguez, Victoria E., and Peter M. Ward. 1995. *Opposition Government in Mexico,* 1st edition. Albuquerque: University of New Mexico Press.

Rodríguez-Raga, Juan Carlos. 1999. "Posibilidades y riesgos de la actual reforma electoral en Colombia: un análisis del sistema electoral colombiano." *Pensamiento Jurídico* 11: 203–214.

Rodríguez-Raga, Juan Carlos. 2001. "¿Cambiar todo para que nada cambie? Representación, sistema electoral y sistema de partidos en Colombia: capacidad de adaptación de las élites políticas a cambios en el entorno institucional." In *Degradación o cambio: Evolución del sistema político colombiano,* edited by Francisco Gutiérrez. Bogota, Colombia: IEPRI-Norma.

Rodrik, Dani. 1989. "Credibility of Trade Reform: A Policy Maker's Guide." *World Economy* 12 (1): 1–16.

Rodrik, Dani. 1995. "Taking Trade Policy Seriously: Export Subsidization as a Case Study in Policy Effectiveness." In *New Directions in Trade Theory,* edited by Alan V. Deardorff, Robert M. Stern, and James A. Levinsohn. Ann Arbor: University of Michigan Press.

Romer, Thomas, and Rosenthal, Howard. 1978. "Political Resource Allocation, Controlled Agendas, and the Status Quo." *Public Choice* 33 (4): 27–43.

Romer, Thomas, and Rosenthal, Howard. 1979. "The Elusive Median Voter." *Journal of Pub La Nueva Economía Política Economics* 12 (2): 143–170.

Romer, Thomas, and Rosenthal, Howard. 1982. "Median Voters or Budget Maximizers: Evidence from School Expenditure Referenda." *Economic Inquiry* 20 (4): 556–578.

Rose-Ackerman, Susan, and Jana Kunicova. 2002. "Electoral Rules as Constraints on Corruption." Department of Political Science, Yale University, New Haven, CT. Mimeo.

Ross, Michael. 2001. "Does Oil Hinder Democracy?" *World Politics* 53 (3): 325–361.

Saiegh, Sebastian. 2005. "The Role of Legislatures in the Policymaking Process." Presented at the Inter-American Development Bank Workshop on State Reform, Public Policies and Policymaking Processes, Washington, DC.

Saiegh, Sebastian, Pablo Spiller, and Mariano Tommasi. 2007. "Federalism, Argentine Style." In *The Institutional Foundations of Public Policy: A Transactions Theory and an Application to Argentina*, edited by Pablo Spiller and Mariano Tommasi. New York: Cambridge University Press.

Saiz, Martin, and Hans Geser, eds. 1999. *Local Parties in Political and Organizational Perspective*. Boulder, CO: Westview Press.

Sala-i-Martin, Xavier, and Avrind Subramanian. 2003. *Addressing the Natural Resource Curse: An Illustration from Nigeria*. NBER Working Paper no. 9804. Cambridge, MA: National Bureau of Economic Research.

Salazar, Natalia, and Diego Prada. 2003. *Hay que recuperar la política fiscal.* Carta Financiera No. 124. Bogota, Colombia: Asociación Nacional de Instituciones Financieras.

Samuels, David. 2000a. "Ambition and Competition: Explaining Legislative Turnover in Brazil." *Legislative Studies Quarterly* 25 (3): 481–498.

Samuels, David. 2000b. "The Gubernatorial Coattails Effect: Federalism and Congressional Elections in Brazil." *Journal of Politics* 62 (1): 240–253.

Samuels, David. 2003. *Ambition, Federalism and Legislative Politics in Brazil.* New York: Cambridge University Press.

Samuels, David, and Richard Snyder. 2001. "The Value of a Vote: Malapportionment in Comparative Perspective." *British Journal of Political Science* 31 (3): 651–671.

Sánchez de Dios, Manuel. 1999. "Parliamentary Party Discipline in Spain." In *Party Discipline in Parliamentary Governments,* edited by Shaun Bowler, David Farrel, and Richard Katz. Columbus: Ohio State University Press.

Sanchez, Nolte, and Mariana Llanos. 2005. *Bicameralismo, Senados y senadores en el Cono Sur latinoamericano.* Barcelona, Spain: Publicaciones del Parlamento de Catalunya, Barcelona.

Sartori, Giovanni. 1976. *Parties and Party Systems: A Framework for Analysis.* New York: Cambridge University Press.

Sawers, Larry. 1996. *The Other Argentina. The Interior and National Development.* Boulder, CO: Westview Press.

Scartascini, Carlos, and Mauricio Olivera. 2003. "Political Institutions, Policymaking Processes and Policy Outcomes: A Guide to Theoretical Modules and Possible Empirics." Design Paper no. 2 for the Red de Centros Project "Political Institutions, Policymaking Processes and Policy Outcomes." Inter-American Development Bank, Washington, DC.

Scherer-García, Julio, and Carlos Monsiváis. 2003. *Tiempo de saber.* Mexico, D.F., Mexico: Editorial Aguilar.

Schwarz, Carl. 1977. "Jueces en la Penumbra. La Independencia del Poder Judicial en los Estados Unidos y en México." *Anuario Jurídico* 2: 143–219.

Schwarz, Carl. 1990. "El Papel del Precedente como Factor Institucional en la Toma de Decisión Judicial: Los Estados Unidos y México." In *Derecho Constitucional Comparado México-Estados Unidos,* edited by J. F. Smith. Mexico, D.F., Mexico: Universidad Nacional Autónoma de México.

SCI (Servicio de Consultoría Informativa). (Various years). *Análisis del Mes.* Asunción, Paraguay: BASE.

Scott, John. 2004. "¿Quién se beneficia del gasto social en México?" In *Impuestos y Gasto Público en México desde una Perspectiva Multidisciplinaria,* edited by Juan Pablo Guerrero. Mexico, D.F., Mexico: CIDE/Miguel Angel Porrúa.

Scott, John. 2005. "Protección Básica, Cobertura Universal: Seguridad Social y Pobreza en México." *Bienestar y Política Social* 1 November.

Serna, Juan Guillermo. 1988. *Aspectos de la política presupuestal en Colombia 1886–1987.* Bogota, Colombia: Ministerio de Hacienda.

Serrafero, Mario. 2005. *Exceptocracia, ¿Confín de la democracia?* Buenos Aires: Lumiere.

Shepsle, Kenneth, and Mark Boncheck. 1997. *Analyzing Politics: Rationality, Behavior and Institutions.* New York: W. W. Norton.

Shepsle, Kenneth, and Barry Weingast. 1981. "Structure-Induced Equilibrium and Legislative Choice." *Public Choice* 37 (3): 503–519.

Shepsle, Kenneth, and Barry Weingast. 1987. "The Institutional Foundations of Committee Power." *American Political Science Review* 81 (1): 85–104.

Shepsle, Kenneth, and Barry Weingast. 1995. *Positive Theories of Congressional Institutions.* Ann Arbor: University of Michigan Press.

Shields, David. 2003. PEMEX: *un futuro incierto.* Mexico, D.F., Mexico: Editorial Planeta.

Shugart, Mathew. 1995. "The Electoral Cycle and Institutional Sources of Divided Presidential Government." *American Political Science Review* 89 (2): 327–343.

Shugart, Matthew, and John Carey. 1992. *Presidents and Assemblies: Constitutional Design and Electoral Dynamics.* Cambridge, UK: Cambridge University Press.

Shugart, Matthew, E. Moreno, and L. Fajardo. 2005. "Deepening Democracy by Renovating Political Practices: The Struggle for Electoral Reform in Colombia." In *Institutional Reforms: The Case of Colombia,* edited by Alberto Alesina. Cambridge, MA: MIT Press.

Smith, Peter H. 1979. *Labyrinths of Power: Political Recruitment in Twentieth-Century Mexico.* Princeton, NJ: Princeton University Press.

Snyder, Richard, and David Samuels. 2001. "Devaluing the Vote in Latin America." *Journal of Democracy* 12 (1): 146–159.

Sousa, Mariana. 2005. "Judicial Reforms, the PMP, and Public Policy." Inter-American Development Bank, Washington, DC. Mimeo.

Spiller, Pablo, Ernesto Stein, and Mariano Tommasi. 2003. "Political Institutions, Policymaking Processes and Policy Outcomes: An Intertemporal Transactions Framework." Design Paper no. 1 for the Red de Centros Project Political Institutions, Policymaking Processes and Policy Outcomes. Inter-American Development Bank, Washington, DC.

Spiller, Pablo, and Mariano Tommasi. 2003. "The Institutional Foundations of Public Policy: A Transactions Approach with Application to Argentina." *Journal of Law, Economics, and Organization* 19 (2): 281–306.

Spiller, Pablo, and Mariano Tommasi. 2005. "Instability and Public Policy-Making in Argentina." In *Argentine Democracy: The Politics of Institutional Weakness,* edited by Steven Levitsky and María Victoria Murillo. University Park: Pennsylvania State University Press.

Spiller, Pablo, and Mariano Tommasi. 2007. *The Institutional Foundations of Public Policy in Argentina.* Cambridge, UK: Cambridge University Press.

Spiller, Pablo, and Santiago Urbiztondo. 1994. "Political Appointees vs. Career Civil Servants: A Multiple-Principals Theory of Political Institutions." *European Journal of Political Economy* 10 (3): 465–497.

Stein, Ernesto. 1999. "Fiscal Decentralization and Government Size in Latin America." *Journal of Applied Economics* 2 (2): 357–391.

Stein, Ernesto, and Mariano Tommasi. 2005a. "Democratic Institutions, Policymaking Processes, and the Quality of Policies in Latin America." Paper presented at the International Seminar Una Nueva Agenda de Desarrollo Económico para América Latina, Fundación CIDOB, Salamanca, Spain.

Stein, Ernesto, and Mariano Tommasi. 2005b. "Political Institutions, Policymaking Processes, and Policy Outcomes: A Comparison of Latin American Cases." Inter-American Development Bank, Washington, DC. Mimeo.

Stratmann, Thomas, and Martin Baur. 2002. "Plurality Rule vs. Proportional Representation. How Much of a Difference Do Electoral Rules Make? Evidence from Germany." *American Journal of Political Science* 46 (3): 506–514.

Strom, Kaare. 1995. "Parliamentary Government and Legislative Organization." In *Parliaments and Majority Rule in Western Europe,* edited by H. Döring. New York: St. Martin's Press.

Székely, Miguel. 2005. "Pobreza y desigualdad en Mexico entre 1950–2004." *El Trimestre Económico* 72 (4): 913–931.

Tapia Palacios, Palmira. 2003. "El Nuevo Papel de la Suprema Corte de Justicia en México." Bachelor's thesis. Mexico, D.F., Mexico: CIDE.

Taylor, Michael. 1997. "Why No Rule of Law in Mexico? Explaining the Weakness of Mexico's Judicial Branch." *New Mexico Law Review* 27 (1): 141–166.

Taylor-Robinson, Michelle, and Christopher Diaz. 1999. "Who Gets Legislation Passed in a Marginal Legislature and Is the Label Marginal Legislature Still Appropriate? A Study of the Honduran Congress." *Comparative Political Studies* 32 (5): 589–625.

Thacker, Strom C. 2000. *Big Business, the State and Free Trade: Constructing Coalitions in Mexico.* New York: Cambridge University Press.

Tommasi, Mariano. 2006. "Federalism in Argentina and the Reforms of the 1990s." In *Federalism and Economic Reform. International Perspectives,* edited by Jessica Wallack and T. N. Srinivasan. New York: Cambridge University Press.

Tommasi, Mariano, and Pablo Spiller. 2000. *Los Determinantes Institucionales del Desarrollo Argentino.* Bueno Aires, Argentina: PNUD & Eudeba.

Torre, Juan Carlos. 2003. "Los Huérfanos de la Política de Partidos. Sobre los Alcances y Naturaleza de la Crisis de Representación Partidaria." *Desarrollo Económico* 42 (168): 647–665.

Transparency International. 2003. *Corruption Perceptions Index 2003.* Berlin, Germany: Transparency International.

Tsebelis, George. 1995. "Decision Making in Political Systems: Veto Players in Presidentialism, Parliamentarism, Multicameralism and Multipartyism." *British Journal of Political Science* 25 (3): 289–325.

Tsebelis, George. 2002. *Veto Players: How Political Institutions Work.* Cambridge: Cambridge University Press.

Tsebelis, George, and Jeannete Money. 1997. *Bicameralism.* Cambridge: Cambridge University Press.

Tullock, Gordon. 1997. *The Case Against the Common Law.* Durham: North Carolina University Press.

Ugalde, Luis Carlos. 2000. *The Mexican Congress: Old Player, New Power.* Washington, DC: Center for Strategic and International Studies.

Urrutia, Miguel. 1991. "On the Absence of Economic Populism in Colombia." In *The Macroeconomics of Populism in Latin America,* edited by Roger Dornbusch and Sebastian Edwards. Chicago: University of Chicago Press/National Bureau of Economic Research.

Valecillos, Héctor. 1993. "Estadisticas Socio-Laborales de Venezuela." *Series Historicas 1936–1990*. Colección Cincuentenaria. no. 8 Banco Central de Venezuela.

Vernon, Raymond. 1965. *The Dilemma of Mexico's Development: The Roles of the Private and Public Sectors*. Cambridge, MA: Harvard University Press.

Vial, Joaquín. 2001. *Institucionalidad y Desempeño Fiscal: Una Mirada a la Experiencia de Chile en los 90*. Programa de Investigaciones de la Corporación de Estudios para Latinoamérica (CIEPLAN). Santiago, Chile.

Villasmil, Ricardo, Francisco Monaldi, German Rios, and Marino González. 2004. "Understanding Reforms: The Case of Venezuela." Unpublished manuscript. Global Development Network.

Wallack, Jessica Seddon, Alejandro Gaviria, Ugo Panizza, and Ernesto Stein. 2003. "Political Particularism around the World." *World Bank Economic Review* 17 (1): 133–143.

Wantchekon, Leonard. 2000. "Credible Power Sharing Agreements." *Constitutional Political Economy* 11 (4): 329–352.

Ward, Peter M., Victoria E. Rodríguez, and Enrique Cabrero Mendoza. 1999. *New Federalism and State Government in Mexico*. Austin, TX: Lyndon B. Johnson School of Public Affairs, University of Texas at Austin.

Ware, Alan. 1996. *Political Parties and Party Systems*. Oxford: Oxford University Press.

Warman, Arturo. 2001. El campo mexicano en el siglo XX. Mexico, D.F., Mexico: Fondo de Cultura Económica.

Weaver, R. Kent, and Bert A. Rockman. 1993. *Do Institutions Matter?* Washington, DC: The Brookings Institution.

Webb, Steven. 2004. *Fiscal Responsibility Laws for Subnational Discipline: The Latin American Experience*. Policy Research Working Paper Series 3309. Washington, DC: World Bank.

Weingast, Barry, and William Marshall. 1988. "The Industrial Organization of Congress; or, Why Legislatures, Like Firms, Are Not Organized as Markets." *Journal of Political Economy* 96 (1): 132–163.

Weingast, Barry R. 1997. "The Political Foundations of Democracy and the Rule of Law." *American Political Science Review* 91 (2): 245–263.

Weitz-Shapiro, Rebecca. 2007. "Political Competition, Poverty, and Incentives for Good Government and Clientelism in Argentina." Paper presented at the annual meeting of the Midwest Political Science Association, April.

Weldon, Jeffrey. 1997a. "The Political Sources of Presidencialismo in Mexico." In *Presidentialism and Democracy in Latin America*, edited by Scott Mainwaring and Matthew Shugart. New York: Cambridge University Press.

Weldon, Jeffrey. 1997b. "El presidente como legislador, 1917–1934." In *El Poder Legislativo en las décadas revolucionarias, 1908–1934*, edited by Pablo Atilio Picato. Mexico, D.F., Mexico: Universidad Nacional Autonoma de Mexico, Instituto de Investigaciones Legislativas.

Weyland, Kurt. 1999. "Economic Policy in Chile's New Democracy." *Journal of Interamerican Studies* 41 (3): 67–96.

Wibbels, Erik. 2000. "Federalism and the Politics of Macroeconomic Policy and Performance." *American Journal of Political Science* 44 (4): 687–702.

Wiesner, Eduardo. 1995. *La descentralización, el gasto social y la gobernabilidad en Colombia*. Bogota, Colombia: Departamento Nacional de Plantación, Asociación Nacional de Instituciones Financieras and Financiera de Desarrollo Territorial.

World Bank. 1992. *Paraguay: Country Economic Memorandum*. Washington, DC: World Bank.

World Bank. 2003. *Paraguay: Creando las Condiciones para un Crecimiento Sustentable*. Washington, DC: World Bank.

World Bank. 2004a. *Doing Business in 2004: Understanding Regulation*. Washington, DC: World Bank/Oxford University Press.

World Bank. 2004b. *Mexico Public Expenditure Review, Vol. 2, Main Results*. Report 27894-MX.Colombia, Mexico Country Management Unit, Poverty Reduction and Economic Management Unit, Latin America and the Caribbean Region. Washington, DC: World Bank.

World Bank. 2004c. *Ecuador Poverty Assessment*. Washington, DC: World Bank. http://web.worldbank.org/WBSITE/EXTERNAL/COUNTRIES/LACEXT/0,,contentMDK:20415456~page PK:146736~p iPK:146830~theSitePK:258554,00.html.

World Bank Institute. 2004. *Governance Data*. Washington, DC: World Bank. www.worldbank.org/wbi/governance.

World Economic Forum (various years). *Global Competitiveness Report—Executive Opinion Survey*. Available at http://www.weforum.org/.

World Economic Forum. 2003. *The Global Competitiveness Report 2002–2003*. New York: Oxford University Press.

Yashar, Deborah J. 1998. "Contesting Citizenship: Indigenous Movements and Democracy in Latin America." *Comparative Politics* 31 (1): 23–42.

Zapata, Juan Gonzalo, Olga Lucía Acosta, and Adriana González. 2001. "Evaluación de la descentralización municipal en Colombia. ¿Se consolidó la sostenibilidad fiscal de los municipios colombianos durante los años noventa?" *Archivos de Economía* no. 165. Bogota, Colombia: Departamento Nacional de Planeación.

Zuvanic, Laura, and Mercedes Iacovello. 2005. "El rol de la burocracia en el PMP en América Latina." Inter-American Development Bank, Washington, DC. Mimeo.

Index